Drive Around

Australia

YOUR GUIDE TO GREAT DRIVES

Titles in this series include:

- Andalucía and the Costa del Sol
- Australia
- Bavaria and the Austrian Tyrol
- Brittany and Normandy
- Burgundy and the Rhône Valley
- California
- Canadian Rockies
- Catalonia and the Spanish Pyrenees
- Dordogne and Western France
- England and Wales
- Florida
- Ireland
- Italian Lakes and Mountains with Venice and Florence
- Languedoc and Southwest France
- Loire Valley
- New England
- New Zealand
- Portugal
- Provence and the Côte d'Azur
- Scotland
- Tuscany and Umbria
- Vancouver and British Columbia
- Washington DC, Virginia, Maryland and Delaware
  and

- Selected Bed and Breakfast in France (annual edition)

For further information about these and other Thomas Cook publications, write to Thomas Cook Publishing, PO Box 227, The Thomas Cook Business Park, 15–16 Coningsby Road, Peterborough PE3 8SB, United Kingdom.

Drive Around
Australia

The best of Australia's diverse
landscapes, from the surfing beaches
of the Gold Coast to the sub-
tropical rainforests of Queensland
and the deserts of the outback

Cathy Bolt, Bina Brown, Rick Eaves,
Jacob Greber, Deborah Howcroft,
Damien Murphy, Sue Neales, Dominic
O'Grady and Robin Taylor

Thomas Cook
Publishing
www.thomascookpublishing.com

Published by Thomas Cook Publishing,
a division of Thomas Cook Tour Operations Limited
PO Box 227,
The Thomas Cook Business Park
15–16 Coningsby Road
Peterborough PE3 8SB
United Kingdom

Telephone: +44 (0)1733 416477
Fax: +44 (0)1733 416688
E-mail: books@thomascookpublishing.com

For further information about
Thomas Cook Publishing, visit our website
www.thomascookpublishing.com

ISBN 1-841575-17-8

Text: © 2005 Thomas Cook Publishing
Maps and diagrams:
Road maps supplied and designed by Lovell Johns Ltd., OX8 8LH
Road maps base mapping © Hema Maps Pty Ltd 1999, www.hemamaps.com.au
City maps prepared by RJS Associates © The Thomas Cook Group Ltd

Head of Thomas Cook Publishing: Chris Young
Series Editor: Linda Bass
Production/DTP Editor: Steven Collins

Written, researched and updated by:
Cathy Bolt, Bina Brown, Rick Eaves, Jacob Greber, Deborah Howcroft, Damien Murphy, Sue Neales,
Dominic O'Grady and Robin Taylor

About the authors

This book has been written by a team of Australia-based travel writers and photographers, who are all enamoured of their own vast country.

Robin Taylor, who wrote the five driving chapters on Victoria, is a freelance journalist based in Melbourne, with a special interest in science, travel, food and rural writing. **Bina Brown**, who wrote three of the NSW chapters and the one on central Australia, is a Sydney freelance journalist specialising in finance and travel writing. **Rick Eaves**, a Tasmanian photojournalist who lives in one of the most lovely, if remote, west coast villages in the Apple Isle, wrote the three Tasmanian chapters.

Cathy Bolt is a Perth-based journalist who writes for the national daily the *Australian Financial Review* and spends as much of her spare time as she can exploring WA's lovely southwest region in search of the best wines. She wrote two of the chapters for Western Australia.

Deborah Howcroft, who explored and researched some of the South Australia driving tours for this book, lives in rural Victoria close to the border with SA.

Jacob Greber is a daily newspaper journalist based in Brisbane, who wrote the chapter on the Gold Coast and Scenic Rim, while **Damien Murphy** is a Sydney-based newspaper journalist, who spends as much of his spare time as possible surfing the spectacular NSW north coast beaches in search of the perfect wave. **Sue Neales**, who wrote the introductory section and the spectacular driving tours in outback and remote Australia, is a former newspaper foreign correspondent and feature writer. **Dominic O'Grady** is a freelance journalist specialising in travel, food and wine.

Acknowledgements

Little of the factual information included in these driving tours could have been compiled by the writers without the assistance of the Australian Tourism Commission and the various state and regional tourism organisations. Thanks too to the State driving associations and the Federal Government's Office of Road Safety, who assisted so willingly with road safety and driving information and tips, especially orientated for overseas independent travellers.

Contents

About Drive Around Guides

Key to Maps

  Place of interest

- - - - - Railway line

———— Monorail

(1) Road number

🎋 Picnic area

Symbol Key

❶ Tourist Information Centre

❷ Advice on arriving or departing

❿ Parking locations

◉ Advice on getting around

➲ Directions

⓫ Sights and attractions

◖ Accommodation

⓫ Eating

⬭ Shopping

⑨ Sport

◖ Entertainment

Thomas Cook's Drive Around Guides are designed to provide you with a comprehensive but flexible reference source to guide you as you tour a country or region by car. This guide divides Australia into touring areas – one per chapter. Major cultural centres or cities form chapters in their own right. Each chapter contains enough attractions to provide at least a day's worth of activities – often more.

Star ratings
To make it easier for you to plan your time and decide what to see, every sight and attraction is given a star rating. A three-star rating indicates an outstanding sight or major attraction. Often these can be worth at least half a day of your time. A two-star attraction is worth an hour or so of your time, and a one-star attraction indicates a site that is good, but often of specialist interest. To help you further, individual attractions within towns or theme parks are also graded, so that travellers with limited time can quickly find the most rewarding sights.

Chapter contents
Every chapter has an introduction summing up the main attractions of the area, and a ratings box, which will highlight the area's strengths and weaknesses – some areas may be more attractive to families travelling with children, others to wine-lovers or people interested in finding castles, churches, or good beaches.

Each chapter is then divided into an alphabetical gazetteer, and a suggested tour. You can select whether you just want to visit a particular sight or attraction, choosing from those described in the gazetteer, or whether you want to tour the area comprehensively. If the latter, you can construct your own itinerary, or follow the author's suggested tour, which comes at the end of every area chapter.

The gazetteer
The gazetteer section describes all the major attractions in the area – the villages, towns, historic sites, nature reserves, parks or museums that you are most likely to want to see. Maps of the area highlight all the places mentioned in the text. Using this comprehensive overview of the area, you may choose just to visit one or two sights.

One way to use the guide is simply to find individual sights that interest you, using the index, overview map or star ratings, and read what our authors have to say about them. This will help you decide whether to visit the sight. If you do, you will find plenty of practical

Practical information

The practical information in the page margins, or sidebar, will help you locate the services you need as an independent traveller – including the tourist information centre, car parks and public transport facilities. You will also find the opening times of sights, museums, churches and other attractions, as well as useful tips on shopping, market days, cultural events, entertainment, festivals and sports facilities.

information, such as the street address, the telephone number for enquiries and opening times.

Alternatively, you can choose a hotel, perhaps with the help of the accommodation recommendations contained in this guide. You can then turn to the overall map on page 10 to help you work out which chapters in the book describe those cities and regions that lie closest to your chosen touring base.

Driving tours

The suggested tour is just that – a suggestion, with plenty of optional detours and one or two ideas for making your own discoveries, under the heading *Also worth exploring*. The routes are designed to link the attractions described in the gazetteer section, and to cover outstandingly scenic coastal, mountain and rural landscapes. The total distance is given for each tour, as is the time it will take you to drive the complete route, but bear in mind that this indication is just for the driving time: you will need to add on extra time for visiting attractions along the way.

Many of the routes are circular, so that you can join them at any point. Where the nature of the terrain dictates that the route has to be linear, the route can either be followed out and back, or you can use it as a link route, to get from one area in the book to another.

As you follow the route descriptions, you will find names picked out in bold capital letters – this means that the place is described fully in the gazetteer. Other names picked out in bold indicate additional villages or attractions worth a brief stop along the route.

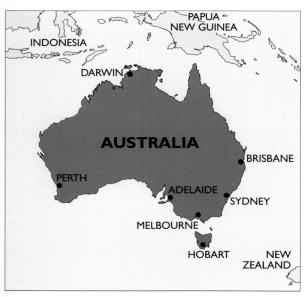

Accommodation and food

In every chapter you will find lodging and eating recommendations for individual towns, or for the area as a whole. These are designed to cover a range of price brackets and concentrate on more characterful small or individualistic hotels and restaurants. In addition, you will find information in the *Travel Facts* chapter on chain hotels, with an address to which you can write for a guide, map or directory. The price indications used in the guide have the following meanings:

$	budget level
$$	typical/average prices
$$$	de luxe.

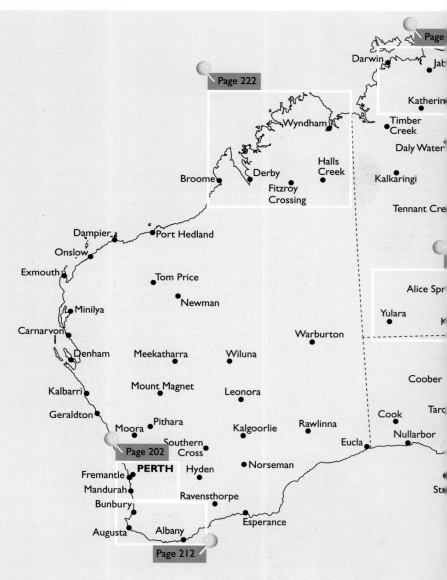

Page

Darwin   Jab

Katherin

Timber
Creek

Daly Water

Page 222

Wyndham

Halls
Creek

Broome   Derby   Fitzroy   Kalkaringi
Crossing

Tennant Cre

Dampier   Port Hedland

Onslow

Exmouth

Tom Price

Alice Spr

Newman   Yulara   K

Minilya

Carnarvon   Warburton

Denham   Meekatharra   Wiluna   Coober

Kalbarri   Mount Magnet   Leonora

Geraldton   Pithara   Cook   Tarc

Moora   Kalgoorlie   Rawlinna   Nullarbor

Southern   Eucla
Cross

Page 202

PERTH   Hyden   Norseman

Fremantle

Mandurah   St

Bunbury   Ravensthorpe

Augusta   Albany   Esperance

Page 212

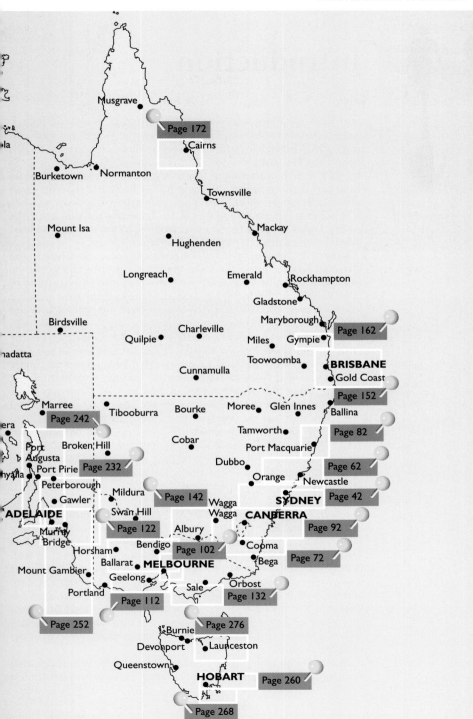

Above
Some stereotypes hold true

Introduction

Australia is one of those places that instantly conjures up vivid images: endless swathes of blue sky, long golden beaches, rugged red rocks and arid outback deserts; the white sails of the Sydney Opera House framed against the blue harbour with its tiny yachts, all dwarfed beneath the famed iron arch of the Sydney Harbour Bridge; the bright underwater coral and flashing fish of the Great Barrier Reef, and the lush green tropical rainforests of Far North Queensland tumbling down to white sand coves and bays; and, of course, the bounding red kangaroos, the cuddly koalas clinging to gum trees and the glorious bright rainbow colours of the parrots, lorikeets and rosellas.

Most of all, Australia is about the feeling of space, timelessness and untamed lands. This is the sixth biggest country in the world – a whole continent, no less, in its own right – yet it has a population of only 19 million people, 90 per cent of whom live clustered within a few kilometres of its coastal fringe. It is a land of wide open spaces and extreme contrasts, of snow-covered mountains in the south and rocky red gorges in the north, of vineyards laden with luscious grapes in the far west, and pounding surf beaches in the extreme east. It is a land where farms are measured in thousands of hectares and square kilometres, where roads stretch on into the distance with nothing else in sight, where the nearest towns are hundreds of kilometres away, and where traditional Aboriginal people and remote communities still live a life not that far removed from their ancestors hundreds of generations ago. It is a country with more than 2000 national parks and 13 World Heritage-listed wonders, from ancient fossil fields and impenetrable rainforests, to the glistening white sands of Fraser Island and the Aboriginal rock art of Kakadu National Park.

For the visitor who has time to explore and enjoy, there is much more to Australia than the beach, wilderness and koala tourist stereotypes. As well as its great icons – Ayers Rock (Uluru), the Great Barrier Reef and Sydney Harbour – the Great Southern Land has many hidden delights to discover and new experiences to savour. Modern Australia is as much about thriving, exciting cities, teeming with cutting-edge festivals, major sporting events, sophisticated restaurants and a well-developed theatre and arts scene, as it is about the bush and outback. It is about fine wines and fresh seafood; about gourmet weekends and idyllic bush retreats; about seasons so disparate across this broad land that you could feasibly be skiing one day in the icy cold of Thredbo and surfing the next in the mellow sunshine of the coastline of Noosa.

The trick with planning any holiday Down Under is to realise that the country is just too big to explore in only one or two weeks. It takes many Australians all their lives just to get to know their own state – and when they've done that, there are still six other states waiting to be discovered. For visitors coming from small European countries, the almost incomprehensible size of Australia is both its attraction and its drawback. Decisions have to be made about what to see and experience this time around – and what to leave for the next holiday. And that often comes down to individual interests, expectations and preferences. Some people will want to visit national parks like Kakadu, camp rough under the glittering stars amidst the red dust and rocky splendour, learn about Aboriginal culture and swim naked in pristine waterholes. Others will prefer to spend time discovering cosy bed and breakfasts, elegant wines, fine meals and glowing autumn colours in the refined splendour and history of Victoria's northeast.

Australia is a land ideally suited to car touring. Driving gives you the freedom to travel at your own pace, experiencing and exploring exactly what interests you, far away from the pushy guides and bustling crowds of the package tours. Distances might be long, but the roads – except in the remote outback – are good and sealed, the road rules are similar to those in Europe and the USA, the driving is safe and navigation easy.

But driving yourself around means having the time to do things, and visit places that are a little off the tourist track. Potter around the vineyards of the Barossa or Hunter Valleys, free-tasting their wine amidst the magnificent countryside. Eat fresh seafood straight from the lobster and fishing boats on Tasmania's east coast, or sample cheese and mustard direct from the kitchen, ovens and factory in Victoria's mellow northeast. It means seeking out the lesser known golden beaches on the NSW north coast where the locals go to surf, rather than just rushing straight to Bondi or the Gold Coast; finding the relaxing natural spas of Hepburn Springs, or the cosiest bed and breakfast with log fires in the Blue Mountains. It means exploring some of Australia's 2000 magnificent national parks and their walking trails, having the time and good fortune to see some of the country's unique native animals in the wild, rather than just at a zoo or the Healesville Sanctuary. It may even mean venturing down for a ski or fly-fish in the soaring Snowy Mountains of southern NSW, horse riding or white-water rafting in the Victorian Alps or going along to a rodeo and campdraft in outback Queensland – experiences and adventures locals take for granted but which overseas visitors don't always have the time, the vehicle or the knowledge to discover for themselves.

But, always remember, Australia is a big country and you can't do and see everything in one go. Take it easy and leave something for the next time. It is one of the world's most ancient lands and, if many of its wonders have been around for millions of years, they will probably still be here for a few more to come. Or at least until the next holiday Down Under.

Travel facts

Accommodation

Australia offers a range of accommodation to suit all budgets, from the classy five-star city hotels with their marble and gilt interiors and the relaxed, but perfectly exclusive resorts on some of the Great Barrier Reef Islands to free outback camping under the stars by a remote river or gorge. In between are everything from budget motels, backpacker dormitories and caravan parks to gourmet bed and breakfasts and enchanting old guesthouses, lodges and historic homes.

Self-catering and self-contained accommodation is another popular option for Australians on holidays, with many beach-side towns and resort destinations offering houses and apartments for rent on a weekly basis. Many caravan parks also have self-contained cabins and rental caravans within their grounds, available for short-term hire for the more budget conscious.

The best sources of accommodation advice are local town tourist information bureaux and regional brochures, while some tourist towns also have special accommodation agencies. During holiday times it can be difficult to arrange perfect accommodation at short notice, so booking is always preferable over the Christmas and January periods and during Easter. However, if travelling at times of the year when Australian families are not on holiday, many resorts offer so-called standby rates, which can be booked at short notice and may often cut between 30 and 50 per cent off normal rates.

If you are travelling around Australia on your own, it is easy to feel disadvantaged and hard done-by. Most hotels still offer rates on a per room basis, with single guests paying almost as much as couples. Other than sharing dormitories or finding a compatible travelling companion, there is not much that can be done.

Airports

Australia's major international air gateways are Sydney, Melbourne, Brisbane, Cairns and Perth, with some direct international flights to Darwin and Adelaide as well. Immigration and customs formalities are undertaken at these airports, and domestic flight links then operate to other major city destinations such as Hobart and Canberra. Most Australian airports are within half an hour's taxi ride from city centres.

Banks and credit cards

Australia has four major banks – the National Australia Bank, Westpac, the ANZ Bank and the Commonwealth Bank. All have direct relationships with major banks in the UK, Europe and the USA. There are also numerous other regional banks and credit unions, most of which offer full customer banking services over the counter or via Automatic Teller Machines (ATMs).

Camping and caravanning

Camping is a great way to explore the real Australia, meet the people and, at the same time, manage a tight travel budget. In the north and more remote parts of Australia, it is normal to pitch a tent by the side of a road or river for free, although permission is needed to camp on private property. In the southern and more settled states of Australia such as NSW and Victoria, many campsites and caravan parks are available. Most national parks have serviced camping grounds, although in some of the more popular ones such as Kakadu and Wilsons Promontory, it is necessary to book in advance.

Caravanning is a national pastime in Australia, with good facilities and a strong fraternity of caravanning compatriots spread across the country. Excellent Australia-wide caravan and campsite guides are available from caravan and camping associations and automobile associations such as the NRMA in New South Wales. These guides are usually available free of charge or at a reduced rate to members of overseas automobile associations.

Children

Australia prides itself on being an egalitarian, family-orientated, relaxed society where casual family picnics, barbecues and outdoor events are all favourite ways of entertaining. Children generally are welcomed at all but the poshest restaurants, and most resorts and hotels offer babysitting and Kid's Club activities, especially during major school holiday times. Most tour operators and museums offer half-price child fares or group family discounts – usually applicable to two adults and two or three children. Breast-feeding in public is acceptable, with some discretion, although it is frowned upon in some high-class restaurants. Most major department stores, airports and public facilities offer breast-feeding rooms, and special baby-changing facilities in rest rooms.

Climate

Due to its vast size and geographical location centred on the Tropic of Capricorn, Australia has a wide range of climates, making it impossible to generalise about the nation's climate. In fact, during winter (June–August) you can ski in the southern states one day and be diving at the Great Barrier Reef in Queensland or surfing at Noosa the next. Australia's seasons are the opposite to those of the northern hemisphere so Christmas is hot, in the middle of summer, which starts in December. Autumn begins in March, winter in June and spring in September. In the south of Australia, from Sydney southwards, the climate is generally Mediterranean, with hot, dry summers and wet, cool winters. But north of Brisbane, way up to the tropics, Darwin and Broome are wettest, hottest and stickiest from November to March. It's this variation that makes Australia, with some forethought and planning, a year-round holiday destination. For example, at the Great Barrier Reef, most rain falls from December to June, while in northern Queensland and parts of the Northern Territory and Western Australia, roads may flood during the 'wet' season, January–April. The ski season runs from June to October in New South Wales, Victoria and Tasmania, but if it's the beaches of NSW and Victoria that you want to enjoy, or hiking in the Tasmanian wilderness, the best, most glorious sunny days occur from December to March.

Currency

Australian currency is decimal with the dollar as the basic unit (100 cents equals one dollar). Notes come in $100, $50, $20, $10 and $5 denominations. Coins come in 5c, 10c, 20c, 50c, $1 and $2 denominations.

Customs regulations

Every traveller over 18 years of age may bring into Australia 1125ml of alcoholic liquor and 250 cigarettes or 250 grams of tobacco products duty free. Allowances of $400 per person aged 18 or over and $200 per person under 18 are granted for other goods intended as gifts.

Departure tax

Australia's passenger movement charge – or departure tax – is the equivalent of $30 and is prepaid with your airline ticket. Exemptions apply to children under 12 years of age, 24-hour transit passengers and transit passengers who stay longer than a day if departure is delayed by circumstances beyond their control.

Electricity

The electrical current in Australia is 240 volts, AC 50Hz. The Australian three-pin power outlet is different from that in most countries so you will probably need an adaptor. If your appliances are 110V, check if there is a 110/240V switch. If not, you will need a voltage converter. Universal outlets for 240V or 110V shavers are usually found in leading hotels.

Emergencies

For serious ambulance, health, fire and police emergency telephone calls, dial 000.

Entry formalities

Anyone wanting to enter Australia must carry a valid passport or similar certificate of identification. Every visitor, except holders of Australian and New Zealand passports, requires a visa to enter Australia. The Australian visitor visa can be obtained from your nearest Australian high commission, embassy or consulate.

Festivals

Australia has its major iconic festivals and events, which are not to be missed if you are in the vicinity:
- Australian Football League (or Aussie Rules) grand final on the last Saturday of September in Melbourne.
- Adelaide Arts Festival in March.
- The Melbourne Cup (horse racing) on the first Tuesday in November at Flemington racecourse.
- Australian Formula One Grand Prix car race at Albert Park, Melbourne in mid-March.
- Australian Tennis Open tournament during late January in Melbourne.
- Mt Isa Rodeo on the first weekend in August.
- Laura Aboriginal Dance Festival held every second year on Cape York (next in 2007).
- New Year's Eve on the Hobart waterfront, celebrating with the sailors from the gruelling Sydney to Hobart yacht race.
- The Bells Beach surf classic held every Easter near Torquay in southwest Victoria.

Below
Sydney's Gay and Lesbian Mardi Gras festival

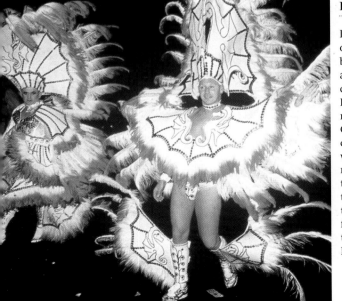

Fire bans and bushfires

In some areas of Australia, open campfires are banned because of the risk of bushfires, a serious threat particularly during the summer months. During a total fire ban no fires may be lit in the open. Campers are always advised to carry portable stoves. Fire ban warnings are issued through newspapers, radio and television and by signs along the roads. It is a serious offence to light a fire on a day of total fire ban, as it poses a grave risk to land, wildlife, property and lives.

NSW: Sydney Visitor Centre *106 George Street, The Rocks, Sydney; tel: (02) 9255-1788; www.tourism.nsw.gov.au*

Victoria: Tourism Victoria Information Centre *Town Hall, cnr Little Collins and Swanston St, Melbourne; tel: 13-2842; www.tourism.vic.gov.au*

Queensland: Tourism Queensland Information *tel: 13-1801; www.qttc.com.au*

South Australia: The South Australian Travel Centre *1 King William St, Adelaide; tel: (08) 8303-2033; www.visit-southaustralia.com.au*

Western Australia: WA Tourist Centre *Forrest Place, Perth; tel: (08) 9483-1111.*

Northern Territory: NT Tourist Information Centre *38 Mitchell St, Darwin; tel: (08) 8981-4300; fax: (08) 8981-0653; www.travelnt.com*

Tasmania: Tasmanian Travel & Information Centre *20 Davey Street, Hobart; tel: (03) 6230-8233; fax: (03) 6224-0289; www.tourism.tas.gov.au*

ACT: Canberra Visitors' Centre *330 Northbourne Ave, Dickson; tel: (02) 6205-0044 or 1800-026-166; www.canberratourism.com.au*

Health

Ensure you have personal insurance or travel insurance with a comprehensive health component to cover the possibility of illness or accident. Visitors from New Zealand, the UK, Ireland, Malta, Sweden, Italy, Finland and the Netherlands are covered by Australia's national health insurance scheme, Medicare. To be eligible, enrol at any Medicare office in Australia (make sure you have the correct documents from your national health scheme before travelling to Australia). Australia's creepy crawlies – and some of its larger, more ferocious sea and river creatures – have given Australia a bad reputation amongst overseas travellers as a dangerous and unpleasant place to visit. Almost all of these reports are exaggerated. With some sensible actions and care taken, it is possible to enjoy a holiday in Australia without any spiders, insects, sharks or stingers impinging on activities and lifestyle. Most spiders are not poisonous, snakes are extremely shy, sharks are rare and saltwater crocodiles only inhabit tropical rivers in the far and remote north of the nation. In the tropics, stingers or box jellyfish make it dangerous to swim from beaches from about October to April; however, swimming on offshore islands such as the Whitsundays or Great Barrier Reef islands is safe all year round.

Information

All capital cities and state governments operate excellent tourist information centres. You may feel swamped by the quantity of leaflets and brochures, but they are a good first port of call when arriving in a capital city as they offer excellent local information. Internet websites are also an easy way to access information about the state and places you plan to visit.

Insurance

Travel insurance is essential whenever travelling overseas; besides giving additional health insurance it will also cover loss of baggage or theft. When hiring vehicles, it is usually worth requesting to pay a few extra dollars per day in collision damage insurance, to reduce the excess amount you would pay in the event of an accident from several thousand dollars to a few hundred dollars.

Opening times

It is impossible to generalise about opening hours in Australia as there are major differences between the big cities, tourist centres and small towns. Banks are open Monday–Friday 0930–1600; post offices 0900–1700. Traditionally, all shops and services were closed on Saturday afternoons and Sunday – a situation that still prevails in many sleepy country towns – but most major cities now have shopping and a thriving business centre at weekends too.

Below left
Australia is a long way from
almost everywhere

Below
Learn to surf

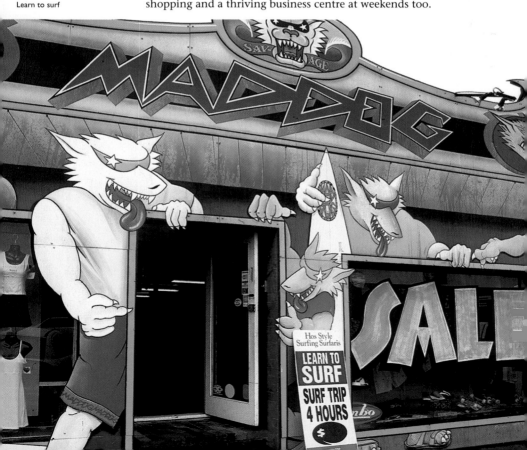

Packing

Check the temperature chart and the weather maps carefully. In the tropics lightweight clothing (natural fibres) is suitable all year round. In the southern temperate regions, summers (December–February) are warm to hot and lightweight clothes are suitable for daytime, but keep a jacket or sweater handy as nights may be cool. For the southern winters (June–August), sweaters, a jacket or light coat and generally warmer clothes are advisable. Australians are informal dressers, but for special occasions, such as business meetings, theatres and dining at good restaurants, men may need a jacket and tie or suit and women a more formal dress. Most of the time just keep clothing light and comfortable. Bring a sunhat, sunglasses and suntan lotion if you expect hot weather. For foot protection when walking on beaches or in the sea, pack your sandshoes.

Postal services

Australia Post provides a domestic letter service and a range of associated postal services handling more than four billion items of mail a year. Most small towns as well as city centres and suburbs have their own post offices. A standard letter within Australia costs 50c to mail, and will usually be delivered within two to three days. The international mail service is reliable and quick for both letters and packages – many letters from Australia make it to their destinations within the UK and the USA less than five days after posting.

Public holidays

As well as the major public holidays, there are other holidays that vary between states, such as Melbourne Cup day in Victoria, the annual agricultural show days in most major cities and towns, and Labour Day. On public holidays, all banks will be closed, most shops shut, and public transport services scaled down to their normal Sunday schedules. Check local newspapers for details.

Safety and security

Australia is essentially a safe travel destination, although in the major cities and tourist destinations there is the inevitable theft of money and personal belongings. To avoid suffering such an unfortunate fate while on holidays, there are a few golden rules to follow:
• Do not carry large amounts of cash.
• Any cash you do carry should be kept in a safe place such as a money belt.
• Do not keep all your money, credit cards or traveller's cheques in the one place.

- Make photocopies of all major travel documents and store them away from the rest of your valuables.
- Always lock parked cars and do not leave valuables in them.
- Do not leave luggage visible in parked cars.
- When driving around inner Sydney, lock doors from the inside: bags have been stolen when a car is stopped at traffic lights.
- Always look confident when walking around a crowded place.
- Avoid dark or deserted locations in cities and towns at night.

Telephones

Public payphones accept a variety of coin denominations and Phonecards. This pre-paid card – for use in public payphones to make local, STD and IDD calls – is available from a large number of retail outlets in denominations of $5, $10, $20 and $50. Australia operates both a digital and modified CMD mobile phone network, with major mobile companies including Telstra, Optus, Vodaphone and Hutchinson. Many international mobile phones will work within Australia. The international country code when calling Australia is 61. All phone numbers have a regional code such as (02) for NSW or (03) for Victoria, followed by an eight-digit number. When calling Australia from overseas, the zero is left out from the regional code, although it is necessary when dialling within Australia.

Below
The Australian Surf Lifesaving
Championships

Time zones

There are three time zones in Australia: Eastern Standard Time (EST) which operates in New South Wales, Australian Capital Territory, Victoria, Tasmania and Queensland; Central Standard Time (CST) in South Australia and Northern Territory; and Western Standard Time (WST) in Western Australia. CST is half an hour behind EST, while WST is two hours behind EST. Except for the Northern Territory, Western Australia and Queensland, there is daylight saving during the summer. It runs in New South Wales, the Australian Capital Territory, Victoria and South Australia from the end of October through to the end of March, and in Tasmania from the beginning of October through to the end of March.

Tipping

Tipping is becoming more frequent in Australia, however service charges are not added to accounts by hotels and restaurants. Porters at airports, taxi drivers and hairdressers do not expect to be tipped although you may do so if you wish. Porters have set charges at railway terminals, but not at hotels. In most restaurants, it is usual to tip food and drink waiters up to 10 per cent of the bill for good service. At any time, tipping is your choice.

Toilets

Australia has high standards of hygiene, with public toilets in all major tourist centres, service stations, department stores, public buildings and hotels usually clean, safe and free.

Right
Billabong in Kakudu

Below
The Blue Mountains

Travellers with disabilities

Access for people with disabilities in Australia has improved significantly in recent years, and it remains a priority. Australian hotels, airlines, attractions and major transport carriers generally provide access for people with disabilities. It is advisable to check with all service providers prior to your visit, ensuring that they are able to meet your particular needs. Advance notice and reservation well ahead will also help ensure that you receive the best possible assistance.

Driver's guide

Automobile clubs

Each state in Australia has its own automobile club and motoring association, all of which are linked and have reciprocal rights among themselves and with most major motoring associations overseas, such as the AA in the UK or the AAA in the US.

Victoria: RACV
tel: 13-1955 (enquiries), 13-1111 (breakdown).

New South Wales: NRMA *tel: 13-2132 (enquiries), 13-1111 (breakdown).*

Queensland: RACQ *tel: 13-1905 (enquiries), 13-1111 (breakdown).*

Tasmania: RACT *tel: 13-2722 (enquiries), 13-1111 (breakdown).*

Western Australia: RACWA *tel: (08) 9421-4444 (enquiries), 13-1111 (breakdown).*

South Australia: RAASA *tel: (08) 8202-4600 (enquiries), 13-1111 (breakdown).*

Northern Territory: AANT *tel: (08) 8981-3837 (enquiries), (08) 8941-0611 (breakdown).*

Britz Australia *tel: 1800-331-454 free phone; www.britz.com*

Accidents

If you are ever involved in an accident when driving in Australia, you must stop and exchange names, addresses and telephone numbers with the other party. Legally, if anyone is injured in the crash, it must be reported immediately to the local police. Both ambulances and the police can be reached on the general emergency telephone number 000. If travelling in a hire car, call the car-hire company as well.

Breakdowns

If you are in the city or in mobile phone range when your car breaks down, the simplest way of getting help is to call the local state motoring association for urgent assistance, assuming you are a member. Most car-hire companies also have their own roadside assistance number, usually written on the car-key ring holder. If you are in outback or remote Australia when you breakdown, never leave your car or vehicle unless a house is actually in sight. This is for your own safety, not for the car's – most tourists who perish in the heat or vastness of outback Australia do so because they abandon their broken- or bogged-down vehicles to get help, never realising how important it is to have protection from the unrelenting heat.

Camper vans and 4WD vehicles

If intending to drive around Australia for an extended period of time, and especially if you are planning to explore some outback routes, it is worth considering hiring a four-wheel-drive (4WD) vehicle or camper-van rather than a conventional vehicle. Camper vans are well equipped, easily parked in campsites, national parks and at the roadside, and have the obvious advantage of saving on hotel costs. The main rental company for camper vans in Australia is Britz Australia who also have some smaller motorhomes for hire although these tend to be too cumbersome and unsuited to gravel roads. All the major car companies rent out 4WDs, often with the option of hiring camping equipment too, although this can be rented or bought relatively cheaply from major camping shops.

Documents

Under Australian law, a bona-fide tourist may drive in Australia on a valid overseas driver's licence although, if the driver's licence is not in

Car-rental companies from overseas and within Australia: **Hertz** tel: 1800-550-067 or 13-3039; www.hertz.com.au **Avis** tel: 1800-225-533 or 13-6333; www.avis.com.au **Budget** tel: 1300-362-848 or 13-2727; www.budget.com.au **Thrifty** tel: 1300-367-227; www.thrifty.com.au

Drinking and driving

Australia has strict drink-driving laws. The maximum driver blood alcohol limit is 0.05 Blood Alcohol Concentration (BAC) and police are allowed to conduct random breath testing of any driver by the side of the road. It is illegal to refuse a breath test. Anyone caught driving over the alcohol limit faces severe fines, loss of licence, a court sentence and even jail. To be sure of staying under the safety limit, it is best for drivers not to drink at all.

Essentials

Two spare tyres are essential and all wheel-changing equipment should be checked. Refuel at every opportunity and keep the tank topped up. Ensure all essential supplies are on board: water, food, first-aid kit, fuel, spare parts, detailed maps, one week's extra supply of food and water and at least 20 litres of water per person, in case of emergency.

English, the visitor must carry a translation with the permit. Driving licences must be carried at all times; a $50 fine can be imposed if you are stopped by police when driving and do not have your licence with you.

When accident and damage insurance is taken out in Australia, it is the car that is covered, rather than the individual driver. It is worth checking the details of the insurance included in your car-rental deal. It is usually well worth paying a few extra dollars a day for loss-damage waiver insurance over and above the standard insurance included in the rental, otherwise you may be liable to pay hefty costs in the case of an accident.

Driving in Australia

Road conditions in Australia vary considerably depending on which part of the country you are driving in. In the cities, all roads are sealed and there are excellent modern freeway and highway systems. Similarly, rural Australia is linked by sealed, well-maintained highways and roads, although not all of the so-called highways are dual carriageway. However, in remote rural areas, many secondary 'bush' roads are still dirt and gravel, although usually well maintained by local councils. Since visitors are often unused to driving on gravel roads, which may be rutted or full of potholes, great care should be taken and excessive speed avoided. Similarly, especially in northern and tropical Australia, it is not uncommon for roads to be blocked by floods for short periods of time. Never drive through a water-covered road unless the bottom of the road can still clearly be seen and the water is no more than a few inches deep and not fast-flowing. Road conditions can change very quickly so it is important to be alert. Watch out for road hazards such as animals and slow vehicles.

Train crossings should also be approached with care, especially those without barriers or other warnings. This may seem an obvious caution to sound, but lives have nevertheless been tragically lost when cars collide with trains at level crossings. If in any doubt, slow down and wait.

It is perfectly safe in a security sense to drive around all of Australia's major cities and country areas at night. However, in many parts of country Australia, such as the Flinders Ranges, night driving can be very dangerous, owing to the large number of kangaroos on the road. In northern and outback Australia, most roads are unfenced and cattle often wander and sleep on the roads at night. For these reasons, avoid driving at night in country Australia unless you really have to; try instead to get to where you are going before dark.

The best time for outback travel is during the drier, cooler months between April and October. Road conditions must be confirmed with local authorities and weather forecasts and fuel availability checked at every opportunity. Take precautions when travelling independently in isolated outback areas. Plan your trip with the aid of a reputable map,

Fines

Heavy fines apply to drivers who exceed the blood alcohol limit, or who commit other drug-related offences. High range blood alcohol levels incur a penalty of up to $3300 and a jail term of up to 18 months.

Drivers caught speeding risk losing their licence on the spot, and incurring a fine of up to $1550.

Fines are also levied on drivers or passengers travelling without a seatbelt. These fines start at $225 and range up to $1175 if four or more people are found to be travelling without seatbelts.

Fines of up to $3300 apply to those who drive without a valid licence; those who drive in a 'reckless or dangerous' manner can incur a fine of up to $2200 and a nine month jail term; and negligent driving resulting in death incurs a fine of up to $3300 and an 18 month jail term.

stay on recognised routes and check facilities and road conditions before departure. Advise someone of your route, destination and arrival time and ask them to notify the police if you have not contacted them by an agreed time. If you break down, stay with your vehicle where there is shade and protection from the heat.

Driving rules

The two most important things to know about driving holidays in Australia are that the distances are vast; and that cars drive on the left-hand side of the road. When driving on a multi-lane road, keep to the left-hand lane wherever possible. Move to the right to overtake and then move back to the left once it is safe to do so.

Crossing the centre line of the road on a blind crest or a curve is prohibited.

Traffic lights are red, amber and green. Red is 'stop'; amber is 'prepare to stop'; and green is 'go'. Arrows indicate whether traffic turning right or left is allowed to go (depending on which direction the arrow is pointed). For example, if the traffic lights are green, but an arrow pointing right is red, then traffic turning right is not allowed to go, but traffic going straight ahead is. In cases where there are no left, or right arrows, a red light will mean 'stop' for everyone, and a green light will mean 'go' for everyone. A flashing yellow arrow means you can turn, but watch carefully for pedestrians and give way to them.

Roundabouts occur frequently in capital cities and residential areas. Give way to all traffic on the roundabout, and only go in a clockwise direction. Always use your indicator when leaving the roundabout.

Buses have the right of way over other traffic.

Fuel

Gasoline (petrol) in Australia comes in super (leaded), unleaded regular and premium unleaded grades and is sold by the litre. Unleaded petrol is a couple of cents cheaper per litre than leaded petrol. Some older 4WD vehicles still use diesel fuel; it too is readily available at all service stations. Some hire vehicles may be fitted with dual fuel systems of LPG gas and unleaded fuel – using gas is cheaper and less polluting. Fuel prices are often higher in remote country areas. Petrol stations are plentiful all around Australia; even on remote highways, there will be one every 200–300km, but on remote dirt tracks, extra fuel should always be carried as towns are few and far between. Most service stations accept international credit cards.

Highways

Most of Australia's roads and major highways are numbered – for example, the Princes Highway that rings Australia is Highway 1 – but

Mobile phones

Drivers are not permitted to use hand-held mobile phones, although use of hands-free mobiles is acceptable. Fines are levied on those drivers who ignore this rule.

Parking

Parking is controlled by the State, Territory and local government authorities. Street parking in capital cities is identified by pole signage, which includes information on time restrictions. Metered street parking is generally limited to one or two hours; fines apply if restrictions are ignored. An easier option, but more costly, is to use one of the many private parking stations found throughout the capital cities. These generally charge around $10 for a half day.

Security

Always lock your vehicle when unattended, and keep valuables out of sight. Do not leave luggage unattended at airports, rental car offices, or other public place.

the system differs between states and lacks the coherence and simplicity of road numbering systems in Europe and the USA; at times it can just be downright confusing. In Australia, most major routes and highways are signed according to their name – such as the Matilda Highway in outback Queensland, the Snowy Mountains Highway in NSW, or the Hume Highway linking Sydney and Melbourne by the most direct inland route.

Most roads and highways in Australia are free, with the exception of a few, recently built roads and bridges that have been privately funded or financed by tolls. Important to remember are the charges for crossing the Sydney Harbour Bridge or the Harbour tunnel (only imposed in one direction), the Gateway bridge linking Brisbane airport with the Gold Coast, and the new private CityLink tollway system in Melbourne which affects almost all major motorways around the city. This CityLink system has its fees charged electronically and invisibly, which means that every car must carry a special card on its dashboard with credit registered on it, to be able to use these roads. Car-hire companies in Melbourne will sell you day passes ($10 each) to enable you to use the network, or they can be bought from booths by the side of the tollway near Tullamarine airport.

Information

Full details of Australian road rules are available from the National Transport Commission at *www.ntc.gov.au*

The New South Wales Road Transport Authority also produces a useful brochure for international visitors to Australia. It can be downloaded free of charge at *www.rta.nsw.gov.au*

Lights

Between sunset and sunrise you must drive with your headlights and rear lights on. In suburban areas you must use low beam. When using high beam on the open road, dip your headlights when an approaching vehicle is within 200m or as soon as the other vehicle's lights are dipped.

Seat belts

Seat belts are compulsory in Australia. The law states that all adults and children in any car must wear a seat belt in both the front and back seats of the vehicle at all times. Smaller children (toddlers) must be placed in an approved child restraint or car seat when travelling in a vehicle, while babies should be in a specially fitted safety capsule.

Speed limits

Speed limits are clearly signposted and strictly enforced. Police use speed cameras, radars and laser equipment to monitor and enforce these speed limits. In towns and city areas the speed limit is usually 60km/h, on a highway it is usually 100km/h–110km/h. The Northern Territory is the only state that has no speed limit on open roads.

Road signs

Road signs should be followed at all times, and are designed to be self-explanatory.

The most common signs are: 'Stop' (drivers must stop completely and give way to all traffic); 'Give Way' (drivers must slow down, approach with caution, and give way to all traffic); 'No U Turn' (it is illegal to make a U turn); 'Roundabout' (travel clockwise in a roundabout and give way to traffic already on the roundabout); 'No Entry' (it is illegal to enter a road or driveway where there is a no entry sign); and 'Speed Limit' (speed limit signs show the speed limit expressed in kilometres per hour, within a red circle).

Below
Sydney Harbour Bridge

AUSTRALIAN ROAD SIGNS

Standard or Commonly-used traffic signs

Area speed limit

End clearway

End area speed limit

Give way

Keep right

Left turn on red light
after stopping

Left turn only

Level crossing

No entry

No left turn

No U-turn

Pedestrians may cross
diagonally

Roundabout

Speed derestriction

Stop

Two-way

Median turning
lane

No stopping
(for an area)

People with
disabilities parking

Hook turn only

Getting to Australia

No matter where you start from, unless you live in New Zealand or Indonesia, Australia is a long way away. And even if your plane is flying over Australian territory, you may still be a long way from your destination; a jumbo jet flying from Asia or Europe can take seven hours from the time it crosses the northern coastline near Derby or Broome before it lands in Sydney or Melbourne. The sheer size of the country, its island status and its southern hemisphere location makes flying the best way to get to Australia, although cruise ships and passenger liners still have their fans. But walking or arriving by bus or car is just not on, although in recent years a few hardy souls have canoed, swum, wind-surfed and island-hopped across Torres Strait from Papua New Guinea to the tip of Cape York.

By air

Australia is a country orientated towards air travel and most of its five million overseas visitors arrive each year by plane. All of Australia's capital cities, with the exception of Canberra, have international airports or gateways, while Cairns in far North Queensland is now a popular arrival point for more than 21 per cent of all visitors.

Planes have become much quicker and, with fewer refuelling stopovers needed, it is now standard to fly from London, Paris, Amsterdam, Frankfurt, Rome and other major European airports in less than 20 hours. From the west coast of the United States, it takes about 14 hours, while from Tokyo it is less than a 10-hour direct flight with no stops.

Most direct flights from Europe to Australia leave late in the afternoon or early evening, thereby arriving in the early morning two days later in Australia owing to the time zones that put Australia between 8 and 11 hours ahead of European time. These schedules give travellers two short 'nights' of sleep and one 'day', a system which has been shown to minimise the effects of jetlag and cause the least disruption to body clocks.

All major airlines fly to Australia, with most of the major European airlines using Singapore or Bangkok as their mid-flight, one-hour refuelling stop, allowing passengers to break their journeys in these countries if looking for an alternative holiday experience. The Australian airline, Qantas, has been flying the Australian–European route for more than 50 years and is recognised as the long-haul flight specialist, as well as being the world's safest airline. It has daily flights, sometimes more, to several major European airports, with daily direct

Above
Darling Harbour monorail

departures from Melbourne, Sydney and Brisbane all linking in Singapore, allowing for great flexibility in departure and arrival points. British Airways, Lufthansa, Singapore Airlines, KLM, Thai Airways and Malaysian airlines are the other major airlines operating the Europe–Australia route daily. Return airfares from Europe can be expensive; cheaper fares are available off-peak, by travelling with less established airlines, through bucket shops and by flying with Middle Eastern airlines that require an overnight stay in the Middle East.

From the USA, most flights to Australia leave from Los Angeles, Vancouver and San Francisco, with refuelling stops in Hawaii, and sometimes in Auckland, NZ, too. All the major American airlines as well as Canadian Air fly to Australia once or twice weekly, although many now share their flights and codes with airlines such as Qantas.

It pays to spend a little time planning which Australian airport should be your first port of call – and then to insist that you fly there as directly as possible. Lazy travel agents often automatically book travellers through the Sydney gateway, without considering their travel plans. This means that travellers who have planned to start their trip in Cairns, Darwin or Perth, for example, are then faced with annoying transfers to the domestic terminal and a subsequent three- or four-hour flight to their destination. Some forethought by their travel agent and a change of aircraft at the Singapore or Bangkok stopover could have got them there much more quickly and without the unnecessary detour to southern Australia.

Given Australia's vast size, it is worth thinking about starting your holiday at Darwin, Cairns or Alice Springs – if these were places on your travel itineraries anyway – and then working your way south or east. That way, the amount of flight back-tracking is minimised.

By ship

Cruise ships that sail the Pacific from destinations such as Hawaii, Fiji or New Zealand offer an alternative way of reaching Australia, although there is always the issue of the return home one-way airfare to deal with. Passenger liners are virtually a mode of transport of the past – their heyday as the main way of travelling between Europe and Australia was the 1950s and 1960s. Now the only way to sail – if you are averse to flying or look forward to four weeks at sea – is on some of the cargo ships that take 10 or 20 paying passengers a trip. Many of these vessels are Russian in origin, so don't expect them to offer luxurious cruising meals and party games, but they do provide a novel way of getting to Australia.

Setting the scene

Geography and location

Australia is the world's largest island and its smallest continent, extending north and south from the Tropic of Capricorn. With an area covering more than 7.6 million sq km, it is the sixth largest country in the world after Russia, Canada, China, the USA and Brazil, yet has a population of only 18.3 million people. Australia is bounded by the clear blue waters of the Coral Sea and the Pacific Ocean to the east, the Arafura Sea to the north, the warm waves of the Indian Ocean to the west, and the mighty waves of the cold Southern Ocean to the south, with a coastline 36,735km long. Its nearest neighbours are Indonesia, with the island of Timor less than 400km northwest of Darwin, Papua New Guinea to the north of Torres Strait and Cape York, and New Zealand off its southeast coast across the Tasman Sea.

Australia is one of the oldest land masses on earth, originally breaking away from the super continent 'Gondwana' and settling in its current position about 15 million years ago. The continent is also one of the most stable of all land masses and has been free of mountain-building forces for 100 million years. Its age also makes it the flattest of all continents, with its highest point, Mt Kosciuszko in the NSW Snowy Mountains, being only 2228m high. Its longest river is the Darling River, which originates in Queensland and eventually joins the mighty Murray River near Mildura, to flow into the sea southeast of Adelaide at Coroong National Park, a distance of 2736km from its source. The highest recorded annual rainfall in Australia, an unbelievable 11.2m, fell on the second highest mountain in tropical Queensland, Mt Bellenden Ker near Cairns, in 1979. Australia's lowest point, the large inland salt lake of Lake Eyre in South Australia, at 15m below sea level, is also its driest, recording an annual rainfall of only 125mm a year. The coldest temperature in Australia, of minus 23°C, was experienced at Charlotte's Pass, near Mt Kosciuszko, amidst the snow and ice of the winter of 1994, while the hottest temperature ever recorded was an extraordinary 53°C at Cloncurry in 1889. The story goes that on the scorching day, birds simply dropped dead out of the sky.

Early Aboriginal history

Scientific evidence and anthropological research both suggest that Aborigines have been living on the Australian continent for the last 50,000–70,000 years, having migrated originally from Indonesia and through New Guinea. The oldest skeleton found in Australia – located at Lake Mungo in southwest New South Wales and believed to be

38,000 years old – bears traces of ceremonial ochre. This is thought to be the oldest sign of ochre use ever discovered. Unlike most other races, Aborigines were not cultivators, relying instead on a form of controlled burning of vegetation known as 'fire-stick farming'. Living in nomadic tribes and family groups and moving land according to the seasons, Aboriginal children were taught from an early age that they belonged to the land and that they had, according to their family and birth totem, responsibility and 'ownership' of certain land features and areas of land. Aboriginal legends, songs and dances tell of powerful spirits who created the land and people during the Dreamtime. There was no written Aboriginal language and, in fact, most of the 600 tribes spoke different dialects and rarely met except on ceremonial occasions. The tradition of the Dreamtime, however, was a unifying force and rock paintings depicting this creation period can be found dotted throughout the country. Some of the most striking and best preserved of these can be viewed at rock galleries in Kakadu National Park and the Kimberley region. Prominent land, river

Below
Aboriginal art

and coastal features were viewed as sacred sites because of their association with the Dreamtime, the time when the earth was formed and cycles of life and nature initiated. It is estimated that there were between 250,000 and 500,000 Aborigines living a nomadic bush lifestyle when Australia was first settled by Europeans in 1788.

The arrival of white people gradually brought an end to the traditional Aboriginal way of life, when settlement began to encroach on tribal lands and white settlers massacred many Aborigines in fierce battles and wars.

European history

Forget all notions of England's Captain James Cook 'discovering' Australia in 1770. Charts in the NT Art Gallery and Museum in Darwin show that Cristovão de Mendoça, the Portuguese explorer, mapped the Top End coastline as early as 1522 and that the earliest European explorers of the mysterious *Terra Australis* were undoubtedly the Portuguese. Mendoça was followed by compatriot Luis Vaeat, who marked the safest area to swim in the strait between the tip of Cape York and New Guinea in the 16th century. Dutch navigators Dirk Hartog, Van Diemen and Abel Tasman all mapped stretches of the coastline but didn't show interest in settling a hostile and barren continent. Consequently, it was not until 1770 that the east coast was sighted by Captain James Cook of the British Royal Navy, in command of his ship, the *Endeavour*. Cook sailed into Botany Bay, south of present-day Sydney, named the fertile land New South Wales and claimed it for the British Crown in the name of King George III, only beating French explorers with similar hopes of conquest and colonisation by a few weeks. On the fragile little *Endeavour* were several scientists and a botanist, Joseph Banks, who during their forays ashore made amazing discoveries of plants and animals, never seen before. After Captain Cook left Botany Bay he travelled north and charted the east coastline, reporting it to be green, fertile and ripe for farming and settlement. But Cook met with disaster on a coral reef near current-day Cairns, and limped into the mouth of the Endeavour River (now Cooktown) for repairs. Not surprisingly, he named many features of this coastline according to his mood of depression, such as Cape Tribulation and Weary Bay. But during his four-week enforced stop at Cooktown, the extraordinary navigator and explorer made contact with the local Aborigines and was quite impressed with the apparent happiness in which they lived. He also spent much of his time trying to find a way out of the coral maze (Great Barrier Reef) within which he feared he, his ship and his crew might have been imprisoned for ever.

Settlement and exploration

Opposite
Cadman's Cottage (1816), the oldest surviving house in Sydney

On 26 January 1788, Captain Arthur Phillip, who became Australia's first governor, led the First Fleet of 11 ships with 736 convicts and

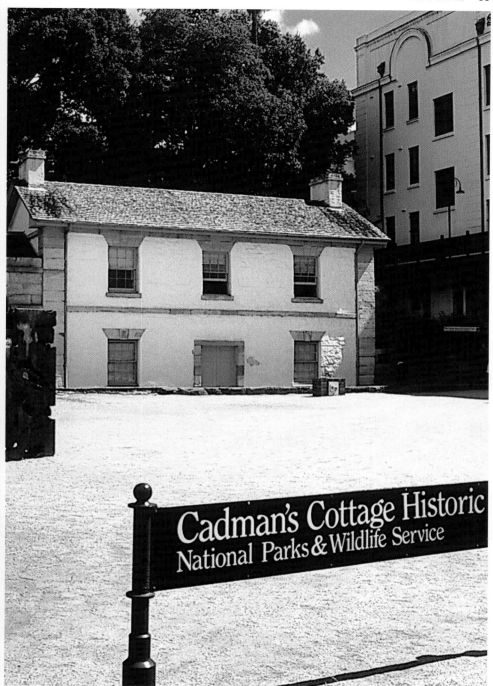

Cities

Contrary to the stereotypes of tanned farmers and outback Crocodile Dundees, Australia is one of the world's most urbanised societies with nearly 90 per cent of the population living in large cities clinging to the coast. The largest and most populous city is Sydney with 4.2 million people, closely followed by Melbourne, its southern rival, counting 3.5 million. The third largest city is Brisbane, 1.7m, Perth 1.4m, Adelaide 1.5m, Canberra 322,000, Hobart 199,000 and Darwin 107,000.

Below
Coogee Beach

their guards into Port Jackson, now known as Sydney Harbour. After the American War of Independence had left it with nowhere to dispose of its criminals and unwanted citizens, Britain had decided that the new colony of New South Wales offered a perfect – and remote – solution. The theory was that a new penal colony staffed by convict labour could produce crops and supply materials for ship-building in England. Those who survived the long voyage were stunned by the isolation and forbidding vastness of their new home. Convicts – many of whom had been transported for life just for stealing a loaf of bread, poaching wildlife or inciting political unrest – were confronted by an untamed land and desperate food shortages for the first 20 years of the Sydney Farm Cove colony.

Nevertheless, the new settlement slowly grew and developed. Many convicts who completed their sentences chose to stay in Australia as farmers and labourers. Free settlers trickled in from 1793, lured by the promise of cheap land and convict labour. Rich grazing land was discovered west of Sydney and wool soon became one of the country's most important industries. At the same time, the colony of Van Diemens Land (Tasmania) was established as a second penal settlement in 1803, followed by settlements on the Brisbane River, Queensland, in 1824, on the Swan River, Western Australia, in 1829,

Beach culture

Australia is very much a beach culture and people's attire reflects an outdoor lifestyle. Today it is hard to believe that at the turn of the century bathing in daytime was prohibited on the grounds of public decency. All state capital cities are built either on or very near the water; even Canberra, although an inland city, is dominated by Lake Burley Griffin.

on Port Phillip Bay, Victoria, in 1835 and on Gulf St Vincent, South Australia, in 1836. The capital cities of five Australian states have grown from those sites.

Meanwhile explorers, driven by an urge to venture inland and by the quest for new grazing land, opened up new country in all directions. At first the rugged Blue Mountains west of Sydney seemed insurmountable until, in 1813, Blaxland, Wentworth and Lawson discovered a passage, and opened the way for inland exploration. Another famed explorer was George Bass who, together with Matthew Flinders, circumnavigated Tasmania. Between 1801 and 1803, Matthew Flinders circumnavigated the Australian continent and completed the mapping of the coastline. Robert O'Hara Burke and William Wills were the first Europeans to cross Australia from south to north in 1860 – an amazing feat that cost them their lives on the way back from the Gulf of Carpentaria to Melbourne. Edward John Eyre, an inland explorer, crossed the continent from Streaky Bay in South Australia to Albany in Western Australia – a long trip of almost 1600km. Hamilton Hume found a route through the Great Dividing Range to the fertile plains of Goulburn and Yass while Ludwig Leichhardt explored inland from Brisbane to Port Essington in the Northern Territory. Charles Sturt discovered the Murray River.

The discovery of gold in the early 1850s at a number of sites across Victoria and NSW brought a fresh influx of immigrants from Europe, China and America, coinciding with an end to England's transportation of convicts in 1852. Some of the richest gold seams were found at Ballarat, north of Melbourne and in central Western Australia at Kalgoorlie while large copper deposits were discovered at York Peninsula in South Australia. The surge of the gold rushes was followed by a building boom and the continuing expansion of wool and cattle wealth. Just 100 years after its first European settlement, Australia's population reached three million. As the cities grew and the roads connecting them were upgraded, a sense of nationalism developed and Australia was declared a commonwealth, a federation of its six founding states, on 1 January 1901.

Australia's system of government

Australia today remains a federation of states, with its own federal parliament based in the nation's capital of Canberra. It is a bicameral system of government following the English Westminster system, with a House of Representatives and a Senate, elected by the people of Australia in a federal election held every four years. Voting in Australia is compulsory for all citizens aged 18 and over, with Australia observing a rich tradition of democracy, being the second nation (New Zealand was the first) to give women the vote in 1902. The Queen of England currently remains the nominal Head of State, represented in Australia by her hand-picked Governor General, and to everyone's surprise, Australians rejected the option to become a Republic in a recent referendum. The Prime Minister of Australia, currently the conservative Liberal Party's John Howard, is the leader of whichever party has control of the House of Representatives after each national vote. There are 148 members of the House of Representatives, with each being elected by a geographical electorate of between 60,000 and 120,000 voters. In contrast, the Senate is the Upper House or House of Review, supposedly in place to defend State rights and to ensure that new laws are fair and equitable. There are 76 senators, 12 from each state and 2 each from the Australian Capital Territory and Northern Territory. Neither of the two major political parties has had a majority in the Senate since 1981, making for interesting political lobbying of independent and minority party senators.

Besides the Federal or Commonwealth government, each state has its own State Government, with a Premier as its head. The states and territories each have their own capital city, flag, flora and fauna emblems, and deal with domestic state affairs such as education, transport, law enforcement, health services and agriculture as well as sharing mutual responsibilities with the federal parliament. The third tier of government in Australia is the municipal council or local government. While the powers and responsibilities of local governments vary from state to state, they encompass community matters such as urban planning, roads, water resources, parks and recreation grounds, and public libraries (sometimes encapsulated in the 3 Rs – roads, rubbish and rates!). With so many politicians and levels of government for a country with a population of 18 million people, it is not surprising that Australia is often declared over-governed and too tied up with red tape and bureaucracy.

Wildlife

With so many people living in the cities, it leaves plenty of space in the country and outback for Australia's other unique and equally flourishing population – its wildlife. Australia's isolation for more than 55 million years has created a sanctuary of animals and plants found nowhere else in the world.

Australia's marsupials did not have to compete with highly developed mammals and there are still over one hundred species which flourish in ideal conditions. Unique animals to watch for include many species of kangaroos and wallabies, the cuddly koala, the nocturnal wombat and the ferocious Tasmanian devil, a carnivorous marsupial found in the wild in Tasmania. Australia also hosts an extraordinary animal group, the monotremes, egg-laying mammals that are often referred to as living fossils. The platypus, for example, is a small river-dwelling animal with a duck bill and an agile furry body resembling an otter. Another representative of this group is the echidna or spiny anteater.

When driving through rural Australia or its national parks, it is common to see kangaroos, emus and wombats, as well as the

Above
A common sight in rural Australia

magnificent array of brightly coloured galahs, cockatoos, lorikeets, rosellas and parrots that live in Australia. However, by visiting a natural wildlife sanctuary such as the famous Healesville Sanctuary near Melbourne, these animals and birds can be observed close up.

There are 520 lizard species in Australia that range from small squeaking geckos to the spectacular frill-necked lizard and the swift moving goanna that can reach a size of 2m. Whales and dolphins frolic in Australia's seas, as do penguins, seals and sea lions in the cooler southern waters, while in northern Australia, freshwater and the feared estuarine crocodiles lounge, laze and snap.

Highlights

Australian experiences that should not be missed (but often are):

- Snorkelling, sailing and fishing on the Great Barrier Reef.
- Seeing the alpine wild flowers of the Snowy Mountains (Jan–Feb).
- Touring the wineries and gourmet restaurants in the NSW Hunter Valley, SA's Clare Valley, McLaren Vale or Coonawarra regions, or in the luscious Margaret River area of WA.
- An adventure week driving through the wild and remote rocky gorge Kimberley country of northern WA.
- Exploring World Heritage Fraser Island near Noosa.
- Outdoor eating at the Mindil Beach markets under the palm trees in Darwin before heading off for a four-day tour of Kakadu National Park and Katherine Gorge (Nitmiluk).
- Climbing to the top of Mt Warning near Byron Bay at dawn.
- Driving Victoria's spectacular Great Ocean Road.
- Marvelling at the real outback of King Canyon, Finke Gorge and the MacDonnell Ranges as well as Uluru (Ayres Rock).
- Consuming oysters and champagne on Circular Quay, next to Sydney Harbour and the Bridge, as the sun goes down.

The following itineraries make the best use of a short trip:

One-week trip

Day 1: Arrive in Cairns early in the morning, afternoon strolling in the rainforest of Mossman Gorge, and visiting the Habitat Animal Sanctuary. Overnight at Port Douglas.

Day 2: Take a day trip to snorkel the coral of the outer Great Barrier Reef with Quicksilver from Port Douglas. Overnight Port Douglas.

Day 3: Fly from Cairns to Uluru (Ayres Rock). Visit the cultural centre, walk around the base of the Rock with aboriginal guides and watch the sunset by the rock. Overnight at Yulura.

Day 4: Early morning climb of Uluru if so inclined. Visit the Olgas and walk up the silent Valley of the Winds. Take an afternoon flight to Sydney.

Day 5: Explore Sydney with a leisurely historic morning walk around the Rocks, the Art Gallery, the Opera House, Circular Quay and the Royal Botanic Gardens. Take a harbour cruise or a ferry to Manly for fish and chips and a surf in the afternoon, or take the Blue Explorer around the eastern harbourside suburbs to famous Bondi Beach. Take in an opera or play at the Sydney Opera House at night.

Day 6: Explore the spectacular Blue Mountains.

Day 7: Slow morning to pack followed by lunch at Watsons Bay next to the harbour, before catching a late afternoon flight home.

Two-week visit

Day 1: Arrive in Cairns early in the morning, afternoon strolling in the rainforest of Mossman Gorge, and visiting the Habitat Animal Sanctuary. Overnight at Port Douglas.

Day 2: Take a day trip to snorkel the coral of the outer Great Barrier Reef with Quicksilver from Port Douglas. Overnight Port Douglas.

Day 3: Hire a car and drive across the Daintree River (include a crocodile spotting trip) up to the rainforest and glorious beaches of Cape Tribulation. Tour back to Cairns over the top of the Atherton tablelands with their waterfalls, tea plantation and little lakes.

Day 4: Fly from Cairns to Melbourne. Afternoon exploring Melbourne's Yarra River area and Botanic Gardens, before a riverside dinner at Southgate.

Days 5–6: Hire a car and take a two-day driving tour to Phillip Island, South Gippsland and Wilsons Promontory National Park or alternatively down the famous Great Ocean Road.

Day 7: Drive to the Dandenongs for a ride through the fern gullies on the little Puffing Billy steam train, then see Australia's native animals at the excellent Healesville Sanctuary and do some wine tasting on the way home in the Yarra Valley.

Day 8: Fly to Sydney. Take a harbour cruise or a ferry to Manly for fish and chips and a surf in the afternoon, or take the Blue Explorer around the eastern harbourside suburbs to famous Bondi Beach. Take in an opera or play at the Sydney Opera House at night.

Day 9: Hire a car or take a bus tour to explore the spectacular Blue Mountains.

Day 10: Explore inner Sydney with a leisurely historic morning walk around the Rocks, the Art Gallery, the Opera House, Circular Quay and the Royal Botanic Gardens, taking in some of the excellent art and tourist shops along the way. Fly to Darwin in the afternoon.

Day 11: Explore Darwin by Tour Tub, visiting old wharf and World War II bombing sites and memorial, its pearl and coral exhibitions, excellent art gallery featuring aboriginal art and maritime museum (a good place for lunch), and botanic gardens. If it's a Thursday night, don't miss dinner at the outdoor Mindil Beach markets, otherwise try one of the many restaurants on waterfront Cullen Bay.

Day 12: Hire a car or 4WD and drive to Kakadu National Park, exploring some of the Adelaide River and Mary River billabongs and beauty spots along the way.

Day 13: Start with a Yellow Waters dawn cruise amidst the inky waters, crocodiles and long marshes; be intrigued by the Warradjan Aboriginal Cultural Centre, visit the rock art sites at Nourlangie Rock, take an Aboriginal cultural cruise with Gulyambi on the East Alligator river, before watching the sunset from Ubirr Rock.

Day 14: Explore Jim Jim Falls, or take a tour of the Ranger Uranium Mine from Jabiru, before driving back to Darwin. Afternoon flight back to Cairns connecting with international flight home.

Sydney

Ratings

Architecture	●●●●●
Restaurants	●●●●●
Scenery	●●●●●
Beaches	●●●●○
Culture	●●●●○
History	●●●○○
Gardens	●●●○○
Shopping	●●●○○

Sydney is spectacularly built around the hills, fingers and coves of a brilliant blue harbour, Port Jackson, the heart and soul of the city. The U-shaped Circular Quay is the centre of most action. There, modern office towers, art deco architecture and iconic buildings such as the magnificent, white-shelled Opera House, blend with the cobbled streets and colonial buildings of The Rocks, a rich reminder of Sydney's convict heritage. For the culturally minded, a performance at the Opera House should not be missed. For the adventurous, there is a climb up the iron-clad Sydney Harbour Bridge, universally known as 'the coathanger'. For children, a trip to award-winning Taronga Park Zoo is a must. And for hedonists, or anyone who just loves sun, surf and seas, don't forget to take a ferry to Manly or a bus to world-famous Bondi Beach.

Sights

ⓘ Sydney Visitor Centre 106 George St, The Rocks; tel: (02) 9255-1788; www.tourism.nsw.gov.au. Open daily 0900–1800.

ⓖ Art Gallery of NSW The Domain; tel: (02) 9225-1744. Open daily 1000–1700. Courtyard café, restaurant and gallery shop ($ for special exhibitions).

Art Gallery of NSW⁺

A fabulous collection of Australian, European and Asian art housed in a superb sandstone building overlooking the Domain parkland and the Royal Botanic Gardens. The Yiribana Gallery presents a comprehensive selection of Aboriginal art, and there is a permanent exhibition showing the changing nature of Australian art from the first settlement to the present day.

Customs House⁺⁺⁺

Fronting the Circular Quay area, **Customs Square** is itself a piece of history. Paving in the square depicts the original tidal zone as it was at the time of the First Fleet landing, long before the construction of the ferry and boat quay. On the square, the Customs House is an imposing building which has undergone a number of transformations, both inside and out, since it was built in 1885 as the first customs

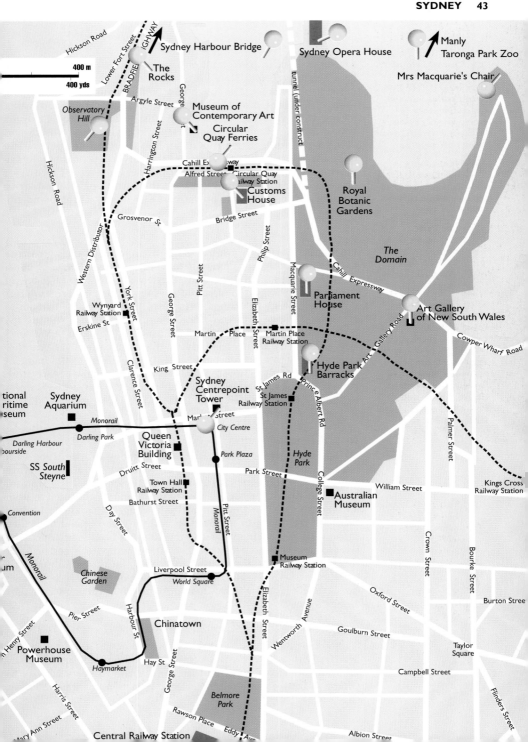

400 m
400 yds

Hickson Road

Lower Fort Street

BRADFIELD HIGHWAY

Sydney Harbour Bridge

The Rocks

Sydney Opera House

Manly
Taronga Park Zoo

Mrs Macquarie's Chair

Observatory Hill

Argyle Street

George Street

Museum of Contemporary Art

Circular Quay Ferries

Harrington Street

Hickson Road

Cahill Expressway

Alfred Street

Circular Quay Railway Station

Customs House

Royal Botanic Gardens

Western Distributor

Grosvenor St

Bridge Street

Philip Street

Macquarie Street

The Domain

Cahill Expressway

Parliament House

Art Gallery of New South Wales

Wynyard Railway Station

York Street

George Street

Pitt Street

Elizabeth Street

Martin Place

Martin Place Railway Station

Art Gallery Road

Cowper Wharf Road

Erskine St

Clarence Street

King Street

Sydney Centrepoint Tower

St James Rd

Prince Albert Rd

Hyde Park Barracks

Palmer Street

National Maritime Museum

Sydney Aquarium

Monorail

City Centre

St James Railway Station

Kings Cross Railway Station

Darling Harbour bourside

Darling Park

Queen Victoria Building

Market Street

Park Plaza

Hyde Park

William Street

SS South Steyne

Druitt Street

Park Street

College Street

Crown Street

Convention

Day Street

Town Hall Railway Station

Bathurst Street

Monorail

Australian Museum

Bourke Street

Monorail

Pitt Street

Liverpool Street

World Square

Museum Railway Station

Oxford Street

Burton Stree

Chinese Garden

Harbour St

Elizabeth Street

Wentworth Avenue

Goulburn Street

Powerhouse Museum

Pier Street

Chinatown

Hay St

George Street

Campbell Street

Taylor Square

Harris Street

Belmore Park

Rawson Place

Albion Street

Flinders Street

Mary Ann Street

Central Railway Station

Eddy Ave

Customs House
Alfred St, Circular Quay; tel: (02) 9247-2285; www.sydneycustomshouse. com.au. Something for everyone with galleries, hands-on exhibitions, great views, cafés and a bar.

Sydney ferry information *tel: 13-1500* for departure times and tour details, between 0600–2200 daily.

Hyde Park Barracks $ *Queens Square, Macquarie St; tel: (02) 9223-8922.* Open 1000–1700. Good coffee shop/restaurant ($$).

The Historic Houses Trust of NSW *tel: (02) 9692-8366; www.hht.nsw.gov.au.* Presents places of cultural and historical significance such as the **Museum of Sydney, Government House, Justice and Police Museum** and **Susannah Place.**

collection point in NSW. Built on land belonging traditionally to the Eora people, Customs House is also where the Union Flag was first raised in the colony. The five floors, built around an atrium, house some of Sydney's best art exhibitions, history displays and eating places. Officially reopened in June 2005, the revamped **Customs House** includes a multimedia library and a new ground floor bar, along with new entertainment and cultural venue spaces. The **Customs House Story** and **Layers of the City** is a permanent display of the historical and architectural perspective of Sydney's development. **Café Sydney ($$)**, on the fifth floor, has indoor or outdoor eating and some of the best views of the bridge and the harbour.

Ferries***
Little green ferries and more modern catamarans criss-cross the harbour as a means of commuting for many residents. But, as so much of Sydney wraps around the central waterway, they also offer one of the best, cheapest and most scenic ways to see the city. Ferries depart upstream to pretty Balmain and Hunters Hill, or across the harbour to Mosman, Taronga Park Zoo and Kirribilli; more special still are the little green ferries to Rose Bay and the seafood restaurants of Watson's Bay. A fast ferry zooms regularly up the Parramatta River. Another runs regularly to the Homebush Bay wharf for access to the home of the 2000 Olympic Games. All ferries and catamarans leave from various well-marked jetties at **Circular Quay**. The longest ferry ride – to Manly – takes about an hour. Tickets can be bought singly, though it is cheaper to buy a set of ten.

Hyde Park Barracks***
Designed by convict architect Francis Greenway, the Hyde Park Barracks housed male convicts between 1819 and 1848 before becoming the Immigration Depot and an asylum for single women. Take a self-guided trip back in time to the dormitory that used to sleep an average of 600 men in hammocks. It is largely thanks to a healthy family of rats living in the barracks and the material and food they squandered that such an accurate museum has been established. The **Greenway Gallery** at the barracks hosts temporary and usually worthwhile exhibitions relating to history, ideas and culture. The barracks is run by the **Historic Houses Trust of NSW** which presents excellent displays of history then and now at 11 different museums around Sydney.

Manly*
Stepping off the ferry or jet-cat at Manly you enter a unique part of Sydney. With a wide, pristine ocean beach on one side and a serene, sandy harbour cove on the other there is almost every activity to choose in between. Among the eclectic collection of shops and cafés

ⓘ **Manly Victor Information Centre** *Ocean Beach, Manly; tel: (02) 9977-1088; fax: (02) 8966-8123.*

⚑ **Manly Arts and Crafts Market** *just off the Corso; open 1000–1700 at weekends and public holidays.*

Ⓟ **Manly Surf School** *tel: (02) 9970-6300.* Drop into any surf shop for details.

Manly Blades *2/49 North Styne, Manly; tel: (02) 9976-3833. Roller blades rental ($).*

Below Circular Quay Ferry

right on Manly Wharf is **Oceanworld** with its giant aquarium, a fun park and paragliding. One of the most stunning walks runs between Manly and the Spit Bridge, overlooking Middle Harbour; the 10-km stretch takes you through unspoiled native bushland and spectacular ever-changing views of the harbour which is usually frantic with boating activity. A colourful mall, the **Corso**, with a mixture of shops and restaurants, links the harbour side of Manly to the ocean. Pick up some fish and chips at any of the many outlets and head for the beach or try one of the many outdoor cafés along North Styne. A promenade heading north along the beach and beneath an avenue of Norfolk pines is as popular with roller-bladers and skateboarders as it is with walkers; it takes you to some of the best surf breaks along the coast including Freshwater and Queenscliff – surf and body boards can be hired from almost any of the many surf shops in the Corso or on North Styne. Marine Parade heads south and follows the ocean foreshore past the delightful Fairy Bower ocean pool to the more secluded and picturesque **Shelly Beach** with its pretty pavilion restaurant. Walk up the hill for superb views of the coast and possibly a southern right whale.

Mrs Macquarie's Chair and the Domain✦✦✦

More comfortable than it sounds, this sandstone rock on the headland above Farm Cove was especially fashioned for Governor Macquarie's wife, Elizabeth, soon after the first settlement, so she could sit on the rock while surveying the wild, empty harbour waiting for ships carrying letters from 'home' to arrive from England. It's now a favourite vantage point for photographers and to enjoy panoramic views of the Bridge. The magnificent harbour view north takes in Garden Island, a large naval base. Most of the navy ships are berthed in Woolloomooloo Bay. Further round from Mrs Macquarie's chair is the superbly located, outdoor **Andrew 'Boy' Charlton Swimming Pool.** Mrs Macquarie's Rd leads to the **Art Gallery of NSW** and the public parkland of the **Domain**, where outdoor

Sydney Sculpture Walk artworks and self-guided tour; tel: (02) 9265-9775.

MCA $ *The Rocks, enter from the front at Circular Quay or from George St; tel: (02) 9252-4033. Open daily 1000–1800. The shop has some innovative and original merchandise.*

Observatory Hill $ *tel: (02) 9217-0485; open 1400–1700 weekdays, 1000–1700 weekends.*

Parliament House *Macquarie St. Open 0930–1600. Free. Tours available.*

Royal Botanic Gardens *tel: (02) 9231-8111. Open 0700–sunset. Free guided walks daily at 1030. Enter near the Opera House, Macquarie St or Mrs Macquarie's Rd. Visitor Centre and Gardens Restaurant tel: (02) 9241-2419.*

Right
Parliament House

concerts and opera nights are often held during summer. You will also pass several glass panels, the Veil of Trees, which is one of 20 contemporary artworks by Australian and international artists around Sydney.

Museum of Contemporary Art and other museums**

On the water's edge at Circular Quay, the MCA is a cutting-edge museum located in a classic 1930s art deco building, featuring changing contemporary art shows and related film and lecture series. Facing north so it gets the winter sun, it has a pleasant café-style restaurant, good for people watching.

The **Powerhouse Museum*** (*Harris St, Darling Harbour; tel: 02-9217-0111*), Australia's largest museum, has 25 dazzling displays of decorative arts, science, technology and social history. The **Australian Museum*** (*College St; tel: 02-9360-6000*) has an excellent display of dinosaur material and a section showcasing Australia's diverse community groups and their culture through music, song, dance and photographs. The **Museum of Sydney*** (*Phillip St; tel: 02-9251-4611*), on the site of the first Government House, covers life in colonial Sydney from 1788 to 1850.

Observatory Hill**

Built in 1858, the Sydney Observatory offers stunning views of the harbour to the west of the bridge, and is a great spot to stop and rest for a quiet hour in the sun, the bustle of the city just a quiet hum in the background. It is now used as a Museum of Astronomy with Planetarium shows every weekend at 1130 and 1530.

Parliament House**

The NSW State Parliament is located on Sydney's historic Macquarie St. Various parts of the building date from different periods in the history of New South Wales, ranging from 1816 through to the mid-1980s. At its Macquarie St frontage it is a small, two-storey Georgian building flanked by the façades of the Victorian-era Parliamentary Chambers. This part of the building is then linked via a 'square doughnut' section around a central fountain to a contemporary 12-storey office block which looks out on to the parkland of **Sydney's Domain** and to the harbour beyond. Watch the NSW politicians in action during question time in both the Legislative Assembly and Legislative Council, the two houses that make up the NSW Parliament.

Royal Botanic Gardens*

Like an oasis, the Royal Botanic Gardens cover 30 hectares of beautifully maintained land in the heart of the city at the edge of the harbour. Established in 1816 on the site of Australia's first farm, they are the oldest scientific institution in Australia.

Cadman's Cottage
110 George St; tel: (02) 9555-09844. Open daily 0900–1700. Sydney's oldest house is now used by the National Parks and Wildlife Service.

Susannah Place *58–64 Gloucester Place; tel: (02) 9241-1893. Open 1000–1700. A terrace of four houses built in 1844 that were part of the rich fabric of early Sydney; now an intimate and colourful corner store.*

Harbour Bridge Museum $ *via Cumberland St, Miller Point; tel: (02) 9247-3408. Open daily 1000–1700.*

Rocks Walking Tours $ *tel: (02) 9247-6678. Starting from the visitors' centre in George St, the 75-minute guided tours run at 1030, 1230 and 1430 weekdays and 1130 and 1430 at weekends.*

BridgeClimb $$$ *5 Cumberland St, The Rocks; tel: (02) 9252-0077; fax: (02) 9240-1122; www.bridgeclimb.com. Open daily 0700–1900. Booking is essential.*

The Rocks*

Adjacent to **Circular Quay**, the Rocks is an artfully preserved slice of Australian history with dozens of cafés and restaurants, boutiques, historic pubs and houses, many of them home to families who have lived in the area for generations. It is here that Captain Arthur Phillip brought the First Fleet of ships in 1788, complete with 750 convicts, sailors and enough supplies and livestock to last two years, and set up the furthest flung outpost of the British Empire. The Argyle Cut, a tunnel excavated through the hill by convicts, stands as an eerie reminder of life in a harsh penal colony. Named after a prominent outcrop of sandstone on the hillside, The Rocks has undergone a series of transformations through the decades, including one after an outbreak of the bubonic plague in 1900, and another in 1925 when whole streets were demolished as work began on the Sydney Harbour Bridge. A substantial redevelopment programme has created a special ambience as well as many sightseeing attractions such as one of Sydney's oldest houses, **Cadman's Cottage***, built in 1816, and **Susannah Place*** (1844). The cannons on the southern side of the bridge are on the site of the military commander's original residence; opposite is **Admiralty House**, once residence for the commander of the navy, now the Sydney home of the Governor General. Most of the pubs, including Australia's oldest, **The Hero of Waterloo**, are usually full of life and entertainment. At weekends, a section of George St is taken over by **The Rocks Market**, with more than a hundred stalls.

Sydney Harbour Bridge***

Commonly referred to as 'the coathanger' (for obvious reasons) or the iron lung because of the large number of people it employed after the great depression, the Harbour Bridge is more than just a north–south access point. The world's largest single arch bridge, with an arch span of 503m, is an engineering miracle offering one of the best views in the world. Thanks to one man's determination, 66 years after its completion in 1932, it is now possible to scale the magnificent arches as part of a unique and unforgettable adventure. Wearing a grey suit to blend in to the bridge, and linked to a static line throughout the climb, you climb about 1500m, venture across catwalks, ladders and arches to reach the top, 134m above sea level, for a 360-degree view of the magnificent harbour and city. The whole experience takes about 3 hours and is well worth the rather steep price. Climbers are breath-tested for alcohol and put through a metal detector; cameras are not allowed but digital pictures are taken for you at the top.

If it is the bridge you are interested in, without the height and adventure, you can climb inside the southeast pylon which houses the ever-improving **Harbour Bridge Museum***.

The Sydney Opera House*

One of the country's greatest icons, the Sydney Opera House and its grand white sails was designed by Dutch architect Jern Utzon, and was opened in 1972 after a decade of controversy surrounding its design, construction and cost. Tours are available of the main concert hall and two smaller theatres, where regular performances are staged by Opera Australia, the Australian Ballet, the Sydney Theatre Company, and the Sydney Symphony Orchestra. Walk around the front of this magnificent building for superb views. A café on the front promenade is a perfect place to soak up the harbour ambience.

Sydney Centrepoint Tower**

The owner of Sydney Tower, insurance giant AMP, has renamed this city centrepiece, AMP Tower Centrepoint. At 305m it offers the best 360-degree views of the city and beyond from its top level. Two revolving restaurants run by Sydney Tower Restaurants offer a choice of à la carte and buffet dining ($$).

Sydney Harbour National Park***

The pockets of bushland around the foreshore and headlands are one of Sydney Harbour's crowning glories. The National Park incorporates views of the majestic entrance to the harbour, natural bushland, secluded sandy beaches, harbour islands and rugged sandstone cliffs with the stark contrast of cosmopolitan Sydney in the background. There are several sections of the park dotted around Sydney Harbour; most are accessible by public transport. It is possible to follow a tour of the harbour islands, including historic Fort Denison off Mrs Macquarie's Point, or Goat Island, west of the Harbour Bridge, where, for over 100 years, people were quarantined at the Quarantine Station to protect Sydney residents against epidemic diseases. You can also take a water taxi to Shark Island off Rose Bay for a picnic. Nielsen Park on the southern foreshore in Vaucluse is particularly beautiful for picnics and swimming (it is shark-netted during summer). Visit South Head for spectacular views and walks – and a drink at the old Watsons Bay Hotel afterwards where you can watch the most beautiful sunsets. Discovery walks, talks and tours are available in all the parks. On the north shore there is Ashton Park near Taronga Zoo, with a 4-km track heading east to Clifton Gardens, another popular picnic and swimming spot.

Taronga Park Zoo*

Some of the animals in Taronga Zoo have the best views in the world, looking across Sydney Harbour towards the city and the Opera House. Located on the edge of the North Shore, the zoo has an extensive collection of Australian animals including koalas, kangaroos, echidnas, dingoes, Tasmanian devils and the nocturnal possums, all in spacious, leafy environments.

Above
Sydney Harbour and the Opera
House

Accommodation and food

Most of the big name, big price hotels are in The Rocks area but there
are also some quaint pubs and old hotels, including **The Mercantile
Hotel $$** *25 George St; tel: (02) 9247-3570*, breakfast included, or **Lord
Nelson Brewery Hotel $$** *19 Kent St; tel: (02) 9251-4044.*

Botanic Gardens Restaurant and Café $$ *tel: (02) 9241-2419.* Set in
the middle of the gardens, the bush and harbour views – away from
traffic – are as good as its food. In winter they light an open fire; the
café is downstairs.

Cockle Bay Wharf has a variety of good eating places to chose from;
recently completed and overlooking Darling Harbour, the area has
attracted some of Australia's best restaurateurs. Try **Chinta Ria $$** for
modern Malaysian and **Coast $$$** for seafood.

Le Kiosk Restaurant $$ *1 Marine Parade, Shelly Beach; tel: (02) 9977-
4122.* Great seafood on the coast in a quite secluded setting, a 10-
minute walk south along Marine Parade from Manly Beach.

Sailors Thai $ *106 George St; tel: (02) 9251-2466.* Upstairs for a bowl of
noodles or flavoursome soup in a modern, comfortable setting; more
expensive restaurant downstairs.

Suggested tour

This is a full day's walking tour, with a ferry ride to either the zoo or Manly. The bridge climb takes about 3 hours.

Start your walking tour at **CIRCULAR QUAY ❶**, heading northeast to the **OPERA HOUSE ❷** and Bennelong Point. Continue through the gates of the **ROYAL BOTANIC GARDENS ❸** and head up the hill immediately to your right to reach Government House. There are several exits to the gardens, but take the gate on the water's edge to the north to continue on to **MRS MACQUARIE'S CHAIR ❹** and some of the best views of the harbour and bridge. Further on you will find the outdoor **Andrew 'Boy' Charlton Pool**, named after an Olympic swimmer. Continue along the reconstructed **Farm Cove** walk which overlooks the **Navy Base** and the revamped **Woolloomooloo Wharf**. At the top of a small rise is another entrance to the Royal Botanical Gardens on the right and the sandstone **NSW ART GALLERY ❺** with its lush green lawns on the left. Opposite the gallery is the **Domain** and Speakers' Corner, should you feel like voicing your opinion or listening to others voice theirs. Continue along Art Gallery Road and head towards **St Mary's Cathedral**. Stay on the right-hand side of the road with the start of **Hyde Park** on your left until you reach the **HYDE PARK BARRACKS ❻** on the corner of Macquarie St and Prince Albert Road. Continue north along Macquarie St towards the harbour, passing the **Sydney Mint Museum, Sydney Hospital, PARLIAMENT HOUSE ❼** and the **State Library**. The Royal Botanic Gardens will be on your right again. When you reach the **Conservatorium of Music**, cross Macquarie St and head left down Bridge St. At Phillip St, the **Museum of Sydney** is on your left. Enter the world of police, law and crime in the **Justice and Police Museum ❽**, right on Phillip St (*open weekends 1000–1700*). You are now back at Circular Quay. The recently refurbished **CUSTOMS HOUSE ❾** on Alfred St is a good place for a break before you take on the historic Rocks precinct. Cut through, under the incredibly ugly Cahill Expressway at the back of Circular Quay, to the **MUSEUM OF CONTEMPORARY ART ❿** and then to George St and **THE ROCKS ⓫**. The best way to get the feel of The Rocks is to go up and down and through as many narrow stairways and alleys as possible.

Below
Period shopping in the Queen Victoria Building on George Street

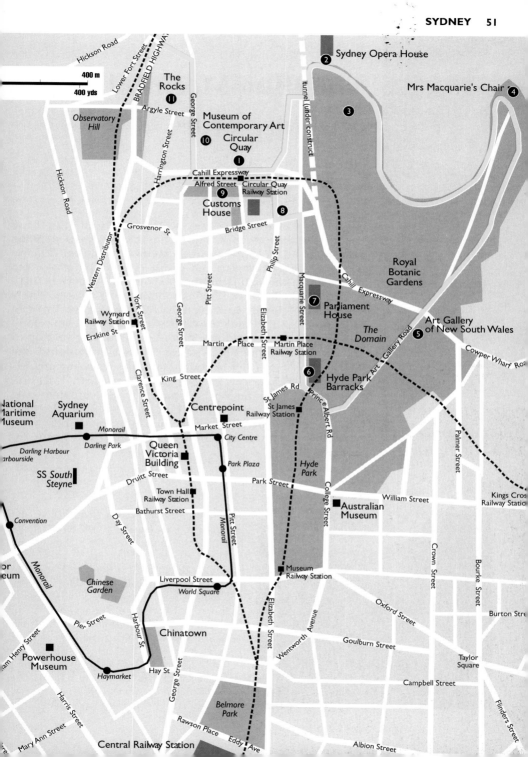

Hickson Road

Lower Fort Street

BRADFIELD HIGHWAY

2 Sydney Opera House

Mrs Macquarie's Chair **4**

The Rocks **11**

Argyle Street

George Street

3

Observatory Hill

Harrington Street

Museum of Contemporary Art

10 Circular Quay

tunnel (under construct

1

Hickson Road

Cahill Expressway

Alfred Street

Circular Quay Railway Station

9 Customs House

8

Western Distributor

Grosvenor St.

Bridge Street

Philip Street

Royal Botanic Gardens

Cahill Expressway

York Street

Pitt Street

Elizabeth Street

Macquarie Street

7 Parliament House

Art Gallery Road

Art Gallery of New South Wales **5**

Wynyard Railway Station

Erskine St

George Street

Martin Place

Martin Place Railway Station

The Domain

Cowper Wharf Roa

Clarence Street

King Street

Centrepoint

Market Street

St James Rd

St James Railway Station

6 Hyde Park Barracks

Prince Albert Rd

Palmer Street

National Maritime Museum

Sydney Aquarium

Monorail

Darling Park

City Centre

Darling Harbour Harbourside

Queen Victoria Building

Park Plaza

Park Street

Hyde Park

College Street

William Street

Kings Cross Railway Statio

SS South Steyne

Druitt Street

Town Hall Railway Station

Bathurst Street

Pitt Street

Monorail

Australian Museum

Crown Street

Bourke Street

Convention

Monorail

Day Street

Burton Stre

or eum

Chinese Garden

Liverpool Street

World Square

Museum Railway Station

Elizabeth Street

Oxford Street

Pier Street

Harbour St.

Chinatown

Wentworth Avenue

Goulburn Street

Taylor Square

Powerhouse Museum

Haymarket

Hay St

George Street

Campbell Street

am Henry Street

Harris Street

Mary Ann Street

Belmore Park

Rawson Place

Eddy Ave

Central Railway Station

Albion Street

Flinders Street

400 m
400 yds

The Blue Mountains and beyond

Ratings

Scenery	● ● ● ● ●
Walking	● ● ● ● ●
Adventure	● ● ● ● ○
Historical sights	● ● ● ● ○
National parks	● ● ● ● ○
Weekend retreats	● ● ● ● ○
Guided tours	● ● ● ○ ○
Wildlife	● ● ● ○ ○

Ninety minutes drive west of Sydney, the Blue Mountains get their name from the haze created by the eucalyptus oil in the air above a seemingly endless expanse of mountain gum forests. The drive essentially follows the route carved through daunting canyons and valleys in 1813 by explorers Blaxland, Wentworth and Lawson. Their discovery of fertile grazing lands to the far west of the mountains ensured the survival of the fledgling penal colony in Sydney. There is evidence that Aboriginal tribes moved to and from the Sydney Plains across the Blue Mountains some 20,000 years ago. Their historic waterholes, grinding grooves and rock carvings can be seen near Wentworth Falls and Glenbrook. The immense National Park also contains some of the country's best bushwalking. Southwest of the Blue Mountains are the cool, fertile Southern Highlands, with rambling homesteads, colonial mansions and beautiful gardens.

BELL'S LINE OF ROAD✦✦✦

Named after 19-year-old Archibald Bell who discovered the route in 1823, the Bell's Line of Road links the historic towns of Richmond and Windsor to the Blue Mountains.

Forming the Grand Circular Drive, the road winds its way along the ridge of the spectacular **Grose Valley** through a mixture of orchards and rugged bush and is an increasingly popular alternative to the Great Western Highway. Originally built by convicts in 1841, the road meanders north from Richmond, through the historic **Kurrajong Village**. Kurrajong is Aboriginal for the *barchychiton populnous* tree which used to grow in the area and whose seeds were roasted as a

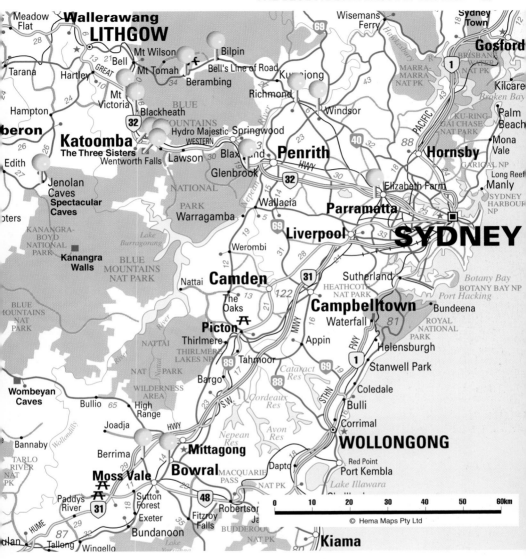

Blue Mountains Adventure Company $$ 84A Main St, Katoomba; tel: (02) 4782-1271; fax: (02) 4782-1277; www.bmac.com.au

substitute for coffee. As well as quaint tea houses, galleries and craft shops, the road passes the Bilpin apple orchards where there are any number of fruit and pie stalls and past Mt Tomah and the Mt Tomah Botanic Garden. Close to the village of Kurrajong Heights is a ski park, offering grass skiing and carting down a grassy slope. Near Bell is the entrance to Pierce's Pass. Walk for about half an hour from the car park to the pass for stunning views of the Grose Gorge down to Blue Gum Forest and the Grose River.

BERRIMA✧✧✧

ℹ Tourist Information and Berrima Courthouse $ *Main Street, Berrima; tel: (02) 4877-1505. Open 1000–1600.*

In the heart of the Southern Highlands, the little sandstone-cottage village of Berrima, established in 1831, is steeped in history, as well as containing a plethora of antique shops, art and craft outlets and tea rooms. It claims to be the only existing example of a preserved Australian Georgian colonial town. There are regular tours to the nearby ghost town of **Joadja**.

BLACKHEATH✧✧✧

ℹ National Parks and Wildlife Service/ Heritage Centre *end of Govetts Leap Rd, Blackheath; tel: (02) 4787-8877; www. nationalparks.nsw.gov.au. Open 0900–1630.* An excellent collection of maps of walking trails in the area plus an interpretative display of the history, flora and fauna of the Blue Mountains; souvenirs and artwork for sale.

Below Bridal Veil Falls

Named by Governor Macquarie in 1815 for its charred, wild, open heath-like appearance, Blackheath is a Blue Mountains colonial town that has some of the Mountains' best bushwalking and views. North of the highway are superb views of the **Grose Valley** and walks to **Neates Glen**, the **Grand Canyon** and **Beauchamp Falls** are accessed from the end of **Evans Lookout Rd.** Off this road is Wall's Cave Rd, leading to the beautiful **Wall's Cave** which was occupied by Aboriginals at least 12,000 years ago. **Govetts Leap Rd**, off the Highway, leads to Govetts Leap Lookout for stunning views of basalt tops (remnants of old volcanoes), **Mt Tomah**, Mt Banks and Mt Hay across the valley. Less crowded than Govetts Leap Lookout but with equally breathtaking views, is **Evans Lookout**, off Evans Lookout Rd. You can also walk to Evans Lookout from Govetts Leap; it is a 3-km one-way, medium walk along the **Cliff Top Track** through dense heathland and mallee gums, banksia trees and wildflowers.

There are several other walks from Govetts Leap, including one to **Perrys Lookdown** and **Pulpit Rock.** Allow 3 hours return for waterfalls, wildflowers, lush rainforest and great views. There is also a walk to the base of **Bridal Veil Falls**. This walk is 1¹⁄₂ hours return straight down and up, and takes in a historic stone stairway, hanging swamps, grand views and the 180-m high waterfall.

BOWRAL*

Bradman Museum
$ *St Jude St; open
1000–1600 daily.* An
enormous collection of
cricket memorabilia plus
cricket souvenirs and
clothing; the start of the
Bradman Walk; tea and
coffee in the Stumps Tea
Room.

Situated in the valley at the foot of Mt Gibraltar, Bowral is one of the main towns in the Southern Highlands. With a population of 20,000 it is best known as the home of Australia's most famous cricketer, Sir Don Bradman. 'The Don' was actually born in Cootamundra in 1908, but went to school in Bowral and spent hours practising cricket here by hitting a golf ball against a corrugated metal water tank with a wicket-wide piece of wood. The tank was demolished years ago, but you can see the house he lived in as part of the 1.7-km self-guided **Bradman Walk** through town. The walk takes in the **Bradman Museum*** – set up in his honour and with an enormous collection of cricket memorabilia.

ELIZABETH FARM*

Elizabeth Farm $
*70 Alice St, Rosehill;
tel: (02) 9635-9488.
Open daily 1000–1700.*
A tearoom serves
Devonshire cream teas
and lunches.

Linden House $ *Lancer
Barracks, Smith and Darcy
St, Parramatta; tel: (02)
9635-7822. Open
1000–1600.*

Not far from Parramatta, Australia's second-oldest European town, Elizabeth Farm is a simple but elegant house built in 1793 by John Macarthur who is often referred to as the father of Australia's wool industry with its deep, shady verandas, Elizabeth Farm became the prototype for the Australian homestead. The interiors contain reproductions of furniture, portraits and objects belonging to the Macarthurs, allowing visitors to 'experience' life in the early 19th century. Elizabeth Farm is situated in a recreated 1830s garden and contains early plants from the Macarthurs' time.

Now a thriving business district, **Parramatta** was a busy rural centre in 1789, its fertile land along the river providing food for the settlement at Sydney Cove. The colony's first orchard, vineyard, tannery and legal brewery were all here. Nearby is **Linden House***, a regimental museum with a fascinating display of colonial-era memorabilia and weaponry. It is the centrepiece of Australia's oldest surviving military establishment.

GLENBROOK**

**Blue Mountains
Tourism Ltd** *Great
Western Highway; tel: (02)
4739-6266; fax: (02) 4739-
6787; www.
bluemountainstourism.org.au.
Open 0900–1700 weekdays
and 0830–1630 weekends.*

**National Parks and
Wildlife Service** *Bruce
Rd; tel: (02) 4739-2950.*

The town of Glenbrook, off the Great Western Highway, has a proud history linked with early exploration of trains. Drive through Glenbrook to reach several special attractions in the Blue Mountains National Park including **Red Hands Cave** – with hand prints and grinding grooves from an Aboriginal culture at least 20,000 years old – **Jelly Bean Pool** and **Euroka Clearing**.

Other local attractions include the delightful **Wascoe Siding Miniature Railway**, open the first Sunday of each month – a hit with children – and the **Ampol Service Station** where there is a beautifully restored former Stationmaster's sandstone cottage.

THE HYDRO MAJESTIC HOTEL**

◐ Hydro Majestic Hotel $$–$$$ *The Great Western Highway, Medlow Baths; tel: (02) 4788-1002; www.hydromajestic.com.au. Recently furbished with gardens and bush walks, sensational views of the Megalong Valley from the Megalong Room (breakfast and lunch) and the Palm Court and Grand Dining Rooms.*

At Medlow Baths, this recently renovated hotel on the escarpment overlooking the Megalong Valley is *the* grand hotel of the Blue Mountains. Built on the site of the home of Edward Hargraves – who discovered the western NSW gold fields – it carries history with charm and elegance. Fire destroyed the original hotel in 1922, along with a hydropathic establishment owned by Sydney businessman Mark Foy. At the turn of the century, Mr Foy returned from a trip abroad where he had benefited from hydropathic treatment received at the popular Derbyshire spa of Matlock Bath in England. Eager to introduce the treatment to Australia, he bought the Hotel Belgravia and Hargraves house, with Tucker's cottage in between, and built the Hydro Majestic Hotel, where the latest therapeutic methods from Europe were used.

KATOOMBA**

ⓘ Blue Mountains Tourism *end of Echo Point Rd; tel: (02) 4782-0756; www. bluemountainstourism.org.au. Open 0900–1700.*

The Edge Cinema $ *Great Western Highway; tel: (02) 4782-8900. A 38-minute documentary on the Blue Mountains, The Edge, on a giant screen. Excellent introduction to the region.*

Katoomba, along with the nearby townships of **Wentworth Falls** and **Leura**, is the most visited, and heavily populated area of the Blue Mountains. Apart from the numerous shops and cafés (which cater extremely well for vegetarians), the main reason for visiting Katoomba is **Echo Point**, about 1km through town, which offers the best views of the **Jamison Valley** and the famous **Three Sisters** rock formation.

Easily the most photographed and famous landmark in the Blue Mountains, the Three Sisters stand at the end of a plateau which drops away into the blue haze of the Jamison Valley, opposite Mt Solitary. Standing 922m, 918m and 906m high, the trio of peaks was formed by the erosion of Triassic sandstone. An Aboriginal legend tells of three sisters whose witch doctor father turned them into stone with his magic bone so as to protect them from a frightening bunyip that lived in a deep hole. The bunyip chased the father, who turned himself into a lyrebird but lost his magic bone before he could turn his three daughters back into girls. As you look at the Three Sisters you can hear the lyrebird calling his daughters as the search for the lost bone continues.

The Three Sisters are best seen from Queen Elizabeth Lookout at Echo Point, about 1km from Katoomba down Echo Point Road. Floodlighting at night makes them look particularly dramatic. There is often an Aboriginal playing the didgeridoo here, a traditional musical instrument made from hollowed wood.

Katoomba is also the starting point for some magnificent walking, from the Three Sisters Walk which takes about half an hour, to the **Giant Stairway-Federal Pass Walk**, which begins at the rear of the Scenic Railway complex and goes deep into the Jamison Valley. The walk descends about 1000 steps through the rainforest with excellent views of Katoomba Falls, the Three Sisters and the Skyway.

Above
The Three Sisters

Next page
Tree tops in the
Blue Mountains

The **Scenic Railway**⁺ (*$ Violet St; open 0900–1700*), on the site of a disused coal-mining operation, drops at a 45-degree angle to the valley floor through spectacular scenery. The **Scenic Skyway** cable car travels about 200m above the valley floor, across Katoomba Falls, and gives a marvellous view of the dense eucalyptus.

Mount Tomah Botanic Gardens❖

**Mt Tomah Botanic Gardens $** *per car; www.rbgsyd.nsw.gov.au. Open daily 1000–1600. Award-winning restaurant ($$): Bell's Line of Road, Tomah; tel: (02) 4567-2154.*

On the Bell's Line of Road, past **Bilpin**, Mt Tomah Botanic Gardens is best known for its stunning collection of cool climate plants. There are also some exotic plant species, and an extensive array of native trees, including the 'wollemi pine', a unique species of tree that was only discovered in 1994.

Mount Victoria❖❖

Mt Vic Flicks $ *tel: (02) 4787-1577. Old-fashioned cinema with mainstream films; on Sat there is a double feature with supper in the interval.*

Jenolan Caves $ *There are about 10 tours a day from 1000–1600 and a night tour at 2000; www.jenolancaves.org.au. Tickets can sell out during school holidays.*

The highest town in the Blue Mountains, at 1043m, Mt Victoria is a small village filled with history. Buildings of interest are the old post office, the 1872 railway gatekeeper's cottage which houses a museum (*open weekends 1400–1700*), the **Victoria and Albert** guesthouse, and the 1849 **Tollkeeper's Cottage** with its especially designed bow windows so the toll keeper could cover the road in both directions. Turn off here for the **Jenolan Caves❖❖❖**, which are amongst the world's best – a veritable labyrinth of caverns and stunning limestone formations. Guarding the entrance are the dramatic **Blue Pool**, **Grand Arch** and **Carlotta's Arch**. Discovered by a convict bush ranger in 1838, the caves make for a spellbinding experience.

RICHMOND❖❖

ⓘ Tourism Hawkesbury *Ham Common, Windsor St, Clarendon; tel: (02) 4588-5895; www.hawkesbury.net.au*

Richmond and **Windsor** are two of the five Macquarie towns in the rich semi-rural **Hawkesbury Valley**. First explored in 1789 and later developed as an important farming area, the twin towns are the Hawkesbury River's gateway to the Blue Mountains. Complete with a village green, Richmond has some good cafés as well as historic attractions such as Hobartville (1828), Bowman Cottage (1821) and St Peter's Church (1841). Windsor, to the east, has lovely old streets, antique shops, eateries and the picturesque Hawkesbury River.

WENTWORTH FALLS❖❖

ⓗ Yester Grange $ *Yester Rd; www.yestergrange.com.au. Open 1000–1600 weekdays and 1000–1700 weekends. A restored home of a 19th-century premier and superb Victorian museum with more spectacular views.*

Apart from the magnificent 300-m cascade of water and the stunning views of the Jamison Valley, the small village of Wentworth Falls is the starting point for a network of fabulous walking tracks, including the **Charles Darwin Walk**. Before you reach the village, Yester Road leads to the magnificently restored **Yester Grange**. Back on Tableland Road, a short drive south leads to Queen Elizabeth Drive and a track which takes you to the haunting **Kings Tableland** Aboriginal site.

Suggested tour

Blue Mountains National Park Heritage Centre *end of Govetts Leap Rd, Blackheath; tel: (02) 4787-8877; www. nationalparks.nsw.gov.au. Open 0900–1630.*

Blue Mountains Visitor Information Centres *Echo Point, Katoomba and Great Western Highway, Glenbrook; tel: 1800-641-227 or (02) 4739-6266; www.bluemountainstourism. org.au*

Tourism Southern Highlands *62–70 Main St, Mittagong; tel: (02) 4871-2888; www. southern-highlands.co.au. Open 0800–1730 daily.*

Blue Mountains Accommodation Booking Service *tel: (02) 4782-2857.*

Free accommodation booking service *tel: 1800-656-176; www.highlandsnsw.com.au*

Jenolan Caves House *$$$ Jenolan Caves Rd, Jenolan Caves; tel: (02) 6359-3322; www.jenolancaves.org.au. Built in 1889, this is a grand old-style guesthouse. Camping is also available.*

Treetops Country Guesthouse *$$ 101 Railway Ave, Bundanoon; tel: (02) 4883-6372; www. treetopsguesthouse.com.au. Be part of an unfolding drama at one of the Super Sleuth Murder Mystery Weekends. Set on the edge of the Morton National Park.*

Total distance: 125km from Glenbrook to Richmond via Katoomba on the Grand Circular Drive, taking in the picturesque Bell's Line of Road. A detour from Mt Victoria in the Blue Mountains to Jenolan Caves is about 56km on a windy road through the stunning Megalong Valley. It is another 77km from Jenolan Caves, with some backtracking, to Lithgow to rejoin the Bell's Line of Road at Bell before continuing a further 65km to Richmond.

Time: One to two days. Allow about an hour to Glenbrook or Richmond from Sydney depending on the traffic.

Route: From the centre of Sydney head west on Parramatta Rd until you reach the M4 tollway then the Great Western Highway from the outskirts of **Penrith**, and over the Nepean River. **GLENBROOK ❶** is the first of 26 townships in the Blue Mountains on the Great Western Highway. Be careful of fog and possibly snow in winter.

The Grand Circular Drive is windy most of the way and is four-lane until **KATOOMBA ❷**. At Katoomba take Cliff Drive, running along the edge of the Jamison Valley, to Leura for some more great views. Return to the Grand Circular Drive which narrows considerably after Katoomba, and continue past **MT VICTORIA ❸**, along the **BELL'S LINE OF ROAD ❹** to **RICHMOND ❺** and nearby **Windsor ❻**. The road is windy and quite narrow in parts but in good condition.

Detour 1: From **BLACKHEATH** railway crossing, drive beneath a memorable canopy of ferns filtered by dappled sunlight and into the majestic **Megalong Valley**, a feast of flora, fauna, amazing sandstone escarpments and rainforest. As well as spectacular walks, through Mermaid, Coachwood or Nellie Glens, this area is great for horse riding. On your way back up Megalong Rd turn left along Shipley Rd for some of the most breathtaking views imaginable. The road forks left to **Hargraves Lookout** for magnificent views of the Megalong Valley and Kanangra Walls. To the right the road takes you to **Mt Blackheath** and stunning panoramas of the **Great Dividing Range**.

Detour 2: From Mt Victoria take Victoria Pass, via **Hartley Historic Village**, to the **Jenolan Caves**. The road to the Caves is windy and slow at the end, but is sealed all the way and takes about 1½ hours from Mt Victoria. After the picturesque hamlet of **Hampton** there are some sensational views of the Blue Mountains escarpment on the left, before you start driving into the Jenolan State Forest and down through hairpin bends until you reach **Blue Pool** and the **Grand Arch**. Either return to the Great Western Highway through Hartley or continue on to **Lithgow**, a thriving town of 20,000 people, where you will find the renowned **Zig-Zag Railway** with its little steam train. From Lithgow return to the Bell's Line of Road via Bell.

Craigieburn Resort
$$$ *Centennial Rd,*
Bowral; tel: (02) 4861-1277;
www.craigieburnresort.com.au.
An imposing county
homestead built in 1887
with 22ha of gardens and a
9-hole golf course.

White Horse Inn $$
Market Place, Berrima; tel:
(02) 4877-1204. Motel
rooms and a fabulous
restaurant which opens
for dinner on Fri and Sat
nights only.

Lilianfels Blue
Mountains $$$ *near Echo*
Point, Katoomba; tel: (02)
4780-1200, 1800-024-452;
www.lilianfles.com.au.
A luxurious resort,
considered one of the best
in the mountains.

From Windsor the quickest way back to Sydney is to follow the
Sydney signs on Windsor Rd until you see the signs to the M2
Motorway or Hills Motorway. Turn left on to the M2 and follow it
through to Chatswood where it runs straight into the freeway leading
on to the Harbour Bridge or Harbour Tunnel and into the City. Allow
about an hour depending on the traffic and time of day.

Also worth exploring

A 2-hour drive southwest of Sydney, the **Southern Highlands** ➐ was
one of the first inland areas to be settled by Europeans in the early
19th century, and has long been used as a summer retreat when
Sydney turns sticky hot in January and February. Rambling
homesteads and colonial mansions, many of which have been
converted into luxury resorts and guesthouses, are evidence of how
the early settlers regarded themselves as landed gentry rather than
Australian farmers. Quaint villages (such as **BOWRAL** and **BERRIMA**)
with beautiful gardens are scattered across this landscape that
resembles England more closely than anywhere else in Australia,
except, perhaps, Tasmania.

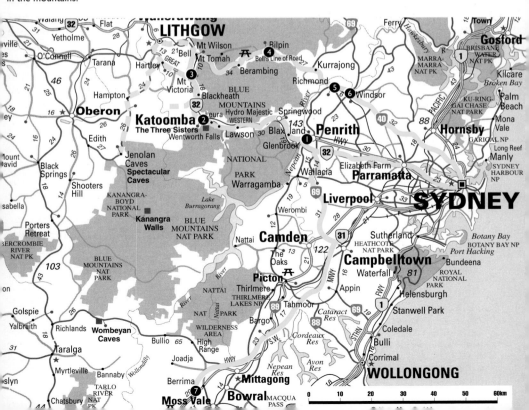

The Hunter Valley

Ratings

Food and drink	●●●●●
National parks	●●●●●
Outdoor activities	●●●●●
Wineries	●●●●●
Beaches	●●●●○
History	●●●●○
Scenery	●●●●○
Wildlife	●●●●○

Relax with a glass of crisp local sémillon and a plate of cheese or olives among the grape vines of the Hunter Valley. Even better, start a day here or in the hills around picturesque Mudgee, and end up later that afternoon with a swim, a surf or a walk along one of the world's best beaches near cosmopolitan Newcastle, the second largest city in NSW. The Hunter Valley with more than 60 wineries tucked in among rolling hills, green pastures and deep valleys of vineyards, also harbours some of the country's most historic colonial towns. Nearby Barrington Tops National Park is a World Heritage-listed subtropical rainforest, home to wallabies, possums and a variety of birdlife. Proximity to Sydney makes the region popular with tourists, yet you can easily be the only people in the tasting room of a small Hunter Valley winery.

BARRINGTON TOPS NATIONAL PARK*

ℹ Barrington Tops Visitor Information Centre
Denison St, Gloucester; tel: (02) 6558-1408; www.gloucester.org.au

🏛 Barrington Tops National Park
Salisbury, via Dungog; tel: (02)4995-3212; www. australiannationalparks.com

🌙 Barrington Guesthouse $$
Barrington Tops National Park, Salisbury, via Dungog; tel: (02) 4995-3212; www. barringtonguesthouse.com.au

One of the most elevated points in Australia, the Barrington Tops reach an altitude of over 1550m and snow is common in winter. The rugged, untamed mountains, cool-climate rainforest, gorges, cliffs and waterfalls, make Barrington Tops a wilderness paradise for walkers, campers, birdwatchers and climbers.

More than 280,000 hectares of forest are protected by the **Barrington Tops National Park***, and the 1000-year-old subtropical rainforest on the southern slopes was declared a World Heritage Area in 1986. This National Park contains some of Australia's tallest and oldest trees; amongst them are forests of giant Antarctic beech trees that give way to magnificent views of the rolling hills and farmlands of the Hunter Valley.

Nestled among the trees just outside the national park is the time-honoured **Barrington Guesthouse**, which is as much a refuge for native animals as human visitors.

CESSNOCK***

One of the younger towns in the **Lower Hunter**, Cessnock sits in a gentle landscape with the magnificent Brokenback Range as its backdrop. Beautifully preserved eucalyptus trees and lofty jacarandas

ⓘ Cessnock Visitor Information Centre *Turner Park, Aberdare Rd; tel: (02) 4990-4477; fax: (02) 4991-4518.*

line the streets of this rural town. Like many other Hunter towns, it developed with the discovery of coal which attracted many people from Wales, Scotland and the north of England to the villages of Kearsley, Kitchener, Aberdare, Bellbird and Nulkaba. It is an excellent starting point from which to explore the Lower Hunter wine region around Pokolbin (*see page 70*).

DUNGOG✦✦✦

ⓗ Tocal Homestead *$ Tocal Rd, Paterson (between Dungog and Maitland); tel: (02) 4939-8965.* Call for opening times; horse-drawn carriage rides, whip-cracking and blacksmithing.

Dungog, north of Newcastle off the New England Highway, has all the charm of an early heritage town with its wide streets and houses with big verandas surrounded by some quite thick bush. The town was established as a military post to help rid the Williams River Valley settlements of bushrangers, and it still has the feel of bushranger country. The cottage belonging to Captain Thunderbolt – one of the most notorious hold-up men – can be seen as part of a tour of **Tocal Homestead**.

HUNTER VALLEY✦

The Hunter Valley contains the oldest commercial vineyards in Australia, established on the fertile flats of the Hunter River in the 1830s. Originally a specialist area for fortified wines, the Hunter Valley is now one of Australia's premium table districts, producing quality red and white wines for both local consumption and the flourishing export market. January to March is harvest time, when the vintage is in full swing, and wineries at their busiest. Shiraz, Sémillon and Chardonnay are now acknowledged as the classic wines of the Hunter.

The Hunter Valley is often divided into two parts: the **Upper Hunter**, around **Muswellbrook** and **Scone**, and the Hunter Valley Wine Country or the **Lower Hunter**, around **Maitland** and **Cessnock**. Most of the wineries are open daily for wine tastings and cellar door sales; several have good restaurants

ℹ **Wine Country
Visitor
Information Centre**
*Turner Park, Aberdare Rd,
Cessnock; tel: (02) 4990-
4477; fax: (02) 4991-4518;
www.winecountry.com.au*

and cafés attached, while golf, horse riding, hot-air ballooning and cycling activities are also available. Towns in the Lower Hunter like **Pokolbin**, **Wollombi** and Maitland have several antique and craft shops, more often than not in renovated colonial style banks or houses in the main street. **Denman** is the heart of the Upper Hunter Wine Country and is known as Hollywood on the Hunter because a number of films and television shows have been filmed there. There is something special about the scenic beauty of this area, with its stark sandstone escarpments glowing gold in the sunset, overseeing the blue-green seas of eucalyptus, pines and acacias and the intimate valleys opening to verdant farmland.

MAITLAND✦✦✦

ℹ **Maitland Visitors'
Centre** *High St; tel:
(02) 4933-2611.* Town
walk maps are available.

Located on the Hunter River, Maitland has been central to the development of the Hunter Valley since it was established in the 1820s by emancipated convicts and free settlers who cultivated the alluvial plains. Its success as a rural centre was boosted with the development of the nearby coal fields in the early 20th century and the wealth and drive of the town is reflected in some of the grand public and private buildings. Maitland has a host of heritage buildings, including the **Courthouse** (1895) and the **Church of St Mary the Virgin** (1860).

Eight kilometres northeast of Maitland is **Morpeth**, the major port of the Hunter Valley and surrounding districts between 1843 and 1890. Morpeth is now under a heritage order and a walk down its streets is like a step back in time.

MUDGEE✦✦✦

ℹ **Mudgee Visitor
Information
Centre** *84 Market St;
tel: (02) 6372-5875;
fax: (02) 6372-2853;
www.mudgee.nsw.gov.au.
Open Mon–Fri 0900–1700,
Sat 0900–1530, Sun
0930–1400.*

🏛 **Colonial Inn
Museum $** *126
Market St, Mudgee; tel: (02)
6372-3078. Open Sat
1400–1700, Sun and public
hols 1000–1700.*

'Don't miss Mudgee' is the advice of discerning travellers in Australia. It is a magnificent old rural town, with classic landscapes, fine wines, good eating and a sense of history. The 150-year-old township is set amid rolling blue hills, green pastures, red-dirt sidetracks and valleys of vineyards. Grand stately buildings line its main street, largely protected by the National Trust. Historic buildings to be visited on the town walk include the **Regent Theatre** in Church St, almost all of the churches, banks and town buildings in **Market St**, and the railway station, as well as the restored West End Hotel that now houses the excellent **Colonial Inn Museum✦**.

Mudgee is also famous for its wineries. The volcanic soils of the region produce some of the best Shiraz and Chardonnay wines in Australia. The labels to look for – and buy at local cellar doors – are Poet's Corner, Rosemount, Huntington, Botobolar, Craigmoor and Montrose.

MUSWELLBROOK✧✧✧

ⓘ Muswellbrook Visitors' Centre
Hill St; tel: (02) 6541-4050;
www.muswellbrook.org.au.
Open daily 0900–1700.

This town in the Upper Hunter is surrounded by wineries and stud farms as well as the coal fields, which are the mainstay of its population of 10,000. Muswellbrook characterises the productivity of the region, an area of considerable physical diversity that ranges from fertile river flats to the massive sandstone formations and rugged mountains of the **Wollemi National Park**. The town is full of beautiful homesteads and restored buildings, which reflect the prosperity of some of the early settlers in the area.

NEWCASTLE✧

ⓘ Visitor Information Centre *The Old Station Master's Cottage, 92 Scott St; tel: (02) 4929-9299;*
www.visitnewcastle.com.au.
Open 0900–1700 weekdays and 1000–1530 weekends.

Newcastle (population 265,000) has transformed itself from an industrial city built around coal mining and a steelworks to a bustling, cosmopolitan city by the sea. Its historic beauty is partly owed to a moderate earthquake in 1989, which measured 5.6 on the Richter scale, but left 14 people dead and destroyed 70,000 properties. The quake prompted a decision by Newcastle authorities to restore the city rather than reshape it with faceless, modern, high-rise apartments and office blocks. New planning decisions dictate that developments comply with the heritage style of the picturesque town; old rail yards, foundries and warehouses are renovated rather than knocked down.

**Bike hire/
Grapemobile $**
corner of McDonalds and
Gillards Rd near Pokolbin; tel:
(02) 4998-7639.

**Lake Macquarie
Holiday Cruises $–$$**
tel: (02) 4973-5770 has a
range of boats for hire as
does **The Charter Base
on Lake Macquarie**
$–$$ 89 Soldiers Rd,
Pelican; tel: (02) 4972-0790.

Disused waterfront land has been turned into a vibrant eating and shopping district in the **Queens Wharf** complex.

There are plenty of reminders that this was a place for the most intractable of convicts. The breakwater out to **Nobby's Head** was built by convicts and leads to the **Bogey Hole** swimming pool which was cut, by convicts, into the rock on the ocean's edge below **King Edward Park**. **Newcastle Beach** is the main beach and is only a few minutes' walk from the city centre. Walk across the plaza from Hunter St, through the time tunnel with its murals of Newcastle's beach-life history.

A popular getaway for Newcastle residents, **Lake Macquarie** nestles behind the beaches and sand dunes south of the city and is Australia's largest saltwater lake. At 109 sq km, it is four times the size of Sydney Harbour and is popular for sailing, houseboating, fishing and water skiing.

Scone*

Scone Stud Tours
$$ tel: (02) 6545-
3337. By arrangement;
includes visits to a sheep
station, thoroughbred stud
farms and polo matches.

Noted for its thoroughbred stud farms, Scone is one of the richest farming areas in the region. It is also one of the prettier towns, with several historic buildings including the **Historical Society Museum** which was built in the 1860s as a lock-up. The very grand homestead of **Belltrees**, belonging to the well-established pastoral White family – relations of Australia's only Nobel Prize-winning writer Patrick White – is about 25km northeast of Scone. The house itself is private but there is a guesthouse and a café on the property.

Singleton**

**Singleton Visitors'
Centre** 6 Castlereagh
St; tel: (02) 6571-2499.
Open 0900–1600 weekdays.
At weekends look for the
caravan on the New
England Highway when you
arrive from the east.

Given the large amount of coal mining around Singleton it is surprising that the town's historic buildings have survived. The **Historical Museum** was built by Benjamin Singleton as a courthouse and a gaol in 1841 and was used by the Municipal Council Chambers until 1941. Singleton is home to the **Royal Australian Infantry Corps Museum*** (*$ Singleton Military Barracks; tel: (02) 6570-3427; open Wed–Sun 0900–1600*). This has a world-class collection of military firearms, uniforms, medals, badges and equipment.

Accommodation and food

The Hunter Valley is full of great restaurants and accommodation, ranging from luxury guesthouses to self-contained cottages and B&Bs. A good information source is **Wine Country Tourism**, *tel: (02) 4990-4477; www.winecountry.com.au*

Belltrees Country House $$ *Scone; tel: (02) 6546-1123.* Mouth-watering morning and afternoon teas; country-style lunch and dinners; also accommodation ($$).

Craigmoor $$ *Mudgee, tel: (02) 6273-4320.* The gourmet restaurant at the cellar of this century-old vineyard serves traditional and modern Australian food. Dining is on tables made from old wine casks.

Elton's $$ *81 Market Street, Mudgee; tel: (02) 6372-0772.* An old chemist shop complete with art-deco copper trim and bevelled windows now dishes out great breakfasts, lunches and afternoon teas. Picnickers can stock their hampers at the mouth-watering deli.

McGuigan Hunter Village $$–$$$ *Hunter Valley Gardens, Broke Rd, Pokolbin; tel: (02) 4998-7600.* Something for everyone at one of the more commercial wineries. As well as a driving range there are Aboriginal cultural experiences at the Native Touch gift shop and gallery. Also wine tasting, a range of restaurants including **The Cellar Restaurant $$**, **Sangas on the Hill $** for gourmet sandwiches and the **Vineyard Kitchen $** coffee shop and takeaway food. Resort-style accommodation (**$$–$$$**).

Palatinos $$ *142 Bridge St, Muswellbrook; tel: (02) 6541-2211.* Award-winning restaurant which trades as a café by day; located in the historic sandstone Loxton House which is one of Muswellbrook's oldest buildings, originally built around 1840.

Pepper Guest House $$$ *Ekerts Rd, Pokolbin; tel: (02) 4998-7596.* A warm and friendly guesthouse, furnished in colonial Australian style with rustic bric-à-brac. Set in stunning gardens with tennis court and pool. Also has a four-bedroom homestead for groups. Award-winning restaurant **Chez Pok $$$**.

Pokolbin Cabins $$–$$$ *Palmers Lane, Pokolbin; tel: (02) 4998-7611.* For peace and quiet in your own cabin (three to six bedrooms), each are fully equipped with kitchens and log fires.

Suggested tour

Total distance: 150km from Newcastle to Scone; 120km from Scone to Mudgee, or 153km from Newcastle to the Barrington Tops.

Time: Newcastle to Scone on the New England Highway takes between $1^1/_2$ and 2 hours. Allow another 2 hours to Mudgee on narrow country roads from Scone. A drive from Newcastle through the Hunter can be done in a day, but if you want to drink a bit and relax, then a night in either the Lower Hunter, around Pokolbin or the Upper Hunter, around Scone or even Mudgee, is suggested. Allow at least a day for walking and exploring the Barrington Tops National Park.

Links: The Lower Hunter Valley is a natural detour to the North Coast of NSW (*see page 82*). Taking in more of the Hunter Valley, it also links with the Blue Mountains (*see page 52*), via the central west town of Bathurst where you join the Great Western Highway through Lithgow and over the Blue Mountains back to Sydney.

Route: From **NEWCASTLE** ❶ take the New England Highway towards Hexham and **MAITLAND** ❷. Turn left on to the Kurri Rd to Kurri Kurri, **CESSNOCK** ❸ and **Pokolbin**. It is about an hour from Newcastle to Pokolbin.

Detour: From Pokolbin it is about half an hour to **Wollombi** through some spectacular state forest and picturesque farmland. Take the Broke Rd for about 30km to the town of **Broke**, a semi-rural community and an official sub-region of the Hunter. As well as extensive coal operations there are some good wineries. A fairly windy narrow road will take you around the Pokolbin State Forest to the main road back to the New England Highway.

From Pokolbin, Allandale Rd heading north and Broke Rd will get you on to the Brokenback Wine Trail along Broke Rd. Or head out of Cessnock on the Wollombi Rd and turn right into Mount View, left

Pokolbin

In the heart of the older wineries and not far from **Cessnock** (see page 63), Pokolbin is basically a shop and a motel set in the rolling hills of vineyards. The **Golden Grape Estate** on **Oakey Creek** has a museum which gives a good history of wine-making in the area from the 1820s, when the first vines were planted. A group of family businesses have got together to form the **Brokenback Wine Trail**, taking in wineries, eateries, horse-drawn coaches, galleries and quaint guesthouses.

on Marrowbone Rd and on McDonalds Rd for a more circuitous route through some superb wine country. The roads may get pretty narrow and are unsurfaced in places. Take the Hermitage Rd to return to the New England Highway and continue west through Belford for about 23km to **SINGLETON** ❹.

Detour: From Singleton it is about 65km or 40 minutes' driving along narrow roads, through rolling hills and vineyards, across the Hunter River, through Jerry's Plains to **Denman. Arrowfield Wines**∗ (tel: 02-6576-4041; open daily 1000–1600), discovered and named by the pioneering settler George Bowman in 1824, is on the left. Bowman was a winemaker as well as a horse breeder and several champions have been bred here. From Denman it is a short drive to another award-winning winery, **Rosemount Estate** (end of detour).

From Singleton it is about 47km or almost an hour to **MUSWELLBROOK** ❺, straight up the New England Highway, and then a further 27km to **SCONE** ❻.

Detour: GULGONG ❼ and **MUDGEE** ❽ may be outside the Hunter Valley proper but still have magical country settings, with rolling hills and rugged outcrops to the southwest. From either Denman or Muswellbrook it is about 2 hours along narrow, sometimes rough roads through the picturesque town of Merriwa. The drive is through some spectacular farming country toward the Central West Goldfields and has plenty of history. The town of Mudgee with its wide streets and restored heritage buildings won't disappoint. From here you could continue south past Lake Windemere, through gold-mining country of Wattle Flat to the Central West town of Bathurst where you join the Great Western Highway through Lithgow and over the Blue Mountains back to Sydney.

Also worth exploring

As a detour for this trip, or as a separate trip from Newcastle, the subtropical rainforest of Barrington Tops is a highlight, with Mount Barrington, at 1544m, one of the highest points in Australia.

The drive north of the New England Highway from Hexham or **Maitland** (or northeast from **Singleton**) is along narrow roads, mostly in good condition, over one-lane bridges and through spectacular rolling hills. It takes about 2 hours to travel the 153km from **Newcastle** to **Barrington Tops**. Big clumps of untamed state forest give way to farming land, mainly dairy, and offers perfect spots for camping and picnics until you reach the natural beauty of the World Heritage-listed Barrington Tops National Park. You can also take the Pacific Highway to Raymond Terrace (about 20km from Newcastle), heading north to Clarencetown and **DUNGOG** ❾ and 40km on to **Salisbury** ❿ and **BARRINGTON TOPS NATIONAL PARK** where there is magnificent walking and serious hiking to be done amongst some true wilderness. Lake Chichester, the main source of water for the Hunter, is also a beautiful spot for walking, with spectacular waterfalls and streams. You can rejoin the New England Highway at Singleton via the town of **Gresford** ⓫. The road is windy and quite narrow in parts, but generally in good condition and takes in stunning scenery.

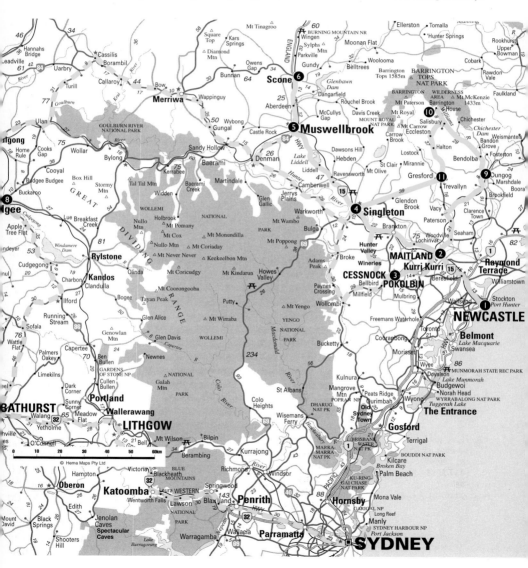

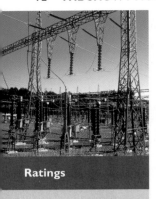

The Snowy Mountains

Ratings

Fishing	●●●●●
Mountains	●●●●●
Outdoor activities	●●●●●
Scenery	●●●●●
Skiing	●●●●●
Walking	●●●●○
Wildflowers	●●●●○
Food and wine	●●●○○

Just six hours' drive south of Sydney, the Snowy Mountains is a place of majestic, snow-capped peaks, tumbling mountain streams and crisp, clean air. This is a harsh, wild and breathtakingly beautiful region with its gnarled snow gums, wild brumby horses, untouched snow plateaux and flower-flecked mountain fields. The heart of the Snowy Mountains is the 690,000 hectares of the vast Kosciuszko National Park, containing Australia's highest mountain, Mt Kosciuszko, and all of NSW's major ski resorts. Besides skiing, there is superb walking, mountain climbing, mountain horse riding, white-water rafting, and cold creek fly-fishing. The region also has a rich history, from the days when Aboriginal tribes used to gather in the mountains to feast on the delicacy of Bogong moths, to the rip-roaring days of the 1859 gold rush, the summer mountain cattle drives and the legendary Snowy Mountains Scheme.

CHARLOTTE PASS✥

ℹ️ **Charlotte Pass Village Administration Centre** tel: (02) 6457-5247.

🌙 **Kosciuszko Chalet $$** Charlotte Pass; tel: 1800-026-369 or (02) 6457-5245; www.cool-ether.net.au/kos_chalet

Charlotte Pass is the highest village in the Snowy Mountains (1760m), marking the start of the summit walk to Mt Kosciuszko and the circuit Main Range walk via Carruthers Peak and glacial Blue Lake. It was named after Charlotte Adams, the daughter of the NSW surveyor-general who, in 1881, was the first European woman to climb Australia's highest peak.

Charlotte Pass also marks the spot where the first winter ski chalet was built in the Snowy Mountains and skiing was 'invented' in Australia by European labourers working on the Snowy Mountains Scheme. Nestled just under the rise of Mt Kosciuszko, Charlotte Pass, with its lovely old chalet, has an emphasis on fun family skiing in winter, with its lack of cars and buses making it a gentle, quiet holiday place where you can ski right from the chalet door. In summer, it is a mecca for mountain walkers.

Cooma ❖

ℹ️ **Cooma Visitors'**
Centre *119 Sharpe*
St; tel: 1800-636-525 or
(02) 6450-1742;
www.visitcooma.com.au

Once the base for the extraordinary Snowy Mountains Scheme with its thousands of European migrant workers, Cooma is now a busy rural town servicing the treeless Monaro tablelands and acting as the gateway to the NSW Snowy Mountains, Kosciuszko National Park and the ski-fields. It has an abundance of ski shops and fly-fishing stores,

ⓘ Snowy Mountain Scheme Information Centre
Snowy Mountains Authority, Yulin Ave, Cooma North; tel: (02) 6453-2004 or 1800-623-776; www.snowyhydro.com.au: for information about the scheme and for booking tours to the power stations.

as well as some splendid historic buildings and old pubs that can be visited on three heritage walks, each with its own accompanying information booklet.

Cooma is also home to the **Snowy Mountains Scheme Information Centre**. Completed in 1969 after 20 years of construction, the Snowy Mountains Scheme is recognised as one of the greatest projects undertaken in Australian history, and one of the engineering wonders of the modern world. A staggering 100,000 workers from more than 30 different countries – many were refugees and immigrants from a war-torn Europe – laboured in appallingly rugged and forbidding terrain to divert snow-melt water from the mighty Snowy River, across the watershed of the Great Dividing Range to the Murray River valley. The ambitious scheme, designed both to generate electricity and irrigate the dry inland, was born in the 1930s, commenced in 1949 and finished in 1969, at a cost of $820 million and 33 lives. Today, it is impossible to travel through the Snowy Mountains without being aware of the pipes, pylons, tunnels, roads, dams and power stations that criss-cross this once-pristine wilderness (there are 7 power stations, 16 major dams, and 140km of tunnels).

DEAD HORSE GAP ❖❖

This magnificent mountain pass on the Alpine Way is a favourite starting point for cross-country ski touring in winter and summer walking. Dead Horse Gap – so named after 17 brumbies (wild horses) perished in a snowdrift here in the last century – is also a good stop for a driving break by the bubbling Crackenback River and for some of the first views down towards Victoria and the seemingly endless Victorian Alps. The pass marks the start of one of the great walking tracks into the more remote areas of the Kosciuszko National Park, the **Cascade Trail**, which can be followed as a relatively easy, but rewarding, 16-km return, day walk to **The Chimneys** and headwaters of the Crackenback River.

FLY-FISHING❖❖❖

Mike Spry's School of Fly Fishing $$$
Khancoban; tel: (02) 6076-9511.

John Sutton Fly-fishing $$$ Adaminaby; tel: (02) 6454-2656.

Steve Williamson's Lake Jindabyne Trout Fishing Adventures $$
Lake Jindabyne; tel: (018) 024-436.

Some of the best trout fishing in Australia can be found in the creeks and rivers of the central Snowy Mountains, in lakes such as Lake Eucumbene and Blowering Dam, and in the basalt streams of the Monaro plains such as the Maclaughlin, the Kybeyan, the Bobundara and the Delegate River. Trout fishermen from around the world come to fly-fish in the Snowy Mountain lakes and rivers for salmon, rainbow and brown trout. Recreational fishermen now need a licence ($ monthly or yearly) to fish in NSW freshwater rivers and dams; this is available from the Snowy Region Visitor Centre in Jindabyne. For the novice keen to learn fly-fishing, it is best to be taught technique from an expert and be shown some of the Snowy Mountains' hidden trout spots. One of the best is **Mike Spry**, who runs his well-known School of Fly Fishing from Khancoban. Specialist **John Sutton** also offers fly-fishing tours and lessons from near Adaminaby, as does **Lake Jindabyne Trout Fishing Adventures** with Steve Williamson.

JINDABYNE❖❖❖

Snowy Region Visitor Information Centre (incorporating **Kosciuszko National Park Visitor Centre**)
Kosciuszko Rd, Jindabyne; tel: (02) 6450-5600; fax: (02) 6456-1249; email: srvc@npws.nsw.gov.au; www.snowymountains.com.au. Open daily 0800–1800.

The modern resort town of Jindabyne hosts the new and excellent Snowy Region Visitor Information Centre on the edge of Lake Jindabyne. Built during the construction of the Snowy Mountains Scheme when the Snowy River was dammed to create the lake, Jindayne is also a major centre for the ski industry. It offers much-needed accommodation – the resort lodges of Thredbo, Perisher and Charlotte Pass have finite room – with modern motels and apartments built around the lake's rim, all close to local restaurants, pubs, ski-hire shops and tourist information. There is a vibrant nightlife and some good restaurants in this year-round holiday town.

KIANDRA AND THE LONG PLAIN ROAD❖❖

The discovery of gold in 1859 turned cold and windswept Kiandra into a gold-rush boom town – but the gold ran out after two years and the town slowly dwindled, until it became a ghost town by the mid-1960s. Located on the Snowy Mountains Highway halfway between

Near Kiandra is the small, family-orientated downhill ski resort of **Mt Selwyn**, geared towards downhill skiing novices and families, although its lower altitude means it is often the last to get and the first to lose its snow. It is also an excellent place for cross-country skiing. For further information, contact **Selwyn Snowfields** *Cabramurra Rd, via Kiandra; tel: (02) 6454-9488.*

Cooma and Tumut, the hills of Kiandra now have a short, marked walking trail around the historic ruins and sad little graves, with details of the old mountain gold rush. Not far from Kiandra are the **Mt Selwyn Snowfields**. On a fine summer day, take a drive up the dirt track of **Long Plain Road** (dry weather only) through a lovely alpine valley. See old cattlemen's huts, explore the old rooms of the deserted **Coolamine Homestead**, before reaching Cave Creek and the limestone gorges and caves of the **Blue Waterholes** (about a 40-km drive). The deep blue pools flanked by steep gorges and caves make for spectacular swimming. There are many signs of seasonal aboriginal camps in this area, and the caves are fascinating to explore with their stalactites, stalagmites, slender columns and limestone waterfall formations. The eerily named Murderer's Cave where a body was found in 1890 was believed to have once been home to a member of bushranger Ben Hall's gang.

KOSCIUSZKO NATIONAL PARK✦✦✦

The **Snowy Mountains** are famous for being the home of the greatest bush rider of all, Jack Riley or the *Man from Snowy River* immortalised in Banjo Paterson's bush ballad. Relive his race through the alpine pastures, mountain streams and snow gums by riding in the Snowy Mountains with some of the very experienced trail riding companies, which include **Reynella Rides** *Adaminaby; tel: (02) 6454-2386;* and **Snowy River Horseback Adventures** *Round Mountain; tel: (02) 6453-7260.* Most rides operate from Nov to May.

The 690,000 hectares of thick bush wilderness, rocky mountain peaks, rushing thaw rivers and grassy mountain meadows that make up Kosciuszko National Park together form one of Australia's greatest natural treasures. It contains the country's highest mountain (Mt Kosciuszko, 2228m), the only glacial lakes on the mainland, most of Australia's snow country and more than 200 plant and animal species found nowhere else in the world. The headwaters of Australia's greatest rivers – the Murray, the Snowy and the Murrumbidgee – all lie within the park, as do six commercial downhill ski resorts – including picturesque Thredbo village – and the spectacular Alpine Way drive linking Victoria and NSW across the Dead Horse Gap pass. To protect the rare plants and animals that live in the park, and to balance its many recreational and commercial uses, Kosciuszko National Park has been divided into different zones, with six declared wilderness areas where all activities other than bush hiking are limited. In other zones, horse riding and mountain-bike riding are allowed and commercial operators may be given permits for their own activities. The park is managed by the NSW National Parks and Wildlife Service, with a fee ($) being charged per person, per day for 24-hour access. This fee grants use of all Kosciuszko National Park facilities and there is no extra charge for camping.

MT KOSCIUSZKO✦✦✦

Australia's tallest mountain (2228m) was first climbed by a European on 15 February 1840, when surveyor and explorer Count Paul Strzelecki climbed it from the west and named it after a Polish general who had fought against the partitioning of Poland in 1794. For the next 150 years it was mis-spelt as Mt Kosciusko, until the correct spelling of the general's difficult name was reinstated by the Geographical Names Board in 1997, to include the missing 'z'.

Despite lacking a significant peak, the relatively easy climb to the highest point in Australia remains an ambition for many, either on cross-country skis in winter, or by walking through the rocks and wildflowers in summer. It is most simply achieved by taking the Crackenback chairlift from the Thredbo ski resort in summer, and then strolling for 6km along a raised boardwalk with marvellous views, to reach the summit. An alternative, but longer, walk (9km each way) is to reach the top from Charlotte Pass, crossing the Upper Snowy River and passing the little stone **Seaman's Hut**, built by the parents of Laurie Seaman, who perished on a cross-country skiing trip to the top of Mt Kosciuszko in 1928. Just to the northwest, **Mt Townsend** (2210m) is only slightly lower than Mt Kosciuszko and, with a more pronounced summit, is often mistaken for its higher neighbour.

PERISHER BLUE AND SMIGGIN HOLES❖❖

Perisher Blue Road Resort tel: 1800-655-844; www.perisher.com.au

Skitube $$ Bullocks Flat, Alpine Way; tel: (02) 6456-2010. Reduced fare for children; travel between the Perisher and Blue Cow Ski slopes is free with a valid ski-lift pass.

Perisher Blue is the largest ski resort in the Snowy Mountains, with the four former resorts of **Blue Cow**, **Guthega**, **Smiggin Holes** and **Mount Perisher** now combined as Perisher Blue to give this modern development a skiable area of 1250 hectares of snow linked by 50 lifts across 7 mountain ranges. The highest point is the top of the Mt Perisher chairlift at 2034m, with skiing down to 1600m. Perisher is the best place for intermediate skiers, with 60 per cent of its runs classed as red or blue; however its steep **Kamikaze** and **Double Trouble Runs** for expert skiers are the only double black runs in Australia. It is also a favourite resort for snowboarders, with a special Boardriders' School and new areas being developed just for snowboarders. Particularly good **snowboarding** can be found at the new Devil's Playground area, Terrain Parks at Perisher, and at the special half-pipe at Blue Cow where there is always plenty of action and spills.

SNOWY MOUNTAINS❖❖❖

The Snowy Mountains are part of Australia's romance, magic and extraordinary geographical diversity. In the world's driest continent, it is often hard to imagine a massive strip of mountains – the Great Dividing Range – covered with deep snow for four to five months of the year, stretching 500km from Canberra to the north deep into Victoria in the south. Uplifted from the sea floor more than 250

million years ago, many of the landmark mountains – including Australia's highest, Mt Kosciuszko – are not jagged peaks but rounded mounds with the country's only glacial lakes. However, the western face of the range is deep and lined with gorges and steep cliffs. The beauty is riveting all year round, from the spectacular views and wildflowers that carpet the alpine meadows in summer, to the white days of winter when gnarled snow gums bend beneath their snow burden, and icy granite boulders stand sentinel against the cold winds and clear blue skies.

THREDBO❖❖❖

ℹ Thredbo Information Centre tel: 1800 020-589 or (02) 6459-4100; www.snowymountains.com.au

Thredbo is the favourite ski resort for old timers and experienced skiers, with its pretty village nestled in the Thredbo River valley at 1365m, and the steep sides of Mt Crackenback, Ramshead and Mt Kosciuszko rising above. What it lacks in size – there are 175 hectares of skiing – it makes up for in length, height and steepness of run, and the beauty of the valley.

YARRANGOBILLY CAVES❖❖

Deep in the heart of Kosciuszko National Park near Kiandra, the Yarrangobilly Caves were formed when a 440-million-year-old coral limestone reef was uplifted, compacted and gradually dissolved by rainwater over the past 750,000 years to create a system of large cracks, tubes and caverns. Five of the 70 Yarrangobilly caves are open to the public and are run by the NSW National Parks and Wildlife Service. The **Jersey Cave**, believed to be the oldest in the group, is the most highly decorated, with clear white columns, cascading orange waterfalls, underground pools and dog's tooth spar crystals forming an unforgettable underground fairyland. Visitors can also explore the **Glory Hole Cave**, where stockman John Bowman found his cattle sheltering in 1834 when he discovered the unique cave system.

Accommodation and food

Kosciuszko Mountain Retreat $ *Sawpit Creek, Kosciuszko National Park; tel: (02) 6456-2224.* Former headquarters of the National Park, has comfortable cabins and chalets for rent, as well as a camping ground with hot showers.

Above
Thredbo ski resort

The Lodge $$$ *Smiggin Holes; tel: (02) 6457-5341.* De luxe ski lodge

Kosciuszko Accommodation Centre tel: 1800-026-354; www.visitnsw.com.au

with big open fires and an excellent restaurant, right in the heart of the Perisher Blue ski resort.

Mt Kosciuszko Chalet $$ *Charlotte Pass; tel: (02) 6457-5245.* Bavarian-style family accommodation in the quiet village of Charlotte Pass. Full board, winter tariff also covers all ski hire, tows and equipment use.

Novotel Lake Crackenback Resort $$$ *Lake Crackenback, tel: (02) 6456-2960*; a luxurious resort 10 minutes' drive from Thredbo village and next to the Skitube for access to the Perisher Blue snowfields. Luxury self-contained apartments and hotel suites.

The Outpost Fly Fishing Lodge $$$ *Murrumbidgee River, Yaouk; tel: (02) 6454-2293.* Exclusive fishing lodge hidden away in the bush, maximum of six guests; great food and wine, and fishing tuition.

Reynella Rides and Country Farmstay $$ *via Adaminaby; tel: (02) 6454-2386.* Working farm located on the edge of Kosciuszko National Park; comfortable base from which to explore the park or go horse riding.

Royal Hotel $ *Cooma; tel: (02) 6452-2132.* Typical budget country pub with its wide two-storey veranda and cosy bar.

Sante Restaurant $$ *Squatter's Run, Thredbo; tel: (02) 6457-6083.* Modern Australian cuisine featuring quality local produce and fresh seafood from the south coast of New South Wales. Popular for both dinner and lunch.

Thredbo Alpine Hotel $$$ *Thredbo Village; tel: (02) 6459-4200.* Central location for both ski and *après-ski* action. This first-class hotel, conference and entertainment complex in the ski village, next to the Thredbo River, is ideal winter and summer.

Suggested tour

Distance: Two routes are recommended in the Snowy Mountains, both setting out from the town of Cooma: it is 184km up the Snowy Mountains Highway from Cooma to Tumut, and 174km from Cooma to Khancoban via Jindabyne, Thredbo and the Alpine Way. Both the Snowy Mountains Highway and the Alpine Way are sealed roads. But be very careful driving in the Snowy Mountains in winter, when there may be snow, sleet and ice on the roads. Chains must be carried at all times, and night driving is not a good idea.

Time: It would take about 3 hours to drive the Snowy Mountains Highway route direct, and about four on the often steep and winding Alpine Way. But this tour is about stopping to ski, walk and explore – that way it makes a lovely and relaxing two- or three-day getaway.

White-water rafting

Some of the best white-water rafting in Australia is found on the Upper Murray River where the snowmelt waters of the Murray are forced through a narrow gorge amongst enormous boulders, waterfalls and cascades. Several tour companies, including the locally based Upper Murray White-Water Rafting (tel: (02) 6076-9566), operate out of Khancoban and offer thrilling one- or two-day trips through the spectacular and wild Murray Gorge between Tom Groggin and Colemans Bend. Pick-ups can also be arranged from Thredbo. This white-water rafting trip is an October-to-Easter summer-only venture and is no gentle paddle. But it is the thrill of tackling, and beating, the notorious Murray Gates, The Wall and the Headbanger rapids that make shooting this remote gorge (only accessible by raft) such a fantastic experience.

ⓘ What's On in the Snowy Mountains tel: (02) 6450-5549.

Ski NSW tel: 13-2030.

Snowy Mountains road conditions tel: (02) 6450-5551.

Snow report (winter) and fishing report (summer) tel: (02) 6450-5553.

Links: The Snowy Mountains can be explored after touring Canberra (*see page 92*), only 110km to the north of Cooma. The Alpine Way at Khancoban leads across into Victoria, linking up with the Northeast Victoria route (*see page 142*).

Snowy Mountains Highway: Set out from **COOMA ❶**, after visiting the excellent **Snowy Mountains Scheme Visitor Centre**, and take the Snowy Mountains Highway heading northwest towards Tumut. The towering **SNOWY MOUNTAINS** can soon be seen ahead and to the west. It is about 50km to **Adaminaby**, close to **Lake Eucumbene** and one of the Snowy Mountains' best **FLY-FISHING ❷** centres. Just before Adaminaby is a turn-off to **Reynella**, the main horse-riding property in the region.

Continue 40km up the Snowy Mountains Highway, to the old gold-rush ghost town of **KIANDRA ❸**. The Cabramurra Rd leading to the **MT SELWYN SNOWFIELDS ❹** soon turns off to the left. It is another 20km on to the **Long Plain Road** turn-off (summer only) to the right, leading to **Coolamine Homestead** and the **Blue Waterholes**. The spectacular **YARRANGOBILLY CAVES ❺** are just a bit further down the Highway, before its starts to descend into **Talbingo** and the **Tumut River** valley.

Alpine Way: An alternative tour from Cooma is to head west for 65km towards **JINDABYNE ❻** and the main **Snowy Region Visitor Centre** for information on the **KOSCIUSZKO NATIONAL PARK**.

The left fork outside Jindabyne leads along the famous **Alpine Way** heading towards the ski resort of **THREDBO ❼**, just 36km away, and up the Thredbo River valley. In summer, the easiest way to climb **MT KOSCIUSZKO**, Australia's highest mountain, is by taking the Crackenback chairlift from Thredbo village. There are many other lovely day walks including one to **Blue Lake** that can be reached from either Thredbo or Charlotte Pass.

Continuing on the Alpine Way past Thredbo, it is just 3km to the spectacular **DEAD HORSE GAP**. From here, the mountain road twists and winds for another 40km before reaching the river crossings at **Tom Groggin** and **Geehi Flat**. These are the staring points for some excellent **White-Water Rafting** along the Upper Murray River. The Alpine Way continues for another 30km – don't miss **Scammels Lookout** with its fantastic views of the towering **Townsend** range – before arriving at the mellow little town of **Khancoban** on the NSW–Victoria border.

Getting out of the car

The only way truly to appreciate the views, scenery and rare flora and fauna of the Snowy Mountains is at close range – on foot. Walking and hiking in Kosciuszko National Park is always a magnificent

ℹ️ **NSW Tourism**
www.tourism.nsw.gov.au

Australian skiing
SnoInfo www.ski.com.au

Yarrangobilly Caves
National Parks and Wildlife
Service, off Snowy Mountains
Highway via Kiandra; tel:
(02) 6454-9597. Open daily
0900–1700.

⛑️ **Opening of the Ski**
Season: June

🌐 **Upper Murray**
White-Water
Rafting *Khancoban; tel:*
(02) 6076-9566.

experience, whether for a day expedition to the top of Australia's highest mountain, or simply for a gentle stroll across the alpine meadows admiring the brilliantly coloured summer wildflowers. The National Park is well served with walking tracks and considerable effort has been put into ensuring that tracks on the highest points of the Main Range – well above the tree-line – do not damage the fragile alpine ecosystems.

The best day walks are a hike to the summit of **MT KOSCIUSZKO**, via the Thredbo Crackenback chairlift, or a walk from Charlotte Pass to **Blue Lake**, Australia's only mainland glacial lake lying pristine and clear in a deep and sheer ice-quarried basin 28m deep, one of the true treasures of Kosciuszko National Park. Within the **THREDBO** ski resort, the 5-km **Merritts Nature Trail** winds downhill, passing thick bush vegetation, fern gullies and bubbling mountain streams. Trained botanical guides and flower experts also take guided walks starting from Thredbo village during January and the Thredbo Wildflower Festival early in February, which is a great way to learn more about the unique and lovely mountain wildflowers.

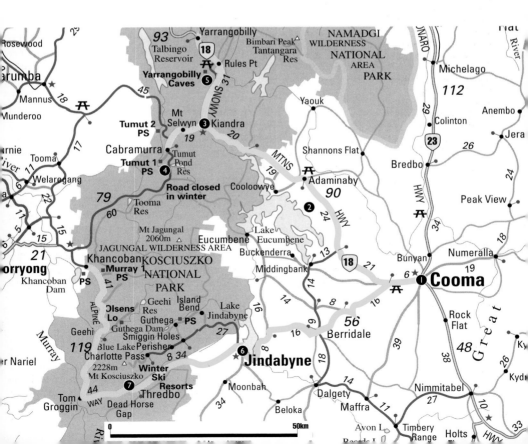

The North Coast

Ratings

Beaches	●●●●●
Scenery	●●●●●
Surfing	●●●●●
History	●●●●○
Romantic weekends	●●●●○
National parks	●●●●○
Food	●●●○○
Markets	●●●○○

Highway One out of Sydney heads north into sub-tropical warmth, endless sun, marvellous surf beaches, and the land of the big Northern Rivers. Away from the Pacific Highway the coastal strip wedged between the hills of the green Great Dividing Range and blue of the Pacific Ocean offers much to the visitor. As well as a choice of river cruises, fun parks and theme parks, there is canoeing, bushwalking, four-wheel driving, deep-sea or game fishing, scuba diving, whale and dolphin watching, horse or even camel riding. Beyond Coffs Harbour, the Northern Rivers region becomes tropical, with blue waters and volcanic mountains offset by wide rivers, lush countryside and brightly flowering trees. But more than anything, the 1000-km strip of coast between Newcastle and the Queensland border has become the keeper of the truest of Australian experiences, the beach.

BELLINGEN AND DORRIGO*

ⓘ Bellingen Tourist Information Centre *Yellow Shed, cnr High St and Prince St; tel: (02) 6655-1189; www.visitorinformation.net*

Dorrigo National Park Rainforest Centre *Dome Rd, Dorrigo; tel: (02) 6657-2309.*

Set peacefully on the fertile banks of the Bellingen River, the beautiful inland town of Bellingen is the region's art and craft capital. Originally a timber and ship-building village in early pioneer days, much of the town and its tree-lined streets are now listed by the Heritage Commission. The Yellow Shed, historic Wheatley Emporium and the old Butter Factory complex are well worth a look. Bellingen's monthly market features talented local craftspeople and artists and has become a respected institution for locals and visitors alike. About 20km inland from Bellingen is the spectacular escarpment leading to the New England tablelands and Dorrigo, a pretty, sub-tropical rainforest town with great views and a good steam railway museum. **Dorrigo National Park*** is part of NSW's World Heritage-listed rainforest park. It has good walks, excellent trout fishing, an elevated Skywalk amongst the tall treetops and an award-winning rainforest centre.

Byron Bay***

Byron Bay Tourist Information Centre
*Old Station Master's Cottage, Jonson St; tel: (02) 6685-8050;
www.visitorinformation.net*

Recognised by Captain James Cook on his voyage past in 1770 as the most easterly point of the Australian mainland, Byron Bay was once a sleepy whaling town. It died when whaling finished, but in the past three decades has come back to life on the strength of its beautiful surf beaches which first attracted surf nomads in the late 1960s. After the town made it into the US surf magazines, developers moved in and have been arm-wrestling with the Greenies ever since. Byron Bay, has a laid back, anything-goes atmosphere, where New Age disciples mix alongside ageing hippies and blonde surfies, while the sprinkling of famous residents adds just a touch of sophistication. The plentiful cafés, pubs and restaurants offer excellent dining and fun night life.

And the waves remain the same: perfect tubes at the **Wreck** on the town's main beach; the **Pass**, on the point, can roll out 400-m rides; while around **Watego's Beach** beneath Cape Byron and its Lighthouse, Malibu riders can stand tall. Sheltering beneath the cape's southern side, **Tallows Beach** offers another wave. Five kilometres further south, **Broken Head** can turn on heart-breakingly perfect surf, and beyond that is **Lennox Head** and **Boulder Beach**. This is surf heaven. But at Byron Bay you can also go whale watching, try a Tai Chi class or have a diving lesson at Julian Rocks. The East Coast Blues Festival, Australia's best, is staged in Byron each Easter. The Byron Bay hinterland has been Australia's 'alternative lifestyle' capital for decades. The market stalls of nearby **Nimbin** (*see page 86*), **Murwillumbah** and **Mullumbimby** offer home-grown and organic tropical fruits and vegetables, while the **Billinudgel** Village Pub serves old-fashioned Aussie hospitality.

Below
Byron Bay mural

COFFS HARBOUR*

 Coffs Harbour Tourist Information Centre cnr Marcia St and Pacific Hwy; tel: (02) 6652-1522; www.visitorinformation.net

The halfway mark between Sydney and Brisbane, Coffs Harbour has long been a favourite holiday spot as well as one of NSW's busiest ports. Famed as the centre of the banana industry, the vast Big Banana was built on the outskirts of the town long before theme parks became part of holidaymakers' fun. At one time, tourism was focused along Park Beach Rd with its easy access to the sweeping beach and beautiful stark islands anchored offshore. But in the 1980s development hit Coffs harder than any other NSW coastal town and it now boasts upmarket resorts and high-rises. The town centre is modern and unattractive, but venture down to the ocean beach with its fishing harbour and marina for the real treasures of Coffs Harbour. Here, fresh fish can be bought direct from the boats and the fishermen's co-op. Just across the railway line, the strip of more than 15 cafés and restaurants – serving a mix of Thai, Italian and modern Australian cuisine – offers some of the best food along the north coast of NSW.

CRESCENT HEAD**

A headland bearing a picturesque and improbable six-hole golf course creates precision waves that break for several hundred metres along the sandy sea bottom making Crescent Head the Mecca for surfers riding longer Malibu-style boards. Developers have not crushed the town's old-time feel and the 5-hour drive from Sydney deters weekenders so Crescent Head retains secrets city folk never discover. Driving south, an unmade road offers surfing, fishing and silence and a great hot day getaway if the town beach becomes too crowded. **Racecourse Headland**, **Delicate Nobby**, **Big Hill** and finally **Point Plomar** (where a historic Aborigine rock fish trap lies on the beach) are untapped gems. North of town, **Hat Head National Park** offers even more solitude; the huge goannas that wonder through the camping area make mealtimes interesting.

GRAFTON*

South Grafton Visitor Information Centre cnr Spring St and Pacific Hwy; tel: (02) 6642-4677.

The highway almost bypasses Grafton, the old cattle and timber city famous for its jacaranda trees that turn the town and its wide, gracious streets purple each October. Situated well inland on the Clarence River, Australia's sugar industry starts just downstream from Grafton. The landscape changes here into flat green flood plains dotted with white peeling-paint houses on stilts that seem the essence of tropical Australia and punctuate the coast all the way up to Cairns. About 15km north, the village of Ulmarra is an old river port, from the days when ships were the lifeblood of the coast.

MORPETH*

Morpeth was at the navigation head of the Hunter River during the early colonial days when sailing ships ferried goods back and forth to Sydney. Parts of Morpeth seem preserved in time with many buildings retaining Georgian elements. Although a dormitory village now to both Maitland and Newcastle, Morpeth comes alive at weekends with hundreds of visitors picking though the arts, crafts and antiques. There is a weekend jazz festival in June.

NIMBIN**

ⓘ Lismore Visitor Information Centre cnr Ballina St and Molesworth St, Lismore; tel: (02) 6622-0122; www.visitorinformation.net

Mt Warning National Park NPWS district office, Colonial Arcade, Main St, Alstonville; tel: (02) 6628-1177.

World Heritage Rainforest Centre Budd Park, Murwillumbah; tel: (02) 6672-1340 or 1800-674-414.

Nimbin is the town the hippies saved. When 'The Big Scrub' was cleared in the 19th century, Nimbin, in the bush inland from Byron Bay, boomed as a dairy centre. But by the late 1960s the town was in decline. Seeking a safe place to grow marijuana, hippies took over, celebrating their conquest with 1973's Aquarius Softlicks festival. Media coverage and the local backlash enshrined Nimbin as Australia's alternative lifestyle capital while wily city dwellers bought bush blocks and turned their lifestyles into a tourism industry. Cullen St is still loaded with psychedelic restaurants and shops. The surrounding hills are filled with craftspeople who sell their wares at the Showground market on the fourth Sunday of each month or at the Channon Craft Market on the second Sunday.

The World Heritage-listed **Nightcap** and **Mount Warning*** national parks are within easy drive. Climbing the 1157-m Mount Warning at dawn to see the rising sun first strike the Australian mainland is a memorable achievement. South of Nimbin, **Lismore** is a slightly alternative university city surrounded by World Heritage rainforest national parks. The Rotary Rainforest Reserve near the centre of this bustling regional centre is worth visiting. North of Nimbin at Murwillumbah is the **World Heritage Rainforest Centre***, open daily to the public.

PORT MACQUARIE*

ⓘ Port Macquarie Visitor Information Centre cnr Clarence St and Hay St; tel: (02) 6583-1077; www.visitorinformation.net

 Timbertown historic village Oxley Hwy, Wauchope; tel: (02) 6581-8633.

Port Macquarie, a former penal settlement, is one of the country's oldest towns and now one of its most popular family holiday destinations, with a climate considered by many to be the best in Australia. Situated at the mouth of the Hastings River, 420km north of Sydney, it has many early 19th-century buildings, nature reserves and spectacular beaches. Offshore fishing is one of the area's specialities. Less than 20km inland from Port Macquarie is Wauchope, an old logging town where life in the 1880s has been recreated in the **Timbertown historic village***.

PORT STEPHENS✧✧

ⓘ Port Stephens Visitor Information Centre
Victoria Pde; tel: 1800-808-900;
www.visitorinformation.net

A quiet, relaxed beach and seaside area away from the highway and the major holiday centres like Port Macquarie, the small villages grouped around Port Stephens harbour have now collectively become known by the name of the bay they face. Tea Gardens and Hawks Nest epitomise middle-class Australia at play over the summer holidays – there are kids, caravans, fishing rods and little boats galore. Away from the towns, the coastal beaches leading up to famed **Seal Rocks** offer great surf and are protected as part of **Myall Lakes National Park**. The coastal lakes themselves are serene places ideal for houseboating, bird watching and fishing.

TRIAL BAY GAOL✧✧

ⓘ Kempsey Tourist Information Centre *Pacific Hwy; tel: (02) 6563-1555.*

Above
Port Macquarie

One of the stranger relics of Australia's past, **Trial Bay Gaol✧**, on the coast just north of the town of **Kempsey**, is one of the world's best-sited prisons. Perched on west-facing headland, the gaol is a great pink and grey granite ruin designed in 1877 as an experiment in penal reform and to supply labour to build a breakwater after 243 lives were lost at sea along this coast. The convicts built the breakwater, the sea

Trial Bay Gaol and Museum $ *South West Rocks; tel: (02) 6566-6168. Open daily 0900–1700.*

quickly smashed it, so in 1903 the authorities closed the gaol. It re-opened in 1914 to house 500 German internees during World War I. A monument to the Germans was blown up in 1919 and rebuilt in 1959. Today the gaol houses a museum and there is a pleasant camping ground beneath its walls overlooking the calmer waters of Trial Bay. Not far away is the popular surfing area of **South West Rocks** and the beautiful coastal national park of **Hat Head**.

YAMBA*

Clarence River Visitor Information Centre *Pacific Highway, South Grafton; tel: (02) 6642-4677; www.clarencetourism.com*

A prawn trawler town with a large fishing fleet, Yamba sits at the mouth of the **Clarence** halfway between Coffs harbour and Ballina. During the days of the coastal traders Yamba was a considerable port; now the town is enjoying a boom as a retirement favourite.

Five kilometres south, the unprepossessing village of **Angourie** has what many surfers believe to be Australia's best right-hand breaking wave. A generation of Australian surfers had Angourie to themselves until surfing films opened it up to outside eyes. Nowadays when Angourie breaks, the world is waiting to crowd the take-off but its stark haunting beauty still makes it a must-see. On the southern side of the point is the **Blue Pool**, a freshwater pool of unknown depth just above the sea which always used to offer a refreshing swim but has been stricken with blue algae in recent years.

Accommodation and food

The Anchorage $$$ *Corlette Point Rd, Corlette, tel: (02) 4984-2555.* Upmarket resort located in the stunning surrounds of Port Stephens, with its glistening blue waters, long beaches and excellent fishing. Luxury rooms and suites, all with great views of the sheltered bay. Good for conferences.

Beach Caravan Park $ *Byron Bay Headland, Byron Bay, tel: (02) 6685-6496;* camping caravans and cabins in marvellous location overlooking the surf beach, about 3km along the beach to town.

Beachwood Café $ *15 The Crescent, Angourie, tel: (02) 6646-9258.* Fashionable Mediterranean restaurant with great food and good prices, where all the locals and Sydney blow-ins gather to talk about the great barrel waves.

Byron Bay Beach Club $$ *Bayshore Drive, Byron Bay, tel: (02) 6685-8000.* A private and quiet resort set in 93 hectares of natural parkland, with secluded white-sand beach frontage, its own nine-hole golf course and wallabies, echidnas and native birds galore. The town is a lovely 2-km stroll away along the surf beach; all accommodation is in self-contained cabins, studios and villas, scattered among the gardens.

Above
Dorrigo National Park

Crown Hotel $ *Grafton, tel: (02) 6642-4000.* Classic Australian hotel overlooking the Clarence River; its huge veranda is a delightful dining spot.

Fins $ *Pacific Highway, Brunswick Heads, tel: (02) 6685-1876.* The best seafood restaurant in the region with interesting Portuguese touches, all overlooking the Brunswick River.

Kim's Beachside Retreat $$$ *Charlton St, Toowoon Bay; tel: (02) 4332-1566.* Only an hour north of Sydney, Kim's weekend getaway is talked of in reverential tones by almost all Sydneysiders in the know – for its gourmet food, its tropical gardens, its absolute white-sand beachfront and its luxurious private bungalows.

Lord Byron Resort $$ *120 Jonson St, Byron Bay, tel: (02) 6685-7444.* Medium-sized resort in a tropical garden setting and only a short stroll from the beach and town centre. Has motel room accommodation or large, family self-contained apartments.

Pelican Beach Travelodge Resort $$ *Pacific Highway, Coffs Harbour, tel: (02) 6653-7000.* This large family resort enjoys a perfect beachfront position adjoining the Coffs Harbour ocean beach. It also features a magnificent free-form pool by the beach, and it has extensive children's facilities, including a Kids' Club, which operates during holidays and weekends.

Rae's on Watego's $$ *8 Marine Pde, Byron Bay, tel: (02) 6685-5366.* Classy establishment overlooking perfect Watego's Beach at Byron Bay. Asian-influenced cuisine.

Shelleys on the Beach $ *Shelley Beach Rd, Ballina, tel: (02) 6686-9844.* Casual atmosphere and reasonable prices for superb fresh seafood.

Wombat Beach Resort $–$$ *Crescent Head, tel: (02) 6566-0121.* Low key and relaxed family resort with units, camping and cottages.

Suggested tour

Distance: It is about 850km from Sydney to Byron Bay.

Time: The Pacific Highway is a good sealed road, a multi-laned freeway in its early stages, but often single-lane around the Northern Rivers districts. It can be slow; allow at least 12 hours if intending to drive without stops.

① NSW Tourism Visitor Information Centre 106 George St, The Rocks, Sydney; tel: 13-207.7 or (02) 9931-1111; www.tourism.nsw.gov.au

NSW National Parks Information Service tel: 1300-361-967; www.npws.gov.au

NSW NPWS Regional Office 152 Horton St, Port Macquarie; tel: (02) 6584-2203. For information on Hat Head National Park.

Links: This drive links in with the Hunter Valley circuit (*see page 62*) crossing over at Newcastle and Maitland. It is only 100km from Byron Bay north to the Queensland border and the Gold Coast, linking up with the Gold Coast and Scenic Rim drive (*see page 152*).

Route: Head north out of Sydney along the F3 freeway, by-passing industrial **Newcastle**. At the end of the F3 (160km north of Sydney) the right-hand fork is the Pacific Highway continuing north, while the left hand fork leads along the New England Highway to the early colonial town of **Maitland ①** (*see page 65*), 6km inland. After touring Maitland, head back along the New England Highway towards the Pacific Highway junction, calling in at the historic river village of **MORPETH** on the way. Continue north on the Pacific Highway for 50km, then turn right to the **PORT STEPHENS** region, and the seaside holiday villages of **Tea Gardens** and **Hawks Nest**. Take the small coastal road to explore **Myall Lakes National Park** and **Seal Rocks**.

Back on the Pacific Highway, it is 145km to the large holiday town of **PORT MACQUARIE ②**, with the re-created Timbertown village 15km inland at **Wauchope**. From Port Macquarie, it is another 49km, again heading north on the Pacific Highway, to the southern edge of **Kempsey**, where there's a right turn to **CRESCENT HEAD ③** and the coast, 21km away. After a great surf, head back towards Kempsey and take the turn-off north of the town centre, to get to **Hat Head National Park**, and the extraordinary **TRIAL BAY GAOL** at **South West Rocks**. Back on the Pacific Highway via the Jerseyville Bridge Rd, it is another 80km through the fishing and surf-mad coastal resort of **Nambucca Heads**, before the turn-off to the left leading to the picturesque river town of **BELLINGEN ④** and the **DORRIGO NATIONAL PARK**, perched on the escarpment rim. It is then just 25km along the Pacific Highway to the thriving holiday and banana centre of **COFFS HARBOUR ⑤**, with its lovely town surf beach, offshore islands and excellent wharf restaurant strip. From Coffs Harbour to **GRAFTON ⑥** is another 83km on the Pacific Highway. This is the start of the great Northern Rivers country and the true tropics. About half an hour's drive from Grafton, before crossing the mighty Clarence River, there is a right-hand turn-off leading to the prawn and surf towns of **YAMBA ⑦** and **Angourie**.

Continue north for 130km; the highway winds through bush and across big rivers before crossing the Richmond River at **Ballina**. Leave the Pacific Highway here – you will probably be heartily sick of its slow trucks and caravans by now – for a spectacular 33-km run along the coast to **BYRON BAY ⑧**, ogling at great surf breaks, sandy beaches and rocky headlands as you potter. Enjoy the surf and a few coffees at Byron Bay, then venture inland for a day via **Lismore**, to giggle at hippie **NIMBIN ⑨** and to watch a new dawn break from the top of **Mt Warning**.

Canberra

Ratings

Architecture	●●●●●
Art	●●●●●
Children's activities	●●●●●
National monuments	●●●●●
Politics	●●●●●
Flowers	●●●●○
History	●●●●○
Scenery	●●●●○

The sheep station of 'Canberry', at the foothills of the Snowy Mountains and vaguely halfway between Sydney and Melbourne, was chosen in 1908 as the unlikely location for a brand new city, the capital of the newly established Australian nation. Canberra has since grown to become an elegant and graceful city, built around a lake and nestled between bush-covered mountains that are snow-capped in winter. Despite its importance as the centre of political and administrative power in Australia, Canberra has retained its 'bush capital' tag; it has a population of less than 500,000, its suburbs are ringed by gum trees, and kangaroos still occasionally hop down its suburban streets. Outside the city but still within the borders of the Australian Capital Territory lie more of the capital's natural attractions at the Tidbinbilla Nature Reserve, the Murrumbidgee River or the wild Namadgi National Park.

Getting around

ⓘ Canberra Visitors' Centre
330 Northbourne Ave, Dickson; tel: (02) 6205-0044 or 1800-026-166. Information, tour bookings, maps and accommodation assistance.

Canberra tourism
www. canberratourism.com.au

ⓐ ACTON bus information
tel: 131710.

The frequent complaint of visitors to Canberra is that all its roads seem to go in circles, they never stumble across a petrol station or grocery shop by chance and that while there is little traffic and they can see where they are trying to get to, it always seems to be across the other side of the lake!

All these complaints are valid; Walter Burley Griffin deliberately designed Canberra as a series of circular roads linked by a major axis entwined at its heart around elongated Lake Burley Griffin and its four central hills – Black Mountain and Mt Ainslie to the north and Capital Hill and Red Hill south of the lake.

For this reason, the Parliament Triangle – on both sides of the lake and containing most of the major monuments, institutions, museums and attractions – is best explored on foot, or by taking the **Canberra Explorer Red Bus**, which serves as a transport link between the city's sights.

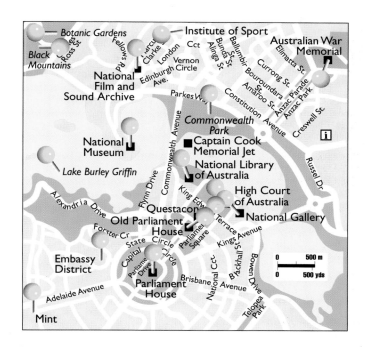

Map labels: Botanic Gardens, Institute of Sport, Australian War Memorial, Black Mountains, Ross St, Church, Clarke St, London St, Cct, Bunda St, Ballumbir St, Alinga St, Bulumbir St, Bourandara St, Currong St, Ellmatta St, Anzac Parade, Anzac Park, Fellows Rd, Vernon Circle, National Film and Sound Archive, Edinburgh Ave, Parkes Way, Constitution Avenue, Amaroo St, Creswell St, Commonwealth Avenue, Commonwealth Park, Captain Cook Memorial Jet, National Library of Australia, Russel Dr, National Museum, Lake Burley Griffin, Flynn Drive, King Edw, High Court of Australia, National Gallery, Alexandria Drive, Questacon, Terrace Avenue, Forster Cr, Old Parliament House, Parliament Square, Kings Ave, Kings Ave, Embassy District, State Circle, Capital Circle, Parliame Drive, Bowen Drive, Parliament House, Brisbane Avenue, Backhall St, National Cct, Mint, Adelaide Avenue, Telopea Park, 0 500 m, 0 500 yds

Sights

Australian Institute of Sport Visitor Centre $$
Leverrier Crescent, Bruce; tel: (02) 6214-1444. Tours 1130 and 1430 Mon–Fri, 1000, 1130, 1300 and 1430 Sat, Sun and school holidays.

Australian National Botanic Gardens Clunies Ross St, Black Mountain; tel: (02) 6250-9540. Open daily 0900–1700, guided walks 1100 weekdays, 1100 and 1400 weekends.

Australian War Memorial Anzac Parade, Campbell; tel: (02) 6243-4211. Open daily 1000–1700.

Australian Institute of Sport**

This is a tourist attraction that most young children dream of – being shown around the world-class Australian Institute of Sport. Take a tour of the AIS, built in 1981, and see where the nation's élite athletes sleep, train and eat, watch some of the great moments of Australian sport on video in their excellent museum and test your skills and fitness in a variety of sports at the interactive centre, Sportex.

Australian National Botanic Gardens*

Located on the bush slopes of Black Mountain, the Australian National Botanic Gardens hold the finest living collection of Australian plants, with more than 6000 native species. Explore the special Rainforest Gully, the Rockery, Eucalypt Lawn, Aboriginal Trail and Tasmanian Garden, or just picnic and play on the lawns.

Australian War Memorial**

The nation's tribute to its 102,600 war dead is also a remarkable museum recording the participation of Australians in war, both at home and at the front. Although it sounds a boring, sombre place, it is actually a fascinating museum that has just benefited from a $20-million facelift and that brings history back to vibrant life with compelling personal stories, film, paintings, photos, relics and diaries.

Telstra Tower $
*Black Mountain Drive,
Acton; tel: 1800-806-718.
Open daily 0900–2200.*

Blundell's Cottage $
*Wendouree Drive, Parkes;
tel: (02) 6273-2667. Open
daily 1000–1600.*

Government House
*Dunrossil Drive, Yarralumla.
Closed to the public.*

In front of the War Memorial **Anzac Parade** – the main avenue leading towards the lake – is lined with nine memorials, including some spectacular modern sculptures, commemorating the different campaigns, wars and places where Australians have died for their country. An excellent view of Canberra, giving a good understanding of Walter Burley Griffin's parliamentary triangle design, can be gained from the top of Mt Ainslie, behind the War Memorial.

Black Mountain and the Telstra Tower*
For the best view of Canberra, drive up Black Mountain and climb to the viewing platforms of the Telstra Tower, known affectionately by locals as the 'giant syringe'. This, the best possible vantage point, soars 195m above the summit of Black Mountain and houses state-of-the-art communication equipment and an exhibition on the history of telecommunications in Australia. From its three viewing platforms and revolving restaurant there are spectacular 360-degree views of Canberra and the surrounding countryside both day and night.

Blundell's Cottage*
Built in 1858 by the Campbells of Duntroon Station for their head ploughman and later occupied by bullock driver George Blundell, his wife Flora and their 10 children, this small sandstone cottage once looked out over sheep paddocks, now Lake Burley Griffin. It provides an excellent example of the hardships of early life on a remote farm.

Civic Square*
The commercial heart of Canberra is the Civic Centre, on the north side of Lake Burley Griffin close to the northwest corner of the Parliamentary Triangle. It is the centre of shopping and many administrative, legal and local government functions in Canberra, and a meeting place for locals. Despite the uninteresting architecture of the surrounding buildings, it is dominated by a graceful bronze statue of Ethos by Australian sculptor Tom Bass, and nearby Times Fountain. In adjoining **Petrie Plaza** is an antiquarian merry-go-round for children with wooden horses, a much-loved Canberra landmark.

Commonwealth Park*
This large park on the edge of Lake Burley Griffin next to Regatta Point, is ablaze with colour in September and October when it hosts Canberra's famous spring flower festival, **Floriade**, which features more than one million annuals and bulbs blooming in specially designed beds, reflected in the still lake.

Government House*
Government House, or Yarralumla as it is colloquially known, is the official residence of the Governor-General, the representative of the Queen in Australia and the nominal head of State (until Australia

High Court *King Edward Terrace, Parkes Place; tel: (02) 6270-6811. Open daily 0945–1630.*

Burley Griffin Cruises $–$$ *Canberra Southern Cross Club; tel: (02) 6283-7200; www.cscc.com.au*

Canberra Steam Boats $ *National Library Jetty; tel: 014 685-684; fax: (02) 6291-2340. A 100-year-old wooden steam boat, complete with coal boiler and steam whistle. Trips leave daily at 1100, 1200 and 1300.*

National Film and Sound Archive $$ *McCoy Circuit, Acton; tel: (02) 6248-2000 or 1800-067-274; www.nfsa.gov.au. Open daily 0900–1700.*

becomes a republic). Until 1927 – when it became the residence – Yarralumla was part of a large sheep station first settled in 1828. The sprawling homestead is closed to the public but a lookout point on Lady Denman Drive, south of the Scrivener Dam wall, gives good views of the residence and gardens, where wild kangaroos abound.

High Court*

Hundreds of years of British and Australian legal tradition find a home in this imposing glass and concrete structure by the lake, opened in 1980 by Queen Elizabeth II. This is the highest court of justice in Australia, with the final court of appeal and the court where landmark cases of national significance involving federal law and the Australian Constitution are heard by its seven judges. Designed to instil awe and respect in the nation's justice system, the High Court is centred around a vast glass public hall featuring two striking six-panelled murals by artist Jan Senbergs. The murals represent the Australian Constitution, the role of the states in the Federation and the significance of the High Court at the apex of the judicial system. A speckled granite waterfall running the full length of the ramp leading to the High Court is symbolic of how the decisions taken in this institution trickle down to all Australians.

Lake Burley Griffin**

The focal point of Canberra's elegant design, Lake Burley Griffin was artificially created between 1959 and 1964 by damming the Molonglo River. A walk or bike ride around the trail that rings the lake's perimeter is highly recommended, or in summer when it is warmer try a picnic. The **Captain Cook Memorial** jet fountain, and a bronze, copper and enamel globe at the water's edge. These were added to Canberra's monuments in 1970, to commemorate the bicentenary of Captain James Cook's exploration and claiming of Australia's east coast in 1770. Wind permitting, the elegant fountain next to Commonwealth Bridge blasts six tonnes of water 137m out of the lake from 1000–noon and 1400–1600 daily; it is a spectacular sight. A boat trip on Lake Burley Griffin, especially in autumn when the capital's colours are at their best, is a lovely way to spend a leisurely afternoon.

National Film and Sound Archive*

Housed in one of Canberra's finest art-deco buildings, Australia's great film and sound history comes alive at the National Film and Sound Archive. The collection contains many rare and early films, most of which can be

*Below
Lake Burley Griffin*

National Gallery of Australia $ *Parkes Place, Parkes; tel: (02) 6240-6502; www.nga.gov.au. Open daily 1000–1700, except Good Friday and Christmas Day. Free tours of the permanent collection available daily at 1100 and 1400.*

National Library *Parkes Place, Parkes; tel: (02) 6262-1111; www.nla.gov.au. Open Mon–Thur 0900–2100, Fri–Sun 0900–1700. Guided tours Tue–Thur 1400.*

National Museum of Australia *Lawson Crescent, Acton Peninsula; tel: (02) 6208-5000; email: information@nma.gov.au; www.nma.gov.au. Open daily 0900–1700. Free admission.*

Old Parliament House $ *King George Terrace, Parkes; tel: (02) 6270-8222; www.oph.gov.au. Open daily 0900–1700.*

National Portrait Gallery $ *Old Parliament House, King George Terrace, Parkes; tel: (02) 6270-8210; www.portrait.gov.au. Open daily 0900–1700. Also at Commonwealth Place; open Wed–Sun 1000–1800. Free admission.*

watched using individual touch-screens and headphones, including Australia's first feature film, *The Story of the Ned Kelly Gang* (1906). Watch old advertisements, historic news footage, learn about Australia's first Oscar and marvel at the intricately hand-painted pre-1920s films.

National Gallery of Australia***

If there were just one reason to visit Canberra, it would be to see the exceptional permanent collection of Australian colonial, impressionist and aboriginal art, as well as significant contemporary and older works from Europe and Asia at the National Gallery of Australia. Opened in 1982 to house Australia's young but growing art collection, it now contains more than 95,000 artworks as well as an excellent range of touring international 'blockbuster' exhibitions.

National Library*

The five-storey National Library is a temple to Australia's literary, cultural and documentary heritage, housed in an imposing lakeside building now considered an icon of 1960s architecture. Items such as Captain Cook's original diaries from his *Endeavour* voyages are on display and selected old cine-films are regularly shown.

National Museum of Australia*

Established by an Act of Parliament in 1980, the $100-million National Museum opened on the Acton peninsula of Lake Burley Griffin in March 2001, as a highlight of the national Centenary of Federation celebrations. It has three main themes: Aboriginal and Torres Strait Islander history and culture; Australian society and history since European settlement in 1788, and our interaction with the Australian environment. In 2005, the museum was declared Best Major Tourism Attraction in the Australian Tourism Awards.

Old Parliament House (National Portrait Gallery)**

Built in 1927 as the first, but temporary, parliamentary building in the new national capital, Old Parliament House was the centre of Australian politics for more than 60 years, until the opening of its grand successor in 1988. Now open to the public, it is well worth visiting graceful Kings Hall, the old House of Representatives and Senate chambers, and the lovely old carved Speaker's chair. A highlight is the excellent sound and light show *Order, Order* which relives some of the building's greatest moments. The new **National Portrait Gallery***, with its paintings, cartoons, busts and sculptures of famous Australians is also located here, while the rose gardens, courtyards and historic non-members bar can also be toured. The gallery has a second location in Commonwealth Place, focusing on contemporary portraits and photography.

🛈 **Parliament House**
$ *Capital Hill,
Canberra; tel: (02) 6277-
5399 for information desk.
Open daily 0900–1700, or
later when parliament is
sitting.* Free guided tours
are available every 30
minutes. Public galleries in
both parliamentary
chambers are open
0900–1700. Feisty debates
can be heard during
Question Time at 1400
each afternoon when
parliament is sitting.

**Questacon National
Science and
Technology Centre $$**
*King Edward Terrace,
Parkes; tel: (02) 6270-2800.
Open 1000–1700 daily.*

Below
Parliament House

Parliament House***

When the imposing $1.1-billion 'New' Parliament House, built on and within Capital Hill, was opened in 1988, it became the fourth home of the national parliament since 1901, when Australia first became a federation. The home of government and democracy in Australia, and the hotbed of feisty national politics, magnificent Parliament House is home to more than 5000 politicians, political staffers, public servants and the media entourage, making it one of the largest buildings in the Southern hemisphere. Australia is governed by elected representatives based on the British political system, with both a House of Representatives (147 elected members) and a Senate (76 senators representing their own States). Under the green lawns of Capital Hill and the vast 81-m high flag mast – the tallest stainless steel structure in the world – are both chambers of Parliament, the Prime Minister's offices, the Cabinet Room, the offices of all national politicians and the Great Hall, where State and ceremonial functions are held. The building was designed by Romaldo Giurgola of Mitchell, Giurgola and Thorp Architects, after an international competition attracted 329 entries from around the world. It took eight years and 10,000 workers to build new Parliament House using Australian timbers and local granite. Inside, there are tapestries, paintings and aboriginal art, as well as one of only four surviving 1297 copies of the Magna Carta, signed by King Edward I of England on 12 October 1297.

Questacon**

The action-packed Questacon or National Science and Technology Centre is a favourite with both kids and adults of all ages. With 200 hands-on exhibits in six different galleries arranged around the 27-m high central 'drum' of the building, science need never be dull again.

Royal Australian Mint $ *Denison St, Deakin; (02) 6202-6819. Open weekdays 0900–1600 (with coin production).*

Royal Australian Mint*

The Royal Australian Mint produces 600 million coins a year, or two million coins a day, and has made more than eight billion decimal coins since it opened in 1965. Watch coins being made out of silver, gold and metal blend blanks, see designers at work and visit the coin museum to learn about the history of coins and money in Australia. Mint your own personal $1 coin, see truckloads of money or discover why a 1930 penny is worth $6000. There is an excellent coin shop.

Red Hill Lookout

Cars can be driven to the top of Red Hill for an excellent view over Lake Burley Griffin, Parliament House, Manuka and the embassy suburb of Yarralumla. Behind Red Hill stretch the southern suburbs of Canberra with the Brindabella Ranges to the west. After enjoying the view, visit the nearby chic shopping village of **Manuka** for the best coffee and cakes in Canberra.

Yarralumla Embassy District**

The suburb of Yarralumla is home to more than 80 foreign embassies and diplomatic residences, many designed in the style of their national architecture. A drive through the tree-lined streets of Yarralumla gives a fascinating and fun glimpse of foreign culture. Distinctive embassies to view include the vast Chinese embassy with its yellow and blue curved roof tiles, red columns, dragon statues and pagoda shaped roofs, the stately red-brick Georgian-style compound of the United States of America, the Indian embassy with its pools, shallow moat and white temple building of the Mogul architectural style with a gold spire on top, and the High Commission of Papua New Guinea, built as a Spirit House with rising wooden ends, painted motifs and carved totem poles outside. Just across Adelaide Avenue behind tall white walls is The Lodge, the Canberra residence of the Australian Prime Minister and his family.

How Canberra was born

In 1911, after more than 10 years of wrangling about where a new inland national capital should be built, the Australian government (then sitting in Melbourne) decided on Canberra as the best site and launched an international competition for a city plan. Models of the Canberra site, with its central hills, the Molonglo River basin and recommendation that a dam on the Molonglo would create an excellent ornamental lake, were exhibited in cities around the world. After much debate, first prize was awarded to a 35-year-old landscape architect from Chicago, Walter Burley Griffin, who had studied under avant-garde architect Frank Lloyd Wright. His plan was for a garden city of 25,000 people, with a series of lakes, a great triangle of avenues enclosing the major government buildings and radiating boulevards and circular suburbs, and a series of terraces rising to the focal point of Parliament House atop Capital Hill. Influenced by the design of both Washington and Versailles, and assisted by the elegant plans and drawings of his wife, architect Marion Lucy Mahony, Burley Griffin predicted 'it would be unlike any other city in the world'. On 12 March 1913, an official foundation stone for the city of Canberra was laid by the Prime Minister, Andrew Fisher. Lady Denman, the wife of the governor-general, Sir Thomas Denman, announced the new city would be known as Canberra (pronounced by her, and forever after, as Can'bra). Bureaucratic arguments, procrastination and World War I then intervened. By 1921 little of the new city had been started and Burley Griffin was dismissed from his post as Federal Capital Director of Design and Construction. He stayed in private practice in Australia, designing the NSW cities of Leeton and Griffith until in 1935, reduced to designing municipal incinerators, he left for India, dying there two years later at the age of 60 in relative obscurity and totally disillusioned with Australia.

Above
Canberra's Australian National Gallery

Accommodation and food

A Foreign Affair $$ *8 Franklin St, Manuka; tel: (02) 6239-5060.* A chic Italian restaurant that has set new standards in Canberra dining.

Asakusa $$$ *Green Square, Jardine St; tel: (02) 6295-3608.* Authentic Japanese restaurant located near the Parliamentary Triangle; its bento boxes (traditional Japanese packed lunches) are great favourites.

Blue and White Lodge $ *524 Northbourne Ave, Downer, tel: (02) 6248-0498.* Reputedly Canberra first and most friendly bed and breakfast, the Blue and White Lodge provides a variety of budget and family accommodation and a full cooked breakfast. About 4km north of the city centre on the main road to Sydney.

Brassey Hotel $$ *Belmore Gardens, Braddon; tel: (02) 6273-3766.* Set amidst flower gardens and peaceful lawns, this unusual hotel was once a large private home and later a training ground for Australia's budding young diplomats. Now it is a boutique hotel with old-world charm and attached conference facilities.

Brindabella Station $$$ *Brindabella Valley, Brindabella, tel: (02) 6326-2121.* Nestling in the mountains 45km from Canberra between Kosciuszko and Namadgi National Parks, this luxury farm homestead retreat built in the 1900s is surrounded by bush, birds and native animals. Activities include bush-walking, birdwatching, horse riding, 4WD-tours and trout fishing. Famous for its comfort and hospitality. All meals are included.

Canberra Hyatt Hotel $$$ *Commonwealth Ave, Yarralumla; tel: (02) 6270-1234.* This five-star 1920s-style heritage-listed hotel located on the south edge of Lake Burley Griffin is one of Canberra's showpieces.

Canberra International Hotel $$$ *242 Northbourne Ave, Dickson; tel: (02) 6247-6966.* A large hotel popular with corporate and conference guests for its reasonable rates and efficient service, located north of the lake not far from the city centre.

Canberra YHA $ *191 Dryandra St, O'Connor; tel: (02) 6248-9155.* The Canberra Youth Hostel offers top-class budget accommodation in a lovely bush setting, north of the lake on the side of Black Mountain, about 2km from the town centre.

Carrington at Bungendore $$$ *21 Malbon St, Bungendore, tel: (02) 6238-1044.* A weekend stay at the Carrington at Bungendore, a relaxing country-style homestead in a rural village just outside the ACT, is popular with local Canberrians and visitors alike. Browse in antique shops and soak up the atmosphere of this early bush town.

Fringe Benefits $$$ *54 Marcus Clarke St, Canberra City; tel: (02) 6247-4042.* Named after the new tax introduced in the 1980s that meant

ⓘ Regatta Point Visitors' Centre and the National Capital Exhibition
Commonwealth Park; tel: (02) 6257-1068. Open daily 0900–1700, 1800 during summer months.
The rotunda housing the National Capital Exhibition on the north side of Lake Burley Griffin at Regatta Point is recommended as a starting point for any tour of Canberra. Inside are models, videos, old pictures and slides showing the history and growth of Canberra as the federal capital of Australia, providing an excellent orientation of the city's major features and buildings before any tour is undertaken. From the windows of the rotunda is a clear view of Lake Burley Griffin and the Parliamentary Triangle.

St John the Baptist Church and School House Museum
Constitution Ave, Reid; tel: (02) 6248-8399.
The oldest buildings in Canberra are the Anglican church of St John the Baptist and its adjoining schoolhouse, built of local sandstone and bluestone in 1854. The beautiful high-steepled church has been a focal point of the district for 150 years. Memorials on the walls of the church commemorate many statesmen, scientists, scholars and servicemen, while headstones in its graveyard bear the names of many old Canberra pioneering families.

work lunches were no longer tax deductible, Fringe Benefits remains a favourite Canberra restaurant serving modern Australian cuisine in a bubbly, tasteful atmosphere.

Kythera Motel $$ *98–100 Northbourne Ave, Braddon, tel: (02) 6248-7611.* Comfortable affordable family hotel on the main road to Sydney, close to the city centre, with both Italian and Malaysian restaurants.

The Oak Room $$$ *Hyatt Hotel, Commonwealth Ave, Yarralumla; tel: (02) 6270-8977.* Canberra's most formal, discreet and special occasion restaurant, the Oak Room belies its 1920s surrounds and silver and crystal décor by serving modern Australian food which has won many national awards.

Ottoman Cuisine $$ *Upstairs, 8 Franklin St, Manuka; tel: (02) 6239-6754.* Award-winning Turkish restaurant with vast speciality menu, and great uses of seafood and spice. Often described as Australia's best Turkish restaurant.

Passmore Cottage Homestay $$ *3 Lilley St, O'Connor, tel: (02) 6247-4523.* Traditional bed and breakfast accommodation is unusually located in a quiet and leafy part of suburban Canberra, only 3km from the city centre and close to the university.

Ruby's Chinese Restaurant $ *18–20 Woolley St, Dickson; tel: (02) 6249-8849.* Traditional Chinese restaurant in outlying Dickson, with all the heavy décor and potted palms; has a fascinating reputation as being the place where spies of all nationalities rendezvous.

Tang Dynasty $$$ *27 Kennedy St, Kingston; tel: (02) 6295-0102.* Stylish modern Chinese restaurant complete with black horse statues, bamboo partitions and dark fittings, that is serious about its gourmet Chinese food.

Vivaldi $$$ *Arts Centre, Australian National University, University Ave, Acton; tel: (02) 6257-2718.* Set in the leafy grounds of the ANU, Vivaldi serves great food with emphasis on local Canberra regional wines.

Suggested tour

Distance: Most of the Canberra attractions listed above are within a few hundred metres of each other, located around Lake Burley Griffin and the so-called Parliamentary Triangle. Most can be explored on foot.

Time: Exploring the Parliamentary Triangle and its imposing edifices can take one day or two half days if you divide the tour into two parts: north and south of the lake.

Links: Continue south of Canberra to link up with Cooma and the start of the NSW Snowy Mountains drive (*see page 72*).

Route 1: The first route explores the south side of the lake starting with a tour of the remarkable **PARLIAMENT HOUSE** ❶ on Capital Hill, followed by **OLD PARLIAMENT HOUSE** and the **NATIONAL LIBRARY**. After a break from the serious stuff at the **QUESTACON** science centre, move on to the **HIGH COURT** and the artistic wonders of the **NATIONAL GALLERY OF AUSTRALIA** ❷.

Route 2: The second tour starts with the excellent **Regatta Point National Capital Exhibition** ❸ detailing Canberra's history, followed by a walk through lovely **COMMONWEALTH PARK**, home to the spring Floriade festival. Visit historic **BLUNDELLS COTTAGE** ❹ and **St John the Baptist Church** before tackling the might of the **AUSTRALIAN WAR MEMORIAL**. Relax with a cruise on **LAKE BURLEY GRIFFIN**, or perhaps a bike ride around its edge. After that, you are entitled to collapse exhausted at Canberra's central shopping area, **CIVIC SQUARE**, for a bite to eat and a rest.

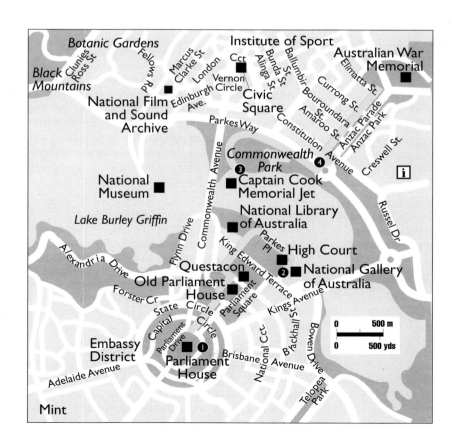

Melbourne's Dandenongs and the Yarra Valley

Ratings

Food and wine	●●●●●
Vineyards	●●●●●
Outdoor activities	●●●●○
Scenery	●●●●○
Children	●●●○○
National parks	●●●○○
Walking	●●●○○
Wildlife	●●●○○

In less than an hour from the centre of Melbourne you can be spotting lyrebirds in Sherbrooke Forest, wandering through magnificent mountain gardens or riding on a vintage steam train. In the Yarra Valley, not far away, vineyards stretching as far as the eye can see are evidence of Australia's booming wine industry. The valley's proximity to Melbourne markets has also attracted specialist food producers who supply everything from hand-made cheese to venison, trout and pick-your-own raspberries. A day or weekend drive combining both these areas and a visit to the famous Healesville Sanctuary makes for a magnificent, relaxing and gourmet time away from the bustle of central Melbourne. If it is hot and the beaches beckon, try driving to Port Phillip Bay for swimming and sailing and Mornington Peninsula National Park for clean sandy beaches, dolphin watching or wild clifftop walks.

DANDENONG RANGES NATIONAL PARK✦✦✦

ⓘ Visitor Information Centre *1211 Burwood Highway, Ferntree Gully 3156; tel: 1800-645-505; fax: (03) 9758-7533.*

The 3215 hectares of the Dandenong Ranges National Park covers some superb scenery with spectacular mountain ash forests and lush fern gullies and walking tracks to suit all levels of fitness. Even if you don't want to leave your car, the roads winding through Sherbrooke Forest provide beautiful and surprising views. Although many of the tall mountain ash trees growing in the forest today are the result of regeneration following bushfires in the 1890s and early 1900s, some of the forest giants are thought to be up to 200 years old. Despite pressures from the encroaching suburbs and domestic animals, the park has more than 130 native bird species, including many lyrebirds. Visitors will often hear them mimicking the sounds of other birds, but the best chance of seeing them is on the 7-km **Eastern Sherbrooke Lyrebird Circuit** walk through Sherbrooke Forest. One of several pleasant picnic spots in the park is the site of the old Doongalla

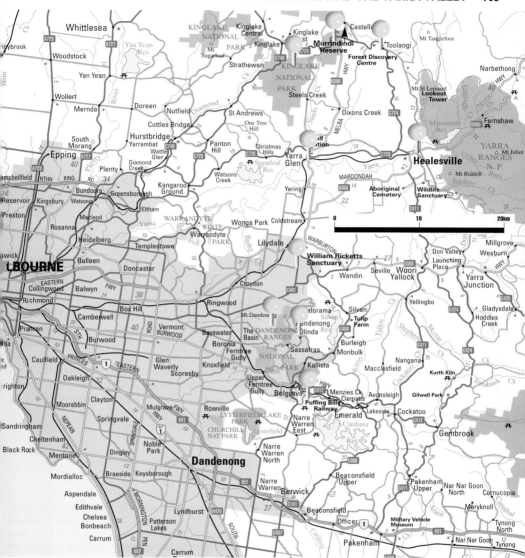

homestead, where open lawns, giant camellias and rhododendrons contrast with the surrounding bush. Stop here for lunch and you are likely to be joined by several friendly kookaburras in the trees above. A longer 20-km walking circuit starts and finishes in the park near Fern Tree Gully, connecting One Tree Hill with Mt Dandenong, the Olinda State Forest, Kallista, Sherbrooke Forest and Belgrave. Another green and tranquil walk is the 11-km path from Sassafras to Emerald along the ferny gully of **Sassafras Creek**.

HEALESVILLE SANCTUARY✦✦✦

This is one of Victoria's tourist highlights, the most famous and natural place to see some of Australia's unique native wildlife species. The sanctuary has a great bird display, famous platypus exhibit and more than 200 species of Australian native animals in 31 hectares of bush. There are excellent keeper talks and special animal exhibitions – the wedge-tail eagle flights are an unmissable highlight.

Behind the displays, the sanctuary is involved in veterinary, research and education programmes which place it at the forefront of wildlife conservation. It takes part in breeding programmes for more than 20 threatened species, including Victoria's faunal emblem, the endangered helmeted honeyeater. The Healesville Sanctuary is the only place in the world to have successfully reared young lyrebirds in captivity and in 1999, for the first time in 50 years, a platypus gave birth at the sanctuary. The twin youngsters are now on display in the Sidney Myer Platypus Exhibit where visitors enjoy a platypus-eye view of the world.

ℹ Healesville Sanctuary $$ *Badger Creek Road, Healesville, open daily 0900–1700; 24-hr information line: 1902-240-192; email: hs@zoo.org.au; www.zoo.org.au*

As you wander between the different exhibits you will cross paths with free-ranging animals such as cheeky emus, curious kangaroos and wallabies and the raucous sulphur-crested cockatoos. Each year many injured birds of prey are brought to the sanctuary. If they can be rehabilitated, they are returned to the wild but some are permanently damaged and unable to survive in their natural habitat. These birds are included in a special display, giving visitors the chance to observe their awesome power at close range.

KINGLAKE NATIONAL PARK✦✦✦

ℹ Kinglake National Park Visitor Information *National Park Road, Pleasant Creek, 3757;* **Parks Victoria Information Centre** *tel: 13-1963; www.parks.vic.gov.au*

Plunging waterfalls, fern gullies and the superb lyrebird are some of the attractions that draw people to Kinglake National Park. The park, on the outskirts of Melbourne, covers 21,600 hectares of eucalyptus forest on the slopes of the Great Dividing Range. This type of forest, dominated by messmate (a type of eucalyptus) and narrow-leaved peppermint, was once common in central Victoria.

The usually shy lyrebird can often be seen near the **Masons Falls** picnic area, scratching for grubs in the old sawdust mound; if you are lucky, you may even see the male performing his courtship dance. The other main picnic area is at **Jehosophat Gully**. From both these sites visitors have a choice of several walks. The northern section of the park has more open forest and the trees are more stunted due to drier conditions and poorer soils. One short walk in this area leads to the **Wombelano Falls**, a beautiful and relatively pristine waterfall which is spring fed and flows for most of the year.

Above
White Kookaburra

MURRINDINDI RESERVE✧✧✧

With their tumbling waterfalls, soaring mountain ash and damp, fern filled gullies, the forests of the Murrindindi Scenic Reserve just off the Melba Highway, are home to a variety of native animals including wombats, echidnas and shy swamp wallabies. It is just a short way along the River Walk track from the reserve car park to the **Murrindindi Cascades**, where the river drops steeply over granite boulders, through beautiful cool temperate rainforest of myrtle beech and sassafras trees. It makes a great picnic spot and, for kids playing in the tumbling creek, summer is best.

NATIONAL RHODODENDRON GARDENS, OLINDA✧✧

National Rhododendron Gardens $$ The Georgian Road, Olinda. Open daily 1000–1630, Oct–Mar closes 1730; **Parks Victoria Information Centre** tel: 13-1963; www.parks.vic.gov.au

Tesselaars Tulip Farm $ Silvan; tel: (03) 9737-9811.

It is hard to drive around the Dandenongs and Yarra Valley in spring and not be struck by its mass of colours and flowers. In September, the 40-hectare **National Rhododendron Gardens** at Olinda are a mass of bright azaleas, pure white camellias and daffodils. Two months later, the rhododendrons, high amongst the Dandenong mountain air, have burst into dappled pinks, purples and whites. Although they are not native to the region, the rhododendrons in this garden look at home beneath their canopy of Mountain Ash. They thrive on the deep acidic mountain soil and the cooler high-altitude climate of the ranges. The collection of individual gardens contains many stunning and unusual plant species from exotic mountainous regions, all linked by the rhododendron theme. The protea garden, with a superb collection of plants from the South African and Australian Proteaceae family, is well worth seeing. Other features are a cherry walk, a dogwood path and an extensive alpine garden. Follow the paths for a delightful view over the Yarra Valley and distant mountains. Friendly kookaburras may follow your progress and ducks and geese wander on the lawns near the Visitors' Centre. The colourful Vireya rhododendrons, from regions such as northern Australia, New Guinea and Indonesia, flower sporadically throughout the year and often provide a colourful display when other species are not in bloom. To see flowers around the Dandenongs and Yarra Valley, visit the famous **Tesselaars Tulip Farm**✧ at Silvan, which is alive with colour and swaying heads in early spring.

PUFFING BILLY STEAM TRAIN✧✧✧

The shrill whistle and the bits of ash puffed out by the steam engine have been a favourite holiday experience for generations of Melbourne children. The little Puffing Billy steam train, once an important link for mountain dwellers to transport timber and farm produce to the

Above
Puffing Billy

🔘 **Puffing Billy $$** *Old Monbulk Rd, Belgrave; tel: (03) 9754-6800; 24-hr recorded timetable information 1900-937-069; fax: (03) 9754-2513; email: pbr@pbr.org.au; www.pbr.org.au. Open daily except Christmas Day.*

city, is now the Dandenongs' top tourist attraction. Every day Puffing Billy carries visitors in open carriages and closed restaurant cars, kids' legs dangling out the windows, chuffing through hills, untouched bush, fern gullies and across tall wooden trestle bridges from Belgrave Station to pretty Emerald Lake for a three-hour round trip. For many years only this 13-km section of the original track remained, but since 1990 volunteers have been rebuilding the rest of the track and in 1998 the section from Emerald Lake to Gembrook was re-opened, adding another 40 minutes to the previous one-hour one-way journey. Volunteers have also restored many of the original carriages and in the steam museum at Menzies Creek railway station their work can be seen in a collection of early steam locomotives and machinery. This is an adventure not to be missed.

TOOLANGI FOREST❖❖❖

🔘 **Toolangi Forest Discovery Centre** *$ Main Road; tel: (03) 5962-9314. Open daily 1000–1700.*

Singing Gardens *98 Kinglake Road; tel: (03) 5962-9282. Open Sat–Thur, 1000–1700; closed Aug.*

A striking building made of timber, glass and steel, the **Toolangi Forest Discovery Centre❖** tells the story of tall forests and the timber industry in the Yarra Ranges, an area which teemed with pioneers, loggers and extraordinary little timber tramways at the turn of the century. The centre is a good starting place for exploring the Toolangi State Forest. The famous poet, C J Dennis lived at Toolangi and wrote about local characters in his poems. He was the proprietor of a local sawmill and today his old home, and his well-known 'Singing Gardens', created in 1915, are now a Devonshire tea house.

WILLIAM RICKETTS SANCTUARY❖❖

William Ricketts Sanctuary $$ *Mt Dandenong Tourist Road, Mt Dandenong; tel: (03) 9751-1300. Open daily 1000–1600; closed Christmas Day.*

The intricate clay figures carved by sculptor William Ricketts blend in with the rocks and trees as if they had grown there. His sanctuary on top of Mt Dandenong is dotted with nearly 100 sculptures depicting aboriginal and animal figures moulded into rocks and tree stumps with inscriptions painstakingly engraved on clay tablets. The sanctuary, which was Ricketts' home from 1934 to 1993, reflects his passion for the environment and concern about its destruction.

YARRA RANGES NATIONAL PARK❖❖❖

Parks Victoria Information Centre *tel: 13-1963; www.parks.vic.gov.au*

Visitor Information Centre *The Old Court House, Harker St, Healesville 3777; tel: (03) 5962-2600; fax: (03) 5962-2040.*

Between Healesville, Yarra Junction and Marysville, the Yarra Ranges National Park has something for everyone. In the Black Spur and Dom Dom Saddle area, the 12-km **Morleys Track** from Fernshaw Park to the Dom Dom Saddle car park offers an exceptional Australian experience of walking through thick, dark mountain ash forest with a rich understorey of wattles, ferns and myrtle beech. A new hiking track is the '**Top of the Ranges walk**', a spectacular 22-km one-way scenic walk linking Mt Dom Dom with Mt Donna Buang to the south. Other popular walks include the ski trails around Mt Donna Buang, Echo Flat and Lake Mountain. A shorter route is the 4-km loop near Powelltown to see the **Ada Tree**, a 300-year-old mountain ash that towers over the forest, 76m tall; the walk passes through fern gullies, groves of ancient sassafras, myrtle beech and other temperate rainforest species.

YARRA VALLEY WINERIES❖❖❖

Domaine Chandon winery and tasting room *Maroondah Hwy, Green Point; tel: (03) 9739-1110.*

Yering Station Produce Store *38 Melba Hwy, Yering 3770. Offers locally produced foods and preserves.* **Old Dairy** *Yarra Glen; tel: (03) 9739-0023.*

Yarra Valley Grape Grazing Festival *tel: (03) 9761-8474; fax: (03) 9761-9488. First weekend in Mar.*

Less than an hour after you leave Melbourne you can be sipping your first glass of wine in one of the Yarra Valley's renowned wineries. In many ways the Yarra Valley has grown up with the wine industry which now flourishes in the rolling hills of this long-established farming area. Early in the morning hot-air balloons drift over the valley ready to float down for a winery champagne breakfast. Of more than 50 wineries in the Yarra Valley, about 30 offer cellar door tasting and sales. Many also have their own restaurants or cafés; the glass-walled tasting room at **Domaine Chandon** is not to be missed for a lunchtime glass of sparkling wine.

The Yarra Valley regional food trail takes in more than 60 epicurean delights ranging from chutney and hand-made chocolate to lavender honey. You can buy some of these delicacies from the produce store at **Yering Station**, the valley's oldest winery, or at the evocative **Old Dairy** near Yarra Glen. There are regular festivals at Yarra Valley wineries, including musical afternoons at Domaine Chandon.

Accommodation and food

Australis $$ *939 Don Road, Healesville 3777; tel: (03) 5962-4260; fax: (03) 5962-6077.* Cosy cottage 400m above the Yarra Valley.

Baytree House $$ *11 Ida Grove, Olinda, 3788; tel: (03) 9751-1836; fax: (03) 9751-2265.* Self-contained cottage.

Bianchet Winery $$ *187 Victoria Road, Lilydale 3140; tel: (03) 9739-1779; fax: (03) 9739-1277. Café open daily 1000–1800, dinner Fri and Sat.* Continuous food with Mediterranean and Asian influences.

Ranges $$ *5 Main St, Olinda; tel: (03) 9751-2133.* A contemporary café-restaurant amidst a plethora of 'tea shoppes'.

Singing Gardens of C J Dennis $ *98 Kinglake Road, Toolangi 3777; tel: (03) 5962-9282. Open Sat–Thur, 1000–1700 (closed Aug, Christmas Day).* Devonshire teas and light lunches.

Sweetwater Café $$ and **Eleonore's Restaurant $$$** *Chateau Yering, 42 Melba Highway, Yering 3770; tel: (03) 9237-3333; fax: (03) 9237-3300.* Enjoy freshly baked snacks and meals in magnificent surroundings.

Valley Guesthouse $$ *319 Steels Creek Road, Yarra Glen, 3775; tel: (03) 9730-1822; fax: (03) 9730-2019; email: valguest@alphalink.com.au.* Luxurious suites display the work of the guesthouse's master potter proprietor.

Australia's native animals

Australia's isolation from the rest of the world for more than 50 million years has blessed it with a strange and unique mix of native fauna. Some animals such as the platypus and crocodile are living remnants from the ancient dinosaur world, while others have adapted so well to their natural environment, that they can survive in dry or hot areas that other animals find uninhabitable. The most instantly recognisable animal is the marsupial kangaroo, of which there are many different species; its companion on the national coat of arms is the emu, a tall flightless bird similar to the ostrich and the cassowary of the north Australian rainforests. Most remarkable of all are the Australian monotremes – the shy river platypus and the echidna or spiny anteater – the only mammals in the world that also lay eggs. Both species are regarded as living fossils, their life cycles displaying their early reptilian origins. The much-loved koala (it is not a bear) can be found along the east coast of Australia, feeding and sleeping high in the gum trees. Other special Australian fauna – all of which can be seen at Healesville Sanctuary – include the slow and sturdy wombat, the dingo or native dog, the ferocious little Tasmanian Devil and many fascinating species of shy and tiny nocturnal bandicoots, bilbies and desert rats. Australia's birds are as magnificent and special as its fauna; its colourful lorikeets, rosellas, cockatoos, kookaburras, and galahs are among the best known and most frequently seen.

Suggested tour

Total distance: 165km.

Time: 1 or 2 days.

Links: Instead of returning to Melbourne, from **KINGLAKE**, head west through **Upper Plenty** to the Hume Highway and continue north to Benalla and the northeast Victoria tour. Alternatively, from **Sorrento**, take the car ferry to the pretty seaside town of **Queenscliff**, and continue to **Geelong** and the Great Ocean Road.

Route: From Melbourne take the South Eastern Highway and Burwood Road to **Upper Ferntree Gully**, a distance of about 34km. Continue on the main road to Belgrave and go for a ride on the **PUFFING BILLY STEAM TRAIN ❶**.

Drive through Sherbrooke Forest and the **DANDENONG RANGES NATIONAL PARK** to rejoin the main route.

After stopping at the Ferntree Gully Visitor Information Centre, continue along the winding **Mt Dandenong Tourist Road**, through the picturesque towns of **Sassafras** and **Olinda**, stopping at the nurseries and craft shops, and at the **NATIONAL RHODODENDRON GARDENS ❷**, which has colourful displays all year.

Detour: Leave the main road at Kallista and join the Monbulk Road to explore some interesting gardens; the Pirianda Garden is at its most spectacular in autumn when the exotic trees are a mass of colour and the R J Hamer Arboretum has 100 hectares of woodland refuge. Visit the National Rhododendron Gardens and rejoin the Mt Dandenong Tourist Road at Olinda (*end of detour*).

Continue along the scenic Tourist Road to the **WILLIAM RICKETTS SANCTUARY**. Admire the view at the **Kalorama Lookout** before descending the mountain to **Montrose** and joining the Maroondah Highway at **Lilydale**. From here you will see signs to the **YARRA VALLEY WINERIES**. Drive on 23km to Healesville and the **HEALESVILLE SANCTUARY ❸**.

Detour: Take the Melba Highway 14km to **Yarra Glen** if you want to visit the Yering wineries. Return to the main route on the Yarra Glen-Healesville Road.

At Healesville, join Myers Creek Road to **TOOLANGI ❹** and the **MURRINDINDI SCENIC RESERVE**, a distance of 18km.

Enjoy a scenic return to Melbourne via **KINGLAKE NATIONAL PARK ❺**, 20km away and then through St Andrews, Hurstbridge and Greensborough, about 50km back to the city.

ℹ Peninsula Visitor Information Centre tel: 1800-804-009; fax: (03) 5981-0462.

Point Nepean Visitor Information Centre, Nepean Rd, Portsea; tel: (03) 5984-1586. Open daily 0900–1700.

🏞 Mornington Peninsula National Park Parks Victoria; tel: 13-1963.

🚡 Arthur's Seat chairlift $ Arthur's Seat Rd, Dromana; tel: (03) 5987-3095. Chairlift available daily mid-September to end of April, all weekends, public and school holidays.

⛺ Red Hill Market Sept to May, first Sat of the month. **Mornington Racecourse Craft Market** 2nd Sun every month. **Balnarring Emu Plains Market** Coolart Rd, Balnarring; Nov to May, 3rd Sat every month.

Below
Brighton beach on Port Phillip Bay

Also worth exploring

If you feel like heading for the beach rather than the hills, a visit to Sorrento and the Mornington Peninsula is an easy day trip from Melbourne. Take the Nepean Highway and Frankston Freeway to Dromana and a winding road that leads up to **Arthur's Seat** lookout, where the 302-m peak gives a panoramic view over **Port Phillip Bay**, Bass Strait and the hinterland. In summer, a chairlift up the mountain provides visitors with thrilling tree-top vistas. A short drive away is the town of **Red Hill**, home to Victoria's oldest continuous community market. The area is also well known for its wineries, craft shops and restaurants. Fresh fruit from local orchards is a speciality with opportunities to pick your own berries in season. **Cape Schanck**, the southern-most tip of the peninsula and part of the **Mornington Peninsula National Park**, has a wild, rugged coastline. A boardwalk leads from the clifftop lookout to Pulpit Rock. One of the best coastal walks leads from the cape to **Bushrangers Bay**. A 27-km walking track goes all the way from Cape Schanck to Portsea, taking in spectacular and exhilarating scenery as it passes the ocean beaches of Rye, Gunnamatta, and Sorrento with access available at various points along the way.

As you enter **Sorrento** a small memorial and pioneer cemetery marks the site of the first, doomed, white settlement in Victoria, at Sullivan Bay. Sorrento has many fine buildings, some of them made from local limestone which gives them an attractive honey colour. This popular holiday town has cafés, boutiques, galleries and other shops which cater to visitors all year round. Bottlenose dolphins frolic in the waters of the bay and one of the most delightful ways to see them and admire the clifftop **Portsea** mansions is to take the small passenger ferry to **Queenscliff**, a 40-minute trip. An alternative is to put your car on the larger vehicle ferry, and to cross more directly to Queenscliff and **Geelong** (see page 113) on the western side of The Heads narrow entrance to Port Phillip Bay.

The **Point Nepean** section of the Mornington Peninsula National Park includes historic **Fort Nepean** and the quarantine station. After being off limits to the public for more than 100 years, most of the tip of the peninsula was opened in 1988 and visitors can now explore the area on foot or by a transporter.

The Great Ocean Road

Ratings

Beaches	●●●●●
Scenery	●●●●●
Surfing	●●●●○
Coastal towns	●●●●○
Fishing	●●●●○
Geology	●●●●○
Nature	●●●●○
Shipwrecks	●●●●○

After a visit to Melbourne, head for The Great Ocean Road, probably Australia's most famous driving route, which leads from Torquay to the wild landscapes of Victoria's southwest. Huge cliffs and roaring seas, fishing villages and marvellous beaches on one side of the road and magnificent rainforest on the other make this one of Australia's most scenic drives. In summer, the beaches can be golden and serene, with gentle curling surf and endless blue seas, while in winter the rugged coastline is transformed with white caps and mountainous waves. Offshore, the towering, marooned rock islands surrounded by wild seas that make up the Twelve Apostles are one of Victoria's most majestic sights. North of the Great Ocean Road, this route heads towards the major wool-growing centre of Hamilton and the magical Gariwerd or Grampians National Park, a favourite spring and summer haunt for walkers, bush-lovers, rock climbers and wildflower enthusiasts.

APOLLO BAY❖❖❖

ℹ **Great Ocean Rd Visitor Information Centre**
Foreshore, Apollo Bay; tel: (03) 5237-6529; fax: (03) 5237-6194;
www.visitvictoria.com

Once a sleepy fishing village, this is now a popular base for tourists to explore the Otway cool climate rainforests and attractions of the coast. Approaching the town, the road offers spectacular views back along the cliffs and plunging coast of the twisting Great Ocean Road. Crayfish is a speciality of the area and the fishermen's co-operative at the edge of the wharf sells fresh fish every day. The Otway rainforest and many walking tracks are easily accessible from Apollo Bay.

GEELONG❖❖❖

The city of Geelong, tucked in the southwest corner of Port Phillip Bay about 80km from Melbourne, has a rich past, linked to its role as the wool-export city for the productive and wealthy grazing properties of Victoria's Western District basalt plains. The historic 1872 bluestone

ℹ Visitor Information Centre *Geelong and Great Ocean Rd, Stead Park, Princes Hwy; tel: (03) 5275-5797, or toll free: 1800-620-888.*

🏛 National Wool Museum $ *26 Moorabool St; tel: (03) 5227-0701.*

woolstore, now home to the **National Wool Museum***, houses a series of interactive displays, working examples of old machinery and the sights and sounds of an industry central to Australia's economic success. Geelong has many fine National Trust properties and historic country gardens, as well as fine botanical gardens on a headland overlooking the Bay. Eastern Park, with its beautifully restored art-deco baths on Corio Bay, is a peaceful spot for a stroll, swim or a picnic. In recent years the waterfront, Steampacket Place, has been given a new lease of life with restaurants, shops and a marina.

GRAMPIANS NATIONAL PARK❖❖❖

ⓘ **Grampians National Park Visitor Centre** *Grampians Rd, Halls Gap; tel: (03) 5356-4381; fax: (03) 5356-4446.*

ⓗ **Brambuk Aboriginal Living Cultural Centre** *Halls Gap; tel: (03) 5356-4452; fax: (03) 5356-4455. Open daily. Includes bush tucker restaurant, display, souvenir shop and auditorium.*

Stunning views, hidden valleys, waterfalls, rocky outcrops and Aboriginal culture as well as outstanding wildflower displays are what you can expect to find in the Grampians, one of Victoria's best bushwalking locations and world famous as a site for rock climbing. The Aborigines know the Grampians as Gariwerd and descendants of the original inhabitants continue to have a strong association with the area today. At the excellent **Brambuk Living Cultural Centre** just south of the central hamlet of Halls Gap you can learn about the culture of the Aboriginal communities of southwest Victoria and find out the location of rock art sites. The undulating shape and earthy colours of the building blend with the natural surroundings. Koalas can often be seen in the gum trees around Halls Gap, while the kangaroos at **Zumsteins** picnic area are very tame. Most visitors stay in Halls Gap which has excellent day tour options including a walk up **Mt Abrupt** overlooking Dunkeld, and a day drive down the magnificent **Victoria Valley**, especially when the wildflowers are out.

GREAT OCEAN ROAD❖❖❖

The eastern edge of the surf town of Torquay marks the official start of the Great Ocean Road, Australia's most spectacular and rugged coastal driving route. From here it is a continuous procession of sand, surf,

ℹ **Visitor Information Centre** 144 Mountjoy Parade, Torquay; tel: (03) 5289-1152; fax: (03) 5289-2492.

Information Centre Morris St, Port Campbell; tel: (03) 5598-6382.

🌙 **Great Ocean Road Accommodation Centre** 136 Mountjoy Parade, Torquay; tel: (03) 5289-1800 (24-hr holiday hotline); email: lornere@ne.com.au; www.lornereal estate.com.au

towering cliffs, thick forests and resort destinations. World-famous **Bells Beach**, just a few kilometres from Torquay, is a regular venue for international surfing championships. From Airey's Inlet to Lorne, the coastal scenery is spectacular, rising from beach level to dizzying heights around **Cinema Point**. A memorial arch at Eastern View commemorates those who built the road in the 1920s. Swimming is excellent at **Kennett River**, while a drive up the **Gray's Road Ridge** for a few kilometres, usually reveals a plentiful koala colony. Past Apollo Bay, the road turns inland and winds through the Otway National Park, with magnificent mountain-top lookouts. It returns to the coast at **Castle Cove**, near the site where fossilised remains of dinosaurs 100 million years old have been discovered. Further along, near **Port Campbell**, is the most spectacular stretch of the coast, famous throughout the world for its striking rock formations. London Bridge, the Twelve Apostles, Loch Ard Gorge and the Blowhole are the best known. A self-guided walk at Loch Ard introduces you to the coastal geology.

LORNE✦✦

ℹ **Victoria Visitor Information Centre** Town Hall, cnr Little Collins and Swanston Sts; tel: (03) 9790-2121.

With its trendy cafés, restaurants, boutiques and shops, Lorne has more of a seaside resort flavour than any of the other towns along the Great Ocean Road. It was a popular holiday town even before the road was built and has never lost its appeal. The mountains behind Lorne create a stunning background and give the town a mild, sheltered climate. A long, protected beach provides swimming and surfing conditions for all ages. Popular **Erskine Falls** is just a short drive away and the heathland and eucalyptus forest of the **Angahook-Lorne State Park** offer many other easily accessible walks.

MELBOURNE✦✦✦

🏛 **Royal Botanic Gardens $** Visitor's Centre and Gate F, Birdwood Ave, Melbourne; tel: (03) 9252-2300. Open daily Nov–Mar 0730–2030, Apr–Oct 0730–1730.

The first capital of Australia, Melbourne is renowned for its theatre, art, festivals and music, fine food, elegant fashions and sport.

Once a bustling waterway, the river is still an important focus for Melbourne, as it meanders past bustling Southgate and the beautiful **Royal Botanic Gardens✦✦**. On a summer night, you can take a rug to the gardens and watch theatre being performed under the stars. A range of leisure craft offer **cruises✦** down the Yarra River for a different perspective on Melbourne. Stop at Herring Island, just upstream from the city, where art and nature merge into one at the Environmental Sculpture Park.

On St Kilda Road by the Yarra River, discover the imposing

Left
Loch Ard Gorge from the Great Ocean Road

Melbourne River Cruises $$ *Princes Walk, cnr Princes Bridge and Batman Ave (opposite Flinders St Station), Melbourne; tel: (03) 9614-1215; fax: (03) 9614-1252.*

The Victorian Arts Centre *100 St Kilda Rd, Melbourne; tel: (03) 9281-8000; www.vicartscentre.com.au.* Houses the **State Theatre**, decorated in the reds and golds of traditional grand theatre. In the same complex is the Playhouse, which is used for drama productions, mainly by the Melbourne Theatre Company, the **Melbourne Concert Hall** and the **Performing Arts Museum.**

The National Gallery of Victoria $$ *180 St Kilda Rd, Melbourne; tel: (03) 8620-2222; www.ngv.vi.gov.au. Open daily 1000–1700.* This location houses NGV International; there is a second gallery, NGV Australia, at Federation Square, cnr Flinders and Swanston Sts.

Immigration Museum $$ *400 Flinders St, Melbourne; tel: (03) 9927-2700. Open daily 1000–1700.*

Victorian Arts Centre**, home to the Australian Ballet, Opera Australia and the Melbourne Symphony Orchestra. The **National Gallery of Victoria***** houses the largest collection of art in the southern hemisphere, including many indigenous works and studies by the early Australian masters. Next to the arts precinct is Southgate, where restaurants and shops provide theatregoers with a place to go after the show.

Waves of migrants from different parts of the world have made Melbourne into the city it is today. The **Immigration Museum**** in the Old Customs House, Flinders Street, portrays fascinating stories of immigration to Victoria since the early 1800s. Thanks to its multi-cultural society, Melbourne offers a fantastic range of food, from the cheap Turkish and Lebanese eateries of Sydney Road to traditional Italian in Lygon St, the famous cakes and pastries of St Kilda to Little Bourke Street's Chinatown and Vietnamese in Victoria Street. Melbourne also has many lovely parks and gardens to take time out and recharge your batteries; stroll through the Treasury and Fitzroy Gardens on the eastern side of the city and be amazed at the city wildlife as possums scurry past your feet.

Many of Melbourne's buildings reflect the state's gold boom heritage – Parliament House, the old Treasury Building, the State Library with its domed reading room and the original Exhibition Building built for the great exhibition of 1880. The free City Circle tram can drop you off and pick you up near these attractions.

On the corner of Flinders and Swanston Streets is the strikingly modernist Federation Square. It occupies an entire city block, and offers a mix of attractions that the city believes embodies all that is great about Victoria: fine art, hospitality, bold design, innovation and vibrant events.

Above
Melbourne high-rises

A great way to see Melbourne is by the free City Circle Tram, refurbished and decked out in burgundy and gold. Trams travel around the city, along Flinders St, Spring St, Lonsdale and Spencer Sts, operating every 10 minutes daily, 1000–1800, touring the city in both directions, with 25 stops along the route.

They say you can buy anything at the **Queen Victoria Market**, *cnr Victoria and Elizabeth Sts, Melbourne; tel: (03) 9658-9601; open every day except Mon and Wed*, where more than 1000 traders offer everything from live poultry to leather handbags. Explore by yourself or take a guided tour.

Accommodation and food in Melbourne

Adelphi Hotel and restaurant $$ *187 Flinders Lane, Melbourne; tel: (03) 9650-7555; fax: (03) 9650-2710; email: info@adelphi.com.au.* With a much-photographed rooftop swimming pool that juts out over Flinders Lane, the Adelphi is a small, contemporary hotel in the heart of the city. The restaurant offers a superbly cooked, innovative menu.

Babka Bakery Café $ *358 Brunswick St, Fitzroy; tel: (03) 9416-0091.* The Russian heritage of the owners is evident from the menu – borscht and cabbage rolls. Patrons don't mind queuing for a table while enjoying the aroma of freshly baked bread. Nothing over $12. Great breakfasts.

Caffe e Cucina $$ *581 Chapel St, South Yarra; tel: (03) 9827-4139.* Authentic Italian atmosphere, good coffee and cakes and aloof waiters; breakfast, lunch and dinner. Mon–Sat.

The Como Hotel $$$ *630 Chapel St, South Yarra; tel: (03) 9825-2222 and 1800 033400.* Close to the shops and cafés of Chapel St, the Como provides all the facilities of a modern hotel.

Magnolia Court Boutique Hotel $$ *101 Powlett St, Melbourne; tel: (03) 9419-4222.* Ask for the old rooms in this quiet hotel, conveniently located a short walk from the city through the Fitzroy and Treasury Gardens.

Walter's Wine Bar $$ *Level 3, Southgate; tel: (03) 9690-9211.* A popular Southgate eatery where diners can enjoy a selection of modern Australian cuisine while sitting on the balcony overlooking the Yarra and sipping a glass of wine from the extensive list.

OTWAY NATIONAL PARK✢✢

Otway Eco-Guides offer an interesting range of walks; *tel: (03) 5237-7240; fax: (03) 5237-6622; email: sue@otwayeco-guides.com.au; www.otwayeco-guides.com.au*

Lush rainforest and beautiful scenery stretch inland and along the coast between Apollo Bay and Princetown. The Great Ocean Road, bordered by giant trees and graceful ferns, runs through the middle of the park. The Otways were formed 150 million years ago when the great southern landmass known as Gondwana began to break up. European settlers cleared much of the land but extensive forest remains. The **Mait's Rest** rainforest walk takes you on a short meandering trip through a beautiful and tranquil fern garden and past huge moss-covered trunks of old beech and myrtle trees, some of them thought to be more than 300 years old.

Right
Otway National Park

PORT FAIRY❖❖❖

ⓘ Visitor Information Centre 22 Bank St, Port Fairy; tel: (03) 5568-2682; fax: (03) 5568-2833.

✪ Port Fairy Folk Festival: first weekend in Mar; **Spring Music Festival:** Oct.

This seaside village is justifiably a favourite with everyone who visits. Walk along Port Fairy's historic wharf with its quaint harbourside dwellings and colourful fishing boats and you are transported to another country. Early in the morning local fishermen unload their harvests of crayfish, abalone and shark. The town used to be known as Belfast and the area's Irish heritage is still present in the names of local landmarks – the Moyne River, the Belfast Emporium, Dublin Inn, etc. Numerous old colonial buildings remain – stone cottages once occupied by whalers, sealers and fishermen, and bluestone warehouses and mills – many now converted into tourist accommodation. Port Fairy also has wide, sandy swimming and surf beaches and on **Griffiths Island**, tens of thousands of mutton birds (short-tailed shearwaters) land each year and nest from September to April. In March, Port Fairy bulges at the seams, for the hugely popular **Port Fairy Folk Festival**❖, Victoria's largest music festival.

TORQUAY❖❖

ⓘ Surfworld Australia $ Surf City Plaza, Beach Rd; tel: (03) 5261-4606; fax: (03) 5261-4756; www.surfworld.org.au

Australia's 'surf city' and home to some of the world's best-known surfing industry manufacturers, Torquay is a busy holiday town with a mixture of styles. The front beach, with its tall Norfolk pines dotting the shoreline, offers a quiet, protected foreshore while nearby fisherman's beach attracts a wide cross-section of beach-goers; further on waves come crashing in from Bass Strait on to the main surf beach. **Surfworld Australia**❖, a museum dedicated to surfing, is packed with memorabilia, including photographs of the sport's pioneers, and surfboards from the long, heavy models of yesteryear to the lightweight designs of today. Engaging interactive displays draw visitors of all ages. Not far away are the world-famous surfing temples of **Bells Beach** and **Jan Juc**.

WARRNAMBOOL❖❖

ⓘ Visitor Information Centre 600 Raglan Parade (Princes Hwy), Warrnambool; tel: 1800-637-725.

ⓘ Flagstaff Hill Maritime Museum $$ Merri St, Warrnambool; tel: (03) 5564-7841.

Tourists driving through Warrnambool should turn off the Princes Highway or they will miss the beauty of this gracious town with its long beaches and historic buildings. Warrnambool is also the nursery for the rare southern right whale and every year these magnificent creatures – up to 15m long – journey from the Southern Ocean to calve in the shallow waters of **Logans Beach**. They often swim within 100m of the shore and can be viewed from a platform in the sand dunes. Whale-watching season runs from May to September.

The **Flagstaff Hill Maritime Museum**❖ recreates the sights and

Spirit of the Sea
(Music Festival): Jan;
**Wunta Wine and Food
Fiesta**: Feb.

sounds of a 19th-century port, complete with original lighthouses and replicas of buildings of the time, including sailmaker's loft, bank, town hall and chapel.

WERRIBEE PARK❖

Werribee Park $$
*K Rd Werribee; tel:
(03) 9741-2444. Mansion
open from 1000 every day
except Christmas Day.*

**Werribee Park Open
Range Zoo $$** *tel: (03)
9731-9600; www.zoo.org.au.
Open every day 0900–1700,
safari tours depart from
1030.*

The 60-roomed Italianate mansion at Werribee Park was built in the 1870s by the enormously wealthy Scottish brothers, Thomas and Andrew Chirnside, who established a massive pastoral empire in Australia. The ornate sandstone house, furnished with magnificent period pieces, gives visitors an impression of what life was like for rich Victorian graziers in the boom years of the 1870s and 1880s. There remains a working farm with animals and herb gardens to see, while polo matches are still played in November and February on its polo lawns. The large formal gardens include the Victoria State Rose Garden with 4000 rose bushes blooming from November to May. Next to the mansion is **Werribee Zoo**❖, an open range zoo teeming with cheetahs, hippopotamuses, lions and other inhabitants of the African savannah, as well as Australian natives. The animals roam free while visitors stay in tourist vehicles.

Accommodation and food

Beacon Point Lodges $$ *Skenes Creek Rd, Apollo Bay; tel: (03) 5237-6218; fax: (03) 5237-6196.* Stunning views across the ocean from these moderately priced, self-contained units.

Cape Otway Lightstation $$ *Via Great Ocean Rd, Cape Otway; tel: (03) 5237-9240; fax: (03) 5327-9245; email: keeper@lightstation.com.* Self-contained lightkeepers' cottages and studio accommodation in mainland Australia's oldest lighthouse (1848).

Chris's Beacon Point Restaurant and Villas $$$ *Skenes Creek Rd, Apollo Bay; tel: (03) 5237-6411; fax: (03) 5237-6930.* Glorious views, and fine self-contained accommodation or eat at Chris's excellent restaurant.

Merrijig Inn $$ *1 Campbell St, Port Fairy; tel: (03) 5568-2324; fax: (03) 5568-2723; email: merrijig@standard.net.au.* Sensational breakfasts are a feature of this historic inn, which also has a fully licensed restaurant. Tall people should ask for a downstairs room.

Quamby Homestead $$ *Caramut Rd, Woolsthorpe; tel: (03) 5569-2395.* Picturesque accommodation and restaurant in a historic homestead setting between Warrnambool and Port Fairy.

Queenscliff Hotel $$$ *42 Gellibrand St, Queenscliff; tel: (03) 5258-1011; fax: (03) 5258-3712.* Faithfully restored old hotel with fine cuisine in

Cape Otway Lightstation $$ *tel: (03) 5237-9240; fax: (03) 5237-9245; email: keeper@lightstation.com; www.lightstation.com. Guided tours 0900–1700 daily.*
The winding road down to the Cape Otway lighthouse meanders through stunted eucalyptus and tea tree, interspersed with cleared areas where dairy cows graze on bright green pastures. The lighthouse stopped working in 1994 when it was replaced by a small solar-powered signal, but you can still climb it to look out over the 90-m-high cliffs. The oldest lighthouse on mainland Australia, it was built in 1848 and is now operated as a tourist venture, even offering accommodation options (*see page 119*).

the grand dining room and excellent fish and chips (and other meals) in the cheaper Boat Bar restaurant.

Skye Beachfront Retreat $$ *72 Griffiths St, Port Fairy; tel: (03) 5568-1181; fax: (03) 9482-9409; email: holiday@skye-retreat.com.au; www.skye-retreat.com.au.* Charming self-contained beachfront apartments.

Suggested tour

Total distance: 776km.

Time: This makes an excellent three- to five-day tour.

Links: At Ballarat, the drive links up with the Central Goldfields tour (*see page 122*). If you take the diversion to Queenscliff, you can travel by car ferry to Sorrento and link up with the Mornington Peninsula day trip from Melbourne (*see page 115*).

Route: From Melbourne take the Princes Freeway west over the Westgate Bridge and after 30km take the second exit to **WERRIBEE PARK ❶**. You will rejoin the freeway further on and continue past the You Yangs range which rises above the flat plain to the west, and the turn-off to **Serendip Sanctuary**, which recreates the natural habitat of the western plains. Victoria's second largest city **GEELONG ❷** is 75km from Melbourne.

Detour: Only 20 minutes from Geelong, the historic town of **Queenscliff** was a popular seaside retreat in the late 19th and early 20th centuries. The town has retained its Victorian architecture, graceful old hotels and guesthouses, and is a popular place for gourmet and romantic weekend getaways.

From Geelong follow the signs to **TORQUAY ❸** 23km away and continue along the **GREAT OCEAN ROAD**. After another 69km of winding road and spectacular views you reach the coastal resort of **LORNE ❹**. Follow the coast for 45km to **APOLLO BAY ❺** and another 22km to the turn-off to **CAPE OTWAY ❻**. It is a 14-km drive from here down to the **lighthouse**.

Return to the Great Ocean Rd which veers inland to **PORT CAMPBELL NATIONAL PARK** and then back to the **TWELVE APOSTLES ❼**, 83km away. Continue along the Shipwreck Coast for 66km to **WARRNAMBOOL ❽**, and another 29km to **PORT FAIRY ❾**.

Detour: Heading north from Port Fairy towards Hamilton, don't miss a visit to **Mt Eccles National Park**, close to **Macarthur** which is about 48km from the Princes Hwy just west of Port Fairy. This beautiful bushland northeast of Portland once ran red-hot with molten lava. Today, Mt Eccles' three main craters hold the spring-fed waters of Lake

Surprise in a much cooler environment with a lush green heathland and forest of manna gums. This is a perfect park to see koalas in the wild. The park also has a number of interesting geological formations to explore including craters and stony rises, while the lava cave is a cool retreat on a hot day.

Back on the main route, head north to **Dunkeld** ❿, the southern gateway to the **GRAMPIANS**, travelling through typical Western District wool-growing country for 74km. Continue to the magnificent **Halls Gap** ⓫ area which has many walks to explore including Silverband Falls (30 minutes return) and Splitters Falls (45 minutes return). A short distance along the Halls Gap Tourist Rd, walking tracks lead to the summits of Mt Sturgeon and Mt Abrupt, both of which have great views. Return to Melbourne via the Western Highway, a distance of 258km.

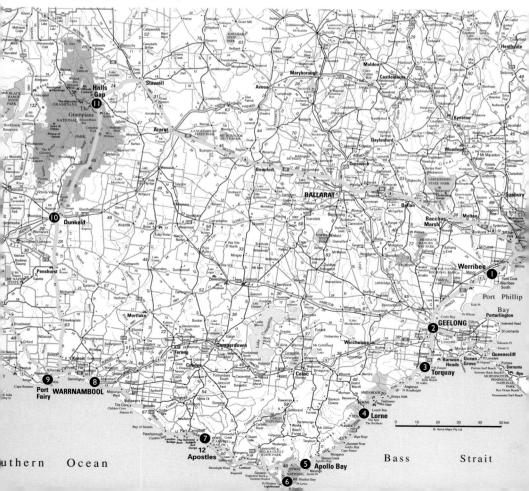

Victoria's Gold Fields and Spa Country

Ratings

Architecture	●●●●●
History	●●●●●
Art	●●●●○
Children	●●●○○
Food and wine	●●●○○
Gardens	●●●○○
Outdoor activities	●●●○○
Scenery	●●●○○

Victoria is a small state that is easy to explore by car, with natural, historic and cultural treasures tucked around every corner. Gold was discovered here in 1851, and by 1853 the Bendigo gold rush had attracted 20,000 diggers, making it Australia's largest gold field. The magnificent and authentically re-created Sovereign Hill, in the town of Ballarat, transports visitors back to the days of the gold diggings, complete with an old town, shops, stagecoaches and panning for gold. Bendigo and Ballarat are now busy towns still graced by grand 19th-century buildings.

This part of central Victoria also takes in tall eucalyptus forests, beautifully tended gardens, aromatherapeutic mineral spas and rolling hills with sheep farms and orchards. And there are some charming smaller towns too, such as Maldon, Kyneton, Castlemaine and Daylesford as well as antique shops, art galleries, excellent restaurants and B&Bs.

BALLARAT✦✦✦

ⓘ Ballarat Visitor Information Centre *39 Sturt St; tel: 1800-648-450.*

ⓝ Ballarat Fine Art Gallery $ 40 *Lydiard St North. Open daily 1030–1700.*

Montrose Cottage and Eureka Museum $ *111 Eureka St, Ballarat; tel/fax: (03) 5332-2554.*

The historic town of Ballarat has wide tree-lined streets, beautiful gardens and grand architecture. The heritage of its gold fields is evident in the ornate decoration and imposing design of many of the buildings including **Her Majesty's Theatre** – Australia's oldest purpose-built, continually operating theatre – and the **Ballarat Fine Art Gallery✦**. The gallery contains the original Eureka flag, which was flown over the nation-forming **Eureka Stockade** rebellion against the British colonial authorities (*see page 127*). The largest inland city in Victoria, its name is derived from two Aboriginal words 'Balla' and 'Arat' meaning literally 'resting on one's elbow'. The Aborigines used the rich countryside of the district as a resting place. The area was originally settled by pastoralists but with the discovery of gold in 1851 people from all walks of life came to seek their fortunes.

Eureka Street✦, the original road leading into Ballarat from

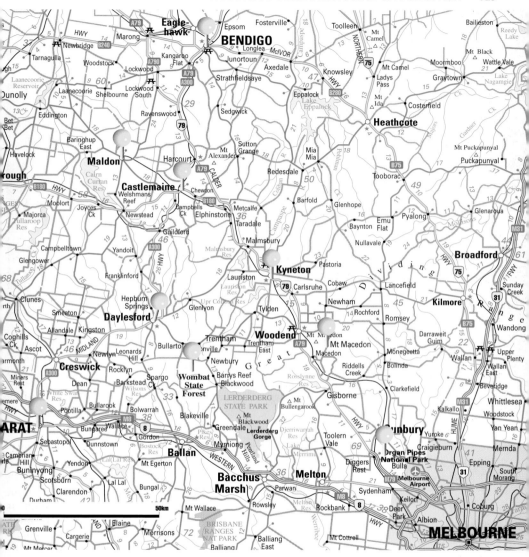

(see page 129)

Smythesdale gold fields *southwest of Ballarat on the Glenelg Highway. Visit the gold fields at any time. An old gold-mining town, with a courthouse dating back to gold-rush days.*

Melbourne, is filled with old miners' dwellings, such as **Montrose Cottage**◊, the first bluestone dwelling to be built on the gold fields, now open to the public. In the forests and bushland of the **Smythesdale gold fields**◊, 17km south of Ballarat, you can tour the old diggings which have names like Jubilee Mine, Misery Creek, Devil's Kitchen and Hard Hill. Ballarat's most famous tourist attraction is the excellent **Sovereign Hill**, an award-winning re-creation of the working gold fields of the 1850s (*see page 129*).

Craig's Royal Hotel
$$ *10 Lydiard St South,*
Ballarat; tel: 1800-648-041;
fax: (03) 5331-7103.
Historic grand hotel in the
centre of Ballarat.

Bodlyn B&B $$ *9 Errard*
Street North, Ballarat; tel:
(03) 5332-1318; fax: (03)
5332-2899; email:
kittelty@netconnect.com.au;
www.ballarat.com/bodlyn.htm.
Edwardian charm within
walking distance of lake and
city centre.

Hermiston Retreat $$
109 Chisholm Street,
Ballarat; tel/fax: (03) 5332-
6880. B&B or fully self-
contained accommodation.

Right
Ballarat stagecoach

BENDIGO✦✦✦

**Bendigo Visitor
Information** *51–67
Pall Mall; tel: 1800-813153
or (03) 5444-4445; fax: (03)
5444-4447;
www.bendigotourism.com.
Open daily 0900–1700.*

**City Circle
Heritage Tour $$**
*tel: 0500-544-169; fax:
0500-844-169.* Tour
departs from Central
Deborah Gold Mine hourly
from 1000 weekends,
school and public holidays;
1000 and 1400 normal
weekdays.

A thriving regional centre with a population of 85,000, Bendigo is
large enough to offer some excellent visitor facilities yet small enough
to explore at your leisure, perhaps on one of the city's unique vintage
tram tours. Laid out in 1854 with broad and regular boulevards, the
city of Bendigo has opulent gold-boom architecture and **Pall Mall**,
with its decorative Alexander Fountain, is one of the most beautiful
Victorian-era streetscapes in Australia. But the bush of **One Tree Hill**
or the **Whipstick Forest** are only minutes from the city centre. The
74-km Bendigo bushland trail provides cycling and walking tracks
which link the city to its surrounding forests. The trail may be walked
or cycled in small sections.

Bendigo has many fine antique shops and galleries. The recently
redeveloped **Bendigo Art Gallery**✦ – one of the oldest and finest
regional galleries in Australia – houses outstanding permanent
collections of 19th-century European art, and Australian art from the
19th century to the present. Visitors can experience the city's gold-
mining past at the **Central Deborah Gold Mine**✦ which stopped

Bendigo Art Gallery $ *32 View St; tel: (03) 5444-0007. Open Wed to Sun 1000–1700.*

Central Deborah Gold Mine $$ *76 Violet St; tel: (03) 5443-8322. Tours daily from 0930.*

Golden Dragon Museum $$ *5–11 Bridge St; tel: (03) 5441-5044. Open 0930–1700.*

operating in 1951; a one-hour guided tour of the mine descends 61m below ground. Central Deborah is also the starting point for a tour on one of Bendigo's vintage 'talking' trams, the **City Circle Heritage Tour**. A recorded commentary covers the town's mining and cultural history. Stay aboard, or get off and reboard at any of the designated stops which include the Chinese Museum, Bendigo Pottery, Discovery Centre and the Railway Station. At the **Golden Dragon Museum** and Classical Chinese Gardens you can experience a living history of the Chinese people of Bendigo from the Gold Rush of the 1850s to the present day. On permanent display is 'Sun Loong' the longest imperial dragon in the world.

Accommodation and food in Bendigo

Bazzani $$–$$$ *Howard Place; tel: (03) 5441-3777; fax: (03) 5443-9995.* Open daily. Bar, café and restaurant; a popular and stylish eatery.

Goldmines Wine Bar, Café, Restaurant $$ *49 Marong Rd, Bendigo; tel: (03) 5443-6175.* Fine dining restaurant and café, with wine bar featuring wine and local produce from the Bendigo region.

JoJoes $$ *4 High St; tel: (03) 5441-4471. Open every night from 1700 till late.* From pizza and pasta to more upmarket meals, dine in and takeaway.

Marlborough House B&B $$ *115 Wattle St; tel/fax: (03) 5441-4142.* Elegant guesthouse, a short stroll from the city centre.

Shamrock Hotel $$ *Cnr Pall Mall and Williamson Streets; tel: (03) 5443-0333; fax: (03) 5442-4494.* Superb gold-rush architecture.

CASTLEMAINE

Castlemaine Market Visitor Information Centre *Mostyn St; tel: 1800-171-888; fax: (03) 5471-1746.*

Buda Historic Home and Garden $$ *Hunter St. Open daily 0900–1700.*

Castlemaine/ Maldon Accommodation Booking Service *tel: 1800-171-888; fax: (03) 5471-1746.*

The pretty town of Castlemaine, with its hilly streets and splendid old sandstone buildings, is a hub of art and folk music. At its last biennial **Festival of the Arts**, 47 art galleries sprang up almost overnight, many of them artists' own studios open for the occasion. The festival takes place over 10 days in April–May (next one in 2007).

During the gold rush, Castlemaine became the marketplace for all the gold fields of central Victoria. Unlike many of the other small towns nearby, it has survived as a regional centre. You can see reminders of the gold fields in the huge mullock heaps which mark the sites of deep reef mines. One of its highlights is the **Buda Historic Home and Garden**, with a pavilion set among flowering bulbs and an aviary, both charming examples of garden architecture from the 19th century. The best time to visit is in spring, or to coincide with Castlemaine's annual **Festival of Gardens** in October–November (*PO Box 758, Castlemaine, Vic 3450; tel: (03) 5472-2086*).

Accommodation and food in Castlemaine

Togs Place Café and Gallery $ *58 Lyttleton St; tel: (03) 5470-5090. Open Sun–Fri 1000–1700, Sat 0900.* Trendy salads, freshly baked pies and home-made cakes; dine in the gallery or the leafy back courtyard.

The Yellow House B&B $$ *95 Lyttleton St; tel: (03) 5472-3368.*

Orana $$ *2 Stewart St; tel: (03) 5470-5589.* Fully self-contained cottage.

DAYLESFORD AND HEPBURN SPRINGS***

ⓘ **Visitor Information Centre** *49 Vincent St, Daylesford; tel: (03) 5348-1339.*

Ⓟ **Hepburn Spa Resort $$** *Mineral Springs Reserve, Hepburn Springs; tel: (03) 5348-2034; fax: (03) 5348-1167; www.hepburnspa.com.au. Open weekdays 1000–2000; weekends 0900–2000.*

◓ **Pantechnicon Gallery** *34 Vincent St, Daylesford.* Local art at reasonable prices.

Don Wreford Glass Studio *39 Albert St, Daylesford; open daily.* Watch one of Australia's leading glass artists at work.

◓ **Swiss Italian Festa** *tel: (03) 5348-3512. Last weekend in May.* A weekend of food, music, wine, art and film.

The large number of mineral springs flowing around Daylesford and Hepburn Springs give this area its reputation as the heart of Victoria's spa country. These charming towns, set among the lakes and forests of the central highlands are very popular with tourists. The Aborigines knew the healing properties of the mineral springs, and early this century European settlers came to take the waters to treat disorders such as rheumatism and gout. The springs (they are not naturally hot) went out of fashion during the 1960s and 1970s, but in the last 20 years they have enjoyed a massive revival. The **Hepburn Spa Resort** is Australia's only mineral water bath facility. It contains a large relaxation pool, as well as private mineral baths where you can soak with your choice of aromatherapy oils. Mineral water, gushing out of old pumps and mountain springs, can also be gathered (free). Other attractions include boating on Lake Daylesford, a visit to the **Wombat Hill Botanic Gardens**, the monthly Saturday markets, a Sunday afternoon train ride through the Wombat State Forest, and the town's numerous bookshops, galleries and cafés. There are literally hundreds of places to stay in Daylesford and Hepburn Springs and if you can visit mid-week some very good packages are available. The accommodation is divided into four main types: restored homes, miners' cottages, bed and breakfast and hotel/motel.

Accommodation and food in Daylesford and Hepburn Springs

The Boathouse Café $$ *Lake Daylesford.* Breakfast at weekends, lunch and dinner daily; good coffee and great views; the nearby playground makes it ideal for people with young children.

Cosy Corner Café $$ *3 Tenth Avenue, Hepburn Springs.* Homely café that has become very popular. Serves brasserie-style food Thursday– Monday for lunch and dinner; breakfast/brunch from 0930 at weekends.

Dorothy's Apartments $$ *114–18 Main Rd, Hepburn Springs; tel: (03) 5348-1448.* Pleasant self-contained accommodation.

◐ Daylesford Accommodation Booking Service 27 Vincent St, Daylesford; tel: (03) 5348-1448; fax: (03) 5348-4149.

The Spa Country Holiday Shop 86 Vincent St, Daylesford; tel: (03) 5348-1255; fax: (03) 5348-3606; email: daylecot@netconnect.com.au

Dudley House $$ *101 Main Rd, Hepburn Springs; tel/fax: (03) 5348-3033; email: dudley@netconnect.com.au; www.netconnect.com.au/~dudley.* Bed and breakfast in an Edwardian guesthouse.

The Food Gallery $$ *77 Vincent St, Daylesford; tel: (03) 5348-1677.* A coffee shop and deli and a smart place for breakfast.

Lake House $$$ *King St, Daylesford; tel: (03) 5348-3329.* Fine dining, beautiful views and luxurious accommodation in award-winning surroundings by the lake.

Two Rooms $$ *27 Albert St, Daylesford; tel: (03) 5348-2752.* Café, restaurant and takeaway.

EUREKA STOCKADE✦✦

🏛 Eureka Stockade Centre Eureka St, Ballarat; tel: 1800-648-450 for more information and a free information kit.

Gold was the cause of the only armed conflict on Australian soil in the country's history. The Eureka Stockade was a miners' uprising in December 1854 against police and colonial authorities. The outcome of the short but fierce battle, in which more than 30 miners and 5 troopers died, was the freedom to mine without harassment, the lowering of licensing fees, and the right of Australian miners to live as law-abiding citizens with a representative parliament. The Eureka flag – bearing Australia's distinctive Southern Cross star constellation instead of the colonial English flag – was flown for the first time at the wooden stockade where the miners and their leader Peter Lalor fought that nation-building night. The site of the stockade now houses the **Eureka Stockade Centre✦** where state-of-the-art multimedia and interactive displays bring this vibrant and torrid piece of history to life. The original, if somewhat moth-eaten and tattered, Eureka flag is on display at the Ballarat Fine Art Gallery (*see page 122*).

Below
Melbourne school uniforms evoke Peter Weir's atmospheric film

HANGING ROCK✦✦

This remarkable volcanic rock formation rising abruptly as a solitary peak amid surrounding farmland near **Woodend** is steeped in Aboriginal legend. Over the years it has provided a refuge for bush rangers and a venue for picnic races and other sports events. The rock provided the inspiration for Joan Lindsay's book *Picnic at Hanging Rock* and Peter Weir's 1975 film of the same name. At that mysterious picnic one shimmering hot summer's day, three schoolgirls dressed in white disappeared in the rock without

○ **Hanging Rock Picnic Races** New Year's Day and Australia Day (26 Jan). **Harvest Picnic Festival** last weekend in Feb.

trace, one of them to reappear, equally mysteriously, three days later. Hanging Rock and the land around it have been a park reserve since 1886, and kangaroos and wallabies are plentiful. Visitors can walk to the top on several different paths which give something of a feel for the mystery of the Rock. Tea rooms, picnic shelters and barbecue facilities are all available at the bottom.

KYNETON❖❖

❶ **Kyneton Visitor Information Centre** East End Playground, High St; tel: (03) 5422-3532.

○ Sept: **Kyneton Daffodil and Arts Festival**; Mar: **Kyneton Country Music Festival**.

The tea rooms, restaurants, mills and antique shops of Piper Street are part of an authentic period streetscape. The Kyneton district was settled in the two decades before the gold rush when squatters took up large tracts of land around Carlsruhe, Barfold, Mt Macedon and Malmsbury. Many bluestone buildings of this era remain in and around the town today. The opening of the Melbourne to Bendigo railway in 1862 ensured Kyneton's rapid commercial expansion.

Surrounded by wineries, Kyneton is a popular spot for day-trippers from Melbourne who enjoy browsing around the many antique shops. The bakery provides good food and coffee. The 3^1/₂-km **Kyneton Heritage Walk** covers civic offices, banks, churches, shops and private homes dating back to the 1850s. Famed for their daffodils, the **Kyneton Botanic Gardens** (and those at Malmsbury) were inspired by colonial botanist and creator of the Royal Botanic Gardens in Melbourne, Baron Ferdinand von Müeller.

MALDON❖❖

❶ **Maldon Information Centre** High St; tel: (03) 5475-2569; fax: (03) 5475-2007; www.maldon.org.au

❶ **Victorian Gold Fields Railway $$** Hornsby St; tel: (03) 5470-6658; fax: (03) 5470-6272. Open Sun, public holidays and Boxing Day–mid-Jan 1130, 1300 and 1430; Wed 1100 and 1300.

Maldon is largely unchanged since its days as a 19th-century gold-mining town. The well-preserved banks, shops and hotels still bear their original signs. The Victorian streets are lined with fine houses, pretty cottages and shops full of antiques, bric-à-brac, local arts and crafts, and home-made food. In 1966, the National Trust classified Maldon as Australia's first 'Notable Town', citing its 'most unique and well-preserved variety of historic architecture'. Other attractions are old mining sites, a lookout tower and a **steam railway**❖. Maldon stages a fair at Easter and a Folk Music Festival in October (tel: (03) 5475-2166).

Accommodation and food in Maldon

Gowar Homestead B&B $$ Castlemaine Rd; tel: (03) 5475-1090; fax: (03) 5475-1600; email: gowar@jaycom.net.au; www.jaycom. net.au/gowar. Just outside the township of Maldon, historic homestead in quiet setting.

Heritage Cottages of Maldon $$ 26 Adair St; tel/fax: (03) 5475-1094. A range of accommodation, from miners' cottages to Victorian homes.

MT MACEDON❖❖

ⓘ Mt Macedon Information Centre *Nursery Rd; tel: (03) 5426-1866.*

Mt Macedon is well known for its grand homes and magnificent gardens as well as its native forests and historic monuments. Its hill-station environment has provided a retreat from Melbourne for more than a century. Bush fires, especially the Ash Wednesday fires in 1983, destroyed many buildings and devastated the forest. There are a number of scenic drives including the roads to the summit and to **Hanging Rock** (*see page 127*). Autumn and spring are good times to visit as many of the Mt Macedon mansions open their gardens – famous for their rhododendrons and spring-flowering bulbs. Other private gardens are open to the public at weekends. The peak of Mt Macedon is the ideal vantage point to view the region. Around the mountain, 20km of walking track winds through pretty bush, teeming with wildlife.

ORGAN PIPES NATIONAL PARK❖❖

ⓝ Organ Pipes National Park *Calder Hwy, Diggers Rest; tel: (03) 9390-1082.*

Just 20km northwest of Melbourne on the Calder Highway, the Organ Pipes National Park provides some beautiful picnic spots and walking tracks. The strange 20-m high basalt columns known as the Organ Pipes were formed possibly two to three million years ago from deep lava flows filling creek valleys. These then cracked into hexagonal blocks as they cooled and shrank. The cracks gradually extended downwards and formed the long columns which you can see today. The park contains other interesting volcanic features and over the years has been revegetated with plants indigenous to the area. It is well worth a visit and a short walk or picnic.

SOVEREIGN HILL❖❖❖

ⓝ Sovereign Hill $$ *Bradshaw Street, Ballarat; tel: (03) 5331-1944. Open daily 1000–1700.*

Built on the site of the old Ballarat gold diggings, the award-winning Sovereign Hill authentically re-creates the bustling, hectic, rough and dirty life of the gold-rush days. The hills are covered with tents, real miners (actors) pan for gold in the creeks, and the place hums with life as people perform their chores while dressed in costumes of the time. There are sweet shops, a funeral parlour, a Chinese Joss House, an open school and even a brothel! An excellent evening sound and light show, 'Blood on the Southern Cross', tells the story of the Eureka rebellion. Visitors to Sovereign Hill can pan for gold, ride in a Cobb and Co coach, dress in period costume, and tour the underground mine. The creeks are regularly seeded with gold dust, so real gold can be found – and kept. Australia's first gold museum contains a collection of alluvial gold, nuggets and gold coins. Sovereign Hill is fun, educational and out of the ordinary.

WOMBAT STATE FOREST❖❖

The Wombat State Forest lies between Ballan, Bacchus Marsh, Trentham and Woodend and past Daylesford as far as Mt Franklin. Fern gullies, streams and waterfalls are found among rolling hills, with a profusion of wildflowers in spring. The 65-km Wombat Forest drive, a tourist drive linking the forest with the **Lerderderg State Park**, starts at Daylesford and takes in the scenic sights of the forest. Don't miss a walk to the spectacular **Trentham Falls**, particularly in spring or after heavy rain.

Suggested tour

Garden of St Erth
$$ *Blackwood; tel: (03) 5368-6514. Open daily 1000–1600, closed June, July and Dec.*

Total distance: The main route is about 385km. The detour through Blackwood and the Wombat State Forest adds another 65km.

Time: It will take about one day to explore the main route, not counting stops.

Links: From Ballarat, continue along the Western Highway to Stawell and the Grampians touring route, or from Bendigo, take the McIvor Highway through typical dry eucalyptus forest of the region to Heathcote, where several small wineries are gaining a reputation for their Shiraz. Turn off at Tooborac towards Seymour and the Hume Highway to the Northeast Victoria route (*see page 142*).

Route: From Melbourne, travel along the Western Highway to **BALLARAT ❶**. Once you are past the outskirts of Melbourne, the road bypasses towns along the way, such as the old apple growing area of Bacchus Marsh.

Detour: On the way to Ballarat, turn off the Western Highway just before Ballan and follow the signs to **BLACKWOOD ❷**. Visit the famous **Garden of St Erth**❖, where more than 3000 plant varieties are growing, many of them rare in cultivation. From the car park at the Garden of St Erth the scenic **Lerderderg Heritage River Walk** follows old water races and the Lerderderg River on a 9-km circuit which takes about 3 hours to complete. From here, follow the scenic **WOMBAT FOREST ❸** drive through the pretty little town of Trentham to Daylesford. Alternatively, from Trentham you can join the Calder Highway at Woodend.

From Ballarat, continue on the Midland Highway, through the old gold-mining town of Creswick to popular **DAYLESFORD ❹** and **HEPBURN SPRINGS ❺**, centre of the spa country.

At Daylesford, the **Tipperary Walking Track** follows the course of the many miners' tracks and water races linking Lake Daylesford and

Hepburn Springs. It is a 16-km, 4 or 5-hour walk following Sailor's and Spring Creeks via Tipperary Springs, the Blowhole, Breakneck Gorge and Jackson's Lookout, or it can be done in short sections.

After exploring the delights of Daylesford, continue north through Guildford, another old gold-mining town, to **CASTLEMAINE** ❻. From here it is only a short trip to **MALDON** ❼; link up to the Calder Highway at Ravenswood and continue on to **BENDIGO** ❽. Return to Melbourne via the Calder Highway, with possible stops at **KYNETON** ❾, **HANGING ROCK** ❿, **MACEDON** ⓫, and **ORGAN PIPES NATIONAL PARK** ⓬ on the way.

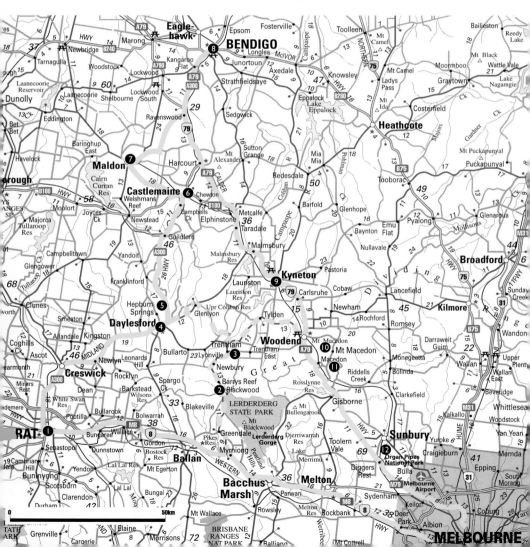

Phillip Island, Gippsland and Wilsons Promontory

Ratings

Beaches	●●●●●
Nature	●●●●●
Scenery	●●●●●
Outdoor activities	●●●●○
Walking	●●●●○
Wildlife	●●●●○
Fishing	●●●○○
Food	●●●○○

No visit to Melbourne is complete without a drive southeast to explore Phillip Island with its fairy penguins and fur seals and Victoria's beautiful, pristine and much-loved Wilsons Promontory National Park. But there is also much more to see in this lush South Gippsland region of Victoria: wide sandy beaches, rocky headlands and tidal platforms around Inverloch and Cape Patterson, the rugged beauty of the Strzelecki Ranges and the cool climate rainforest of Tarra Bulga National Park. This is an area of great natural beauty, with rolling hills, forested mountains and a rugged coastline. The fertile valleys are the centre of Victoria's dairy industry and the area is famed for its fine natural produce and the so-called Gourmet Deli Trail. The drive along the Grand Ridge Road that follows the spine of the Strzelecki Ranges gives magnificent views across the coast and surrounding farmland.

BUNURONG MARINE AND COASTAL PARK✦✦

ⓘ Bunurong Environment Centre *Inverloch; tel: (03) 5674-3738. Open 1000–1600 Thur–Sun, school holidays and public holidays.*

The wild coast between Harmers Haven and Inverloch is part of the Bunurong Marine and Coastal Park, a 17-km narrow coastal strip which extends one kilometre out to sea. Its name comes from the Bunurong people, the Aboriginal tribe who occupied much of the land around the Mornington Peninsula, Port Phillip and Westernport Bay, living off its plentiful fish, shellfish and wallaby populations, before being virtually wiped out with the arrival of white settlers in the early to mid-1800s.

Many of the attractions of Bunurong Marine Park are hidden beneath the sea and it is a popular spot for snorkellers and scuba divers. The rocky platforms, rugged sandstone cliffs and sweeping ocean views create the impression of remoteness despite being within easy travelling distance of the popular holiday town of Inverloch (*see page 135*). During early winter you may glimpse southern right whales travelling through the marine park.

GOURMET DELI TRAIL✦✦✦

Set amid rolling green hills and lush valleys, the well-signed Gourmet Deli driving trail highlights the food and wine treasures of west Gippsland, visiting farms, vineyards, bakeries, galleries and several scenic outlooks along its route. The region's rich soil and consistent rainfall has long been known for producing potatoes, onions,

**Gippsland Food
and Wine Tea
Rooms** *Princes Highway,
Yarragon. Open daily
0730–1730.* Features a
wide range of Gippsland
cheese, condiments and
local wine.

Jindivick Smokehouse
*5838 Jackson's Track,
Jindivick. Open daily,
0900–1700.*

**Tarago River Cheese
Company** *2236 Main
Neerim Road, Neerim South.
Open daily 1000–1700.*

Right
Gippsland

asparagus and dairy products. But many more gourmet delights are
now available through farm-gate outlets and specialist shops. Venison,
smoked meats, fish and berry producers have all opened their gates to
visitors. Highlights of the Gourmet Deli Trail are the **Jindivick
Smokehouse***, where meats and fish are gently cooked over the smoke
from aromatic fruit trees, and the **Jindivick Gardens** and Gourmet
Deli Tearooms where visitors can enjoy panoramic views over Mt
Worth and Westernport Bay. **Neerim South*** is the home of a young
winery and the renowned Gippsland Blue cheeses.

GRAND RIDGE ROAD✦✦✦

The spectacular 150-km Grand Ridge Road winds its way along the
spine of the Strzelecki Ranges from Traralgon to Warragul, past the
mountain ash forests and steep fern gullies of Tarra Bulga National
Park. It is a well-maintained gravel road and it takes about 5 hours
from one end to the other. There are fantastic lookouts over Wilsons
Promontory and South Gippsland along the way. Mt Tassie, the
highest point in the Strzeleckis, provides wonderful views of the entire
La Trobe Valley and beyond. This is a drive to be enjoyed and lingered
over, with frequent stops for picnics and to admire the view.

INVERLOCH❖❖

The pretty seaside village of Inverloch, perched on the end of Anderson Inlet 2 hours southeast of Melbourne, offers a range of beaches to suit the whole family. The Inlet has squeaky clean, calm beaches for safe children's paddling and gentle swimming, and is ideal for windsurfing and dinghy sailing. The Poles is the safest, most popular beach, with lovely views out towards the rougher sea; but for keen surfers, Inverloch Surf Beach offers good rolling waves and is patrolled in summer. It is a lovely drive or coastal walk along the clifftops from Inverloch to Cape Paterson.

The rugged rock shelves, rock pools and caves makes this protected strip of **Bunurong Marine Park** (*see page 132*) popular with children, reef ramblers, snorkellers and scuba divers when the seas are calm enough and the tide low. The Caves, Shack Bay and Eagles' Nest are highlights, while excellent surf breaks for good surfers are dotted along this coast and at Cape Patterson. East of Inverloch, around the rugged tip of Cape Liptrap, are the white sand beaches of Waratah Bay. Try surfing at **Sandy Point** or snorkelling among the plentiful fish and rock shelves at **Walkerville**.

NOORAMUNGA AND CORNER INLET MARINE AND COASTAL PARKS❖❖

The extensive tidal mudflat, island, shallows and channels between Port Welshpool, the northeastern tip of Wilsons Promontory and the beginning of the **Ninety Mile Beach** are covered by the Nooramunga and Corner Inlet Marine and Coastal Parks. These marine parks protect the most southerly mangroves in the world, and are recognised internationally as important feeding and breeding grounds for many species of migratory wading birds and sea birds. Snake Island is the largest island within the park, and the annual muster of cattle from this island across the tidal flats to the mainland each March or April is a sight to behold.

PHILLIP ISLAND❖❖❖

ℹ **Surefoot Explorations**
tel: (03) 5952-1533.
Walking tours with local guides.

Only a short drive from Melbourne, Phillip Island is best known for its **Penguin Parade**, an extraordinary natural spectacle and Victoria's most popular tourist attraction. Every evening at sunset, hundreds of Little Penguins come ashore at Summerland Beach and waddle across the sand to their burrows in the spinifex tussocks, just as their ancestors have been doing for thousands of generations. Seemingly oblivious to visitors watching from raised boardwalks, the penguins

Phillip Island Visitor Information Centre *Penguin Reserve, The Nobbies; tel: (03) 9793-6767; fax: (03) 9793-6868; email: info@sealrocksvic. com.au; www.phillipisland.com. Newhaven; tel: (03) 5956-7447.*

Penguin Parade Visitors' Centre $$ *tel: (03) 5956-8300; fax: (03) 5956-8394; email: penguins@penguins.org.au; www.penguins.org.au*

Sea Life Centre $$$ *Open 1000 to dusk.*

Koala Conservation Centre $ *tel: (03) 5956-8300.*

Right
A local from the Koala Conservation Centre

spend time around their burrows in the dunes preening themselves and, in summer, feeding their hungry chicks.

But there is much more to Phillip Island than its famous penguins. Linked by bridge to the mainland at San Remo, it is a popular holiday spot for Melburnians with fabulous beaches for surfing, swimming and fishing as well as excellent walking and unusual wildlife. Australia's largest colony of 7000 fur seals can be seen sunning themselves at Seal Rocks or playing in the surf off the westernmost tip of the island. They are best viewed from the new **Sea Life Centre**✷ perched next to the rugged cliffs of The Nobbies, or by taking a boat trip. Each year about half a million short-tail shearwaters (often known as mutton birds) fly from the northern hemisphere to land at Cape Woolamai, the highest point of the island. Here they breed in their cliff-top rookeries before making the long return journey.

The best place to see Philip Island's large koala colony is at the **Koala Conservation Centre**✷. Pelicans are often seen at San Remo, waiting for any scraps the fishermen may leave. **Cowes**, the island's main town, is a peaceful place to swim safely in calm waters, relax and dine on the excellent local seafood.

PORT ALBERT❖

The fishing town of Port Albert is Gippsland's oldest village and one of Victoria's earliest settlements. It was the arrival point for thousands of gold-diggers heading for the rich Omeo and Walhalla gold fields during the 1860s, and the supply port for Gippsland farm pioneers until the railway from Melbourne to Sale was completed in 1878. It was also a major centre for whaling, sealing and fishing, and its large old timber jetties often hosted a fleet of commercial and passenger sailing vessels from Europe and America. Today it remains an attractive, but much quieter, commercial fishing port with popular swimming and surfing beaches nearby. Its 1841 pub is a great favourite with the many fishermen who use Port Albert as a base to explore the excellent fishing around Snake Island and Corner Inlet marine park. Every March, Port Albert hosts the $100,000 Fishing Classic.

ROYAL BOTANIC GARDENS, CRANBOURNE❖❖

ⓘ Royal Botanic Gardens, Cranbourne $ *Ballarto Road, off South Gippsland Highway; tel: (03) 5990-2200. Open daily 0900–1700 except Christmas Day and Good Friday. May be closed on days of total fire ban.*

Located on the outskirts of Melbourne, the Cranbourne Gardens are an annexe of the Royal Botanic Gardens, with the land bought in 1970 to develop a garden specialising in native Australian flowers, trees, grasses and shrubs in a natural setting on a large scale. These 'gardens' are actually a slice of remnant bushland and wetland that was once widespread over much of the Mornington Peninsula. A walk through the tea-tree heathland reveals a remarkable variety of wildflowers and birds. There is always something to see: the heath starts flowering in July, producing a carpet of pink and white; the yellow native peas and wattles are next to bloom and during October and November, the bush is a mass of white with the star-like flowers of the wedding bush. Colourful, dainty orchids are a feature of the heathlands and in summer and autumn the silver banksia produces a mass of golden cones.

TARRA BULGA NATIONAL PARK❖❖❖

ⓘ Tarra Bulga National Park Rainforest Information Centre *Grand Ridge Road, Balook; tel: (03) 5196-6166.*

Once the entire rolling slopes of the Strzelecki Ranges of South Gippsland were covered with ancient, dark green, lush and dripping rainforest. Now the 1560 hectares of Tarra Bulga National Park are all that remains after extensive clearing by settlers intent on brutally clearing their farms from the forest's claustrophobic grasp. The remnant National Park features giant mountain ash trees, beautiful fern gullies and ancient myrtle beeches. The Tarra Bulga Visitors' Centre at Balook explains the forest's secrets and its history. The narrow winding roads that provide access to the park offer wonderful

Above
Tarra Bulga National Park

views, and the park has a range of excellent walking tracks to suit all ages and fitness levels. In the Bulga section of the park, stroll the 30-minute Fern Gully nature walk across Corrigans Suspension Bridge, or the slightly more vigorous Mountain Ash scenic track.

WILSONS PROMONTORY NATIONAL PARK❖❖❖

ⓘ **Wilsons Promontory National Park Information Centre**
Tidal River; tel: (03) 5680-9555 or 1800-350-552. Open daily 0830–1630.

Parks Victoria Information Line tel: 13-1963; www.parks.vic.gov.au. Open school and public holidays and various times throughout the year.

☾ **Tidal River cabin and lodge bookings**
tel: (03) 5680-9500.

The jewel of Victoria's national park system is Wilsons Promontory National Park, a 50,000-hectare national park featuring 130km of pristine coastline on the southernmost tip of mainland Australia. Its diversity of landscapes is simply stunning; there are gentle coves, coastal heathland, fern gullies, white sand wild Bass Strait beaches and superb rock formation, all set against a backdrop of majestic, granite peaks. Once a land bridge to Tasmania until the ice caps melted and the sea level rose 15,000 years ago, 'The Prom' has long been of great significance to local Aboriginal people. It is the State's oldest national park and its most popular, with lovely white beaches ringed by warm pink and yellow granite boulders, fantastic scenery and plentiful wildlife. There is an extensive network of day and overnight walking trails with camping grounds. Most walks start from the National Park's headquarters and information centre at the small settlement of **Tidal River**. They take you through scenery which changes from swamps and forests to marshes, valleys of tree ferns, and long beaches lined with sand dunes. The lookout at Mt Oberon car park offers magnificent views across Bass Strait.

For many of The Prom's 400,000 annual visitors, the enduring memory is not simply of the staggering beauty of the park's little beaches and coves, but of its wildlife and flora. Fish and seals abound on its marine-park protected reefs, offshore islands and waters; hundreds of tame crimson rosellas flock around Tidal River, and it is impossible to miss the emus, wombats and koalas and the plentiful swamp wallabies and eastern grey kangaroos hopping across the park's roads.

Tidal River is the only place in the park where camping from vehicles is allowed; cabins, flats and lodges operated by national park staff are also available here. The campsite fronts on to the sweeping **Norman Bay**, which is a safe and popular family swimming beach as it lacks the strong currents that can make other Prom beaches such as nearby Oberon Bay dangerous. The famous white sands of **Squeaky Beach** are only half an hour's walk away from Tidal River, while the **Loo-errn Boardwalk** track, named after an Aboriginal spirit, offers serene views of the river and surrounding peaks to the less active or wheelchair bound. Also recommended is the self-guided **Lilly Pilly Gully nature trail** circuit, a two- to three-hour easy walk through banksias, casuarinas and gum trees where many koalas live, before descending down into the cool verdant gully with its ferns and rainforest.

But most of all The Prom is most loved for its easily achieved overnight hiking trails to beaches as beautiful as **Sealers Cove**, **Refuge Bay** and **Waterloo Bay**. A relatively easy two- or three-day circuit hike reaches these magical white beaches and their little bush camping grounds set behind sheltered coves – all food and equipment must be carried, permits are necessary and no wood fires are allowed. The drier north of the park also has overnight camping facilities, while the northeast corner has been designated a wilderness zone, with the priority on preserving the land, its flora and fauna in as pristine a state as possible.

WONTHAGGI✧✧

State Coal Mine
Garden Street; tel: (03) 5672-3053. Open daily for mine tours 1030–1530.

Wonthaggi has turned its coal-mining history into a tourist attraction. The last coal mine closed in 1968 but two tunnels were reopened at the **State Coal Mine**✦ to give visitors an experience of the miner's life – these are currently closed temporarily for safety reasons. There is still plenty to see above ground though, such as a heritage walk and trips on a steam locomotive. Some of the ex-miners work as tourist guides and a pit pony adds another authentic touch.

Accommodation and food

Chicory Cottage $$ *Church St, Cowes, Phillip Island; tel: (0403) 886-996; www.phillipislandcottage.com.* Lovely self-contained cottage, three minutes stroll to the beach and five minutes from the town centre.

The Fishy Pub $$ *Old Waratah Rd, Fish Creek; tel: (03) 5683-2404; fax: (03) 5683-2550.* Accommodation and meals; this popular hotel has a range of accommodation from backpackers to motel rooms. The meals are home-made with plenty of fresh local seafood.

Narabeen Cottage Guest House and Restaurant $$ *16 Steele St, Cowes, Phillip Island; tel: (03) 5952-2062; fax: (03) 5952-3670.* Quiet location close to beach and all facilities.

Pindari Homestead and Cottage $$ *South Gippsland Hwy, Ruby, via Korumburra; tel/fax: (03) 5662-2005.* A grazing property with superb views, indoor pool and tennis court, about 5km from Leongatha.

Tall Poppies B&B $$ *42–52 Kookaburra Drive, Koonwarra; tel: (03) 5664-2281.* Stylish country house with hearty country breakfast.

Tarra Bulga Guesthouse $$ *Grand Ridge Road, Balook; tel: (03) 5196-6141.* 1930s-style guesthouse and tearooms.

Wilsons Promontory National Park $$ *Tidal River via Foster; tel: 1800-350-552; fax: (03) 5680-9516.* Camping, flats and cabins.

Suggested tour

Total distance: The main route is about 680km.

Time: You will need about three days for the main route. Some of the roads are narrow and unsealed so driving is slow.

Links: From the Gourmet Deli Trail at Neerim South, continue north to Noojee, where the Alpine Trout Farm on the Mt Baw Baw Tourist Road is worth a visit, and continue through Powelltown with its relics of the timber industry, to Yarra Junction and Warburton, linking up with the Yarra Valley tour (*see page 102*).

Route: Take the Monash Freeway (formerly the South Eastern Freeway) to the Cranbourne exit and turn on to the South Gippsland Highway 48km from Melbourne. Just past Cranbourne turn off to **ROYAL BOTANIC GARDENS ❶** . Continue along the South Gippsland Highway for 36km and follow the signs to **PHILLIP ISLAND ❷** via the Bass Highway. The suburbs of Melbourne are left behind and are replaced by grazing land and rolling green hills. After 34km you reach the turn-off to San Remo and Phillip Island and from here it is 24km to **Cowes** at the most northerly point of the island. Return to the Bass Highway, past the historic railway bridge at **Kilcunda** and continue to **WONTHAGGI ❸** , and **BUNURONG MARINE PARK ❹** .

From **Inverloch** it is a scenic 53km to **Foster** and another 61km to **Tidal River** inside **WILSONS PROMONTORY NATIONAL PARK ❺** . The drive from the park entrance at Yanakie to Tidal River is a good introduction to the scenery of the Prom. Return to Foster and continue along the South Gippsland Highway for 23km to Welshpool. Between Port Welshpool and Port Albert are the mudflats and islands of the **NOORAMUNGA MARINE PARK** ❻. From Welshpool, drive 29km to **Yarram**, and another 30km on sealed roads to **TARRA BULGA NATIONAL PARK** ❼.

Detour: From Yarram, continue to Woodside and Seaspray along the Ninety Mile Beach, Golden Beach, Loch Sport and the Gippsland Lakes Coastal Park, the stunning Rotamah Island bird sanctuary, Lakes Entrance and the Lakes National Park. Return to the main route.

To return to Melbourne, follow the winding **GRAND RIDGE ROAD** ❽ – with spectacular views to Mirboo North – 60km on mostly unsealed roads. The route runs through the **Strzelecki State Forest** so watch out for logging trucks. Head north through Thorpdale, heart of potato country, to the Princes Highway at Trafalgar, passing deer farms and berry farms. Pick up a map of the **GOURMET DELI TRAIL** ❾ at **Yarragon**. This trail will take you through **Neerim South** and **Jindivick** to the Princes Freeway about 80km from Melbourne.

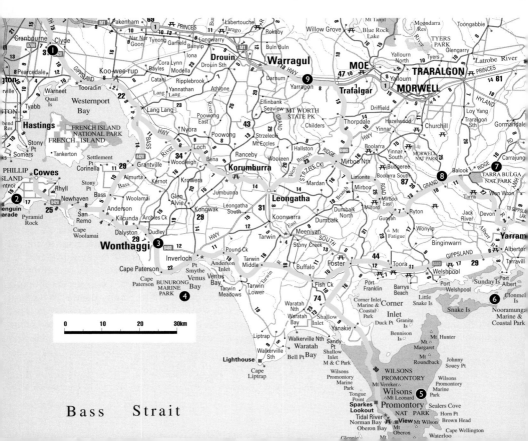

Northeast Victoria

Ratings

Food	●●●●●
Mountains	●●●●●
Outdoor activities	●●●●●
Scenery	●●●●●
Wineries	●●●●●
Art and crafts	●●●●○
Fly-fishing	●●●○
Winter skiing	●●●●○

From the famous wineries of Rutherglen to the bushranger legends of Glenrowan and the beauty of the mountains and high plains, Northeast Victoria offers a whole range of attractions. Some of Australia's oldest wineries are found in the area, and over the past decade many new ones have emerged. The region's gourmet food producers specialise in delicacies such as chestnuts, mustard, trout, lamb, superb cheeses, and unusual varieties of honey. The picturesque towns of Yackandandah, Beechworth and Chiltern, which have remained virtually unchanged for more than a century, are places to view the work of talented local artists. The mountains provide all sorts of opportunities for recreation: in winter the ski-fields come alive and at other times of the year walking over the flower-strewn high plains, trout fishing, horse riding, camping and bird watching are just some of the possibilities.

ALPINE NATIONAL PARK❖❖❖

ⓘ Visitor Information Centre PO Box 145 Mt Beauty; tel: (03) 5754-4718; www.parkweb.vic.gov.au

◉ Falls Creek Food, Wine and Wildflower Festival tel: (03) 5758-3490; 3rd weekend in Jan.
Mt Bogong Conquestathon tel: (03) 5754-4647; early Mar.

Victoria's highest mountains are protected in this vast national park that stretches from central Victoria to join up with Kosciuszko National Park (see page 76) to create a huge alpine wilderness. In spring and summer the wildflowers are glorious and by driving up to the ski resort of Falls Creek and walking from there it is relatively easy to experience the grassy plateaux and stunted snow-gum country of the High Plains. The 400-km Alpine Walking Track traverses the Bogong High Plains from Mt Hotham to Mt Bogong. Banjo Patterson immortalised the life of cattle drovers who grazed their cattle on these High Plains during summer in his famous poem *The Man from Snowy River*. Many of the small wooden huts dotted across the national park and which are now used to shelter weary walkers and lost cross-country skiers were built by the same cattlemen. Access to the Alpine National Park is either via Harrietville and Mt Hotham (Great Alpine Rd) or Mt Beauty and Falls Creek (Bogong High Plains Rd).

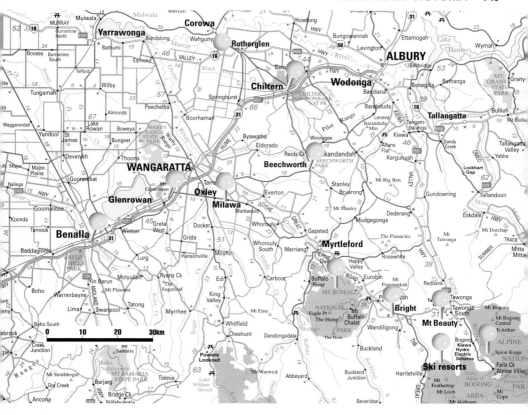

BEECHWORTH***

Visitor Information
Ford St; tel: (03) 5728-3233.

A picturesque town in the scenic Ovens Valley, Beechworth is one of Victoria's best preserved gold-mining towns, with more than 30 of its buildings classified by the National Trust. The town, with its wide, tree-lined streets and honey-coloured buildings is surrounded by forested valleys, waterfalls and rocky gorges. In the 1850s, gold-mining in the Ovens River centred around Beechworth. Visitors can view the cell where Ned Kelly was held before his final trial. The town's **museum** ($$), on Loch St, contains an interesting collection of gold-rush memorabilia and a replica of the main street a century ago. The museum is dedicated to explorer Robert O'Hara Burke, who was the local police chief before leading the doomed expedition to central Australia with William Wills. The Chinese Burning Towers are a reminder of the huge Chinese population which occupied the town during the gold rush era. As well as the numerous antique, bric-à-brac and craft shops, don't miss hot muffins or cakes from the famous Beechworth Bakery.

BENALLA❖❖

ⓘ Benalla Visitors' Information Centre and Costume and Pioneer Museum $
14 Mair St, tel: (03) 5762-1749. Open daily 0900–1700.

Ⓖ Benalla Art Gallery Bridge St.
Open 1000–1700. Easter: **Art Show**; Nov: **Rose Festival**.

The Hume Freeway bypasses the small regional city of Benalla famous for its rose gardens and art gallery. The big old trees in the Botanical Gardens provide welcome shade for picnickers on hot summer days, while during November the city's **Rose Festival** attracts many visitors to the rose garden which was established in the 1860s. Nearby, the **Benalla Art Gallery** sits on the shores of Lake Benalla. The gallery is internationally recognised for its fine collection of Australian art and considered one of Victoria's most important regional galleries. Opposite the gallery is the ceramic mural garden, an on-going project by local artists. Lake Benalla, a man-made lake on the Broken River, is a haven for birds. The **Costume and Pioneer Museum❖** houses Australia's largest collection of period costumes as well as memorabilia of the region's notorious bushranger Ned Kelly and one of the city's famous sons, World War II prison camp survivor, Sir Edward 'Weary' Dunlop.

BRIGHT❖❖❖

ⓘ Bright Information Centre 119 Gavan St; tel: (03) 5755-2275. Walking maps available.

◕ Bright Outdoor Centre 9 Ireland St; tel: (03) 5755-1818. Equipment for camping, fishing, bushwalking and skiing.

In the heart of the Ovens Valley surrounded by snow-capped mountains, Bright has attractions all year round. It is about an hour's drive from the snowfields of Mt Hotham and Falls Creek and only half an hour to Mt Buffalo National Park with its towering cliffs, rocky boulders and gassy snow meadows. The Bright Spring Festival, from late October to early November, provides a showcase for many of the town's lovely gardens. Then in autumn (late April–early May) another festival is held to celebrate the changing seasons when the avenues of deciduous

European trees become a blaze of red and gold. A winding road up the Buckland Valley takes you through grazing land, orchards and wineries to explore the area's gold-mining history. There are a number of walking trails around Bright including Canyon Walk, an easy walk along the Ovens River which passes remains of the old gold workings. During spring and summer, trout fishing is excellent in the region.

Right
Chairlift at Mt Hotham

CHILTERN✦✦✦

Chiltern Visitor Information Centre *Cnr Conness and Main St; tel: (03) 5726-1395.*

Lakeview Homestead $ *Victoria St; tel: (03) 5726-1317. Open weekends, public holidays and school holidays 1000–1600.*

Established when graziers moved into the area, the now sleepy little town of Chiltern, boomed during the 1850s gold-rushes, with a population of 20,000 at its peak. Mining stopped early this century and today life proceeds at a more leisurely pace. Chiltern has been used as a film set for a number of major films and it is not hard to see why, as very few props are needed to recreate a historic atmosphere in this pretty low-key town, reputedly with the oldest grapevine in Australia running (literally) down the posts and shopfronts of its main street. The recently proclaimed Chiltern **Box-Ironbark National Park** nearly encircles the town. This type of forest, once widespread throughout Victoria, is threatened by clearing and logging for firewood. The forest has a number of walks and excellent displays of wildflowers during spring and summer. A 25-km historic drive takes in the Pioneer Cemetery, the old Magenta gold mine and the Donkey Hill lookout. Walk across the bridge over Lake Anderson to **Lakeview✦**, the childhood home of influential Australian author Henry Handel Richardson, famous for her epic novel *The Fortunes of Richard Mahoney*, a saga set on the gold fields.

GLENROWAN✦✦

Glenrowan Visitor Information *Kate's Cottage, Gladstone St; tel: (03) 5766-2448.*

The site of the famous last stand by infamous bushranger Ned Kelly and his gang in 1880, today Kelly is everywhere in Glenrowan. A giant statue of the bushranger greets you as you enter the town, the **Ned Kelly Memorial Museum✦** and a computer animated show of his capture are some of the attractions. Visitors can follow the self-guided historic Ned Kelly trail. The place where the last stand actually took place, where Kelly and his boys attempted to derail a train carrying police from Melbourne, is also being developed, with wooden bollards decorated as police, bushrangers and spectators beginning to dot the area. The ruins of the Kelly family homestead are a few kilometres off the highway at Greta. The countryside around Glenrowan is grazing land with wineries and horticultural crops in the rich river valleys.

MILAWA AND OXLEY✦✦✦

Brown Brothers Winery *tel: (03) 5720-5547; www.brown-brothers.com.au. Open daily 0900–1700.*

The little town of Milawa is a popular stopping place for travellers on their way to the snow-fields and in recent years the number of its gourmet attractions has grown. **Brown Brothers Winery✦** with its free wine tasting has been operating here since 1889. More recently the **Milawa Cheese Company✦**, producing magnificent cheeses and

Milawa Cheese Company tel: (03) 5727-3588. Open daily 0900–1700.

mustards with an interesting range of products, has contributed to the area's reputation for high-quality food. It also runs the renowned King River Café at Oxley. Milawa is located between the King and Ovens valleys, a rich agricultural area where sheep and cattle grazing is interspersed with crops such as hops, wine grapes and berries.

MOUNT BEAUTY**

Visitor Information Centre Kiewa Valley Hwy, Tawonga South; tel: (03) 5754-4024.

Parks Victoria Information Line tel: 13-1963; www.parks.vic.gov.au

The rocky face of Victoria's highest mountain, **Mt Bogong** towers above the town of Mt Beauty. In an ideal holiday location, Mt Beauty owes its origins to the development of the state's hydro-electric scheme. In the 1940s the town provided accommodation for workers on the Kiewa project. Today it is a popular base for skiers in winter and for mountain bike riders and bushwalkers in other seasons. The most popular way of climbing Mt Bogong is via the **Staircase Spur**, a steep 6-km climb which rises from 700m to 1986m at the summit. The **Kangaroo Hoppet** (tel: (03) 5754-310) in late August attracts many international competitors for a variety of cross-country skiing events.

MOUNT BUFFALO NATIONAL PARK***

Rutherglen Wine Region Tourism Office tel: (02) 6032-9166; www.visitrutherglen.com.au

Mt Buffalo Chalet $$ tel: (03) 5755-1500. **Opera in the Alps** is held here in Jan.

The imposing rock face of Mt Buffalo gives it a majesty and character quite different from that of the surrounding mountains. Only a short drive from Bright and Myrtleford, this national park is easily accessible for day visitors who can expect stunning views over mountain valleys, huge granite walls falling to the earth far below, or an afternoon in the languid atmosphere of historic **Mt Buffalo Chalet***. Summer at Lake Catani is delightful with opportunities for swimming, camping and canoeing. Mt Buffalo is a bushwalker's paradise with many well signposted and accessible walking tracks. Summer is also the best time to see the abundant plant and animal life of the tall eucalyptus forest, alpine heathlands and snowgrass plains. In winter the landscape presents a different challenge with gentle slopes for downhill skiing in a small, low-key commercial area and a number of cross-country ski trails. The near vertical walls of the gorge provide some challenging rock climbs and abseiling opportunities.

RUTHERGLEN***

Famed for their fortified wines – such as ports, tokays and muscats – the 16 wineries of Rutherglen are clustered in a triangle around the historic township and along the banks of the nearby Murray River. Most are open seven days a week for tasting and sales. This attractive town, whose main street is lined with old veranda-fronted buildings, comes alive during the immensely popular **Rutherglen Winery Walkabout**, on the first weekend in June. This is also a great region for riding bikes without having to worry about being breathalysed by police while wine tasting and picnicking! Organised bike tours are also available.

Ski Resorts❖❖❖

🛈 Ski resort visitor information and accommodation booking: **Mt Buller** tel: 1800-039-049 or (03) 9809-0291; **Falls Creek** tel: 1800-033-079; **Mt Hotham** tel: 1800-354-555; **Dinner Plain** tel: 1800-670-019; **Mt Buffalo** tel: 1800-037-038.

Alpine Resorts Commission mountain information line tel: 190-2240-523. Snow, roads and weather conditions.

From June to late September, when snow settles on the Victorian Alps, Victoria goes ski-mad and the world-class ski resorts open for serious business. The three big resorts of Mt Buller, Falls Creek and Mt Hotham are all separate villages above the snowline, nestled in the midst of the Alpine National Park. With a vast area of wild national park and high plains available, cross-country skiing is magnificent, although the only groomed tracks are close to downhill resorts; the rest is virgin bush snow for the intrepid to explore. All ski resorts are now accessible by sealed road from Melbourne, and a new mountain airport is being built to service Mt Hotham and Dinner Plain with

direct flights from Sydney and Melbourne. **Mt Buller**, closest to Melbourne and reached through Mansfield, is the most jet-set of the resorts and has the highest proportion of day visitors. Being further from Melbourne, **Falls Creek** (reached via the town of Mount Beauty) and **Mt Hotham** (reached via Omeo or Bright) are for skiers with a long weekend or week to enjoy the snow. **Dinner Plain** is an attractive, bush-architect designed, cross-country ski village, only a 20-minute drive from the downhill runs of Mt Hotham. **Mt Buffalo** (reached via Bright) is geared towards gentle skiing and young families. In all downhill resorts, groomed ski runs – paid for with a day or week pass and serviced by chairlifts and T-bars – are not generally as long as runs in Europe or the US. But the weather is not as cold, and skiing among beautiful snow-gums with blue sky and sun above, magnificent views over the High Plains all around, light powder snow underfoot is an experience not to be missed. *Après-ski* night life is a key element of any Australian ski holiday; good restaurants and bars with music abound.

YACKANDANDAH❖❖

ℹ Yackandandah Visitor Information Centre
High St; tel: (02) 6027-1222.

◆ Yackandandah Folk Festival
second weekend in Mar.

The small gold-mining town, tucked away in the scenic Indigo Valley, has a strong community of artists whose work can be seen at local galleries and studios. Stroll down the main street and stop at the bakery or one of several cafés while you admire the many Victorian-era buildings listed by the National Trust. A scenic drive through the surrounding forest takes about half an hour and may be a good place for a picnic. You will see evidence of mining along the drive and if you decide to take a walk watch out for mine shafts and tunnels. In the early morning or late afternoon, the trees come alive with honeyeaters, rosellas, willy wagtails and other birds.

Accommodation and food

All Saints Winery $$$ *All Saints Rd, Wahgunyah; tel: (02) 6033-1922.* Cellar door and restaurant inside the walls of a 130-year-old castle.

Beechworth Bakery $$ *27 Camp St, Beechworth.* An irresistible array of cakes and pastries.

Beechworth Provender $$ *18 Camp St, Beechworth.* Open daily; café-delicatessen; local cheeses, mustard, smoked meats and relishes.

Black Springs Bakery $$ *Beechworth; tel: (03) 5728-2565.* Self-contained accommodation in stone barn, garden open at weekends.

Bogong Alpine Village $$ *27 Main St, Bogong; tel: (03) 5754-3300; fax: (03) 5754-3391.* Holiday cottages between Mt Beauty and Falls Creek, overlooking Lake Guy.

The Kelly Gang

The northeast of Victoria is 'Kelly Country' where Australia's most famous outlaw, bushranger Ned Kelly, roamed free with his gang for more than five years, robbing banks and terrorising local police officers. Despite killing three policemen, Kelly has entered the annals of Australia's folklore; rightly or wrongly, he is now regarded as a highly intelligent working-class hero who stood up for the rights of the common man (mainly poor Irish bush settlers) against the overbearing colonial authorities (mainly English). His story is scattered across northeast Victoria. In Benalla, where the Kelly family grew up, Ned first appeared in court at the age of 15. At Mansfield, a memorial in the main street commemorates the death of three troopers shot by the Kelly gang at nearby Stringybark Creek in 1878, the crime for which he was eventually hanged. Glenrowan is the famous site of the Kelly Gang's last stand, where in a shoot-out with police in 1880 by the railway station, Ned Kelly was finally captured and the rest of his gang shot dead. It was at Beechworth courthouse that Ned Kelly was committed for trial in Melbourne, where he was hanged in the Old Gaol in 1881 with the famous last words, 'such is life'.

King River Café $$ *Snow Rd, Oxley; tel: (03) 5727-3777.* Casual eatery with regional produce.

Kinross B&B $$ *34 Loch St, Beechworth; tel: (03) 5728-2351; fax: (03) 5738-3333.* Return to a log fire in your room after dinner in the house restaurant.

Lake Moodemere Homestead B&B $$ *Rutherglen; tel: (02) 6032-8650; fax: (02) 6032-8118.* A historic homestead on the banks of Lake Moodemere. The property produces grapes, cereal crops and sheep.

Mt Buffalo Chalet $$ *Mt Buffalo National Park; tel: 1800-037-038; fax: (03) 5755-1892; email: buffaloc@netc.net.au.* A historic guesthouse offering a range of packages.

Parlour & Pantry $$ *69 Ford St, Beechworth.* Gourmet deli and restaurant.

Suggested tour

Total distance: The main route is 251km. The detour up Mt Buffalo is 56km return.

Time: It will take about two days for the main route, not counting stops.

Route: From **BENALLA ❶**, head northeast along the Hume Freeway for 45km and exit to the Snow Rd before Wangaratta.

Detour: Leave the Hume Highway at **GLENROWAN ❷**, a distance of 23km, and explore the Ned Kelly Memorial Museum or visit some of the Glenrowan wineries, such as **Baileys**; from here you can also head across the Warby Range, or continue north along the route.

Twenty-one kilometres from the Wangaratta turn-off, visit the King River Café and Cellar at **OXLEY ❸** and sample the gourmet delights of **MILAWA**, before continuing along the Snow Rd. The route joins the Great Alpine Rd and a pleasant meander past the small farms which line the Ovens Valley selling seasonal local produce, such as asparagus, nuts, vegetables and berries of all kinds. Vineyards, hops and tobacco crops carpet the valleys and hills surrounding **Myrtleford**, a township 26km further on which is fast gaining fame as a gourmet food producer. Myrtleford is also the gateway to the Alps. Enjoy spectacular views of **Mt Buffalo** and the narrow ridgeline of Mt Feathertop.

Detour: Turn off the Great Alpine Rd at **Porepunkah** and drive up to

Baileys of Glenrowan *Taminick Gap Rd, Glenrowan; tel: (03) 5766-2392. 1000–1700.* Renowned for its fortified wines, this is one of the oldest wineries in the district, established in 1870; it has barbecue facilities and weekend gourmet lunches.

Rosewhite Vineyard *RMB 2650, Rosewhite via Myrtleford; tel: (03) 5752-1077. Open 1000–1700 weekends and public holidays; daily during Jan.*

Tobacco, Timber and Hops Festival, Myrtleford *tel: (03) 5752-2737. Mar.*

MT BUFFALO ❹ for spectacular views and walks in the national park. Return to the main route.

Continue on to **BRIGHT** ❺, only 6km away, and **MT BEAUTY** ❻, a further 30km.

Right
Eucalyptus forest and wild flowers

Detour: From Bright – November to May only – continue through **Harrietville** along the **Great Alpine Rd**, over **Mt Hotham** and **Dinner Plain** (a charming all-year-round resort) to **Omeo**, for spectacular views and High Plains meadow walking. Don't miss seeing old cattlemen's huts like Wallace's Hut near Falls Creek, and walking among the wild mountain flowers. But beware, the weather can change at any time.

From Mt Beauty here you can explore the **ALPINE NATIONAL PARK ❼**. Return via another scenic route, passing dairy farms and large eucalyptus along the Kiewa Valley Highway, turning off to **Dederang ❽**, which is 27km from Mt Beauty. Drive through the beautiful **Indigo Valley** to **YACKANDANDAH ❾** (34km) and **BEECHWORTH ❿** (a further 21km), leaving the mountains behind. From here it is 26km to **CHILTERN ⓫** and another 18km through flat, open farming land to **RUTHERGLEN ⓬**.

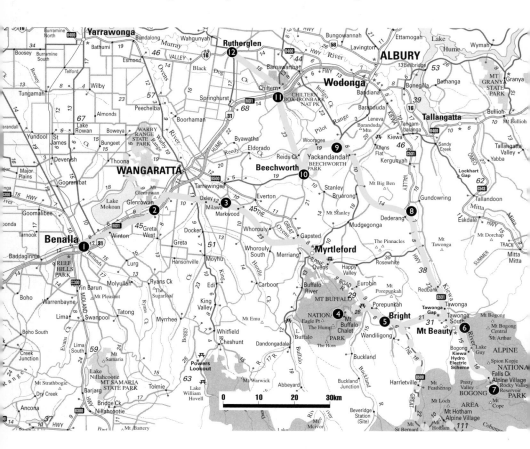

Ratings

Beaches	●●●●●
Children	●●●●●
Nightlife	●●●●●
Surfing	●●●●●
Rainforests	●●●●○
Restaurants	●●●●○
Walking	●●●●○
Wildlife	●●●○○

The Gold Coast and Scenic Rim

The Gold Coast is Australia's most vibrant coastal playground: a world of iconic sweeping sand beaches, classic Aussie surf-lifestyle, with the vivacious city of Brisbane close to beautiful rainforest-clad mountains. The coast stretches south from Brisbane past several famous surf breaks and beaches. Home to children's theme parks, a casino, world famous marinas, high-rise apartments, snaking waterways and a glitzy nightlife, the Gold Coast is also a gateway to the lush sub-tropical rainforests of Springbrook and Lamington National Park. Tumbling from the mountains are stunning waterfalls that feed delicate ecosystems of rare plants, animals and birds. A paradox of natural beauty and man-made fun, the Gold Coast has become a tourist mecca, and the centre of one of Australia's largest migrations of retirees, dreamers and sun-lovers. A popular holiday destination for chilled Southerners since the late 1800s, the region now prides itself on being pioneering, outward looking and unashamedly bold.

BRISBANE✦✦✦

ⓘ Gold Coast Tourism Bureau
tel: free call on 1800-655-066; www. goldcoasttourism.com.au

Queensland Government Travel Centre *Edward and Adelaide Sts; tel: (07) 3833-5412.*

Brisbane City Council Information Booth *Queen St Mall; tel: (07) 3229-5918.*

Brisbane lies inland on the Brisbane River. At Moreton Bay, where the river enters the sea, there is said to be an island for every day of the year. Some of these are large sandy islands that shelter the coast from incoming storms. Brisbane came of age when it hosted the World Expo in 1988. Once derided by southern states as a sun-baked backwater, buildings were refurbished, restaurants opened, the whole South Bank, which had been an ugly warehouse and industrial area close to the city centre, was brought to life.

The Brisbane River meanders through the centre of the city and, with its bank-side gardens and developments, gives the city shape and character. **City Hall**✦, in King George Square, contains an art gallery, museum, concert hall and public library. It was built over a period of 10 years starting in 1920, and its centrepiece is the clock tower, which was, for many years, the highest structure in the city. **Parliament House**✦, opened in 1868, is a fine example of French Renaissance

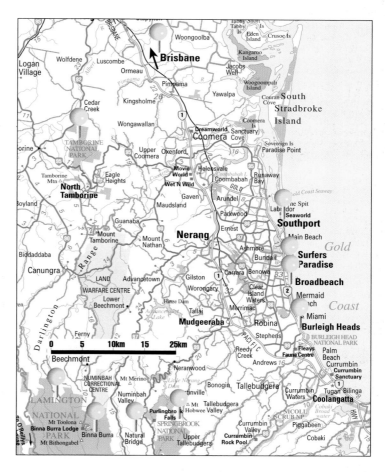

City Hall $ *King George Square.*
Open daily from 0700.

Parliament House
Public gallery open to visitors when Parliament is sitting.

Botanic Gardens $$
Alice Street; tel: (07) 870-8136. Open daily sunrise to sunset.

architecture. It is set in parkland opposite the **Botanic Gardens✦✦**.

Brisbane has a wide range of museums and art galleries. The **Queensland Cultural Centre✦✦✦** contains the **Queensland Art Gallery✦✦**, which has serious collections of Australian art as well as European and Asian antique furniture, silver, glassware and pottery. **South Bank Parklands✦✦** consists of 16 hectares of landscaped parklands on the south bank of the river, with restaurants, an open-air beach area, boat rides and entertainment. Adjacent is the **Queensland Museum✦✦**, which houses a vast range of exhibits relating to anthropology, geology, zoology, history and technology. The nearby **IMAX Theatre Complex✦** shows large-format adventure and nature films. Another attraction in Parklands is the world's largest collection of Australian butterfly species in their own flowering forest environment at the **South Bank Butterfly House✦✦**.

🏛 Queensland Cultural Centre
South Bank; tel: (07) 3414-7303; www.qpat.com.au. Open daily 1000–1700, Wed late closing at 2000.

South Bank Parklands
tel: (07) 3867-2051.

Queensland Museum $$ *Cultural Centre, S Brisbane; tel: (07) 3840-7635; www.qmuseum.qld.gov.au. Open daily 0900–1700, Wed late closing at 2000.*

IMAX Theatre Complex $$ *The Avenue, South Bank, S Brisbane; tel: (07) 3844-4222. Open daily 0900–2300.*

South Bank Butterfly House $ *South Bank, S Brisbane; tel: (07) 3844-1112/1137. Open daily 1000–1800.*

🛈 Brisbane is a small city, easy to explore on foot. Brisbane also has an excellent public transport system, although this ceases at midnight. The best buy is the **DayRover** ticket ($), which gives you unlimited travel (on bus, ferry and CityCats) for one day. Brisbane is bisected by the river and ferries and super-fast commuter catamarans run across it from several places.

Food in Brisbane

Circa Restaurant $$ *483 Adelaide St, Brisbane; tel: (07) 3832-4722.* Stylish but unpretentious modern Australian cuisine.

Daniel's Steakhouse $$ *145 Eagle St; tel: (07) 3832-3444.* Lunch and dinner Monday–Saturday. Licensed.

E'CCO $$$ *100 Boundary St; tel: (07) 3831-8344.* Lunch and dinner Tuesday–Saturday. Licensed. Award-winning Australian cuisine.

Il Centro $$ *1 Eagle Street Pier; tel: (07) 3221-6090.* Lunch Sunday–Friday. Dinner daily. Licensed. Italian cuisine.

Michael's Riverside $$$ *Waterfront P1, 123 Eagle St; tel: (07) 3832-5522.* Licensed. High quality – perhaps the best in Brisbane.

Mt Coot-tha Summit Restaurant $$ *Sir Samuel Griffith Drv; tel: (07) 3369-9922.* Open daily 1100 till late. Wonderful views.

Right
Nepalese temple in Brisbane's South Bank Parklands

BROADBEACH✧✧

Conrad Jupiters Casino $$$ *Gold Coast Hwy; tel: free call 1800-074-344; open 24 hours. Free parking.*

In competition with Surfer's Paradise to attract the Gold Coast's perennial fun seekers, Broadbeach boasts the dazzling landmark of **Conrad Jupiters Casino✧**. The casino is open 24 hours and has some 80 gambling tables which draw up to 13,000 punters every day. Worth visiting, even if only to take in the super-charged atmosphere.

Accommodation and food in Broadbeach

Evergreen's Coffee Pavilion $ *corner Bundall Rd and Ashmore Rd, Sorrento; tel: (07) 5531-6146.* Mediterranean-influenced food in relaxed venue attached to a nursery complex.

Grand Mercure Hotel $$$ *Surf Parade; tel: (07) 5592-2250.* Luxury hotel linked to Conrad Jupiters Casino by a hotel monorail.

Mario's Italian Restaurant $ *Ground floor, Oasis Shopping Centre, Broadbeach Mall; tel: (07) 5592-1899.* Ever-popular family restaurant with casual feel and good pizzas.

BURLEIGH HEADS, CURRUMBIN AND COOLANGATTA✧✧✧

Information Booth *Beach House Plaza, Marine Pde, Coolangatta; tel: (07) 5536-7765. Open weekdays 0800–1400 and 1500–1600, or 0800–1500 on Sat.*

Burleigh Heads National Park *Gold Coast Hwy near Tallebudgera Bridge, Burleigh Heads; tel: (07) 5535-3032. Open daily 0900–1600.*

Currumbin Sanctuary $ *Tomewin St, Currumbin; tel: (07) 5534-1266. Open daily 0800–1700.*

Burleigh Heads, Currumbin and Coolangatta are home to some of the world's finest beaches, internationally renowned for their surf breaks. The river inlet at **Currumbin Beach✧** has a swimming area relatively sheltered from direct surf, ideal for less-experienced swimmers. All three destinations abound with cheap accommodation and restaurants. Although less glitzy than their northern neighbours, these beaches are typical of much of Australia's coastline: relaxed, unpretentious and egalitarian. Burleigh Heads is buttressed by a small but diverse **National Park✧** with good walks and views. A beloved and prolific wildlife park at **Currumbin Sanctuary✧** is filled with rainbow coloured lorikeets and other bird life. **Coolangatta** marks the border with NSW, and enjoys a sleepy small-town ambience thanks to classic surf beaches such as Kirra, Point Danger and Greenmount.

Accommodation and food in Burleigh Heads

Hillhaven Holiday Apartments $$ *Goodwin Terrace; tel: (07) 5535-1055.* Good-value apartment-style rooms with excellent views north of the coast to Surfer's Paradise.

Oscars on Burleigh $$ *Goodwin Terrace; tel: (07) 5576-3722.* Pleasant varied menu on an open deck perched over the sea with long coastal views.

GREEN MOUNTAINS AND BINNA BURRA***

O'Reilly's Guesthouse $$ Green Mountains; tel: (07) 5544-0644; fax: (07) 5544-0638.

Binna Burra Mountain Lodge $$ Canungra Rd, Green Mountains; tel: (07) 5533-3622, or toll-free 1800-644-150. For campsite bookings, tel: (07) 5533-3758.

These delightful mountain retreats both lie in the heart of Lamington National Park. Green Mountains is intimately linked to the O'Reilly family who pioneered this rugged landscape in the early 1900s. Over subsequent generations the family has gradually returned much of its land to the National Park, but still runs the famous **O'Reilly's Guesthouse**, a beautiful lodge that serves as a western base for Lamington's famed walks. On the eastern side of the park lies the intriguing **Binna Burra Mountain Lodge**, coveted by visiting city-dwellers for its cosy log cabins and tasty meals served in a restaurant blessed with spectacular views.

LAMINGTON NATIONAL PARK***

Lamington National Park Ranger Station Green Mountains, Lamington; tel: (07) 5545-1734.

One of southeast Queensland's most remarkable National Parks, **Lamington** covers 20,200 hectares of thick sub-tropical rainforest, blanketing the rugged McPherson border ranges with NSW. A haven for bushwalkers and wildlife lovers, the park boasts over 150km of walking trails, including an impressive suspended canopy walk through the forest crown. Stunning views of Mt Warning to the south, and the Numinbah Valley to the east are among the many highlights.

MT TAMBORINE*

National Parks Visitor Information Centre Doughty Park, North Tamborine; tel: (07) 5545-1171.

Songbirds Rainforest Retreat $$ Tamborine Mountain Rd, North Tamborine; tel: (07) 5545-2563.

Mt Tamborine is a 600-m high plateau with attractive rainforests and walks, relatively well developed but close to the Gold Coast. Perched on the northernmost tip of the 60-km long McPherson Range, Mt Tamborine has lovely views to the east of the Gold Coast and to the west where the majestic sweep of Queensland's border ranges vanish into the distance. A series of waterfalls and rainforest parks known as **Witches Falls*** and **Cedar Creek Falls*** have enjoyable walks and views. Mt Tamborine, and its adjoining townships are filled with guesthouses, arts and craft galleries, Devonshire tea houses and eco-resorts, including the good **Songbirds Rainforest Retreat***. The area is perfect for day trips from the Coast.

NATURAL BRIDGE**

Natural Bridge National Park Numinbah Valley Rd, between Nerang and Murwillumbah; tel: (07) 5533-6156. Free.

A hidden gem, the **Natural Bridge National Park*** is a rock archway spanning a creek buried deep within the lush rainforests that tumble down the western slopes of Springbrook Plateau to the Numinbah Valley. Discovered by timber workers around 1893, it remains in pristine condition, and is well known for a colony of glow-worms clinging to cavern roofs under the arch. A welcome swimming hole sits at the bottom of the waterfall gushing through the Bridge.

SOUTHPORT***

Sea World $$
Broadwater Spit, Main Beach; tel: (07) 5588-2222. Open daily 0930–1700.

Marina Mirage
Shopping Centre Broadwater Spit, Main Beach; tel: (07) 5577-0088; www.marinamirage.com.au

Below
Heading for the surf

The northern end of the Gold Coast's famous bleached beaches are based around the towns of **Southport*** and **Main Beach***. Bounded by a sparkling river estuary with its picturesque 'seaway' opening into the Pacific, and the first of several magnificent beaches, Southport also boasts Queensland's well-established **Sea World**** theme park. Stop and enjoy daily dolphin-feedings, water-skiing displays and the obligatory roller coasters and water slides. On the same sandy finger of land known as the **Broadwater Spit*** lies a popular indulgence of luxurious resorts, endless shopping and delightful restaurants. The best include Sea World's **Nara Resort** and the nearby **Marina Mirage**, both prime examples of the Gold Coast's highlife.

Accommodation and food in Southport and the Gold Coast

Palazzo Versace $$$ *Sea World Dr, Main Beach; tel: (07) 5509-8000.* A high-style, high-gloss resort with all the trimmings you'd expect from the Versace tribe. The in-house dining is outstanding, thanks to restaurants Vanitas and Vie.

RPR's $$ *Royal Pines Resort restaurant Ross St, Ashmore; tel: (07) 5597-1111.* Magnificent rooftop restaurant perched above this popular golfing resort with unrivalled views of the hinterland and coast.

Sea World Nara Resort $$ *The Spit, Main Beach; tel: (toll-free) 1800-074-448.* Excellent family hotel in the heart of things, with tariffs linked to free Sea World entry. The resort is also tied to the park via a monorail.

Sheraton Mirage Gold Coast Resort $$$ *Sea World Dr, Main Beach; tel: (07) 5591-1488.* High-level luxury (and expense) close to Sea World and Surfer's Paradise.

SPRINGBROOK PLATEAU***

ⓘ Springbrook National Park Information Centre *Springbrook Rd; tel: (07) 5533-5147. Open daily 0800–1600.*

A startling contrast to the sometimes overwhelming razzle-dazzle of the Gold Coast, Springbrook is a fertile plateau bounded by moist temperate rainforests, escarpments of volcanic rock and rolling fields. **Springbrook National Park**** is known for its lush walks, breathtaking views and the beautiful **Purling Brook Falls*** which plunge 100m into rainforest. Springbrook's greenery comes courtesy of the hinterland's enormous rainfall; a torrent averaging roughly 3000mm a year, most falling during the summer months. The plateau is often shrouded in spectacular mists, while in winter its many visitors climb the hill to enjoy cosy guesthouses well insulated from the surprisingly cool nights. Don't miss the perfectly named **Best of All Lookout**** at the end of a 350-m trail through ancient trees.

Accommodation and food in Springbrook

Hardy House $ *Springbrook Rd, Springbrook; tel: (07) 5533-5402.* A friendly B&B run by Graham and Patricia Hardy, members of a family with a long and interesting history in Springbrook.

Lyrebird Ridge Café and Gallery $ *Lyrebird Ridge Rd, Springbrook Mountain; tel: (07) 5533-5195; open 1000–1700 and Sat evening.* Great food in a magnificent rainforest setting, offering glimpses of the coast.

The Mouses' House $$ *Springbrook Rd; tel: (07) 5533-5192; fax: (07) 5533-5411.* A hinterland institution. Features a series of cosy cabins set deep inside a rainforest literally on top of several bubbling creeks. Complete with saunas and spas, a real treat. Booking is vital.

Below
Sun, sea and skyscrapers in Surfer's Paradise

Springbrook Mountain Chalets $ *Springbrook Rd, Springbrook; tel: (07) 5533-5205.* These are comfortable and private bush hideaways, with several stand-alone chalets surrounded by wildlife and flora. Can be difficult to find a vacancy at weekends.

Summer House Themed Lodges $$ *Springbrook Rd, Mudgeeraba; tel: (07) 5530-4151; fax: (07) 5530-7277.* Quirky hideaway with several themed lodges of varying capacity, including a pyramid $^1/_{20}$th the size of the Cheops Pyramid in Egypt. Very handy launch pad for tours into the hinterland, yet still close enough to the coast.

SURFER'S PARADISE✣✣✣

ⓘ Gold Coast Tourism Bureau
Cavill Ave; tel: (07) 5538-4419.

🎸 Hard Rock Café $
corner of Cavill Ave and the Gold Coast Hwy; tel: (07) 5539-9377. Open 0900–1100.

This is the Gold Coast's heartland: a compact strip of land dominated by spectacular beaches and ocean-front high-rise apartments and hotels. First developed shortly before World War II, Surfer's Paradise is the unrivalled epicentre of Gold Coast nightlife and glitz. Worth visiting day and night, the area is held together by **Cavill Ave Mall✣✣**, a vibrant pedestrian district filled with countless shops, duty-free stores, and several themed restaurants including the **Hard Rock Café✣**. Running perpendicular to the Mall is Orchid Avenue, the coast's leading nightclub quarter. Stroll along **The Esplanade** for a crash course in Australian beach culture studded with bronzed surfers, beach bums and visiting sun-worshippers.

Accommodation and food in Surfer's Paradise

Amalfi Bistro & Wine Bar Restaurant $$ *3032 Gold Coast Hwy, Surfer's Paradise; tel: (07) 5588-8305.* Casual dining, Italian-style, with extensive wine list.

Omeros $$ *corner of Frederick St and the Gold Coast Hwy; tel (07) 5538-5244.* Terrific seafood and very popular.

Surfer's Paradise Marriot Resort $$$ *Ferny Ave; tel: (07) 5592-9800.* An over-the-top five-star resort minutes from Cavill Ave and endless beaches.

THEME PARKS***

Dreamworld $$
*Pacific Hwy, Coomera;
tel: (07) 5588-1111;
www.dreamworld.com.au.
Open daily 1000–1700.*

Movie World $$ *Pacific
Hwy, Oxenford; tel: (07)
5573-8485;
www.movieworld.com.au.
Open daily 0930–1730.*

Wet 'n' Wild $ *Pacific
Hwy, Oxenford; tel: (70)
5573-2255;
www.wetnwild.com.au. Open
daily 1000–1600 in winter,
to 1700 in summer and
2100 in late Dec and Jan.*

The Gold Coast's northern reaches boast a veritable fantasy-alley of theme parks. Highlights include **Dreamworld's**** stomach-churning 'Tower of Terror' roller coaster where hapless participants reach speeds of up to 160km/h in a 38-storey plunge. Centred on ten themed areas with names like Tiger Island, Gold Rush County and Ocean Parade, the park buzzes with rides and variety shows. Nearby lies the Hollywood-make-believe of **Movie World*** where roller-coaster rides like the aptly-titled 'Lethal Weapon' and a host of oversized cartoon characters vie for the attention of the park's visitors, a population averaging over a million per year. Immediately next door lurk the cooling thrills of **Wet 'n' Wild's**** adrenalin-soaked water slides.

Suggested tour

Total distance: Brisbane to Burleigh Heads is 120km. Binna Burra and Mt Tamborine are between 90 and 150km further, depending on chosen roads.

Time: Brisbane to Burleigh Heads is 3 hours. The total journey takes 6 hours.

Links: This route is an excellent link to the Byron Bay region via the Murwillumbah Rd south of Natural Arch (*see page 84*). Mt Tamborine is also well connected to Brisbane via Oxenford and the new Southeast Freeway. North of Brisbane connect with the Sunshine coast and hinterland drive (*see page 162*).

Route: Drive south from Brisbane along the Pacific Highway. About 20km south of **Beenleigh** you will reach the **THEME PARKS** area. Just after Movieworld, the highway forks. The left road becomes the Gold Coast Highway leading to **SOUTHPORT ❶**, with its highlights of Broadwater and **Broadwater Spit**, **Seaworld** and **Main Beach**. Just a few kilometres further on, you will reach the high-rise apartments, restaurants and night life of **SURFER'S PARADISE ❷**.

From Surfer's Paradise, head south along the Gold Coast Hwy for about 3km, before passing under the monorail linking **BROADBEACH ❸** to **Jupiters Casino**. Continue along the Highway for another 6.5km, passing several excellent beaches until you reach the craggy buttress of **BURLEIGH HEADS ❹**. Turn right on to Reedy Ck Rd (Burleigh-Connecting Rd) and to Mudgeeraba via the Pacific Highway (10km).

Back on the Mudgeeraba freeway, take the exit on to Springbrook Rd. For the next 25km the road leaves the coastal suburbia and climbs on to **SPRINGBROOK PLATEAU** ❺ via a delightful winding drive through steep eucalyptus forests. Several of Springbrook's attractions lie on a ring road that circles the plateau near the town of **Springbrook**, passing **Purlingbrook Falls**, the **Hardy's Lookout**, and **Best of All Lookout** and several superb picnic grounds.

From Springbrook backtrack towards the coast for 5km, and turn left on to Pine Creek Rd and a steep drop into **Numinbah Valley**. Turn left at the Nerang-Murwillumbah T-junction and travel for 12km towards **NATURAL BRIDGE** ❻. Return to the Gold Coast and Surfer's Paradise via Nerang, a 57-km leg.

The wonders of **LAMINGTON NATIONAL PARK** can be accessed in two main ways. Either take the **Beechmont Rd** from **Advancetown** (on the road to Nerang) for a delightful 33-km (one-way) drive through dense forests passing several excellent lookouts, and a hang-gliding ramp leading to **BINNA BURRA** ❼. Or travel to **Canungra** instead and enjoy the lush 36-km drive up Lamington National Park Rd leading to the **GREEN MOUNTAINS,** part of the National Park and the famous O'Reilly's guesthouse. On the way back to Brisbane or the Gold Coast, visit **MT TAMBORINE** ❽ from Canungra up Mt Tamborine Rd (14km), returning to the Gold Coast via the Tamborine-Nerang Rd, a 55-km homeward journey.

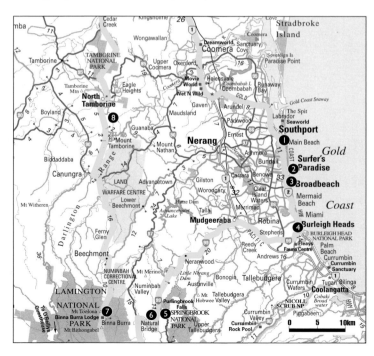

The Sunshine Coast

Ratings

Beaches	●●●●●
National parks	●●●●●
Surfing	●●●●●
Walking	●●●●●
Wildlife	●●●●●
Children's activities	●●●●○
Festivals and markets	●●●●○
Food	●●●●○

As well as a wonderful climate, the Sunshine Coast is blessed with beautiful beaches, coastline, national parks and hinterland hills. Tourism is well developed in the area, and tours usually involve outdoor activities such as boating, fishing, horse riding, walking or visiting some of the region's extensive national parks. The elegant resort town of Noosa Heads is one of Australia's top holiday destinations, combining beaches, surf, sea views and sandy national park walking tracks with sophisticated restaurants, smart boutiques and chic cafés and bars. But there is much more to do in the Sunshine Coast region: visit Fraser Island, the largest sand island in the world, take a boat trip up to the floating grass islands and inky black waters of the Noosa Everglades, go on golf excursions to world-class resorts, and discover goldrush and colonial history at Gympie and Maryborough.

BLACKALL RANGE RIDGE ROAD AND THE HINTERLAND❖❖

ⓘ Tourism Sunshine Coast
tel: (07) 5443-6400; www.sunshinecoast.org

Tourism Queensland Information
tel: 13-1801; www. queensland-holidays.com.au

The hills and ranges behind the Sunshine Coast are full of quaint villages, colourful markets, art galleries, tea houses, gourmet B&Bs and lovely gardens. And there are hinterland national parks with short walks through lush rainforest to scenic lookouts and cascading waterfalls. The **Blackall Range Ridge** road passes through the pretty mountain villages of Mapleton, Flaxton, Montville and Maleny, and gives magnificent views south to the Glass House Mountains, east to the golden beaches, and west to the lush Mary Valley and Conondale Mountains.

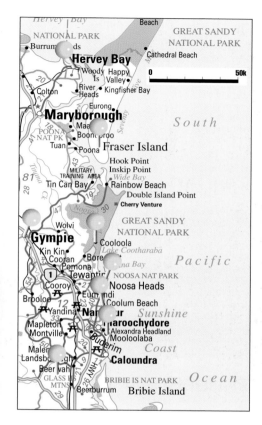

Below
The Noosa River

COOLOOLA AND THE NOOSA EVERGLADES✢✢

ⓘ **National Park**
Queensland National Parks and Wildlife Service;
tel: (07) 5449-7364.

Ⓝ **Everglades Water Bus Company $$**
Noosa; tel: (07) 5447-1838.
Boats leave from the Noosa Sheraton pier and Tewantin marina at least twice daily.

North of Noosa, the **Cooloola National Park✢** – the Cooloola section of the Great Sandy National Park – is the wild bush region set around the beautiful Noosa River system, Lake Cootharaba, Lake Cooribah and the sand dunes and coloured cliffs of the Teewah coastline. The magnificent 56,000-hectare park between Noosa and Rainbow Beach is the largest tract of natural coast and bush on Queensland's southern coast, virtually untouched by development. It includes the long golden-sand 40-Mile Beach, the vast sand mountain of the Cooloola Sandpatch, the rusty red and yellow cliffs of the Teewah Coloured Sands, patches of verdant rainforest, the catchment of the Noosa River and the inky waters and mirror-like reflections of the floating-grass **Noosa Everglades**. The Everglades, where the tributaries meander across the plains towards the oceans, are an extensive part of the

The Jetty Restaurant $$
Boreen Point; tel: (07) 5485-3167. On the edge of Lake Cootharaba, ebullient owner Edi Brunetti serves long and elegant set five-course lunches. Return home to Noosa by romantic boat.

Noosa River system. Its waters are dark reddy-black, as a result of tannins from the paperbarks and bloodwood trees and the reflections of huge sprawling swamp box and bloodwood, creepers, ferns and birdlife are magnificent. Much of the saw-tooth sedge grass on the edge of the rivers is not attached to the banks, but grows in floating clumps, more common in the famous Florida Everglades. It is possible to hire a canoe or small boat from Boreen Point or Elanda Point and paddle gently upstream to Harry's Hut, an old logging camp, for a swim, fish and lunch. Coastal Cooloola, with its dunes and coloured sands, can also be explored from **Teewah Beach**.

COOLUM❖

Hyatt Regency Coolum $$$ *Mt Coolum; tel: (07) 5446-1234. World-class resort with a focus on health, sporting and family interests. Relaxed bush setting, central food Village Square with bars and restaurants, 9 swimming pools, an 18-hole golf course and own surf beach.*

The solid bulk of monolithic Mt Coolum rises above the coast like a guarding beast, and has been special to Aboriginal tribes for thousands of years. Its name is derived from the Aboriginal word *gulum*, meaning without a head, since the rock top is blunt. The steep rock can be climbed for magnificent views of the Sunshine Coast from Noosa to Caloundra, the Maroochy River and surrounding canefields, and in spring the wildflowers are lovely. At the foot of the rock nestled in the bush, is the peaceful, health-oriented **Hyatt Regency Coolum** resort, its championship 18-hole golf course one of the best in Australia. Member of other Australian or overseas golf clubs can play ($$$) on Thursdays (resort guests every day).

FRASER ISLAND❖❖❖

Fraser Island-Great Sandy National Park *National Parks and Wildlife Service, Rainbow Beach park headquarters, Rainbow Beach Rd; tel: (07) 5486-3160, for permits.*

Fraser Island NPWS *Eurong, Fraser Island; tel: (07) 4127-9128.*

Department of Environment head office *160 Ann St, Brisbane; tel: (07) 3227-8185.*

Alongside Uluru, Kakadu and the Great Barrier Reef, World Heritage-listed Fraser Island is one of Australia's most remarkable and beautiful natural sites; indeed, it is one of the great natural wonders of the world. Over 120km long, and with an area of 163,000 hectares, it is the largest sand island in the world and contains half the world's perched freshwater dune lakes, all now protected as the Great Sandy National Park. Fraser Island has long white beaches, dramatic coloured sand cliffs, natural sand blows, crystal clear white-sand freshwater lakes and stands of tall rainforest satinay giants.

A trip to Fraser Island should include visits to **Pile Valley** and its massive 1000-year-old satinay trees – the only place in the world where rainforest trees grown on sand dunes – and the lovely little fern and palm-studded **Wanggoolba Creek** with its boardwalk at Central Station. The island's main campsite is based at dazzling **Lake McKenzie**, one of the beautiful freshwater mirror lakes with white sand fringes, paperbark trees and clear water that is lovely for swimming. **Lake Wabby** on the island's east coast is a tea-coloured perched lake, gradually being filled by an advancing giant sandblow.

Fraser Island Adventure Tours *Noosa Heads; tel: (07) 5444-6957;* **Fraser Island Excursions** *Noosa Heads; tel: (07) 5474-8622;* **Fraser Island Suncoast Safaris** *Noosa Heads; tel: (07) 5474-0800;* **Fraser Island 4x4 Getaway Tours** *Tewantin; tel: (07) 5474-0777;* **Trailblazer Tours** *Noosaville; tel: (07) 5474-1235;* **Inskip Point to Hook Point ferry/barge** *tel: (07) 5486-3154;* **Mary River Heads to Kingfisher Bay resort ferry/barge** *tel: (07) 4125-5511;* **Urangan to Moon Point ferry/barge** *tel: (07) 4125-3325.*

Driving on the east coast **75-Mile Beach** is great fun, and clear **Eli Creek** with its pandanus trees is a popular picnic and swimming spot. Fishing off 75-Mile Beach is great, but not swimming as currents are dangerous and there are many sharks. Stop and admire the coloured sand cliffs at The Cathedrals, the wreck of the old ocean liner **Maheno**, and **Indian Head**, the rocky bluff named by Captain Cook when he saw it lined with 'indians' (Aborigines) watching the *Endeavour* sail past in 1770. Beyond Indian Head are the wave-splashed **Champagne Pools** for exhilarating low-tide swimming and, beyond the little settlement of **Orchid Beach**, the wild, rarely visited northern reaches of the park.

Accommodation and food on Fraser Island

Kingfisher Bay Resort $$ *Fraser Island; tel: (07) 4120-3333 or 1800-072-555.* Upmarket resort on Fraser Island with a friendly, ecotourist thrust. Excellent value accommodation, including boat transport to Hervey Bay, free breakfasts and lunches, and free day tours of Fraser Island with trained ranger-guides.

Above
Fraser Island

GLASS HOUSE MOUNTAINS✤✤

ⓘ Glass House Mountains National Park *tel: (07) 5494-6630.*

The Glass House Mountains were named by Captain James Cook as he sailed past on the fine morning of 18 May 1770, on account of their domed, conical structure, which he thought resembled glass kilns and foundries. Rising out of the flat plains to heights of 556m, these 13 old

Above
Glass House Mountains

Moby Vic's
Roadhouse *Bruce
Highway; tel: (07) 5496-9666 for tour buses.*

volcanic plugs are an extraordinary sight and hold great Aboriginal Dreamtime significance. Best viewing points for the Glass House Mountains are from Mary Cairncross Park near Maleny or from the spectacular glass **Wild Horse Lookout** off the Bruce Highway, with free bush shuttle trips every hour from Moby Vic's Mobil service station on the highway for those without their own transport.

GYMPIE*

**i Cooloola and
Gympie
Information Centre**
Bruce Highway; tel: (07) 5482-5444.

**Gympie Historical
Museum $ 2/5**
*Brisbane Rd, Gympie; tel:
(07) 5482-3995. Open: daily
0900–1630.*

Gympie is the major centre in this region on the Bruce Highway, servicing the surrounding rural district and with a history as a rich gold rush town from the 1860s. It has an excellent **Historical Museum**＊ and a good tourist office which issues permits for Fraser Island and Cooloola National Park. Also worth exploring near Gympie is the **Mary Valley Scenic Way**, and **Cedar Grove State Park** with its red cedar trees and lovely swimming holes. During the last weekend in August, thousands of campers descend on the **Amamoor Creek State Forest Park** for the **National Country Music Muster**, better known as the Gympie Muster, and famous for its great country music concerts under the stars, set among the gum trees, bush and mountains.

HERVEY BAY⬦

ⓘ **Fraser Coast-South Burnett Regional Tourism Office** *388–96 Kent St, Maryborough; tel: (07) 4122-3444 or 1800- 444-155.*

Hervey Bay Central Booking Office *363 Charlton Esplanade; tel: (07) 4124-1300. Whale-watching enquiries and bookings.*

There is officially no such town as Hervey Bay, but the collection of seaside villages such as Urangan, Pialba, Boat Harbour and Torquay clustered around the shores of Hervey Bay, have now grown together to be given their combined name and reputation as one of Australia's favourite holiday spots. The fishing is good and there's a relaxed, sunny atmosphere in Hervey Bay, but its main claim to fame is as the humpback whale-watching capital of Australia. Between August and early November, giant humpback whales move down the inner east coast of Australia to feed on the abundant fish and krill in Antarctic waters. Sheltered Platypus Bay provides a large, safe area for these humpback giants to regroup and regain their strength for a few days before continuing their 12,000-km journey south. Groups of young males arrive early in the season, and play in the bay, while many mothers with calves can be seen in this large bay during September and October. The best time to watch whales is in the early morning; most operators leave from the Urangan pier and boat harbour from 0700 to 0800.

MOOLOOLOBA⬦⬦

ⓜ **Underwater World $$** *The Wharf; tel: (07) 5444-2255.*

Just south of Maroochydore is the much more attractive beachside town of Mooloolaba, and the famous surf beach at **Alexandra Headland**. It has a good beachfront strip of upmarket cafés and restaurants, and is popular with yachties. The large marina and harbour up the mouth of the Mooloolah River, come alive each March with the finish of the Sydney to Mooloolaba yacht race. But Mooloolaba is best known as the home of one of the Sunshine Coast's star tourist attractions, the award-winning **Underwater World**⬦, Australia's largest tropical oceanarium and an excellent mix of education and family fun. In a fascinating two- or three-hour visit, you can hear wildlife experts give talks on crocodiles and sharks, see baby stingrays, turtles and sharks growing up, and touch all sorts of strange anemones, starfish and sea slugs in a colourful touch-tank.

NOOSA HEADS⬦⬦⬦

ⓘ **Noosa Information Centre** *Hastings St roundabout; tel: (07) 5447-4988; www.tourismnoosa.com.au*

Noosa National Park *tel: (07) 5447-3243.*

Noosa Heads is one of Australia's premier holiday resorts. It is a bustling little village gloriously positioned between the main surf beach, a lagoon and the Noosa River mouth, with a bush headland of small coves, koalas and sandy paths preserved as Noosa National Park. Developers have not yet spoilt this beach paradise, although up the hill away from Noosa Heads and its café strip along **Hastings St**, the sprawl of other suburbs known as Noosaville, Noosa Sounds, and Noosa Junction continues unabated. But Noosa Heads still manages to

Festival of Surfing
Mar; Hot and Spicy Food Festival *June.*

Free Accommodation Services

Accommodation Noosa, *tel: (07)* 5447-3444; Holiday Noosa, *tel: (07)* 5447-4011; Noosa Holidays, *tel:* 1800-629-949; Noosa Destinations, *tel: (07)* 5449-2999; Noosa Visitors' Centre, *tel: (07)* 5447-4222; Noosa Getaways, *tel: (07)* 5447-5355; Noosa Resort Management, *tel:* 1800-066-672.

Below
Granite Bay, Noosa National Park

combine the hedonism of good coffee, good food and good conversation, with a lie or swim on the surf beach, and an active, outdoor lifestyle. Visitors can wander the bush tracks of the Noosa National Park, fish, play golf, ride a horse by Lake Weyba or take a boat trip up through the still Noosa Everglades (*see page 163*). Most of all Noosa is regarded as the culinary capital of the Sunshine Coast and of Queensland. It has an extraordinary number of top-quality restaurants, bistros, bars and cafés that are always changing and trying new and exciting dishes, flavours and styles. Fortunately, top-quality food doesn't mean stiff, formal and expensive dining; this is innovative food to be enjoyed in casually elegant outdoor surroundings, with a mix of informality and fun. And yet just down the road from sophisticated Hastings St, a world away from the bustle and café lattes, is the unspoilt headland of **Noosa National Park***. A coastal walk from the car park to the plunging Hells Gate coastal gorge is a gentle and popular 2.7-km stroll past pretty and private Tea-Tree Bay; walk back via the broad sweep of Alexandria Bay (a nudist beach with good surf), and the quiet bush beauty of the Tanglewood Track (4.2km). Since it is only a small national park of 432 hectares, there are no roads and camping is not allowed. Watch out for koalas, goannas, rosellas and bush turkeys.

Accommodation and food in Noosa Heads

Berado's Restaurant and Bar $$ *Hastings St; tel: (07) 5447-5666.* Top end restaurant in a French Riviera style, serving fresh regional produce in high style.

Filligan's $$ *Munna Point; tel: (07) 5449-8811.* Casual restaurant in the old wooden general store, which serves Carabin food and is always bursting with fun and laughter. Open late.

Halse Lodge $ *tel: (07) 5447-3377.* Great classy budget accommodation in lovely old Queenslander house, right in the heart of Noosa Heads.

Ricky Ricardo's $$ *Noosa Wharf; tel: (07) 5447-2455.* A casual bar and light bistro on the edge of the Noosa Sound, perfect for sunset, wine and tapas.

Saltwater $$$ *Hastings St; tel: (07) 5447-2234.* Best seafood at Noosa Heads.

Seahaven Resort $$ *tel: (07) 5447-3422.* Self-contained luxury apartments on the beachfront at Noosa Heads.

The Sebel Resort $$ *32 Hastings St; tel: (07) 5474-6400.* One of the newest kids on the block, boutique self-contained apartments in stylish surrounds.

Sheraton Hotel Resort $$$ *tel: (07) 5449-4888.* Expensive five-star hotel accommodation in the heart of Noosa Heads; massive pool and excellent Hastings St restaurant and bar, Cato's.

Soleil $$ *Sunshine Beach; tel: (07) 5474-5533.* Marriage of seafood, duck and lamb with African-Asian flavours, all reasonably priced although the wine list is expensive.

Suggested tour

Total distance: 350km, mostly sealed road, but some long driving on beach sand for four-wheel-drive vehicles only.

Time: This is a lovely two- to three-day trip, but could take longer with stops and detours, especially if you decide to spend a couple of days at Noosa Heads or on Fraser Island.

Links: The route can start or end in Brisbane, just 100km south of the Glass House Mountains. Through Brisbane, it will link up with the Gold Coast and Scenic Rim tour (*see page 152*).

Route: Starting at the gateway to the Sunshine Coast holiday city of **Caloundra ❶**, head north along the Kawana Waters coastal road towards **MOOLOOLABA ❷**, just over 12km away, with its terrific Underwater World, yachting harbour and surf beaches. Stick to the

No one holidaying on the Sunshine Coast can miss going to the New Age weatherboard village of **Eumundi**, in the hills behind Noosa, for its thriving Saturday morning (and Wednesday) market. This is not just another market; for clothing, woodwork, knick-knacks, candles, crystals and food it's really good value and good quality and there's a great atmosphere too. Try the cooked breakfasts on the veranda at the Imperial Hotel on Saturdays, and taste the local Eumundi lager. Parking can be a problem, but buses leave regularly from Noosa Heads every Saturday morning from 0630.

coastal road, passing the Alexandra Headland surf beach, for another 10km to **Maroochydore** ❸ . Next, drive on to the Sunshine Motorway to cross the Maroochy River bridge, but turn right at the first exit, and head back along the coast past the airport to **COOLUM** ❹ just another 10km away. Still on the coastal road, drive towards Peregian Beach and the delights of lovely **NOOSA HEADS** ❺ , a total distance of 56km from Caloundra. While in Noosa, don't forget to take a boat trip up the Noosa River and through its shallow lake system to explore **COOLOOLA** and the **NOOSA EVERGLADES** ❻ .

After enjoying the sophistication and scenery of Noosa Heads, the adventure section of this drive starts. Hire a 4WD vehicle (or take an organised Fraser Island tour), drive a short distance down the Noosa River to Tewantin and take the ferry across to Noosa North shore. Once across, head for the long sand strip of **40-Mile Beach, Teewah Beach** and **Cooloola Coloured Sands**. Make sure you are within three hours on either side of low tide before driving the 50-km length of this superb beach to the small town of **Rainbow Beach**, and the Inskip Point vehicle ferry barge just beyond. Cross over to **FRASER ISLAND** ❼ and explore its lakes, beaches, forests and World Heritage National Park (4WD vehicles only). After a day or two, take another ferry from **Kingfisher Bay** resort on the west side of Fraser Island across to **HERVEY BAY** ❽ , the whale-watching capital of the world.

From Hervey Bay, there is a good sealed road for 33km to the elegant city of **Maryborough** ❾ , and then another 85km down the main Bruce Highway to **GYMPIE** ❿ . About 50km south from Gympie, turn left to the small towns of **Cooran** and **Pomona**. Visit the old silent movie house, then head another 10km south on the same back road towards the little New Age market town of **Eumundi** ⓫ . It is then less than 20km down the Bruce Highway to **Yandina** with its ginger factory, and the Big Pineapple at **Nambour**. At Nambour, turn right towards Mapleton and the **BLACKALL RANGE RIDGE ROAD** and the **HINTERLAND**, stopping at spectacular Dulong Lookout on the way up the escarpment from Nambour. It is about 56km along the ridge road with its walks, waterfalls and little villages, before reaching Maleny. View the **GLASS HOUSE MOUNTAINS** ⓬ from **Mary Cairncross Scenic Reserve**, before descending to **Landsborough**. From here, the Glass House Tourist Route heads south to the little town of Glass House Mountains, with side roads giving access to the strange, curious peaks of Mt Ngungun, Mt Beerwah, Mt Tibrogargan and the main lookout in their midst. After **Beerburrum**, rejoin the Bruce Highway, and head back to Brisbane.

Also worth exploring

At the far north end of Hervey Bay, about 100km from the Urangan boat harbour whale-watching centre, is the **Mon Repos** beach near the city of **Bundaberg**. This is the site of Australia's most accessible mainland giant turtle rookery. Four types of turtle – loggerhead, green, leatherback and flatback – lay their eggs in shallow sand nests here from November to January, although loggerheads predominate. From mid-January to March, the young tiny turtles break through their buried eggs and find their way to the surface of the sand in a relentless and often doomed march to the sea.

To watch the eggs being laid and the young turtles hatching are both extraordinary spectacles. Visitors can observe under the careful control of National Park and Wildlife Service rangers. Most egg-laying occurs around midnight, and the eggs usually hatch during the evening too. **The Mon Repos Turtle Information Centre** (*tel: 07 4159-2628*) is open every night from 1900 until 0600 between November and March; there are informative displays about the turtles, and lit boardwalk access to the beach.

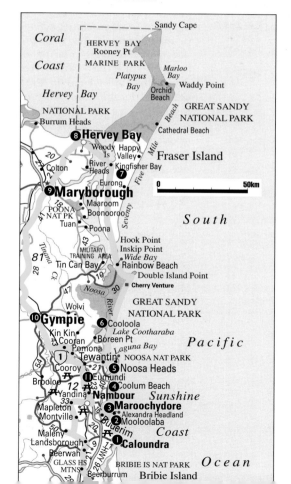

Cairns and beyond

Ratings

Beaches	●●●●●
Coral	●●●●●
National parks	●●●●●
Rainforest	●●●●●
Scenery	●●●●●
Aboriginal culture	●●●●○
Children's activities	●●●●○

Tropical North Queensland 'where the rainforest meets the reef', as the tourist slogan goes, is the coastal strip stretching from relaxed Mission Beach in the south to frontier Cooktown in the north. Home to two of Australia's greatest World Heritage treasures – the Great Barrier Reef and the Wet Tropics Rainforests – the region is one of Australia's premier tourist destinations. Far North Queensland – or 'FNQ' as the locals like to refer to it – combines wilderness and sophistication, offering a range of experiences unrivalled anywhere in the country. One day you may be snorkelling the colourful coral of the Outer Reef, the next day you can be spotting crocodiles and exploring the rainforest wilderness around Cape Tribulation, or learning about Aboriginal culture, or you might be playing golf, lying on the golden beach and sipping cocktails at the laid-back yet sophisticated fishing village of Port Douglas.

ATHERTON TABLELANDS❖❖❖

ⓘ Atherton Tablelands Tourism *Yungaburra;* tel: *(07) 4095-2111.*

Malanda Environmental Centre *Atherton-Malanda Rd, Malanda; tel: (07) 4096-6646.*

One of the most poplar day tours from Cairns is a trip or a circuit-drive up to the cool of the Atherton Tablelands, especially at times of the year when it is hot and muggy on the coast. The tablelands are a fertile and rich farming area above the rainforest escarpment where blue volcanic lakes, waterfalls and quaint little villages blend with a patchwork of coffee, sugar cane, ti-tree, mango and lychee farms. The tablelands can be reached from Kuranda and Mareeba to the north, or via Gordonvale, just south of Cairns. The village of **Tolga** has an excellent wood-carving gallery, while **Atherton** has its thrice-weekly historic steam trains, antique shops, restored Chinese joss house and underground Crystal Caves museum. The picturesque little village of **Yungaburra** is perfect for afternoon tea. There is year-round barramundi fishing in **Lake Tinaroo**, whereas volcanic **Lake Barrine** offers wildlife cruises and popular Devonshire teas. The town of **Malanda** is a dairy-farming centre with its own cheese factory and an excellent rainforest Environment Centre.

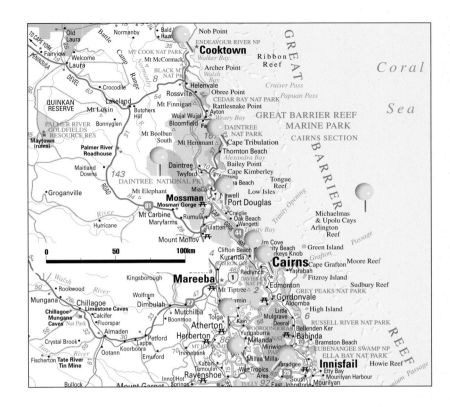

CAIRNS❖❖

Tropical North Queensland Visitor Information Centre
51 The Esplanade, Cairns;
tel: (07) 4051-3588;
www.tnq.org.au

Queensland Tourism Information Line
tel: 13-1801; www.
queensland-holidays.com.au

Queensland National Parks and Wildlife Service Information Centre McLeod St, Cairns;
tel: (07) 4052-3096.

Cairns is a picturesque, modern, thriving and fun city, built around Trinity Bay with a magnificent backdrop of hills and tropical rainforest. To get into the relaxed feel of Cairns, walk along **The Esplanade** path by the mangrove mudflats of the Bay early in the morning or at dusk. This is where everyone in Cairns meets, where the wader birds feed and backpackers sunbake on the grass under the palms. Then explore the Esplanade's shops, restaurants and night markets, the hub of Cairn's activity. The Pier complex on the edge of the wharf hums with life in its 200 shops, hotels, restaurants and famous 'mud markets'. Don't miss the excellent **Regional Art Gallery** in the centre of town and, for more alternative entertainment, try **The Tank**, an avant-garde performing arts centre in the converted World War II oil storage tanks. Nearby, the lovely century-old **Flecker Botanical Gardens** are good for a picnic beside the lily-covered lakes. Grafton St has some of the best cafés and restaurants in town, while The Esplanade has the tourist restaurants, backpacker joints and tour operator centres. After dark, there's the **Reef Casino** to investigate if you are feeling flash and fast, while **Johno's Blues Bar** is rated – along with the reef and rainforest – as one of three places that must be visited while in town.

One thing Cairns lacks – as well as many of its lovely old buildings, which were demolished in the 1970s in the name of progress – is its own beach by the Esplanade, but its golden northern beaches in the suburbs of Palm Cove, Trinity Beach, Machans and Holloways more than make up for that absence.

Accommodation and food in Cairns

Acacia Court Hotel $$ *223–227 The Esplanade, Cairns; tel: (07) 4051-5011*. Medium-price range hotel/motel-style rooms in quiet 10-storey building, fronting the lovely Cairns Esplanade and overlooking the sea. Famous for its nightly seafood buffets at Charlies $ restaurant, that no budget traveller to Cairns ever misses.

Affordable Cairns Bed & Breakfast $$ *396 Draper Street, Cairns; tel: (07) 4051-735; fax: (07) 4051-7352; email: Jennysbb@internetnorth. com.au; www.carinsconnect.com/affordablebandb*. Stay in a charming old Queenslander home, in Cairns' attractive quiet leafy central suburbs, with valley and mountain views. About 15-minutes walk to the city centre, ideal if you have your own car.

Cairns International Hotel $$$ *17 Abbott Street, Cairns; tel: (07) 4031-1300; email: cairnsinthotel@internetnorth.com.au; www.cairns international.com.au*. The Cairns International combines colonial architecture with modern five-star luxury in the centre of Cairns.

Perrotta's $$ *Cairns Regional Art Gallery; tel: (07) 4031-5899*. The trendy spot to be seen for an outdoor drink.

Pesci's on the Water $$ *Marun Marina, The Pier Market Place, Cairns; tel: (07) 4041-1133*. Great seafood dining, with views to match.

Red Ochre Grill $$ *Shield St; tel: (07) 4051-0100*. Awards for its modern Australian food with bush tucker touches.

Sebel Reef House $$$ *99 Williams Esplanade, Palm Cove; tel: (07) 4055-3633; email: info@reefhouse.com.au; www.reefhouse.com.au*. The most luxurious and elegant place to stay at the lovely village of Palm Cove, on Cairns' northern beaches, fronting the beach and surrounded by tall, old paperbark trees. It offers the height of luxury in a cool, relaxed outdoor setting, serving the élite rather than a mass market.

YHA Queensland $ *20/24 McLeod Street, Cairns; tel: (07) 4051-0772; email: cnsyha@yhaqld.org.au; www.yha.org.au*. Youth Hostels of Australia operates two backpacker/budget hostels in Cairns – at McLeod Street and another at 93 The Esplanade. Both are central Cairns' locations, good value and slightly more upmarket than normal backpacker establishments, catering for families and older budget travellers as well.

CAPE TRIBULATION***

Crocodiles and other dangers

Dangerous estuarine or salt-water crocodiles inhabit many river and creek estuaries in the Far North. While crocodiles will not suddenly appear in deep swimming water on a beach or out at sea, care should be taken when walking along mangrove fringed beaches or across creek mouths, especially in more remote areas. Also watch out for coral cuts which can fester. When walking in water near rocks or coral, it is advisable to wear sand-shoes as deadly stonefish can lie hidden in shallow waters. Sea-wasps or 'stingers' with savage, occasionally fatal, stings prevent swimming in the warm seas from November to April, except on offshore islands or on beaches with special 'stinger' nets.

Cape Tribulation, a world-famous name with a reputation for virgin, untouched rainforest, and deserted magical white sand beaches, is in fact a small part of Daintree National Park: it is a beautiful headland with a sweeping curved beach at the end of a sealed road. But it remains a favourite spot for anyone who has been there, with the exception perhaps of Captain James Cook, who named it after holing his ship the *Endeavour* on a nearby coral reef when charting the east coast of Australia in 1770. Just as lovely are the nearby **Cow Bay**, **Noah Beach** and **Thorntons**, while the 800-m Marrdja boardwalk between Oliver Creek and Noah Beach gives a good understanding of the botany of rainforest trees and neighbouring mangroves. At Cape 'Trib' – as it is always known – walk along the boardwalk from the car park out to the headland across the white sand beach, to appreciate the beauty of this unique part of the world where the rainforest really does meet the edge of the sea.

Accommodation and food in Cape Tribulation

Coconut Beach Rainforest Resort $$$ *tel: (07) 4098-0033.* Timber private rainforest villas, white sand beach and seclusion.

Crocodylus Lodge $ *Cow Bay; tel: (07) 4098-9166.* Generations of teenagers have slept in their budget bunks, ridden horses along the beach and swum naked in the lapping seas.

PK's Jungle Village $ *tel: (07) 4098-0040.* Popular backpacker village.

COOKTOWN**

ⓘ James Cook Historical Museum
$ *Helen St, Cooktown; tel: (07) 4069 5386. Open daily Apr–Dec 0930–1600, Jan–Mar check in advance by tel as opening hours vary.*

Cooktown is a frontier town in a wonderful location at the foot of Cape York. Soaked in the history of Captain Cook, the gold rush and the pioneers, it lies on the banks of the Endeavour River where the explorer and his crew spent nearly two months camping in 1770, repairing the *Endeavour* after it had been holed on a coral reef. A sense of this early history still lurks. Visit **Grassy Hill** lookout with its sweeping views; Cook continually climbed this hill searching for a path through the maze of coral reefs. The lovely old-verandahed **James Cook Historical Museum*** is worth visiting for its Cook treasures, diaries, brilliant charts and discarded cannons. The Palmer River gold fields are about 100km inland from Cooktown, and are the

Sovereign Resort Hotel $$ *Charlotte St, Cooktown; tel: (07) 4069-5400.* Small-scale resort offering tourist comforts with Cape York hospitality.

reason the town was established as a port. The town's history is reflected in the little cemetery filled with the graves of so many pioneer babies, Chinese from the Palmer River gold-rush days, and shipwreck victims. Just out of town, **Black Mountain National Park**⁺ appears to be made of jet black rock; in fact it is a heap of giant granite boulders coated with a black algae-lichen – now home to the rare Godman's rock-wallaby.

DAINTREE RIVER AND CAPE TRIBULATION NATIONAL PARK❖❖❖

Daintree Rainforest Environmental Centre $$ *Tulip Oak Rd, Cow Bay; tel: (07) 4098-9171. Open daily 0830–1700.*

Between the Daintree and Bloomfield rivers, the forest slopes of Cape Tribulation National Park plunge to the waters of the Great Barrier Reef Marine Park. The lowland rainforest here is a rare survivor of 100 million years of climatic changes. For most travellers a crocodile-spotting cruise on the Daintree River, is a highly enjoyable way to relax and spend an hour or two on the sunny river. Crocodiles are usually seen, especially at low tide when the sand banks are exposed and during the winter months when they leave the cold river to sunbake on its banks. But the best cruises are much more than just croc-excursions; the top local boat guides are also highly knowledgeable about mangrove and rainforest ecology, as well as being expert birdwatchers. Daintree River cruises start from three places – at the punt crossing, upstream at the Daintree River Cruise Centre, and further upstream at the little village of Daintree itself. From the ferry crossing, the coastal road continues north across Mt Alexandra pass, where a lookout gives great views across the rainforest to the mouth of the Daintree River and the Low Isles beyond. Just after the pass is the excellent, privately run **Daintree Rainforest Environmental Centre**⁺, where an attractive educational facility has been built in the thick lowland rainforest, complete with a tree-top viewing tower, guided boardwalks, rainforest ecology talks and extensive films and display boards on the forest's flora and fauna.

THE GREAT BARRIER REEF❖❖❖

Quicksilver $$$ *Port Douglas Marina; tel: (07) 4099-5500.* **Friendship Cruises $$** *Clump Point jetty, Mission Beach; tel: (07) 4068-7262.* **Quick Cat $$$** *Mission Beach and Dunk Island; tel: (07) 4068-7289.*

Every visitor to Far North Queensland must take a boat trip to snorkel – or at least see from the dryness of a glass-bottom boat – the magnificent corals and bright tropical fish of the Great Barrier Reef. And to fully appreciate this marvellous World Heritage feature of the far north, make sure you allow enough time for a full day trip so that the most spectacular Outer Reef can be reached, rather than simply the closer coastal islands and reefs where the coral can be disappointing. The best Outer Reef expeditions leave, not from Cairns, but from **Mission Beach** and **Port Douglas**.

Above
Snorkelling in the Great Barrier
Reef

Scotty's on the Beach $ *167 Reid Rd, Mission Beach; tel: (07) 4068-8676.* Legendary backpacker lodge with a great bar and beachfront location.

From Port Douglas the two large **Quicksilver** catamarans (each carrying more than 200 people) cruise to their own pontoon and reef observatory on pristine Agincourt ribbon reef on the Outer Edge. These day trips are not cheap, but the snorkelling is unrivalled and the facilities on the large floating reef pontoon are ideal also for those who prefer to view the coral from the safety of a semi-submersible glass-bottomed boat. Much more low key, but a tremendous family-day experience, are the **Friendship Cruise** boat and **QuickCat** service which travel to the beautiful coral and sand beach of Beaver Cay. Both these trips leave from the Clump Point jetty at Mission Beach, the closest town in North Queensland to the Outer Reef.

KURANDA❖❖

Kuranda Scenic Railway $$ *Cairns Station and Kuranda Station; tel: (07) 4093-7115.*

Kuranda Skyrail $$ *Caravonica Lakes, Cooks Hwy, Smithfield; tel: (07) 4038-1555; www.skyrail.com.au*

Butterfly Sanctuary $ *8 Rob Veivers Drive, Kuranda; tel: (07) 4093-7575.*

One of the great features of any Cairns holiday is to spend a day 'doing' Kuranda, the little rainforest village in the cool hills behind the city. But the village with popular markets, a **butterfly sanctuary**✳, bird aviaries and many tourist and art shops is only part of the attraction. For most, the real thrill lies in the journey getting there and back! Since 1891, the historic Kuranda Scenic Railway has delighted passengers as it winds its way for 34km up the steep mountain slopes of the MacAlistair Range, passing through 15 tunnels and crossing several high wooden trestle bridges. From the train, which leaves Cairns twice daily, there are jaw-dropping views of the coast, the Coral Sea and the 260-m Barron Falls and Gorge (where it makes a brief stop). After spending a few hours at Kuranda (the markets are on Wed, Thur, Fri and Sun), a popular option is to return by the new Skyrail

Rainforestation $$
Kennedy Highway,
Kuranda; tel: (07) 4093-
9033.

Kuranda
Backpackers $
tel: (07) 4093-7316. Four
hectares of rainforests.

cable car. It leaves from Kuranda Station and suspends you in small gondolas above the fabulous wilderness of the World Heritage-listed rainforest national park, then plunges down the mountain to its Caravonica Lakes terminal north of Cairns. Also at Kuranda, with frequent bus shuttle services from the station, is **Rainforestation***, a popular tourist property of 40 hectares set in the midst of thick rainforest with a wildlife park, Aboriginal Dreamtime dancing, and a rainforest exploration trip aboard an amphibious Army Duck.

MILLAA MILLAA AND THE WATERFALL CIRCUIT DRIVE**

Eacham Historical
Society Museum
Main St, Millaa Millaa.
Open daily 0930–1300.

Tree House
Restaurant, Silky
Oaks Lodge *Silky Oaks*
Lodge, Finlayvale Rd,
Mossman; tel: (07) 4098-
1666. Fresh tropical foods,
barramundi and mudcrabs,
served overlooking the
river in rainforest tree-top
serenity.

On the south of the Atherton tablelands is a wonderful driving route called the **Waterfall Circuit**, which combines a journey through the Palmerston section of the World Heritage Wet Tropics forests, with seven of Queensland's most spectacular lookouts and waterfalls. They are said to include the widest, the tallest, the longest single drop and most beautiful waterfall in Australia. At **Millaa Millaa**, follow the signs on the waterfall circuit road to **Ellinjaa Falls**, **Zillie Falls** and the world-famous **Millaa Millaa Falls** with their perfect cascade dropping directly into a deep pool. Then head down the Palmerston Highway and the escarpment, through Woonoonooran National Park, taking in the view at **Crawford's Lookout** and **Mungalli Falls** overlooking a beautiful river gorge. There is also a good little pioneering museum, **Eacham Historical Society Museum***, at Millaa Millaa.

PORT DOUGLAS***

Port Douglas
Visitors' Centre
23 Macrossan St;
tel: (07) 4099-5599.

Mirage Marina
Wharf St;
tel: (07) 4099-5355.

Shipwreck
Museum *6 Dixie*
Drive; tel: (07) 4099-5885.

Rainforest Habitat
Sanctuary *Port Douglas*
Rd; tel: (07) 4099-3235.

Dazzling blue skies, long white beaches and warm perfumed air; Port Douglas is a true resort beside the sea. In spite of its popularity and sophistication, the village has kept its close-knit community character, and is a popular getaway destination for incognito superstars and even US Presidents.

The long golden beach is Port Douglas's day playground, coming to life early in the morning when the rich and famous jetset in their lycra jogging gear and Nike shoes mingle with backpackers and campers strolling along the beach in their tatty shorts and flip-flops. During the day, families and sunbakers, often topless, take over the beach. Catamarans can be hired and there is parasailing too. An old gold rush port and fishing town, Port Douglas is now a tourist enclave. Fast cruise trips with the big Quicksilver Cats to the **Outer Reef** from the **Mirage Marina** is one of the most popular activities. While in town, don't miss the fascinating **Shipwreck Museum*** with its maritime relics on the end of the old pier. At the **Rainforest Habitat*** wildlife sanctuary you can see the rare and elusive cassowary, green tree frogs, crocodiles, bright parrots, the red and black Cape York cockatoo, tree kangaroos and the ever-popular koala. A little steam train shuttle for tourists connects many of the resort hotels along the beach with the town and marina, while the bustling Sunday markets are a great place to taste tropical cane juice, or to buy some local art or a new T-shirt.

Accommodation and food in Port Douglas

Macrossan House Boutique Holiday Apartments $$ *19 Macrossan St, Port Douglas; tel: (07) 4099-4366.* Handy self-contained apartments within minutes of café and restaurant strip.

Salsa Bar and Grill $$ *38 Macrossan St; tel: (07) 4099-4922.* Trendy spot to hang out either before or during dinner.

Sheraton Mirage Resort $$$ *Davidson St; tel: (07) 4098-5885.* Tropical beach paradise mixed with luxury and relaxed elegance.

Wharf St Café $$ *Rydges Resort; tel: (07) 4099-5885.* Views over the sea, top spot for brunch or champagne at sunset.

WET TROPICS WORLD HERITAGE AREA✦✦✦

ⓘ Atherton Tablelands Tourism *Yungaburra; tel: (07) 4095-2111.*

Once regarded as the poor cousin to the turquoise blue seas and brightly coloured corals of the Great Barrier Reef, the rainforests of Far North Queensland are now justly seen as one of its dual delights and treasures. Recognised as being of major international ecological and scenic significance (especially since more than half of the world's rainforests have been destroyed), they were granted United Nations World Heritage listing in 1988. These 900,000 hectares of protected Wet Tropics rainforest and tropical vegetation of North Queensland stretch from Townsville to north of Cape Tribulation and are one of the most extraordinarily diverse and complicated ecosystems found in this driest continent on earth. Home to 50 unique rainforest animals, as well as the endangered cassowary bird, they are Australia's richest and most luxuriant forests. Historically, the rainforest has been a source of foods and medicines for the local Aboriginal people. Some of the oldest, most majestic rainforest in the region lies south of Cairns around Queensland's highest mountain, Mt Bartle Frere (1622m high), and along the Palmerston escarpment with its plunging waterfalls west of Innisfail. The Russell and Johnstone are two mighty rainforest rivers, and tucked away near Mission Beach are the magnificent cassowary and licuala palm forests. Walkers can visit the Boulders area at Babinda, and Josephine Falls on the escarpment around Millaa Millaa. More serious hikers can walk the spectacular 19-km Goldsborough rainforest track leading from the Boulders over the spine of Mt Bellenden Ker, down to the Mulgrave River.

The Great Barrier Reef

The World Heritage-listed Great Barrier Reef stretches for an astounding 2300km along the length of Queensland's east coast – from near Cape York at its tip, to Fraser Island in the south. A place of remarkable ecological variety, and extraordinary underwater beauty, the Great Barrier Reef is composed of the world's largest collection of coral reefs and is the only living organism on earth that can be seen from space. The Great Barrier Reef Marine Park in fact protects a wonderland of 2900 individual coral reefs intertwined with idyllic bush islands, white sand coral cays, and 350,000 sq km of turquoise seas.

Australia's greatest natural treasure, with its flashing fish, brightly coloured corals and palm-fringed island resorts attract 1.6 million visitors and more than $1.5 billion tourist dollars each year. Tourism to, and on, the Great Barrier Reef is well developed, with a variety of experiences available in all price brackets. There are more than 30 resort islands, from the exclusive Lizard and Bedarra island resorts, to places like magical Whitehaven Beach in the Whitsundays

(continued)

Suggested tour

Distance: About 500km; add another 150km if Cooktown is visited on the 4WD-only Bloomfield Track.

Time: This loop could be explored in two or three days, either joined together or as separate day trips from Cairns or Port Douglas.

Route: Starting from **CAIRNS ❶**, head north along the Captain Cook Highway. Turn right after about 10km to visit the famous **CAIRNS' NORTHERN BEACHES** from Machans Beach in the south, to Palm Cove in the north. About 22km from Cairns, the Kennedy Highway turns off to the left and winds up the mountain to the little rainforest village of **KURANDA**. Alternatively, continue on the Captain Cook Highway to the shopping centre of Smithfield, the Skyrail cable car departure point for Kuranda and the **Tjapukai Aboriginal Cultural Park**. Critics claim the latter is commercialised, but it provides an introduction to Aboriginal culture and features hi-tech displays explaining Tjapukai creation stories.

The Captain Cook Highway then narrows, and the remaining 50km to **PORT DOUGLAS ❷** is a delightful if slow drive around the cliffs and magnificent beaches of this golden coast. Enjoy Port Douglas for a couple of days, preferably including a **GREAT BARRIER REEF BOAT TRIP**, then rejoin the Captain Cook Highway for 14km to Mossman. Turn left here to marvel at the cool streams and valleys of **Mossman Gorge**, where blue Ulysses butterflies flit across deep rock pools filled with crystal-clear waters.

Continuing north, it is just over 40km to reach the banks of the **DAINTREE RIVER**, with its crocodile cruises, and to put the car on the river punt. Cross the river, then twist and turn into and through the gloomy lush greenness of the coastal section of **DAINTREE NATIONAL PARK**. The sealed road ends after another 20km at the beautiful white sands and headland of **CAPE TRIBULATION ❸**.

Detour: If driving a 4WD vehicle and the road is not closed due to flooding, consider exploring the wild but magical Bloomfield track past Cape Tribulation, to reach the frontier town of **COOKTOWN ❹**, just over 100km to the north, leading up towards Cape York.

Return to Mossman, take the Kennedy Rd turn-off towards **Mareeba**, climb the escarpment up on to the plateau country and pass Southedge Lake before driving through **MAREEBA ❺**. Finally, after a glorious 100-km drive, the road reaches the **ATHERTON TABLELANDS ❻** proper and the little villages of Atherton, Tolga and Yungaburra. Continue south on the Kennedy Highway to Herberton, before reaching **MILLAA MILLAA AND THE WATERFALL CIRCUIT DRIVE ❼**.

The Great Barrier Reef (continued)

where bush camping is allowed ($). Up and down the coast, hundreds of tour operators – all of whom have to operate within strict permit guidelines to preserve the reef – offer sailing, diving, cruising, snorkelling and fishing adventures out to the Reef. But, be warned, some parts of the Reef close to the coastline have recently suffered from severe coral bleaching (whitening) because of too warm sea temperatures; it pays to check in advance the condition of the reef or cay area each tour operator is visiting, before picking a day trip to snorkel the reef.

Wet and warm

Tropical North Queensland is very wet and humid between December and the end of March; one of its highest mountains, Mt Bellenden Ker, near the sugar town of Babinda, recorded Australia's highest annual rainfall of 11.2m in 1979! The best time to travel in FNQ and to enjoy its warm waters and swimming holes is between May and October.

Turn left at Millaa Millaa, heading down the rainforest of the Palmerston Highway for 90km through the spectacular Wooroonooran section of the **WET TROPICS WORLD HERITAGE AREA ❽**. At the Bruce Highway intersection, turn north and after 15km turn left to explore Josephine Falls. At **Babinda ❾** turn left to marvel at **The Boulders** – mystical rocks, pools and waterfalls – before continuing home along the Bruce Highway to Cairns.

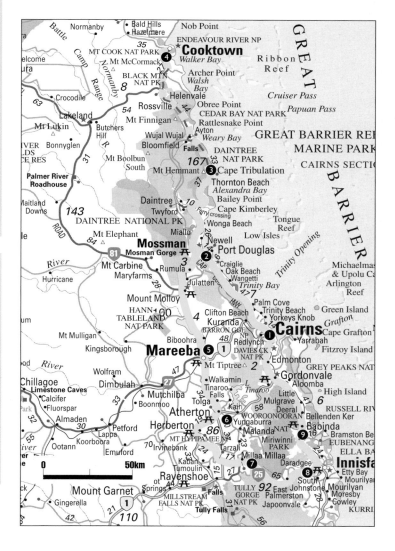

Ratings

Aboriginal history	●●●●●
Geology	●●●●●
Scenery	●●●●●
Walking	●●●●●
National parks	●●●●○
Outdoor activities	●●●●○
Wildlife	●●●○○
Shopping	●●○○○

The Red Centre

Impressive and significant as Uluru (Ayers Rock) is, the Red Centre region of Australia is so much more than just a big red rock in the middle of nowhere. Steeped in Aboriginal history, this outback region around the desert town of Alice Springs combines vast stretches of desert with dramatic rock formations such as the MacDonnell Ranges, Finke Gorge, Kings Canyon, Uluru and Kata Tjuta (The Olgas). The brilliant blue skies provide a stunning contrast to the rich red sandstone cliffs and the white trunks of the ghost gum trees dotted across the landscape. Spectacular natural waterholes at Ellery Creek Big Hole or the Garden of Eden in Kings Canyon are a welcome relief from the desert heat. It is best to avoid the extreme dry heat of mid-summer; April to September are the recommended months to explore Central Australia, although the nights can be cold.

ALICE SPRINGS❖

ⓘ Alice Springs Visitor Information Centre
60 Gregory Terrace;
tel: (08) 8952-5800;
fax: (08) 8953-0295;
www.travelnt.com. Pick up a free copy of the Parks and Wildlife Commission paper for details on guided walks and talks throughout the national parks.

ⓝ Aboriginal Art and Culture Centre $ *86 Todd St.*

With a population of 21,000 Alice Springs is a modern, bustling town that forms the heart of the Red Centre. It is the main access point by both air and road for some of Central Australia's best landscape and, as well as being a convenient shopping hub, contains some important history. The Alice, as it is affectionately known, gets part of its name from a waterhole or spring close to the site of a telegraph station 4km north on the Stuart Highway. The **Telegraph Station Historical Reserve**, which was established in 1872 to relay messages across Australia between Darwin and Adelaide, was the original site of the first European settlement in Alice Springs. The **Todd River**, a distinctive sandy strip through the town where the water flows two feet underground, was named after Charles Todd, the superintendent of telegraphs in Adelaide at the time. Alice was his wife. Buildings, house furnishings and artefacts have been restored at the Reserve and give a good insight into early settlement in the outback. The **Royal**

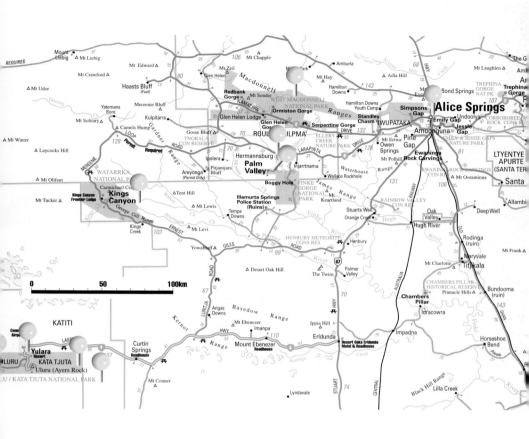

Desert Palms Resort $$ *74 Barrett Drive; tel: (08) 8952-5977; fax: (08) 8953-4176.* Air-conditioned, self-contained units, about 1km from the town centre and 300m from **Lasseters Casino**.

The Henley-on-Todd 'regatta': a riotous festival held where locals and visitors run along the dry river in bottomless 'boats'. Held each year in Sept/Oct.

Flying Doctor Service base close to the town centre, and the **School of the Air**, about 1km north of the town centre, are other attractions open to the public which remind visitors how remote Alice Springs is. Explore **Todd Mall** for shopping, including Aboriginal art and artefacts, and a market every second Sunday. For a good sense of Aboriginal history and an insight into the lives of the local Arrente people, visit the **Strehlow Research Centre** on Larapinta Drive, named after Theodor Strehlow who spent more than 40 years studying the Arrente people. The **Aboriginal Art and Culture Centre**, Aboriginal owned and operated, combines desert discovery tours, didgeridoo lessons, art exhibitions and a museum. Alice Springs is the base for a range of tours including Aboriginal bush-food, camel treks and ballooning. Remember, summer temperatures reach 45°C while winter nights are often below zero.

DESERT PARK❖❖

 Desert Park $$
Larapinta Drive, Alice Springs; tel: (08) 8951-8788; www. alicespringsdesertpark.com.au. Open daily 0730–1800; last entry 1700; allow 3 hours.

The Kata-Anga Tea Rooms double as a museum and art gallery ($) for the community. *Open 0900–1600.*

Opened in March 1997, the $20-million award-winning Park on the outskirts of Alice Springs is the first of its kind to display the plants, animals and landscapes of the Australian arid zone and their traditional use and management by Aboriginal people. It quickly debunks the widely held belief that deserts are lifeless, barren wastelands. The Park immerses visitors in a variety of cleverly blended habitats which display more than 300 hundred native plant species and more than 400 desert animals, several of them extremely rare or on the brink of extinction, and not previously cultivated or held in captivity. The Park covers 1300 hectares at the foothills of the West MacDonnell Ranges, with a core exhibit area of 50 hectares. There are 1.6km of primary and 1.4km of secondary walking paths.

HERMANNSBURG❖❖❖

Hermannsburg Art Gallery $
Hermannsburg Precinct, Hermannsburg; tel: (08) 8956-7402. By tour only, at 10 minutes past the hour, and well worth the visit.

Established by the Lutheran Church in 1877 on the traditional lands of the West Aranda people, Hermannsburg was the first Aboriginal Mission in the Northern Territory. The original church, schoolhouse and mortuary are among the restored precinct that provides employment for the local Aboriginals, including a pottery workshop where the bright, distinctive and much sought-after Hermannsburg pottery and artworks are created. Housed in the Manse, the earliest missionary residence in the area, built during the 1890s, **Hermannsburg Art Gallery❖** contains an extensive collection of watercolours of the area by famous Hermannsburg artists, including Albert Namatjira, who in 1957 was the first Aborigine to be granted Australian citizenship. The most famous white resident was Theodor Strehlow (*see page 183*) who was born here in 1908.

KATA TJUTA*

**Kurkara Tours and
Lilla Tours** *tel: (08)
8956-7442.* Aboriginal-
owned and operated tours.

This large group of domed rocks, once better known as The Olgas, is the most significant site after Uluru inside the **Uluru-Kata Tjuta National Park**. Translated to mean 'many heads', Kata Tjuta is a group of 36 extraordinary gigantic domes of a rust-red sedimentary rock appearing eerily out of nowhere and spanning 35km. The largest dome, Mt Olga, is a staggering 546m high. Much of Kata Tjuta is still used by the traditional owners for meetings and is associated with ritual information and activities which remain the exclusive knowledge of initiated men and is therefore restricted. It is because of this spiritual significance that there is very little written about the rock formations which are conglomerates of pebbles and boulders cemented by sand and mud believed to have formed about 900 million years ago. The Kata Tjuta Dune viewing area located 25km along the Kata Tjuta road inside the National Park gives a magnificent view of these extraordinary formations which geologists believe extend beneath the ground as far as 6km. The prolific tufts of spinifex grass and mulga trees, both important sources of materials to the Aborigines, stand in stark contrast to the orange rock. There are two signposted walks at Kata Tjuta. The longer 7.4-km aptly named **Valley of the Winds*** walk is the best opportunity to discover some of the spectacular landscape and capture views of the surrounding country beyond the towering domes. A few short climbs can make it hard going and for safety reasons the walk is partly closed when temperatures are forecast above 36°C. Walpa, or the **Olga Gorge Walk**, is 2.6km to the end of the gorge where spearwood vines flourish. The walks are along rocky paths and in some cases quite steep. Emergency water is available but it is recommended you carry one litre of water per hour and aim to walk during the cooler morning hours. Flies can be prolific.

KINGS CANYON*

**Kings Canyon
Resort $–$$$**
*tel: (08) 8956-7442;
fax: (08) 8956-7410;
www.kingscanyonresort.
com.au.* The closest
accommodation, 7km
away, with a choice of de
luxe suites or camping.

This dramatic red, sandstone chasm plunges 300m. On the rim of the canyon are extraordinary and seemingly endless beehive-shaped rock domes which create the **Lost City**. Don't be put off by the steep climb to the rim, accessed several hundred metres on the left from the car park. The views of the surrounding countryside, into and across the canyon and of the weathered domes are breathtaking and worth the initial climb. The walk around the canyon takes you down into an exotic oasis of palms and ferns around a permanent water hole, known as the **Garden of Eden**. Rich in fauna and flora, rock pools, sand plains and gullies, Kings Canyon has played an important role in Aboriginal life for more than 20,000 years. Allow $3^1/_2$ hours for the walk around the top, taking in spectacular views and rock formations.

Above left
Kings Canyon

KINGS CREEK STATION**

Kings Creek Station $–$$$ tel: (08) 8956-7474; fax (08) 8956-7468. Camel rides and helicopter flights over Kings Canyon.

Thirty-eight kilometres from Kings Canyon, this station is a working cattle and camel farm that offers alternative accommodation to the Kings Canyon Resort. Sleeping is in permanent canvas cabins set among ghost gums. BBQ Packs can be bought from the station to cook yourself, or they do basic meals. In the morning take your own mug into the station dining room for a solid, home-cooked breakfast with some of the station hands. Sunset and sunrise camel tours through the dunes run regularly.

PALM VALLEY*

Palm Valley and Finke Gorge National Park camping only ($); there are excellent marked walking tracks.

This oasis within the **Finke Gorge National Park***** is a reminder that Central Australia was once covered with water and tropical forest. Stunning rare Red Cabbage Palms, some as tall as 30m, and Cycad palms unique to Central Australia, nestle in a series of magnificent ochre-coloured gorges cut by the Finke River over a period of 100 million years. Permanent water holes and the wide flat bed made the Finke River an important travel and trade route for the Aboriginal people. European explorers also recognised the value of the Finke as a navigation aid. The first white settlers established a pastoral industry around the same reliable waterholes in the 1870s. A mixture of rough sand and rock, the road into Palm Valley from Larapinta Drive is 4WD only but well worth any discomfort of the bumpy ride.

ULURU-KATA TJUTA NATIONAL PARK*

Uluru-Kata Tjuta National Park $$ (free for under-16s). Open half an hour before sunrise to sunset. Permits last for 5 days of multiple entries and cost includes information kit with a guide to walking tracks at Uluru and Kata Tjuta. Note: photographs of the Cultural Centre and the Anangu people are forbidden.

Uluru-Kata Tjuta Cultural Centre Open 0700–1730. The only place to buy food and drinks in the park.

Uluru Kata Tjuta National Park is established on Aboriginal land which, following a landmark agreement in 1985, is leased back to the Commonwealth's National Parks and Wildlife Division. The major attractions in the park are Uluru (Ayers Rock) and Kata Tjuta (The Olgas). Many traditional Aboriginal owners, the Anangu people, still live in the park – mainly around the eastern base of Uluru – and play a key role in its management. In 1987 its cultural and historic significance was recognised with its inscription on the World Heritage List. Within Australia, the park is listed on the Register of the National Estate which recognises its aesthetic, historic, scientific and social significance for present and future generations.

The **Cultural Centre*** inside the Uluru-Kata Tjuta National Park provides an excellent history and *tjukurpa* (traditional law) of the Anangu people. There are also good leaflets produced by Parks Australia on the geology, plants and wildlife in the Park. The Centre contains the Maruku Arts and Crafts Galley and Initi Souvenirs and Café – both displaying traditional Aboriginal art and craftworks. The unusual mediums in the Centre, such as burnt designs on wood, carvings, glass panels and beautifully illustrated floor tiles, show that this is a highly creative and expressive culture. Many of the displays are interactive, with push-buttons bringing to life the words of senior Anangu, in their native Pitjantjatjara language, young people and trainee rangers, bird and animal calls, and distinctive sounds of the desert including the wind in Desert Oak trees.

Uluru✤

Mala and Mutitjulu Walks Purchase a copy of *An Insight into Uluru* brochure from the Cultural Centre for the self-guided walks which take you into and past sacred sites and precious waterholes.

Anangu Tours $$ *tel: (08) 8956-2123.* Run by Aboriginal guides with an interpreter to translate ancient legends. Tours leave twice daily from the Cultural Centre and give an excellent insight into the history of the area and the traditional owners.

There is a 17-km sealed bicycle track beginning opposite Flynns Grave, 7km from Alice Springs along Larapinta Drive.

Uluru, the Aboriginal name for the former Ayers Rock, is 3.6km long and 348m high and is like an iceberg in the desert. The reddish brown rock has reached iconic status in Australia. Its significance is greatest amongst its traditional owners, the Anangu, who request that tourists respect the cultural history of Uluru and their duty of care for your safety, by not climbing the monolith. Self-guided tours along the **Mala Walk**✤✤ (2km) and the **Mutitjulu Walk**✤✤ (1km), or Aboriginal-guided tours around the base of Uluru, are excellent alternatives to the climb and give a more enlightening insight into the Anangu people, their sacred sites, water holes, initiation ceremonies and rock paintings. Learn the ancient stories of the different markings on the rock's surface. The walk around the rock is 9.4km and takes about 3 hours. If you must climb it, there is a marked area near the start of the Mala Walk. It is recommended you allow about 2 hours for the round trip – which is straight up – and that you start early in the morning before it gets too hot. There is a chain to hold on to but it is hardly a safety device, as the memorial plaques at the bottom attest, with more than one fatality a year.

At least one sunset and one sunrise must be spent at the specially marked spots near Uluru. As the sun sets the Rock turns a series of brilliant, deeper and darker reds before it fades into a dull purple while the sky forms a vibrant pink and blue curtain in the background. The parking area gets packed so arrive half an hour before sunset (times are shown everywhere at Ayers Rock Resort) with a bottle of champagne.

Right
Uluru

WEST MACDONNELL RANGE❖

Standley Chasm $
open 0730–1800.

Glen Helen Lodge
has the only commercial facilities. Camping facilities are at **Ellery Creek Big Hole**, **Redbank Gorge** and **Glen Helen**.

Simpsons Gap, Standley Chasm, Ellery Creek Big Hole, Serpentine Gorge, Ochre Pits, Ormiston Gorge and Glen Helen are all part of this region. Pleasant surprises await as you go from one spectacular break in the ranges to another. Head west from Alice Springs along Namatjira Drive, with the Range on your right and the open desert on your left. The best way to experience the views and wildlife in this park is on foot. There is a good choice of walks, from leisurely strolls to adventurous hikes. Short marked tracks with interesting information about the cultural and natural environment are available at each site. The cool scenic gorges are a haven for a variety of plants and animals, and permanent waterholes are ideal for swimming during summer. The drive offers a dramatic ensemble of ancient landscape, rich colours, stark contrast, culture and relict flora and fauna like the distinctive white-trunked ghost gum, pink and grey galahs and rock wallabies.

YULARA❖

Yulara Resort Visitor Information Centre
Yulara Drive; tel: (08) 8956-2240; fax: (08) 8956-2404; www.ayersrockresort.com.au. Open daily 0830–1930.

Ayers Rock Resort Management *tel: (02) 9360-9099 for all tours.*

Museum and Art Gallery of the Northern Territory
Conacher St, Fannie Bay, Darwin; tel: (08) 8999-8201. Open Mon–Fri, 0900–1700, weekends, 1000–1700.

Longitude 131°
www.longitude131. com.au. Offers camping luxury in the wilderness of Uluru-Kata Tjuta National Park, with views of the sun rising over Uluru (Ayers Rock).

Nestled among the spinifex grass and sand dunes, this eco-friendly, low-impact village just outside the National Park is the only place to stay near Uluru. Opened in 1984, it is just 5km from Connellan Airport and provides the closest accommodation and other services including restaurants, cafés and a supermarket, for visitors to Uluru and Kata Tjuta. This is also the place to organise any special events including camel or Harley Davidson motorcycle tours to Uluru, dinner under the stars with the Sounds of Silence, or helicopter or light aircraft flights over Uluru and Kata Tjuta.

Accommodation and food in Yulara

Rapidly growing visitor numbers to Uluru means accommodation is heavily booked in Yulara, but the **Ayers Rock Campground**, where you can pitch your own tent or rent a cabin, has a policy that it won't turn people away (**$** *Yulara Drive; tel: (08) 8956-2055; fax: (08) 8956-2260*).

Outback Pioneer Lodge $$ *Yulara Drive; tel: (02) 9360-9099.* Comfortable hotel rooms, budget cabins and dormitories.

Sails in the Desert Hotel $$–$$$ *Yulara Drive; tel: (02) 8956-2200.* Like an oasis in the desert, Sails has everything you would expect of a five-star hotel.

Sounds of Silence Dinner $$$ *tel: (02) 9360-9099.* Five-star dinner under the stars with an astronomy talk; pick-up from all hotels.

Aboriginal art

Art is an integral part of both ancient and modern Aboriginal culture, providing a connection between Aboriginal people, their land and their belief and law systems. Rock engravings and Aboriginal paintings more than 20,000 years old have been found in many parts of Australia where Aborigines have lived for the past 50,000 years and possibly longer; Arnhem Land, Cape York, the Kimberley and the region around central Australia have the strongest ceremonial art heritage and traditions.

Rock paintings appear to fulfil at least three or four different purposes in traditional nomadic Aboriginal life. Paintings that depict different types of fish and animals that live on the land around the galleries, caves and cliff shelters where tribes often lived and visited, are thought to be 'menu' or 'hunting' boards, giving other travelling tribes an idea of what food is around the area to catch and eat. Other simple paintings, such as the numerous hands that can be found 'blow-painted' or stencilled with ochre spat from the mouth on to gallery walls, may be a way of teaching children about their identities and their own home places, or may be a type of 'visitors book' to record people who arrive and stay at different times. Other paintings, especially more modern ones from the last two centuries which depict white men with guns, and boats with sails, are records of major events in each tribe or family's lives.

But the more complex Aboriginal artworks of mythological beings, spirit figures, giant and strange animal shapes and land forms usually depict 'Dreamings'. These are stories involving supernatural spirits and ancestral beings who created the land and its people, and whose travels, antics and battles provide the 'law', and dictate the framework and structure of Aboriginal society even today, by guiding Aboriginal people through their everyday lives. Each Aboriginal person has their own 'skin' Dreaming, and their own 'totem', and is traditionally ruled by the obligations and responsibilities bestowed by these Creation Beings. This affects all aspects of their lives from who they can marry, which relatives they can mix with, who they can talk to, and which piece of land and features of the landscape they are responsible for taking care of.

Within this complex society, art plays a major role in ceremonies such as initiations, funerals, corroborees and festivals, with traditional Aborigines painting their bodies to dance, and often decorating and re-painting rock art galleries time and time again, overlaying layer upon layer of painting, as part of a particular annual ceremony or special event. Most rock art is painted by mixing rock colourings and ochres with water, although body paint often uses a mix of ochre and sticky plant sap. Coloured ochres have been found painted on ancient gallery walls many hundreds of miles from their source, indicating trading between tribes in ochre paints and dyes. Art styles vary considerably in different parts of Australia, and traditional differences are still evident in modern Aboriginal art today. So called 'dot art' predominates in the Central Deserts area around Alice Springs and is the most internationally recognisable Aboriginal art today. In Arnhem Land, paintings of mimi spirits and x-ray style fish, crocodiles and animals predominate, while in the Kimberley, there are distinctive Wandjina figures representing fertility spirits from the sea and sky.

The **Museum and Art Gallery of the Northern Territory**⁺ in Darwin, with its 2000 pieces of Aboriginal art, ancient and modern, is considered the best collection of its kind in the world. There are ancient rock art paintings, bark paintings and traditional burial poles, as well as magnificent contemporary works by modern Aboriginal artists. To buy Aboriginal art, prices and quality vary widely. Be realistic, you are unlikely to pick up a great work of art by a famous Aboriginal artist for a song and many cheap and poor quality imitations abound. To be on the safe side, the art centres run by some local Aboriginal communities provide the best opportunity of purchasing an authentic work, or, if you are seriously looking for a special piece, stick with the major Aboriginal art galleries in Sydney, Melbourne and Alice Springs. Either way, always ask for authenticating documentation and information about the artists and the Dreamtime story behind the painting to be supplied with the artwork. Cheaper options are to buy attractive painted message sticks or a didgeridoo from an Aboriginal community workshop.

Suggested tour

Total distance: 674km; 826km with detours.

Time: Allow five days (driving about 4 hours a day) with detours.

The suggested route through the Aboriginal-owned Mereenie Loop takes in much more of the real central Australia, with its wide-open plains, spectacular gorges, eerie canyons, meteorite craters, Aboriginal missions and sacred land. However, the quickest way to Uluru-Kata Tjuta National Park from Alice Springs is to head south down the Stuart Highway and then west on the Lasseter Highway. The roads are all sealed and the 461-km route takes about 5 hours.

Links: Alice Springs is an obvious stop for travellers from Darwin to Adelaide. Alternatively, it could be the starting point for the Northern Territory tour (*see page 192*) or the South Australian tour (*see page 242*). It is possible to get from Yulara and the Uluru-Kata Tjuta National Park to Western Australia via Docker Creek, although it is definitely 4WD only and conditions will always be treacherous.

Route: Head west from **ALICE SPRINGS** ❶ to capture the remoteness of the Red Centre. Far from lifeless, barren desert, the drive takes in the spectacular **WEST MACDONNELL RANGE** and Namatjira Drive with its gorges and the mysterious **Tnorala Conservation Reserve or Gosse Bluff** – a 5-km-wide ancient meteorite crater. Namatjira Drive and **Larapinta Drive**, both of which head west out of the Alice, are sealed to **Glen Helen** and **HERMANNSBURG** ❷ respectively. Distinctive white-trucked snow gum trees and shimmering clumps of spinifex grass are a dramatic contrast to the rich red dirt. Black cockatoos and pink and grey galahs dart through the trees along the side of the road.

Detour: From Larapinta Drive, 52km from Alice Springs, travel 9km to **Standley Chasm**, a spectacular, narrow break in the MacDonnell Ranges with bright orange walls. Continue to Glen Helen on Namatjira Drive or take Larapinta Drive to historic Hermannsburg.

Heading further west from Hermannsburg or Glen Helen to Kings Canyon and on to Uluru and Kata Tjuta, you travel on the **Mereenie Loop** through some harsh but dramatic Aboriginal land. A permit is required to travel on the 198km of dirt road which ends at the **Watarrka National Park** and Kings Canyon. There is only one permitted stop about three quarters of the way along the Mereenie Loop. You need a 4WD, particularly if rain turns the sand sticky.

Detour: From Hermannsburg drive 19km to **PALM VALLEY**. The road is 4WD-only and travels through the spectacular **Finke Gorge National Park**, with its red and mauve striped cliffs dotted with spinifex grass, along a rough dirt track and through mostly dry river beds. Allow 3 hours plus time to do some walking through the lush palm grove. There is only one way in and out of Palm Valley. Return to the paved road and turn left along Larapinta Drive to get to the Mereenie Loop and on to Watarrka National Park.

KINGS CANYON ❸ is 6km off the main highway after **Kings Canyon Resort**. Continue south along the Luritja Rd for 38km to **KINGS CREEK STATION** or 167km until you reach the Lasseter Highway to take you 136km west to **YULARA** and the **Ayers Rock Resort**. From the resort, it is 21km to **ULURU ❹** and 54km to **KATA TJUTA**, inside the **ULURU-KATA TJUTA NATIONAL PARK**.

Also worth exploring

The East MacDonnells, east of Alice Springs, are also beautiful with gorges and places of cultural significance. Take the Ross Highway 10km to **Emily and Jessie Gaps**, creek-worn gaps in the ranges. **Ross River Homestead**, 88km east, has some true outback culture, including billy tea and damper and boomerang throwing. **N'Dhala Gorge Nature Park**, 90km east of Alice Springs on unsealed road from Ross River, has rock paintings and carvings dating back 5000 years.

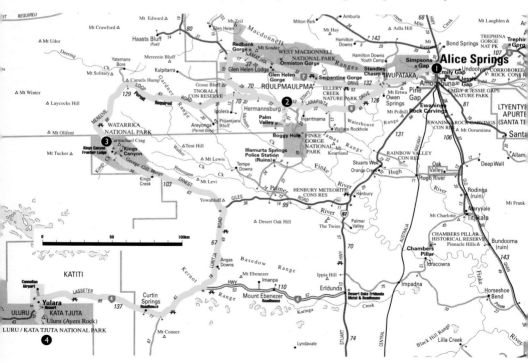

The Top End

Ratings

Aboriginal culture	●●●●●
Birdwatching	●●●●●
Outdoor activities	●●●●●
Scenery	●●●●●
Art	●●●●○
Children	●●●●○
National parks	●●●●○
Wildlife	●●●●○

The Top End is like nowhere else in Australia – tropical and lush in some places, red, rocky and ancient in others. This is a land of Aboriginal culture, ancient landscapes, great rivers, towering sandstone cliffs, plunging gorges, dry plains and verdant wetlands. It is the home of the great crocodiles, and a mass of colourful birds. And it is the place where mythical Aboriginal spirits, Dreamtime ancestors and ghostly hands crowd on the walls of ancient cliff-face art galleries, creating the greatest and oldest collection of rock art in the world. The city of Darwin, capital of the Top End, is a fascinating place too, exuberant, colourful and carefree. It may be small but its cafés and restaurants are among the best in Australia, while its closeness to Asia bestows a multi-cultural, tropical air that sometimes makes it feels like another country.

ADELAIDE RIVER CROSSING REGION**

ⓘ Window on the Wetlands Visitor Centre *Arnhem Hwy; tel: (08) 8988-8188. Open daily 0730–1930. Also information centre for Djukbinj National Park.*

ⓗ Fogg Dam Conservation Reserve *open all year round. Access road may be flooded during the wet season.*

The drive to Kakadu National Park should not be rushed; there are so many places to visit and enjoy on the way. The first region worth visiting is along the Arnhem Highway, where the new **Djukbinj National Park** has been created to protect the Adelaide River wetlands and the grass-swaying Marrakai plains. First turn off to the **Fogg Dam Conservation Reserve***, a great spot to walk among melaleuca swamps and view pied geese, brolgas, jabirus, ducks, herons and other waterbirds from the boardwalks and bird hides. Right next to the Arnhem Highway, perched high on Beatrice Hill, is the spectacular **Window on the Wetlands Visitor Centre***. Run by the NT Parks and Wildlife Commission, it has excellent and free ranger talks, videos, displays and touch screens which give a fascinating insight into the ecology of Top End wetlands, their wildlife and the seasons, as well as local indigenous culture. It is also the information centre for the surrounding Aboriginal-owned Djukbinj National Park. At the

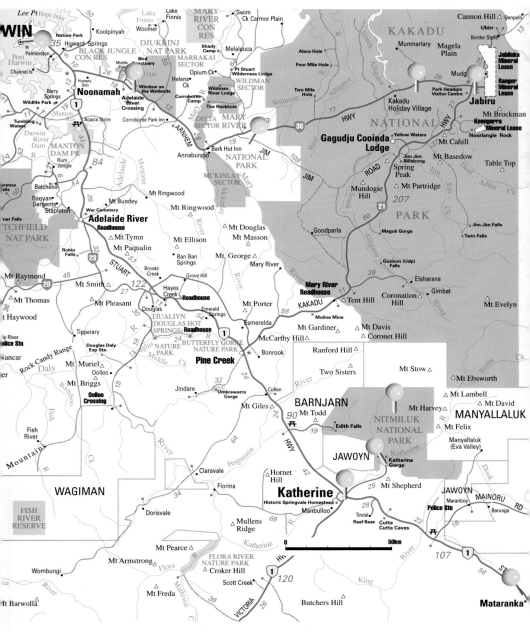

Adelaide River bridge are the **Adelaide River Queen⁺** cruises, which leave four times daily and feature the famous, if slightly bizarre, 'jumping crocodiles' (*tel: (08) 8988-8144*).

DARWIN✦✦✦

ⓘ Northern Territory Tourist Information Centre 38 Mitchell St, Darwin; tel: (08) 8981-4300; fax: (08) 8981-0653. Open daily.

Northern Territory Tourist Commission tel: (08) 8999-3900; www.travelnt.com. Information, brochures and maps before arriving in the Northern Territory.

Northern Territory government www.nt.gov.au

Northern Territory Holiday Centre tel: 1800-621-336. Freecall for more information and bookings.

Northern Territory Police Road Report tel: 1800-246-199 or (08) 8922-3394; for recorded message on current road conditions.

Darwin Tourism Information Centre 38 Mitchell St, Darwin; tel: (08) 8981-4300; fax: (08) 8981-0653.

ⓜ Museum and Art Gallery of the Northern Territory Conacher St, Fannie Bay; tel: (08) 8999-8201. Weekdays 0900–1700, weekends 1000–1700. Free.

Aquascene $ Doctor's Gully, near the northern end of the Esplanade; tel: (08) 8981-7837.

The city of Darwin is perched on a beautiful peninsula, surrounded by turquoise seas and lush vegetation. First mapped in 1839, when British captain John Lort Stokes, commander of the *Beagle*, sailed into its beautiful azure harbour and named it after his friend and former sailing companion, biologist Charles Darwin, it has always had to fight hard to survive, enduring extreme isolation, 64 direct bombing attacks by the Japanese in World War II and the obliteration of the frontier town by the fearful force of Cyclone Tracy in 1974. It has grown to become a flourishing, multi-cultural modern city, with a relaxed tropical atmosphere, great beauty and a distinctly Asian flavour.

Highlights include the outdoor Asian food markets on Thursday and Sunday nights at **Mindil Beach** – where everyone, including the locals, takes tables and chairs and hold impromptu sunset dinner parties – and the **Museum and Art Gallery of the Northern Territory✦**, which houses the best collection of Aboriginal art, both traditional and contemporary, in the world. Other recommended tourist attractions include fish feeding at **Aquascene✦** (four times daily, according to tides), the pearl and coral reef exhibitions at **Stokes Wharf** and the **Botanic Gardens✦** (*$ Gardens Rd; tel: 08-8947-2145; open daily 0730–1900*), with their 400 species of palms and Aboriginal plant medicine trail. There's also the **Australian Aviation Heritage Centre✦** and **Fannie Bay Gaol✦** (*$ East Point Rd, Fannie Bay; tel: 08-8999-820; open daily 1000–1700*), Darwin's main jail from 1883 to 1979, now kept as a museum. The **East Point Military Museum✦** (*$ East Point; tel: 08-8981-9702; open daily 0930–1700*) has footage of the bombings of Darwin during World War II, with photographic and

PALMERSTON TOWN HALL

Right
Bombed remains of the former Town Hall

Australian Aviation Heritage Centre $ *Stuart Highway, Winnellie; tel: (08) 8947-2145. Open daily 0900–1700. Guided tours at 1000, 1400 and 1600 daily.*

Mindil Beach Sunset Markets *Mindil Beach. Thur nights 1700–2200 late Apr–Oct, and Sun 1600–2100 June–Sept. Sixty outdoor food stalls servings specialities from Indonesia, Malaysia, Vietnam, Thailand, India and beyond ($).*

information displays. The best way to see all these sights is by the **Tour Tub**✦ *(tel: (08) 8985-4779)*, an open-sided trolley bus that does an hourly circuit of tourist attractions calling at major hotels and at the Knuckey St end of the Smith St Mall.

Accommodation and food in Darwin

Christos on the Wharf $ *end of Stokes Wharf; tel: (08) 8981-8658.* A classic Darwin dining experience, eating seafood outside on the end of Stokes Wharf, overlooking the harbour and city.

Cornucopia Museum Café $$ *NT Art Gallery and Museum, Conacher St, Fannie Bay; tel: (08) 8981-1002.* A great spot for a light lunch or Sunday brunch, dining outside on a covered deck next to the art gallery and museum and overlooking the tropical headland and bay.

Hanuman Restaurant $$$ *Mitchell St; tel: (08) 8941-3500.* Like no other Thai restaurant, Hanuman melds exquisite flavours and ingredients from Indonesia, Malaysia and Thailand, all in a classy setting.

Saville Park Suites $$ *The Esplanade, Darwin; tel: (08) 8943-4333.* Perfectly located, facing the Arafura Sea, and a few minutes walk from the city centre. Book a room with a view.

Darwin Crocodile Farm✦

Darwin Crocodile Farm $$ *Stuart Highway, Noonamah, just south of Arnhem Highway turn-off; tel: (08) 8988-1450. Open daily 0900–1600.*

The Darwin Crocodile Farm, about 37km south of the city, is well worth a visit. It has about 15,000 saltwater and freshwater crocodiles in residence, including many of the big 'salties' that have been taken out of NT rivers and seas by park rangers after becoming a nuisance or a threat. Crocodiles are farmed here for their meat and their skin, which makes good leather. Feeding time at 1400 daily is the best time to visit.

Right
Don't get too close at feeding time!

JABIRU✤

Ranger Uranium Mine Tours $$
Kakadu Park-link, Jabiru; tel: (08) 8979-2411. Tours leave three times a day.

Just out of Jabiru, excised from the surrounding Kakadu NP, the controversial **Ranger Uranium Mine✤** is one of the largest of its kind in the world. There are daily tours run by the company that owns the mine, ERA, which is planning to open another controversial mine at Jabiluka, also within Kakadu NP. The tours are interesting and informative, even if you disagree for ideological reasons with the mining of uranium in a World Heritage National Park.

Accommodation and food in Jabiru

Frontier Kakadu Lodge and Caravan Park $–$$ *Jabiru Dr; tel: (08) 8979-2422.* Budget dormitory accommodation in a green and spacious campsite near Kakadu National Park's main village of Jabiru. Eat barramundi or crocodile at night around the lovely pool.

Gagudju Crocodile Hotel $$$ *Flinders St; tel: (08) 8979-2800.* Built in the shape of a saltwater crocodile, with the entrance disconcertingly through the wide jaws, this modern Aboriginal-owned hotel has all the luxuries of any major hotel, and the best restaurant in Kakadu – serving crocodile of course.

KAKADU NATIONAL PARK✤✤✤

Kakadu National Park and Bowali Visitor Centre *Jabiru; tel: (08) 8938-1121. Open daily 0800–1700.*

Yellow Water Cruises *Cooinda; tel: (08) 8979-0111.*

Guluyambi River Cruises $$ *East Alligator River near Ubirr Rock; tel: 1800-089-113 or (08) 8979-2411. Three or four times daily.*

Kakadu National Park $$ *children under 15 free. Entry covers 14 days' stay; an excellent map and brochure is provided at the entrance ranger station.*

The 20,000 sq km of Kakadu National Park offer stunningly diverse landscapes and experiences: lush wetlands and waterways teeming with fish, crocodiles and bird-life, red escarpment cliffs cut by plunging waterfalls, grassy green flood plains crossed by wide twisting rivers meandering out to the mangrove coastal flats, and dry scrub country lined with paperbarks and eucalyptus. Huge galleries of ancient Aboriginal rock art painting are dotted throughout the park (several can be accessed by tourists). As well as an excellent Aboriginal cultural learning centre at Cooinda, the park has many interpretative signs that tell the stories of the landscape through local Aboriginal eyes, and cultural walks and tours run by Aboriginal guides.

The best place to start any visit to Kakadu is at its award-winning **Bowali Visitor Centre✤** at Jabiru, where excellent displays describe the animals, Aboriginal culture and geology of the park. A sunrise cruise on the wetlands of **Yellow Water✤** at **Cooinda** is probably the next highest priority. The dawn and dusk scenes reflected in the still waters are magical, complete with lotus lilies, crocodiles, blue-winged kookaburras, magpie geese, jabirus and hundreds of other bird species. At Cooinda, the **Warradjan Cultural Centre** provides a fascinating insight into Gagudju Aboriginal language, its kith and kin laws,

Above
Kakadu rock art

taboos, hunting traditions and creation myths. About 50km north of Jabiru, elevated **Ubirr Rock** provides a magnificent view of the sun setting over the East Alligator River wetlands. At its base are many rock art galleries showing hunting scenes, fish, the rainbow serpent and even possibly an extinct thylacine (Tasmanian tiger). Near Ubirr Rock, take a boat trip on the East Alligator River, with **Guluyambi Cultural Cruises**; learn some of the secrets of traditional Aboriginal medicine, law, sacred ceremonies and creation stories from a local Aboriginal guide. For more bushwalking and rock art is the stunning **Nourlangie Rock**, which shelters a great collection of Aboriginal galleries, including the famous paintings of Namarrgon the Lightning Man and the dangerous spirit Namondjok. Nearby **Angbangbang Billabong** is a magical picnic spot with its carpet of water lilies. **Twin Falls** and **Jim Jim Falls** are two of the spectacular waterfalls that thunder over the edge of the Arnhem Land stony country plateau after the summer rains, down into deep rock pools and on to the billabongs and flood plains of the South Alligator River. Another equally spectacular waterfall can be found in the southern and drier end of Kakadu Park at **Gunlom**, where the large swimming hole at its base featured in the film *Crocodile Dundee*.

KATHERINE**❖❖**

ⓘ Katherine Visitors' Centre *corner Stuart Highway and Lindsay St; tel: (08) 8972-2650.*

The reason most people come to Katherine is to visit the stunning Katherine Gorge, in **Nitmiluk National Park** (*see page 199*), but there are plenty of other places of interest. Just south of Katherine are the **Cutta Cutta Caves❖**, limestone rock formations 15m under the earth's surface formed five million years ago and home to the rare orange horseshoe bat and the brown tree snake. Also south of Katherine is

ⓘ Cutta Cutta Cave Nature Park $$
tel: (08) 8972-1940. Guided tours several times daily.

Manyallaluk Manyallaluk Rd, South of Katherine; tel: (08) 8975-4727 or 1800-644-727.

Manyallaluk*, meaning 'dreaming place', where local Aborigines invite visitors to come and camp, partake in traditional activities and go on organised tours with an Aboriginal cultural guide.

Accommodation and food in Katherine

Aussie's Bistro $ *Katherine Hotel Motel, Stuart Hwy; tel: (08) 8972-1622.* A typical Australian pub meal, or try kangaroo steaks.

Knotts Crossing Resort $ *1375 Cameron St; tel: (08) 8972-2511.* This well-equipped tourist resort, on the road to Nitmiluk National Park, has basic budget family rooms in pleasant surroundings.

Nitmiluk National Park Visitor's Centre bistro $$ *Nitmiluk National Park; tel: (08) 8973-8770.* Enjoy light, modern meals perched on a wide terrace high above the Katherine River.

Springvale Homestead Tourist Park $$ *Shadforth Rd; tel: (08) 8972-1355.* Motel-style accommodation alongside the territory's oldest homestead on the beautiful Katherine River; also camping. Afternoon teas, canoeing, swimming, corroborees.

LITCHFIELD NATIONAL PARK**

ⓘ Litchfield National Park NT Parks and Wildlife Service office; tel: (08) 8976-0282.

Less than two hours from Darwin near the town of Batchelor, Litchfield National Park is another delight which Darwin locals tend to use as their weekend playground. Magnificent waterfalls, gorges and deep flowing pools at Florence Falls, Wangi, Tjaynera Falls and Buley Rockhole – all without crocodiles – make Litchfield a great day or two-day addition to any Top End holiday. Added attractions are the extraordinary giant magnetic termite mounds in the north of the park, which always point exactly north, and the Lost City sandstone column and block formations further to the south, resembling ancient ruins. Most roads are suitable for normal 2WD cars during the dry season.

MARY RIVER NATIONAL PARK**

ⓘ Mary River National Park NT Parks and Wildlife Service office; tel: (08) 8978-8986.

ⓦ Mary River Houseboats and Dinghy hire $$ Corroboree Billabong; tel: (08) 8978-8925.

A new national park has recently been formed on the Arnhem Highway leading towards Kakadu, to protect the extensive Mary River wetlands, considered by many to be the most beautiful area of wetlands in the Top End and to be as special as Kakadu for their bird life, fish and tropical calm. Highlights of the **Mary River National Park** include excellent barramundi fishing at Shady Camp and Corroboree Billabong. Giant saltwater crocodiles flourish in the Mary River, and Shady Camp has the dubious distinction of having the highest concentration of salties in the world. **Crocodylus Wildlife**

Crocodylus Wildlife Cruises $$ *Shady Camp, Mary River; tel: (08) 8927-0777.*

Cruises* runs excellent croc-spotting tours here. North Rockhole and Couzens Lookout are also spectacular spots, while for a bit of comfort and great birdwatching over the flood plains, it is hard to pass up a stay at the **Wildman River Wilderness Lodge**.

Accommodation and food in Mary River National Park

Wildman River Wilderness Lodge $$$ *Off Point Stuart Rd, off Arnhem Hwy, Wildman River; tel: (08) 8978-8912.* In Mary River National Park, comfortable ecotourism lodge, fishing, birdwatching, boat cruises.

MATARANKA✦✦

Elsey National Park *NT Parks and Wildlife Service office and visitor centres; tel: (08) 8975-4560.*

Mataranka Homestead Tourist Resort *tel: (08) 8975-4544.*

An hour's drive south of Katherine lies Mataranka, the heart of Never Never Country made famous by female pioneer, Jeannie Gunn, in her book, *We of the Never Never* about life at Elsey Station at the turn of the century. It is called Never Never country because those who live there and love it, find they can never, never leave it. You can see if this applies to you by taking an invigorating swim in the clear Mataranka Thermal Pool or Rainbow Pool surrounded by rainforest in **Elsey National Park**✦. At the nearby **Mataranka Homestead Tourist Resort**✦, an authentic replica of Jeannie Gunn's Elsey Station homestead made of local cypress pine can be seen, built for the film *We of the Never Never*.

NITMILUK NATIONAL PARK AND KATHERINE GORGE✦✦✦

Nitmiluk National Park Visitors' Centre *Katherine Gorge; tel: (08) 8972-1886. Open daily 0730–2000.*

Nitmiluk Cruises $$–$$$ *North Tours, Nitmiluk National Park; tel: (08) 8972-1253.*

Gecko Canoeing $$$ *Nitmiluk National Park; tel: (08) 8972-2224.*

With its string of 13 separate gorges along 50km of the Katherine River, Nitmiluk National Park is a place of deep pools, silence, grandeur and majesty. The gorges, carved out by torrential summer rains cutting through sheer-sided 100-m high cliffs of red sandstone, are 1650 million years old. **Katherine Gorge** and the surrounding national park teem with magnificently coloured parrots and blue-winged kookaburras; bat colonies hang out of the paperbark trees and barramundi – but no saltwater crocodiles – live in the river. The best way to view the grandeur of the Gorge is from the two-hour, four-hour or all-day boat trips operated by the Jawoyn people who own Nitmiluk NP and run it in conjunction with the NT's Parks and Wildlife Service.

① Territory Wildlife Park $$ *Cox Peninsula Rd, Berry Springs; tel: (08) 8988-7200. Open daily 0830–1800, last entry at 1600.* This award-winning park features 100s of the Northern Territory's unique native species in superb natural surroundings. The park provides an opportunity for visitors to the Territory to learn about and see its animals – many of which are normally nocturnal – in the flesh.

Howard Springs Reserve *Open daily 0800–2000.* Howard Springs is a lovely freshwater spring-fed swimming spot, clean of estuarine crocodiles. The clear cool pools are filled with barramundi and long-necked turtles.

Majestic Orchid Farm $$ *Darwin River Rd, near Berry Springs; tel: (08) 8988-6008.* The largest cut-flower orchid farm in Australia. There are more than 300,000 orchid plants at the farm, and flowers can be bought there directly or arranged to be sent overseas.

Berry Springs Nature Park *Cox Peninsula Rd, Berry Springs (about 50km south of Darwin). Open daily 0800–1830.* At Berry Springs Nature Park a thermal waterfall cascades into a series of deep long pools fringed with lush pandanus and tropical vegetation, making for wonderful family swimming.

Suggested tour

Distance: The total distance of this circuit drive is about 900km, leaving from and returning to Darwin with an additional 106km each way if the extra detour drive from Katherine to Mataranka is taken. All roads are excellent sealed highways, except the gravel roads to Ubirr Rock and Gunlom within Kakadu National Park and the gravel roads inside Litchfield National Park. Some may be impassable during the wet season so check conditions with tourist authorities.

Time: Allowing at least 2 days in Kakadu National Park, a day to explore Nitmiluk National Park and sufficient driving time, this tour will take a minimum of 5 days, and would be a perfect week-long trip.

Links: From Katherine, continue south along the Stuart Highway, driving through Mataranka, Daly Waters and Tennant Creek to get to Alice Springs. Then link up with the circuit route through the Red Centre (*see page 182*). It is 672km from Katherine to Tennant Creek, and 504km between Tennant Creek and Alice Springs.

Route: Drive south from **DARWIN ①** along the Stuart Highway past the turning to the **Howard Springs⁺ ②** swimming reserve after 24km. Ten kilometres later, the Arnhem Highway to **Kakadu National Park**, branches off to left. But first visit the **Territory Wildlife Park⁺**, the **Orchid Farm⁺** and enjoy a dip at **Berry Springs Nature Park⁺**, only 12 more km down the Stuart Highway then right along the major Cox Peninsula Rd for another 10–20km.

After enjoying these excellent parks and attractions, backtrack up the Stuart Highway to the Arnhem Highway turn-off. Just 25km down the track, enjoy the **ADELAIDE RIVER CROSSING REGION ③**, looking for birds at **Fogg Dam** and learning about the wide river plains of **Djukbinj National Park** at the **Window on the Wetlands Visitors' Centre**.

Continuing along the Arnhem Highway for another 30km, and turn left along the dirt road to **Corroboree Billabong** with its fishing dinghies and houseboat hire within **MARY RIVER NATIONAL PARK ④**. Another 50km later, after passing the **Bark Hut Inn roadhouse**, the road turns left to the other Mary River NP areas of **Shady Camp** and **Wildman River**.

Soon you will reach the main entry station to **KAKADU NATIONAL PARK ⑤**, and then it is 121km to the **Bowali Visitors' Centre** park headquarters, just outside **JABIRU ⑥** and the **Ranger uranium mine**. Spend a few days exploring the Park (detailed maps are provided at the entry gate). From Jabiru, it is a 172-km drive to **Pine Creek ⑦** – dropping in at **Gunlom** for a beautiful cool dip on the way – and then another 92km south back on the Stuart Highway to **KATHERINE ⑧**.

Tropical Top End

The Top End can be a seductive place, but remember it is also tropical. Travel in the Top End is best in the cooler, drier months from April to August, although the wet, humid months of January to March give a magnificent alternative view of Kakadu National Park in all its wet season splendour.

Detour: From Katherine, it is 106km south (one way) along the Stuart Highway to reach **MATARANKA** and **Elsey National Park**, with its thermal pools and spring-fed river walks. **Manyalluk** Aboriginal resort is also along the way, as are the **Cutta Cutta caves**.

From Katherine, it is a 30-km drive to **NITMILUK NATIONAL PARK** and the magnificent **KATHERINE GORGE** ❾. Heading north from Katherine on the Stuart Highway, there is a turning to the right about 40km north to the lovely **Edith Falls** ❿. Passing through the towns of Pine Creek and **Hayes Creek**, a detour along dirt roads through **LITCHFIELD NATIONAL PARK** ⓫ can be taken by turning west up the Daly River Rd, although sealed road access to Litchfield NP is best through the town of **Batchelor**, on the Litchfield Park Rd. From the Batchelor turn-off, it is just 112km along the Stuart Highway back to Darwin, calling in on the **DARWIN CROCODILE FARM** ⓬ at **Noonamah** along the way.

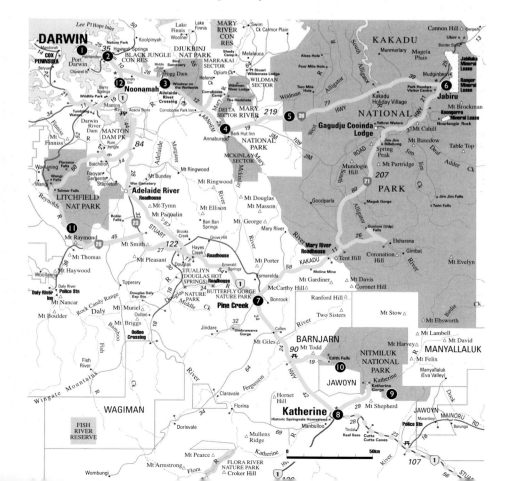

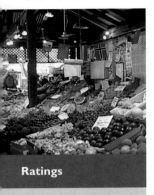

Perth

Ratings

Beaches	●●●●●
Water sports	●●●●●
Colonial architecture	●●●●○
Cycling	●●●●○
Food and drink	●●●●○
Parks and gardens	●●●●○
Walking	●●●●○
Shopping	●●●○○

Perth is the most isolated major city in the world and its personality in many ways reflects this isolation. References to it as the California of Australia are not solely due to the hot summers, mild winters and sun-washed sandy beaches. Its skyscraper-studded skyline and ostentatious riverside and beachside mansions are an indication that power and wealth are not things one needs to be too humble or subtle about here, however temporary they have proved for some. But Western Australians are rightly proud of their capital. It is beautifully set around the wide and usually tranquil Swan River, which flows down from the Darling Ranges into the Indian Ocean at the historic port of Fremantle, cutting the city into northern and southern corridors. The sparkling coastline which marks its western edge also serves up fine swimming, surfing and sailing – and some of the world's best seafood.

COTTESLOE BEACH❖❖

ℹ Western Australian Tourist Centre *Forrest Place, Perth; tel: (08) 9483-1111.*

If Perth has an icon beach, as Sydney has Bondi, then this is it, minus the crowds and the perilous rips. Its grand 1920s changing rooms and surf lifesaving club have now been transformed into the very smart **Indiana Tea House**❖ café and restaurant (*99 Marine Parade; tel: (08) 9385-5005*). Across Marine Parade from the beach are two famous watering holes, the Cottesloe Beach and the Ocean Beach Hotel.

DALKEITH❖❖

Because of its delightful location overlooking the Swan River Dalkeith has the distinction of being the Perth's most expensive residential suburb. Its most famous street, Jutland Parade, is known as 'millionaires' row'. The less well heeled can enjoy the same outlook from the **Point Resolution** reserve at the end of Jutland Parade.

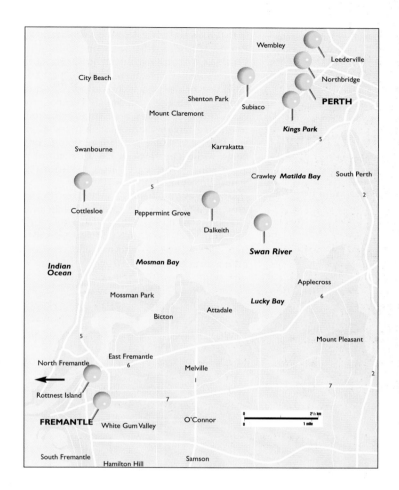

Wembley

Leederville

City Beach

Northbridge

Shenton Park

Subiaco

PERTH

Mount Claremont

Kings Park

5

Swanbourne

Karrakatta

Crawley *Matilda Bay*

South Perth

2

Cottlesloe

Peppermint Grove

5

Dalkeith

Swan River

*Indian
Ocean*

Mosman Bay

Applecross

Mossman Park

6

Lucky Bay

Attadale

Bicton

Mount Pleasant

5

East Fremantle

North Fremantle

6

Melville

2

Rottnest Island

1

7

FREMANTLE

White Gum Valley

7

O'Connor

2½ km

1 mile

South Fremantle

Hamilton Hill

Samson

FREMANTLE❖❖❖

The port of Fremantle is a beautifully preserved heritage precinct in a state which has often shown scant respect for its architectural history. But what makes it more fascinating is that it remains a vibrant working port and city. Its streets and buildings received a complete facelift in the lead up to 1987, when it was host port for the America's Cup, an international yachting trophy won four years earlier by Perth's most notorious businessman, Alan Bond. The cup was lost but Fremantle has not looked back. A walk along its pavements will pass galleries, museums, terrace houses, pavement cafés, markets and many fine examples of architecture from the decades immediately after the

Fremantle's popular undercover markets, a lively mix of stalls selling everything from incense to fresh fish, are open all day Fri to Sun on the corner of South Terrace and Henderson St.

Fremantle Gaol
$–$$ The Terrace; tel: (08) 9430-7177. Open daily 1000–1800. Tours every half hour; candlelight tours Wed and Fri at 1930.

Below
Fremantle

first British settlers established the Swan River Colony in 1829. **The Round House**, a 12-sided stone building at the end of High St, is Western Australia's oldest building, constructed in 1830 as the colony's first civil gaol. Fremantle's West End, flanking the harbour, is rated one of the best Victorian port streetscapes in the world. After a stroll through the past, **South Terrace** offers wall-to-wall pavement cafés and pubs, many reflecting Fremantle's more recent history as home to a large Italian immigrant community. The **Sail and Anchor** was Australia's first pub brewery and continues to serve speciality beers, while **The Norfolk** has a delightful beer garden and generous, good food. More cafés and restaurants are to be found on the waterfront at **Fishing Boat Harbour**.

On the edge of the city centre, the former **Fremantle Gaol**⋆⋆ provides a fascinating if chilling insight into the city's history and an alternative to its prevailing image as a fun seaside town. Built from limestone rock by British convicts sent to the colony, it received its first inmates in 1855 and remained Perth's major maximum security prison until November 1991.

Accommodation and food in Fremantle

Esplanade Hotel $$$ *Corner of Marine Terrace and Essex St, Fremantle; tel: (08) 9432-4000.* The only hotel in Fremantle with four-star facilities. A three-storey establishment with 259 rooms, the Esplanade has an unbeatable location wedged between the South Terrace 'cappuccino strip' and Fishing Boat Harbour.

Gino's Café $ *1 South Terrace, Fremantle; tel: (08) 9336-1464.* Considered by many to serve the best coffee in the port.

Harvest $$ *1 Harvest Rd, North Fremantle; tel: (08) 9336-1831.* A popular and friendly café/restaurant serving fresh seafood and other local produce with a European twist.

The Left Bank $$ *15 Riverside Rd, East Fremantle; tel: (08) 9319-1315.* Restored two-storey mansion alongside the Swan River is now established as one of Perth's most popular bars and cafés. There are few better located beer gardens in the city.

Phillimore's (His Majesty's Hotel) $$ *2 Mouat St, Fremantle; tel: (08) 9335-9596.* In the heart of Fremantle's West End, near the quay, this is one of many old hotels in the port to have been restored with grace and style. The hotel has 25 rooms which, in keeping with its original layout, range from tiny to grand.

KINGS PARK✤✤✤

ⓘ **Kings Park Board**
Fraser Avenue; tel: (08) 9480-3600. General enquiries and information on guided tours.

In 1872, Perth's forefathers preserved 172 hectares on Mount Eliza overlooking the city as permanent parkland. Today, Kings Park covers 400 hectares and is the largest park within the confines of a major city in Australia. It is a peaceful blend of natural bushland, landscaped gardens, walking trails, ponds and playgrounds, in addition to offering a panoramic view over the city of Perth and the Swan River.

OXFORD STREET, LEEDERVILLE✤✤

Northbridge may be better known as the hub of Perth's nightlife, but the area around Oxford St in Leederville, three kilometres northwest of the city, is sleeker these days and at least as popular among students and inner-city inhabitants. A string of cafés and restaurants now occupies the strip south from the popular, independent cinema, **The Luna**. They range from the longstanding Asian budget diner, **Hawkers Hut**, to such ultra-contemporary establishments as **Fourteen 7** noodle bar and **Nucastle**, around the corner in Newcastle St. In a city where good coffee is often hard to find, **Oxford 130** consistently delivers.

NORTHBRIDGE❖❖

Art Gallery of Western Australia
Perth Cultural Center, James St; tel: (08) 9492-6600; www.artgallery.wa.gov.au. Open daily from 1000–1700. Entry fee for special exhibitions only.

Northbridge lies over the railway tracks from Perth City and is the centre of much of the local cultural and night life. It was originally home to many Europeans who migrated after World War II. Over the past two decades a multicultural abundance of cafés, restaurants, pubs and clubs, has sprung up from these origins, some good, some mediocre. The **Re Store** in Lake St and **Kakulas Bros** in William St are examples of the fine European grocery stores which remain, while Kailis Bros fish markets at 100 Roe St gives local consumers access to some of the best seafood caught off Western Australia. Northbridge is also home to the **Perth Cultural Centre** complex, including the **Art Gallery of Western Australia❖** which has a number of significant Australian works. Northbridge can become crowded and a little sleazy on Friday and Saturday nights.

PERTH CITY❖❖

A free bus service, Central Area Transit (CAT), operates around the central Perth area. Red CAT buses do an east–west loop and blue CAT buses run north–south. Routes and times are displayed at clearly marked stops throughout the city. Travel on the regular Transperth bus service is also free to passengers who board and alight within the city area.

Perth is an unashamedly modern city but a walk around its shopping and business area reveals glimpses of its past. Founded in 1829, it was the first settlement in Australia entirely made up of volunteers from England rather than convicts. But that lasted only until 1850 when labour shortages forced the introduction of convicts, who were immediately put to work constructing roads and public buildings. Perth's Town Hall on the corner of Hay and Barrack streets was built by convict labour in the 1870s as was the Gothic-style Government House in St Georges Terrace. Also sandwiched among the Terrace's skyscrapers are the beautiful Cloisters, the first boys' secondary school in Western Australia, and the Old Perth Boys' School, built in 1853, which now houses a National Trust information centre. The main shopping precinct is bounded by Hay, William, Wellington and Barrack streets. Further west, King St, once a shabby home for wholesalers and warehouses, has been transformed over the past decade into one of the city's swankiest areas, lined with galleries, cafés and boutiques.

ROTTNEST ISLAND❖❖❖

Rottnest Island Authority *tel: (08) 9432-9300; www.rottnest.wa.gov.au. Transport and accommodation information.*

If Rottnest was in the Aegean it would be a world famous holiday destination. Instead it lies 20km west of Fremantle and its beautiful rocky bays, white sandy beaches and turquoise waters have largely remained a low-key playground for generations of holidaying Western Australians. The island was named in 1696 by the Dutch explorer, William Vlamingh who mistook the island's unique marsupial resident, the quokka, for a huge rat. Many of its early buildings date

Ferry services run several times a day all year round to Rottnest. Mainland departure points are Perth, Fremantle or Hillarys in the northern suburb. Call **Boat Torque** *(08) 9221-5844* or the **Rottnest Express** *(08) 9335-6406* for ferry bookings.

Bikes and canoes can be hired just off Riverside Drive on the city side of The Causeway. Surfcats and windsurfers can be hired on the other side of the river on the South Perth foreshore.

Above right
Rottnest Island

from 1838 to 1903 when it served as a harsh Aboriginal prison. It became a tourist resort in 1917 but development since then has been limited to low-rise facilities on a small section of the island. No cars are permitted, leaving bicycles, which can be hired, as the main form of transport. The island is only 11km long and 4.5km at its widest point but it is easy to find secluded coves which only need be shared with the gulls. To fully appreciate this unique place requires longer than a day trip.

SUBIACO❖❖

One of Perth's most popular eating, drinking and shopping areas, Subiaco is an interesting atmospheric blend of conservative high street and inner-suburban hip strip. Within a few hundred metres, it ranges from the stark, forbidding outlets of Australia's top designers, to pet shops, antique dealers, dusty drapers and undercover markets. It is also home to one of Perth's most highly regarded Aboriginal art galleries, **Indigenart**❖ *(115 Hay St)*. But Subiaco is perhaps best known as the home of Perth's premier Australian Rules Football stadium, the base of the West Coast Eagles, one of the most successful teams in the national football league and a subject of obsession for most West Australians from April to September. Tickets for Eagles games are hard to come by, but try Red Ticket booking agency on *(08) 9484-1222*.

SWAN RIVER❖❖❖

Perth is often described by visitors as a beautiful city and the main reason is undoubtedly its setting on the Swan. The river glides from the Swan Valley down through the city's eastern suburbs before widening into a vast body of water in front of the Central Business District (CBD) skyline. It then curls its way through the cliffs of Perth's wealthy western suburbs before emptying into the Indian Ocean at Fremantle. In between it is enjoyed by sailors, windsurfers, rowers, canoeists and water skiers, while along its edge, cyclists, joggers and walkers make use of a network of riverside paths. A scenic 10-km circuit connects the city and south Perth via the Narrows Bridge and The Causeway, the main bridges linking Perth's northern and southern suburbs. Other tracks run all the way to Fremantle. The less energetic can just watch it all from a number of riverside cafés, like Jo Jos at the end of the small Nedlands jetty or Moorings at Barrack St jetty at the bottom of the city. Several companies – including **Captain Cook Cruises** *tel: (08) 9325-3341* – offer river cruises from Barrack St jetty down to Fremantle or up to the Swan Valley.

Accommodation and food

Altos $$$ *424 Hay St, Subiaco; tel: (08) 9382-3292.* Modelled on the best cafés of Melbourne or New York, Altos serves fresh, quality produce with skill and style, in a smart environment.

Dusit Thai $$ *249 James St, Northbridge; tel: (08) 9328-7647.* One of Perth's longest established Thai restaurants.

Fraser's Restaurant $$$ *Kings Park, Perth; tel: (08) 9481-7100.* Superb views and some of the best contemporary food in Perth, with an emphasis on seafood.

The Globe $$$ *Parmelia Hilton, Mill St, Perth; tel: (08) 9322-3622.* The Hilton has called on the services of Cheong Liew, regarded as one of Australia's best chef's and the father of east–west food.

Jackson's $$ *483 Beaufort St, Highgate; tel: (08) 9328-1177.* Modern Australian cuisine which consistently impresses locals and visitors alike. Excellent wine list to match.

Jaws $$ *Hay St Mall, Perth Central.* This concept of providing light, delicious, reasonably priced Japanese food to busy workers and shoppers has taken off. There are now three in the city area. Customers sit shoulder to shoulder and select from conveyor belts of sushi or order tempura lunch trays or takeaways.

The Melbourne $$–$$$ *corner of Hay and Milligan Sts, Perth City; tel: (08) 9320-3333.* Classified by the National Trust, this 35-room hotel was restored in the mid-1990s.

Valentino $$ *27 Lake St, cnr James St, Northbridge; tel: (08) 9328-2177.* A typical example of the growing number of airy, café-style restaurants that have sprung up around Perth, which have their roots in Italy but a menu broad enough to satisfy most tastes.

Suggested tour

Total distance: The main driving circuit from Perth to Fremantle and return around the river is approximately 55km. A detour taking in Northbridge, Oxford St, Leederville and Subiaco will add a little over 10km. The detour to Rottnest Island is 19km return by boat.

Time: It will take roughly two hours for the main journey, not counting stops. The detour to the inner suburbs will add about half an hour while the trip to Rottnest from Fremantle will take half an hour each way by ferry provided the seas are not heavy.

Links: This route links with the Great Southwest Drive (*see page 212*), which also leaves from Perth.

Route: Head west out of **PERTH ❶** on St George's Terrace up the hill to a roundabout. Turn left at Fraser Ave to head into **KINGS PARK ❷**. This avenue lined by towering gum trees gives a panoramic view of Perth and the Swan River.

Detour: Alternatively, reach this point via a detour taking in Northbridge, Oxford St, Leederville and Subiaco. Head north over the railway tracks via Barrack St and into the eastern edge of **NORTHBRIDGE**. Because of the one-way system, drive three blocks past the Cultural Centre precinct on your left before turning left into Newcastle St. Turn left again into William St and right into James St to travel through the heart of this busy area. Turn right at Fitzgerald St and turn left after three blocks back into Newcastle St for 1.5km to reach another clutch of cafés and restaurants in **OXFORD ST, LEEDERVILLE**. To travel on to **SUBIACO** turn left at Oxford St and follow the road around to the busy thoroughfare of Loftus St. Turn right and after one kilometre turn right again into Hay St which leads to Subiaco. Turn left at Rokeby Rd to Thomas St. Cross over the traffic lights and enter Kings Park.

Meander through Kings Park's web of roads before exiting on to Winthrop Ave, the continuation of Thomas St. Turn immediately left on Mounts Bay Rd and then right again on to Hacket Drive to begin a riverside tour. Hacket Drive passes the **Matilda Bay Foreshore**, a lovely spot for picnics, while on the right is the

Below
Perth's London Court

beautiful campus of the **University of Western Australia**. After 500m turn left on to The Avenue and continue through **DALKEITH ❸** via Birdwood Parade and Jutland Parade. **Point Resolution Reserve**, another picnic spot, is at the end of Jutland Parade. Drive along Victoria Ave and turn right into Bayview Terrace which leads to the ritzy shopping centre of **Claremont**.

Turn left on to Stirling Highway for a little over one kilometre and turn right into Eric St to reach **COTTESLOE BEACH ❹**. Turn left into Marine Parade and hug the Indian Ocean for about five kilometres to **Port Beach**, another popular swimming area. Turn left into Tydeman St and right into Queen Victoria St which will take you across Fremantle Bridge and into the heart of **FREMANTLE ❺**.

Detour: Depending on the operator, ferries to **ROTTNEST ISLAND** leave from Rous Head, which can be reached by continuing along Port Beach Rd or from C Shed at Victoria Quay in Fremantle itself.

To avoid traffic congestion and one-way streets in Fremantle, turn left from Queen Victoria St at Parry St to reach the southern end of **South Terrace**. Parking and walking is the best way to explore the area and **Fremantle Gaol**. To leave, go back up Parry St and turn right into High St and left after about a kilometre on to Stirling Highway. Turn right on to Canning Highway but immediately left into Preston Point Rd for a tour of the southern riverside suburbs.

Follow Preston Point Rd and turn left into Point Walter Rd to **Point Walter Reserve ❻**, a sheltered swimming and picnic spot. Follow the river around via Burke Drive to return to Canning Highway. About one kilometre after crossing Canning Bridge – where the Canning and Swan Rivers meet – turn left at Thelma St and right on to Coode St. Three kilometres later you will reach the **South Perth Foreshore ❼** and a great view across the river to the City. From Coode St, head east along Mill Point Rd to return to Canning Highway. Within a kilometre turn left on to the Causeway to return to the north side of the river. The Causeway passes over **Heirisson Island**, another pleasant spot for a walk. At dusk it is possible to spot kangaroos here; several have been introduced on to the island, in part to give tourists easy access to Australia's best known native animal. Turn left from the Causeway on to Riverside Drive to return to the heart of the city. **Barrack Square**, the old Perth port at the corner of Riverside Drive and Barrack St, is also good for riverside views from vantage points such as Moorings café and the Lucky Shag bar.

Also worth exploring

Just under 100km east of Perth, **York** is Western Australia's oldest inland town and, like Fremantle, is remarkably well preserved and restored. Settled in 1830, its wide main street is a combination of

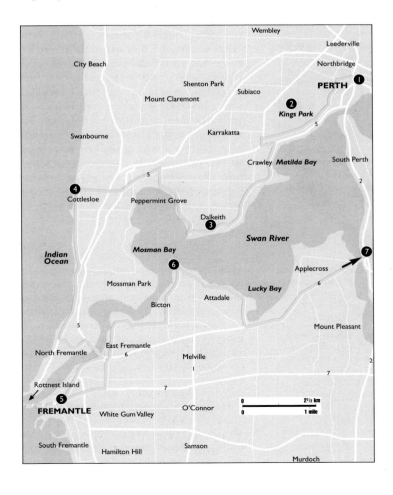

The York Hotel
$$–$$$ *145 Avon Terrace, York; www.theyork.com.au.* Tariff includes dinner, bed and breakfast.

colonial and Victorian architecture. Many of its early public edifices were built by convicts, while the town's growth was fuelled by the discovery of gold in the nearby Yilgarn region in 1889. A fine example of history blending with the present is **The York Hotel**, established in 1908 and recently restored to offer upmarket accommodation and dining. Holy Trinity Church, a short walk via a suspension bridge across the Avon River, was consecrated in 1858 but has striking stained-glass windows by one of Western Australia's best-known contemporary artists, Robert Juniper. Other than farmers, the inhabitants of York are mostly retirees and escapees from city life. To get there from Perth, take the Great Eastern Highway from the Causeway for around 45km and turn left on to the Great Southern Highway for another 47km.

The Great Southwest Drive

Ratings

Beaches	●●●●●
Coastal scenery	●●●●○
Fishing	●●●●○
Food and wine	●●●●○
Geology	●●●●○
Walking	●●●●○
Art and crafts	●●●○○
National parks	●●●○○

Western Australia's southwest corner is quite unlike the rest of this massive state. It is an extraordinarily diverse region of intense natural beauty, combining towering native forests, rolling farmland, rugged coastal cliffs and wild beautiful beaches. With one of the richest floras on earth, the ancient landscape supports around 9000 plant species and many unique wildflowers. In the past two decades, much of the rural landscape has given way to vineyards and wineries which have fostered an increasingly sophisticated hospitality industry. The region also enjoys a relatively mild climate, but be aware that coastal areas are whipped by a strong sea breeze almost daily from late spring to late summer. It can bring welcome relief from the heat but means beaches are often windswept by midday. The suggested drive combines the best of the southwest's forests, beaches, national parks, caves, towns and wineries.

ALBANY✦✦✦

ⓘ Albany Tourist Bureau *Proudlove Parade (old railway station); tel: (08) 9841-1088. Open daily.*

Ⓦ Whaleworld $ *Frenchmans Bay, Albany; tel: (08) 9844-4021. Open daily 0900–1700. Tours hourly.*

Albany lies on the southernmost tip of Western Australia's rugged coastline and overlooks the vast, island-studded Princess Royal Harbour. It is Western Australia's oldest city and port, settled around 30 months before Perth. A replica of the ship *Amity*, which brought the first settlers in 1826, is mounted on the foreshore and the town retains good examples of colonial architecture. Albany's more recent history includes the less glorious distinction of being the last site for commercial whaling in Australia. The former whaling station at Cheynes Beach has now become an interesting if slightly macabre museum, **Whaleworld✦**.

The town has good local beaches, led by Middleton Beach, and plenty of secluded spots further afield. Forty kilometres to the east, **Two Peoples Bay Nature Reserve✦** provides a wildlife sanctuary for such threatened species as the noisy scrub bird and Gilbert's potoroo, a primitive relative of the wallaby. A pretty heritage

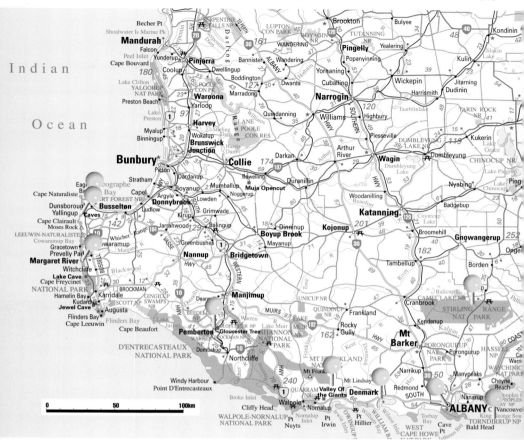

Two Peoples Bay Nature Reserve

40km east of Albany. Take the Lower King Road from Albany. Unrestricted access.

Mt Romance *Mirembenna Park, Lot 2 Down Rd, Albany; tel: (08) 9841-7788. Open daily 0900–1700. Tours available.*

trail cuts through native woodland to lookouts with delightful bay views and passes excellent snorkelling spots. Albany's drawback is the weather – when the sun comes out it is magnificent but cloud and rain seem far more prevalent. For unusual souvenirs, try the **Mt Romance**✦ essential oils cosmetic factory. It specialises in products made from sandalwood, Western Australia's first export industry.

Accommodation and food in Albany

Balneaire Seaside Resort $$–$$$ *27 Adelaide Crescent, Middleton Beach; tel: (08) 9842-2877.* A minute's walk from the beach, Provençal-style Balneaire is a welcome addition to Albany's limited portfolio of stylish, boutique accommodation. Seventeen, two- or three-bedroom apartments face on to a central courtyard.

Cello's Restaurant $$–$$$ *Churchlane Rd, Upper Kalgan; tel: (08) 9844-3370 (about 22km from Albany on the Chester Pass Rd).* Located in a restored stone homestead, Cello's is one of WA's great country restaurants and cafés. It not only has very good food but a wonderful view over a heavily wooded bend in the Kalgan River. Though not to everyone's taste, the menu often includes the exotic Patagonian Toothfish caught in the far Southern Ocean by boats operating out of Albany. The restaurant is unlicensed, so bring your wine and beer. Accommodation is also available.

CAPE NATURALISTE❖❖❖

🍴 Wise Winery and Restaurant $$ *Eagle Bay Rd, Meelup; tel: (08) 9755-3311. Open for lunch daily; dinner Fri and Sat.*

The small peninsula capped by the Cape Naturaliste lighthouse is one of the most beautiful and popular coastal strips in the southwest. That stretch of it facing Geographe Bay is almost unique along WA's coast in having a northern and eastern outlooks, creating an arc of sheltered, pristine bays perfect for swimming, snorkelling, fishing and diving. **Meelup Bay** is one of the prettiest, with an extensive lawn area under shady peppermint trees. Further along Cape Naturaliste Rd are **Eagle Bay** – the most expensive address for a beach house in WA and still relatively unspoiled – and picturesque **Bunker Bay**. At Cape Naturaliste, the land again confronts the Indian Ocean and the environment changes dramatically. From the lighthouse, a network of sandy trails leads to breathtaking views of the rugged coast and powerful swells south to Sugarloaf Rock. In winter and spring, migrating southern right and humpback whales make their way along this stretch of coast and often can be sighted from the lookouts here. Lunch at **Wise Winery❖**, with its magnificent panorama over farm and bushland to Geographe Bay, is not to be missed.

Below
Cape Naturaliste lighthouse

DENMARK❖❖

Denmark is a tranquil little town on the Denmark River, near where it flows into the Wilson Inlet, and is populated by a mix of farmers, alternative lifestylers, and tourists. The signposted **Scotsdale Tourist Drive** (Route 255) takes in many of the surrounding attractions, meandering through rolling hills, imposing stands of karri forest, vineyards and the beautiful beaches and headlands of

William Bay National Park. **Greens Pool** is a magical spot in the park, a large, clear pool of calm water sheltered from the often wild Southern Ocean by a reef of granite boulders. Around the headland is the aptly named Elephant Rocks and, a couple of kilometres further on, **Madfish Bay**, another unusual cove sheltered by a granite island. It is possible to walk through the shallow water to this island, although the attraction is not great – it is a snake-breeding sanctuary.

MARGARET RIVER***

ⓘ Margaret River Tourist Bureau
Bussell Highway; tel: (08) 9757-2911. Open daily.

ⓒ Over the past decade, numerous guesthouses, chalets and B&Bs have opened to service Margaret River's rapidly growing tourist demand. Those rated highly include **Basildene Manor $$$** *Wallcliffe Rd; tel: (08) 9757-3140*, a National Trust-listed building which has undergone extensive refurbishment, and **Bridgefield $$** *73 Bussell Hwy; tel: (08) 9757-3007*, a tastefully restored guesthouse built in 1894 and set in a lush garden near the heart of town.

If you have never heard of Margaret River, either you don't drink or you don't surf. Once a mecca for alternative lifestylers, the Combi vans are now starting to be outnumbered by BMWs as the region takes a distinct turn from hippie to yuppie. But its natural attractions remain intact – spectacular surfing, sandy beaches, towering stands of native forest, vast underground caves, and vineyards which produce some of Australia's best wines. The town is named after a river which enters the sea about 8km away, at **Prevelly**, where some of the best wave breaks in Australia draw surfers from around the world, especially the annual Margaret River Classic. The sheltered beach and open air café at **Gnarabup**, just south of Prevelly, is a great spot for a morning swim and breakfast.

South and west of the town are several of WA's most renowned wineries, led by **Leeuwin Estate**, which enjoys a spectacular setting amid tall karri forest, Voyager Estate, Cape Mentelle and Devil's Lair.

Right
Margaret River coastline

Wine tasting

Western Australia produces only a tiny fraction of Australia's wine but over the past two decades has come to account for more than a quarter of its premium production. Most of that originates from grapes grown in this southwest region where the cool climate and slow ripening produces velvety cabernets and whites bursting with fresh tropical and citrus flavours.

In the past few years, the growth of the industry has accelerated with hundreds of hectares of former livestock grazing country going under vine annually, particularly in relatively new areas like Denmark, Mount Barker and Frankland River. Margaret River remains the supreme appellation, however, and more than 40 wineries which fall into that region – almost from Cape Naturaliste to Cape Leeuwin – are open for cellar door sales.

Tasting is open to the public and is usually free or involves a small fee per person, refundable on any subsequent purchase. Most wineries have an extensive selection of varietals and blends in reds and whites and welcome both wine beginners and enthusiasts to try as many as they like provided they are genuinely interested. Purchases can usually be delivered within Australia and often overseas.

The businesses range from small, one-person operations where the vigneron or winemaker may chat to visitors about the product to multi-million operations employing dozens of staff. Most are worth visiting just for their lovely settings, and many of the larger ones also now have excellent restaurants.

PEMBERTON✦✦✦

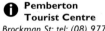

Pemberton Tourist Centre
Brockman St; tel: (08) 9776-1133. Open daily.

Pemberton is known as the kingdom of the karri tree. The town is surrounded by magnificent stands of these pale, smooth-barked giants, the third tallest tree in the world behind California's redwood sequoia and Tasmania's mountain ash. Nearby **Warren** and **Beedelup National Parks** contain three thousand hectares of old growth karri forest and some of the finest forest drives and walks. The trees mature at two hundred years but some live for more than a thousand. Arguably, Pemberton's most popular attraction is the 60-m high **Gloucester Tree** which is reputed to have the highest tree-mounted fire lookout in the world and can be climbed by the more adventurous. Pemberton was a dying timber town but in the past decade has resurrected itself on tourism and the rapidly growing wine industry. **Salitage** and **Gloucester Ridge** are among the better wineries in the region and they have excellent restaurants too. Pemberton also has a number of good woodcraft galleries including **Fine Woodcraft✦** (*Dickinson St, open daily*) which showcases work by nearly 200 woodworkers.

Accommodation and food in Pemberton

Karri Valley Resort $$–$$$ *Vasse Highway, about 20km west of Pemberton; tel: (08) 9776-2020.* This resort is superbly nestled on trout-stocked Lake Beedelup, amid towering karri forest. The lakeside motel units are literally perched over the water, while pine chalets suitable for families are set further into the bush. A walking trail surrounds the lake and links with the short but scenic Beedelup Falls walk in adjacent Beedelup National Park.

STIRLING RANGE NATIONAL PARK✦✦✦

ⓘ WA Department of Conservation and Land Management *www.calm.wa.* Detailed information on most of the state's national parks.

Department of Conservation and Land Management stations sell a variety of passes that can reduce the cost of regular visits to national parks. A holiday pass ($$) allows entry for four weeks to all WA national parks.

The magnificent blue granite peaks of the Stirling Range rise abruptly out of surrounding farmland about 80km north of Albany. It is often likened to the outline of a sleeping woman though Aboriginal Dreamtime legend has it formed from the body of a dead kangaroo. Well-maintained climbing trails and the prospect of dramatic views on clear days as far as the Southern Ocean reward bushwalkers. More than 1500 species of spring and early summer wildflowers are found among the park's heath and shrubland, the most noted being nine species of Darwinias or mountain bells, only one of which can be found outside this park. At 1073m, **Bluff Knoll✦** is the tallest peak in the Southwest and the most popular challenge for walkers. The strenuous return journey from the car park to the summit overlooking its sheer cliff face takes two to three hours. It is worth tackling but be prepared for a cool change and be aware it can frequently and suddenly be covered in streaming low cloud. Though unsealed, the 42-km **Stirling Range Drive✦** is a less arduous way of viewing the park's many scenic and botanic attractions.

TORNDIRRUP NATIONAL PARK✦✦✦

Just 10km south of Albany, on the other side of the Princess Royal Harbour, the Torndirrup Peninsula gives easy access to some of the wildest, most spectacular coast in Western Australia. On the peninsula's southern side, the Southern Ocean surges against giant formations of granite rock formed more than 1000 million years ago when Australia and Antarctica collided (they parted again around 60 million years ago). **The Gap**, a sheer-sided deep gorge in the cliffs, puts on an awesome display even on calm days as rolls of water crash, foam and churn within its walls. Nearby is **Natural Bridge**, a granite arch over the sea, and a short drive and walk away is the **Blowholes**, where air and occasionally spray shoots up through a crack-line in the granite. A little further down the road, a short trail leads to **Stony Hill**, the highest point in the park, and a 360-degree vista.

Left
Ancient Karri forest

VALLEY OF THE GIANTS✦✦✦

Tree Top Walk $$
off Valley of the Giants Rd. Open daily 0900–1700 between mid-Mar and Nov, and 0900–1800 Dec to mid-Mar. Last ticket sold 45 minutes before close.

Located at the eastern edge of the Walpole-Nornalup National Park, this area gets its name from giant red tingle trees which occur only in this very wet, cool part of Western Australia. It also provides another stunning attraction: the opportunity to explore the forest canopy via a 600-m **tree-top walkway**✦. This sympathetically designed engineering marvel is made of steel trusses on steel pylons and gives a bird's-eye view up to 40m above the forest floor. From the same car park, visitors can take a ground-level board walk through a grove of old tingles dubbed the Ancient Empire, some up to 16m in diameter. In many ways the grandeur of the forest is much more overwhelming at this level. Be aware the Tree Top Walk has become one of the Southwest's top tourist destinations. With safety requirements restricting the number of people to 20 per span, delays can occur during the holiday season. An early start will beat the crowds, with the bonus of better birdlife.

YALLINGUP✦✦✦

Ngilgi Cave $$
Caves Rd; tel: (08) 9755-2152. Open daily from 0930.

Below
Cape Leeuwin's meeting of the oceans

Yallingup combines many of the attractions for which southwest WA is justly famous. Its rolling swells attract surfers from around the world, it is close to many of the Margaret River region's renowned vineyards and wineries (probably more than the town of Margaret River), it is home to several fine art and craft galleries and it is a speleologist's paradise. Around 360 caves have so far been discovered in the underground world beneath **Leeuwin Naturaliste National Park**✦, a vast system rated among the oldest and most valuable archaeological sites in Australia. The best known cave, **Ngilgi**✦, is at Yallingup and is one of four in the park where visitors can be guided through vast limestone caverns spiked with stalactites and stalagmites. Most of the wineries in the area are open daily for tasting, usually free. A number also have excellent restaurants in delightful settings, among them Cullens, Vasse Felix, Brookland Valley and Amberley. Just south of Yallingup is **Smiths Beach**, a white, sandy stretch of coast popular with surfers, swimmers, fishers and walkers. A little further down the road is Canal Rocks, a headland of granite outcrops which emerge from the ocean to form a natural canal.

Western Australian Tourist Centre *Forrest Place, cnr Wellington St, Perth; tel: (08) 9483-1111; www.westernaustralia.com*

Accommodation and food in Yallingup

Canal Rocks Beach Resort **$$** *Smiths Beach; tel: (08) 9755-2116.* A range of accommodation right on the beach from higher priced apartments to cheaper chalets and cottages.

Cape Lodge **$$$** *Caves Rd; tel: (08) 8755-6311.* Hosts Joanne and Edward Tait – she an ex-Hyatt employee, he an investment banker – have created at Cape Lodge what is widely regarded as the most sophisticated and stylish retreat in the southwest. Part of the exclusive 'Small Luxury Hotels of the World' portfolio it is set amid 16 hectares of natural bushland, grape vines and English-garden lawns sweep down to a private lake with a natural swimming pool. The establishment has recently been expanded to 20 suites.

Caves House **$$** *Caves Rd; tel: (08) 9755-2041.* One of the Southwest's most historic getaways. It dates from 1903, four years after Yallingup's caves were discovered. A fire in 1935 destroyed the original building, making way for the existing main house, which retains its art deco features including a Grand Terrace, an ideal setting from which to watch the sunset. Beautiful gardens lead down to Yallingup Beach. Caves House is also a great spot for a drink although the Sunday session can draw large, noisy crowds.

Suggested tour

Total distance: The main circuit route is approximately 1250km. The detour to the Stirling Range National Park will add 90km.

Time: The driving time involved is at least 15 hours and an absolute minimum of 3 days will be required to complete the circuit. Realistically, at least 4 days should be allowed, while a leisurely week tour is perfect.

Links: This route starts and ends in Perth and thus links with the tour exploring Perth and Fremantle (*see page 202*).

Route: From Perth, head south on the Albany Highway (State Highway 30) leaving the metropolitan area at Armadale and travelling for 120km to Williams and another 95km to Kojonup before heading to Mt Barker and **ALBANY** ❶.

Detour: To reach Albany via the **STIRLING RANGE NATIONAL PARK** ❷, turn left 62km past Kojonup towards Cranbrook. From Cranbrook, take Route 253 to Amelup for about 20km before turning right on to the unsealed Red Gum Pass Rd. Turn left after about 10km on to the beautiful 42-km Stirling Range Drive which will travel past Mt Magog, Talyuberlup and Toolbrunup. The drive ends at Chester Pass Rd. Turn

Western Australia's carpet of wildflowers

In the spring, between August and November, more than 11,000 species of flowers burst into brilliantly coloured blooms, carpeting dry deserts, rocky plains, beach dunes and the forests of the southwest corner with blazing reds, yellows, purples, pinks and blues. More than three-quarters of these unusual flowers are unique to WA, giving the state one of the richest floras in the world.

Evolution has taken its own course in Australia's west, resulting in some remarkable plants such as the kangaroo paw – WA's floral emblem. The West also has many unique trees, especially its towering jarrah, karri and tingle giants, and the insect-eating Albany pitcher plant.

To guide wildflower tourists, the Western Australian Tourism Commission has produced a special *Wildflower Country* booklet. This divides the state into seven flower 'trails' or driving routes, all starting from Perth, advising on the type of flowers that will be seen, in which national parks and at what time of the season. For those without cars, many tour companies also run flower tours during the spring.

left there and travel for 11km to take the turn-off to the **Bluff Knoll**. Return to Chester Pass Rd and head south again for 88km to reach Albany.

Detour: From Albany, take a right turn on to Frenchman Bay Rd and travel around the harbour for 10km to reach **TORNDIRRUP NATIONAL PARK ❸**. Return the same way.

Take the South Coast Highway 54km to **DENMARK ❹**.

From Denmark, turn right just over the bridge to access the meandering Scotsdale Tourist Drive. Otherwise continue along the highway 12km and turn left to find the sheltered bays of **William Bay National Park**. Return to the highway, drive on for 40km and turn right on to the Valley of the Giants Rd for 6km to access the **VALLEY OF THE GIANTS ❺**.

Return to the highway for 14km to reach the pretty town of Walpole on the Nornalup inlet. Then head up the South Western Highway towards Manjimup and into the southwest's tall timber country. Fifteen kilometres before Manjimup turn left on the Vasse Highway to **PEMBERTON ❻**. Detour at Robinson St and travel 2km to reach **Gloucester Ridge** vineyard and the **Gloucester Tree**. Continue down the Vasse highway from Pemberton for 20km to reach **Beedelup National Park**, or detour 3km out of Pemberton down the Northcliffe road to reach the turn-off to **Warren National Park**. This is the Old Vasse Rd, which reconnects with the Vasse Highway, but take a left at Heartbreak trail to get a better look at the park.

Just over 40km from Pemberton turn left on to the Brockman Highway for Augusta and Margaret River. After 71km this will reach the Bussell Highway. Turn left here and continue if you wish to Augusta and **Cape Leeuwin ❼**, the dramatic granite headland where the Indian Ocean meets the Southern Ocean. Otherwise turn right after about 10km on to Caves Rd. This picturesque route to **MARGARET RIVER ❽**, **YALLINGUP ❾** and Dunsborough provides access to most of the stunning attractions of Leeuwin-Naturaliste National Park, including Boranup Forest, Prevelly and Canal Rocks.

Detour: Take the Cape Naturaliste Rd from Dunsborough for around 10km to reach **CAPE NATURALISTE**. Signposts to the right will point to Meelup, Eagle Bay and Bunker Bay while a left turn will go to Sugarloaf Rock.

From Dunsborough head north for just under 300km to Perth via Bussell Highway to Busselton and Bunbury, the Coast Rd to Mandurah, and Mandurah Rd to Rockingham. While these places are also major holiday centres, they have become victims of sprawling suburbia and are becoming less and less attractive to those looking for a change from urban living. Just after Rockingham, turn right at Thomas Rd and left on to Kwinana Freeway which goes back to Perth.

Also worth exploring

This route can continue on around the coast from Albany to Esperance and beyond – the Great Australian Bight, the Nullarbor Plain and the capital cities of eastern Australia. The coast becomes more arid as it goes east but **Fitzgerald River National Park**, east of Albany, has one of the most important flora reserves in the state with more than 1750 species of plants. **Cape Le Grande National Park**, 60km east of **Esperance**, has some of the most spectacular bays in Australia, with sweeping stretches of impossibly white sand and crystal-clear water.

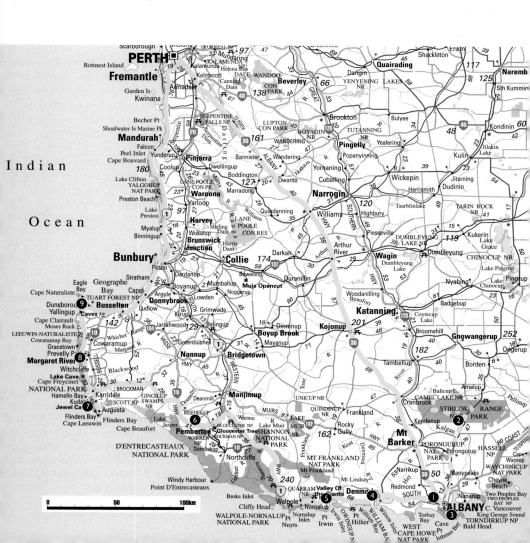

The Kimberley outback

Ratings

Aboriginal culture	●●●●●
Geology	●●●●●
National parks	●●●●●
Scenery	●●●●●
Beaches	●●●●○
Nature	●●●●○
Art	●●●○○
Fishing	●●●○○

A driving tour of the remote and rugged Kimberley region is not for the faint-hearted. This is truly Australia's frontier country where distances are vast, the population minuscule and the remote stillness and antiquity of the land can seem both forbidding and unwelcoming to visitors. But the region has long white sand beaches, ancient Aboriginal rock art, crashing waterfalls, deep red gorges, crocodiles and caves. Broome is a little beach town paradise, with a rich pearl-diving history, while all around are wonderful national parks. Yet tourists are only just starting to discover these tropical treasures, and facilities in the region are beginning to improve. Highlights of this adventure tour include vast rivers, ancient 'beehive' sandstone formations, glistening diamonds, the petrified footprints of a carnivorous dinosaur, a boat trip through Geikie Gorge, and a visit to the second largest meteorite impact site in the world.

ABORIGINAL ROCK ART AND THE BRADSHAW FIGURES❖❖

ℹ **Western Australian Tourist Centre** *Forrest Place, Perth; tel: (08) 9483-1111; www.westernaustralia.com*

Kimberley Tourism Association *PO Box 554, Broome; tel: (08) 9193-6660; www.ebroome.com/kimberley*

Kimberley road conditions and floods *tel: 1800-013-314.*

Aboriginal art in the Kimberley is different from that of most other parts in Australia. Instead of dots, there are the eerie, almost-spacelike **Wandjina** figures of the central Kimberley, and the abstract paintings of ochre, orange, black and white of the Purnululu and Warmun communities based around the Bungle Bungle range. On the **Mitchell Plateau galleries**, the stick-like spirit figures, known as the **Bradshaw figures**, are also fascinating. Older than the co-existing Wandjina art, local Aboriginal groups disclaim all knowledge of their meaning, insisting they were painted by the beaks of birds. One theory is that they were painted by a more ancient race that was obliterated when a newer, and possibly larger, group migrated to the Australian continent from the north. Wandjina paintings and some Bradshaw figures can be found on rock galleries near the King Edward River crossing on the Mitchell Gorge Road, just after it turns off from the Kalumburu Road on the Mitchell Plateau, north of the Gibb River Road.

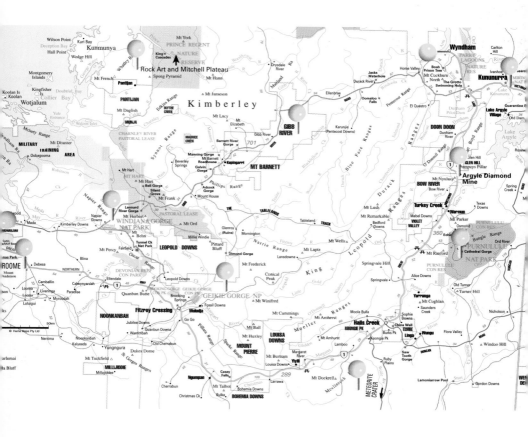

ⓘ **Kimberley Tourist Commission**
www.westernaustralia.net/discover/kimberley/index.shtml

WA Tourist Commission
www.westernaustralia.net

Kimberley's Aboriginal communities

More than two-thirds of the Kimberley population is Aboriginal. And with white settlement only two to three generations old, the Aboriginal culture is one of the strongest, most intact and least destroyed in Australia. Many Kimberley Aboriginal communities have banned alcohol and are educating their children with a strong Aboriginal identity and traditional cultural values, combined with formal white schooling, to enable them to better cope with the pressures of living in a blended society. Some Aboriginal communities now own their own land and cattle stations, and are determined to reduce unemployment, welfare dependence and alcoholism so as to regain control of their own future.

ARGYLE DIAMOND MINE✧✧

Argyle Diamond Mine site tours $$$ *Belray Diamond Tours, Kununurra; tel: 1800-632-533.*

The Argyle Diamond mine, south of Kununurra, is the world's largest diamond mine, producing 34 million carats of diamonds a year, more than one-third of the world's total production. A look around the mine – and at its piles of glittering graded diamonds – is a great experience. The organised tours must be booked at Kununurra; it is not possible just to drop in off the Great Northern Highway as access to the mine is restricted.

BROOME✧✧✧

Broome Tourist Bureau *cnr Broome Highway and Bagot St; tel: (08) 9192-2222; fax: (08) 9192-2063; www. broomevisitorcentre.com.au. Open daily.*

The little tropical paradise town of Broome, has a quaint, slow-moving and historic charm, centred around its fascinating history as a major pearl diving centre from the 1880s. In those days, more than 400 luggers and their crews from Japan, China, Arabia and Europe were based in the port. The Japanese and Chinese influence can still be seen in the town's architecture – its old Chinatown area is now the centre for pearl showrooms – and in the mixed-race origins of many of the locals. Even today highlights of Broome are linked to the pearl industry – take a tour of an operating modern pearl farm, or a champagne cruise on an old wooden pearl lugger out on Roebuck Bay.

CABLE BEACH✧✧

Cable Beach Intercontinental Resort $$$ *Cable Beach Rd, Broome; tel: (08) 9192-0400 or 1800-199-099; fax: (08) 9192-2249.*

About 5km from the township of Broome, stunning and pristine Cable Beach fronts the waves of the Indian Ocean. It is a wonderful 24-km strip of white sand, clear blue waters and gentle surf, in a part of the world where many 'beaches' are no more than mud and mangroves. World-renowned since England's Lord McAlpine built the exclusive but relaxed **Cable Beach Resort✧**, this is the place to lie on the warm sand, ride camels across the sand flats, or watch the sunset from Gantheaume Point, where the 130-million-year-old footprints of a dinosaur are visible on the rockshelf at low tide.

CAPE LEVEQUE✧✧

Kooljaman Resort $–$$ *Cape Leveque; tel: (08) 9192-4970. Open Apr–Oct.*

North of Broome, at the tip of the Dampier Peninsula, are the wonderful red cliffs, white beach and fringing coral reefs of Cape Leveque. A three-hour drive on a boring red dirt road is well-rewarded with a stay at the Aboriginal-owned and run, **Kooljaman Resort✧** at Cape Leveque, either in outdoor bush shelters or more comfortable hut accommodation. Go mud-crabbing with the local Bardi people in the mangroves and mud, or just swim and relax, watching giant

Above
Camel riding on Cable Beach

turtles, dugong and dolphins. **Beagle Bay✴**, halfway up the peninsula, was established as a mission in 1890, and its remarkable little Sacred Heart church built by Trappist monks in 1918 has an ornate interior and altar decorated with local mother-of-pearl.

DERBY✴

ⓘ **Derby Tourist Bureau** / *Clarendon St; tel: (08) 9191-1426 or 1800-621-426; fax: (08) 9191-1609.*

Derby is the major local centre servicing the cattle stations of the West Kimberley and the many outlying Aboriginal communities. It acts as a gateway to the Gibb River Road, the Mitchell Plateau, and the spectacular gorge country to its east. One of its most famous sights is the **Boab Prison Tree✴**, 7km south of the town: the hollow trunk of this giant boab or bottle tree used to serve as an overnight lock-up for prisoners being escorted into Derby for trial.

GEIKIE GORGE✴✴

◉ **Department of Conservation and Land Management**
Geikie Gorge; tel: (08) 9191-5121. Geikie Gorge National Park information; 1 1/2-hour ranger-guided boat trips $ at 0800, 1100 and 1500 daily, Apr–Nov, bookings not necessary.

This magnificent orange, red and gold water-filled gorge, 18km from Fitzroy Crossing, is one of the highlights of any trip to the Kimberley. It is formed where the mighty Fitzroy River slices through the ancient, 350-million-year-old limestone coral beds of the Geikie and Oscar ranges. A boat cruise up the 14-km gorge either with the park rangers or its traditional Aboriginal owners gives a fascinating view of the gorge and its plants, birds and animals. You may spot freshwater sharks and even sharks and stingrays, stranded in this majestic gorge away from the sea where they lived millions of years ago.

GIBB RIVER ROAD***

ⓘ The excellent *Gibb River Road Guide* is available from all tourist offices in the Kimberley. It includes information about cattle stations that welcome guests, favourite camping spots and guides to walking tracks and gorges to be enjoyed along the Gibb River Road.

This remains one of Australia's great adventure drives but is a rough, outback experience that is not to be tackled lightly. Highlights of this dry-season-only, 4WD alternative to the sealed Great Northern Highway linking Derby and Kununurra, include El Questro station (*see page 230*), Manning Gorge, the rampart-like sandstone cliffs of the Cockburn Ranges, the old coral Napier Range and the stunning gorges of Windjana, Bell Creek, Mitchell and Barnett River. This road is gravel only for 586km and can be extremely rutted. It is usually open only from April to November, is always impassable after heavy rain and is not suitable for caravans. Great care must be taken to carry sufficient water, supplies, fuel and breakdown equipment.

KIMBERLEY COASTLINE**

◖ **Cockatoo Island Resort $$$** *via Broome or Derby; tel: (08) 8946-4455.*

Kimberley Coastal Camp $$$ *Admiralty Gulf, North Kimberley; tel: (08) 9161-4410. Open Apr–Oct. Max eight guests.*

The remote north coast of the Kimberley around Admiralty Gulf, the Mitchell Plateau and Prince Regent National Park is almost impossible to access by road. But with its rugged red cliffs, cooling waters, untouched white sand beaches and plunging cliff-face waterfalls, it is a magical place to visit by plane in a scenic air flight or by charter boat, for a sailing or fishing trip. Most tours and charters operating in this region are based in Derby. Often called the 'thousand islands', the **Buccaneer Archipelago*** has massive tides, swirling whirlpools, unlimited oysters, birds and fish. One of its most unusual sights is the **Horizontal Waterfall**, where huge tides funnelling through a narrow neck in Talbot Bay create a 'waterfall' on the sea's surface. Several remote, and generally expensive, resorts operate in this area during the dry season, including one on the former iron ore mine site of **Cockatoo Island***, and another on Admiralty Gulf on the far northern rim of the Mitchell Plateau, both reached only by plane.

KUNUNURRA**

ⓘ **Kununurra Tourist Bureau** *East Kimberley Tourism House, Coolibah Drive; tel: (08) 9168-1177; fax: (08) 9168-2598.*

The green, lush and friendly town of Kununurra, the administrative centre of the east Kimberley, was established in 1960 when the massive Ord River irrigation scheme started. Its origins go back to the famous Durack family of cattle droving fame – their original homestead, then part of Ivanhoe Station, was flooded when the Ord River was dammed to create the immense Lake Argyle. The lake is actually more like an inland sea, containing nine times more water than Sydney harbour. Boat trips are available, and a museum on the lake's shores reconstructs the original Durack homestead. The Argyle Diamond Mine (*see page 224*) south of the lake is a major source of income. In Kununurra itself is the lovely Hidden Valley National Park, while the town also has several airlines offering scenic flights south over Lake Argyle and the Bungle Bungles.

MITCHELL PLATEAU AND KALUMBURU❖❖

The Mitchell Plateau is one of Australia's last untouched wildernesses and an area of significant Aboriginal heritage. Reached via dirt track and in a high-clearance 4WD only, from the Gibb River Road, its highlights are the Wandjina Aboriginal art sites around the King Edward River, the spectacular Mitchell Gorge multiple waterfalls, and the small remote Aboriginal settlement of Kalumburu, renowned for its local Aboriginal artists. All Aboriginal art sites are protected and must not be touched. Beware of dangerous estuarine crocodiles in all rivers in this region, even above major waterfalls.

PURNULULU (BUNGLE BUNGLE) NATIONAL PARK❖❖❖

ⓘ **Purnululu National Park** CALM rangers, Halls Creek; tel: (08) 9168-0200.

These 'tiger-striped beehive mountains' – as the Bungle Bungle rock formations were first called when 'discovered' by the international world in the 1980s – rank as one of the great geological and scenic wonders of the world. Now protected as the Purnululu National Park,

Right
Piccaninny Gorge, Bungle Bungle

the lumpy, weather-moulded mounds of the Bungle Bungle range – 33km long and 23km wide – are most easily viewed by air (from Kununurra or Halls Creek). From the ground they are both fascinating and spiritual; walk among narrow gorges lined with tall palms, 200-m high cliffs among the black and orange domes, and clear pools of water lined with Aboriginal hand prints and rock art.

Windjana Gorge and Tunnel Creek❖❖

These two small national parks on the western end of the Gibb River Road are, together with Geikie Gorge, the best way to get a sense of the immense rocky nature of the Mitchell Plateau and the Kimberley, without tackling the tough Gibb River Road trip itself. Windjana Gorge is part of the 350-million-year-old limestone Napier Range, with the deep fissure of its gorge caused by the flow of the Lennard River. From the national park campsite, there is a lovely 3½-km walk up the gorge where fossils and freshwater crocodiles are often seen. Nearby Tunnel Creek National Park, a 750-m long tunnel running under the same limestone range, makes for adventurous exploring.

Wolfe Creek Crater National Park❖❖

About 150km from the town of Halls Creek, on the start of the Tanami Desert track, is the Wolfe Creek Crater National Park. This is the place where the second largest meteorite known to have hit earth crashed some 250,000 years ago, creating the extraordinary circular

Below
Tidal flats near Wyndham

rim of the Wolfe Crater, some 850m in diameter. The access road crosses the rim and ends up inside the large sheltered interior of the impact site, where it is easy to imagine you are standing on the moon! There are no facilities in this park so water must be carried.

WYNDHAM*

Wyndham Tourist Information Centre *Kimberley Motors, Great Northern Highway; tel: (08) 9161-1281; fax: (08) 9161-1435.*

Visitors to little Wyndham are usually greeted by the view of vast river estuaries and endless mudflats. This port on the Cambridge Gulf is the place where five great rivers of the Kimberley – the King, the Pentecost, the Ord, the Forrest and the Durack – all enter the sea. The Five Rivers Lookout high above the town in the Bastion Range offers the best view. This lookout is also a favourite for hang-gliders who like to fly from here down on to the mudflats – watching out for the numerous crocodiles when they land. The Crocodile Farm is a must for visitors to Wyndham, whereas The Grotto is a lovely natural waterhole free of crocodiles for great swimming. Marglu Billabong in Parry Lagoons Reserve has excellent birdwatching.

Accommodation and food

Cable Beach Intercontinental Resort $$$ *Cable Beach Rd, Broome, tel: (08) 9192-0400 or 1800-199-099; fax: (08) 9192-2249.* The ultimate in relaxed luxury, it was this elegant resort on the edge of the long white sands of Cable Beach that started the Kimberley tourism boom. Great restaurants too.

Cockatoo Island Resort $$$ *via Broome or Derby; tel: (08) 8946-4455.*

Eco-Beach Wilderness Retreat $$ *Yardoogarra, Cape Villaret; tel: (08) 9192-4844; fax: (08) 9192-4845.* Overlooking Roebuck Bay, and 1½ hour's drive from Broome, this award-winning ecotourism resort has birds, turtles, dolphins, whales, self-contained cabins and a friendly, outdoor atmosphere.

Kimberley Coastal Camp $$$ *Admiralty Gulf, North Kimberley; tel: (08) 9161-4410. Open Apr–Oct only.* A luxurious and remote permanent camp on the far edge of the Mitchell River plateau. An exclusive fishing and adventure resort, accessible by air only and expensive.

McAlpine House $$$ *84 Herbert St, Broome; tel: (08) 9192-3886; fax: (08) 9192-3887.* Luxurious guesthouse accommodation in the beautiful old Broome Pearling Master's House.

Ocean Lodge $–$$ *Cable Beach Rd, Broome; tel: (08) 9193-7700; fax: (08) 9193-7496.* Great good-value family motel with self-contained rooms, garden, pool and barbecue. Located halfway between central Broome and Cable Beach, you need a car if staying here.

The **Pearl Festival**, or **Shinju Matsuri**, is held in Broome in Aug or early Sept, depending on the moon's phases. It has a different theme every year connected with the town's pearl history, featuring art and pearl jewellery exhibitions, street parades, ceremonies, free night events and fireworks. For more details, contact the Broome Tourist Bureau (see page 224).

El Questro $–$$$
Gibb River Rd via Kununurra; tel: (08) 9169-1777; fax: (08) 9169-1383; www.elquestro.com.au.
El Questro, a 405,000-hectare cattle station and wilderness park, is a travel experience that can be enjoyed by any tourist, no matter what their budget. There are magnificent gorges, fishing, deep pools, thermal springs and red, rocky, rugged country to be roamed freely and at leisure, whether you are staying in your own tent or caravan at the campsite or at the $600-a-night cliff-top homestead, a permanent luxury tent resort at cool Emma Gorge: unexpected style and elegance in the midst of the Kimberley wilderness.

Suggested tour

Distance: Travelling along the sealed, paved Great Northern Highway, it is 1135km from Broome to Kununurra via Derby, Fitzroy Crossing and Halls Creek. From Kununurra back to Derby via the dirt Gibb River Road is another 705km, only 119km of which are sealed.

Roads are usually open and in good condition in the dry season from April–October, but can be closed – even the Great Northern Highway – during the wet season. To check road conditions, tel: 1800-013-314.

Time: A drive from Broome to Kununurra sticking to the sealed highway, but visiting the sights along the way, will take a minimum of four days, although it could be driven in two days without stops. The dirt Gibb River Road takes at least four days to traverse.

Links: It is about 600km from Kununurra to Katherine in the Northern Territory, heading east along the sealed Victoria Highway, to link up with the Top End driving tour (see page 192).

Route: From the tropical town of **BROOME**, with its stunning white sand **CABLE BEACH**, it is a 221-km drive east on the sealed Great Northern Highway to reach the town of **DERBY** ❶ on King Sound. Derby is the best place to organise air trips and boat charters to visit the remote **KIMBERLEY COASTLINE** and the **Buccaneer Archipelago**, which lies northeast of the town.

From Derby, it is 214km on the sealed Great Northern Highway heading east then north towards **WINDJANA GORGE** and **TUNNEL CREEK NATIONAL PARK** ❷, 105km and 70km respectively.

Continuing along the highway, it is another 42km to the town of **Fitzroy Crossing** and the turn-off to the left to spectacular **GEIKIE GORGE NATIONAL PARK** ❸. Another 288km along the highway is the old gold-rush town of **Halls Creek** ❹, although the gravel road turn-off to **WOLFE CREEK CRATER NATIONAL PARK** ❺ is 16km before Halls Creek to the right. From here it is 111km to see the extraordinary meteorite crater.

Halls Creek is a good place to take a scenic flight over **PURNULULU (BUNGLE BUNGLE) NATIONAL PARK** and to go on an organised one- or two-day 4WD tour. Alternatively, continuing north along the Great Northern Highway from Halls Creek, it is 110km to the 4WD-only turn-off into the **Purnululu National Park** ❻. It is 370km along the sealed highway between Halls Creek and **WYNDHAM** ❼. Although the road to the **ARGYLE DIAMOND MINE** is passed on the way, it can only be visited as part of an organised tour available in **KUNUNURRA** ❽. It is 101km, all on sealed road, from Wyndham to Kununurra, and another 71km from Kununurra heading east to reach

Lake **Argyle** and the narrow but spectacularly deep **Ord River dam wall**.

From Kununurra, the road heads east into the Northern Territory, towards Katherine. If the rough dirt **GIBB RIVER ROAD** ❾ is to be tackled to make a circuit trip, the turn-off is 53km back along the sealed highway, towards Wyndham. From there it is only just over 40km, some of its sealed, to reach the magnificent tourist cattle station of **El Questro** ❿. It is another 210km of dirt road, past the startling **Cockburn Range** and good camping spot of **Jacks Waterhole**, before the rough turn-off ⓫ leading to the remote **MITCHELL PLATEAU** and **KALUMBURU** part of the Kimberley with its special **ABORIGINAL ROCK ART** sites. The Gibb River Rd then continues for another 320km, past Manning River Gorge and the Bell Creek turn-off, before completing the circle to Windjana Gorge and Tunnel Creek National Parks, and the sealed road leading back to Derby and Broome.

Detour: If you have time to spare in Broome, and preferably a 4WD vehicle, take the red dirt road for 220km north to **CAPE LEVEQUE** and Kooljaman Resort at the tip of the Dampier Peninsula, visiting **Beagle Bay** on the way.

Ratings

History	●●●●●
Restaurants	●●●●●
Villages	●●●●●
Vineyards	●●●●●
Outdoor activities	●●●●○
Scenery	●●●●○
Walking	●●●●○
Art and crafts	●●●○○

The Adelaide Hills and Barossa Valley

A drive through the Adelaide Hills and the Barossa Valley is the ultimate in self indulgence; a perfect weekend getaway from Adelaide. The winding road that twists through hills, vineyards and orchards follows the story of European settlement in this beautiful, mellow part of South Australia. In autumn, the trees and vines turn vibrant red and orange and in spring the wild almond blossom, irises and belladonna lilies flower along the roadside. There is just so much to see, drink and taste in this region. Drive from Adelaide through the Adelaide Hills to Mt Pleasant, the Eden Valley and the Barossa, with its world-renowned vineyards and wineries. Visit the little towns of Nuriootpa and historic Tanunda, tasting wines along the way, or drop into the dried fruit factory at Angaston. This is a lush Eden in Australia's driest state.

ADELAIDE✦✦✦

① The South Australian Travel Centre I *King William St, Adelaide; tel: (08) 8303-2033. Open weekdays 0900–1700, weekends 0900–1400.*

South Australian Tourism
www.southaustralia.com

⚠ Adelaide Casino *$ tel: (08) 8212-2811. Open Sun–Thur 1000–0400, Fri–Sat 1000–0600.*

Adelaide is named after William IV's queen, and was laid out in 1836 around a square mile grid of wide streets and squares. The feeling of an elegant city of Victorian solidity prevails. The architecture reflects Adelaide's character, based on old values and old money. Its strong link with a powerful pastoral community contributes to the feeling that Adelaide is a large country town.

North Terrace Boulevard is lined with museums, galleries, the university campus, Government House, Parliament House and a casino. The **Adelaide Casino**✦ is housed in the grand 1920s sandstone railway station. The result is totally stylish and worth visiting, even if you do not intend to gamble one brass razoo. If you happen to wander from the casino late at night, then try a 'Pie Floater', available from pie carts scattered throughout the city. This dish comprises a hot meat pie with tomato sauce, sitting in a bowl of pea soup, and has become an Adelaide institution for many revellers with post-party munchies.

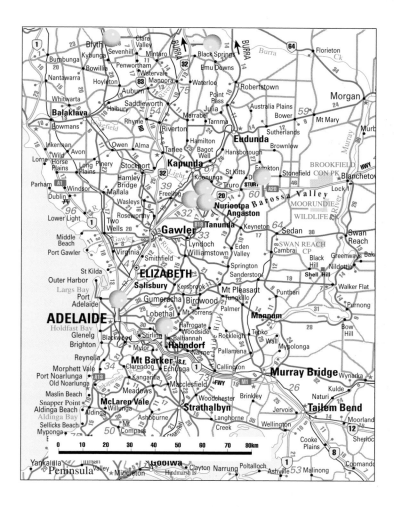

Parliament House
$$ cnr North Terrace
and King William St; tel: (08)
8237-9100. Tours on non-
sitting days 1000–1400; to
see Parliament sitting, visit
from 1400 onwards.

Parliament House✛✛ was built in two stages, 50 years apart, and is a solid pile of Kapunda marble on granite with Corinthian columns. This is the parliament that was shocked to its conservative core when Don Dunstan, the 1960s premier, turned up in pink shorts.

Adelaide prides itself on its cultural heritage, which continues to influence the lives of its populace. The **Adelaide Festival Centre**✛ is the epicentre of the city's festival. The complex includes a concert hall, three theatres, an open-air amphitheatre and a **theatre museum**✛ in the basement, which has more than 40,000 items on display showing the history of the performing arts, using that term in its widest sense. **The Art Gallery of South Australia**✛✛✛ opened in 1871 and has four main areas: prints and drawings, Australian decorative

Adelaide Festival Centre $ *King William Rd; tel: (08) 8216-8600 and the theatre museum $ tel: (08) 8216 8767; www.afct.org.au. Open Mon–Fri 0900–1700.*

The Art Gallery of South Australia $$$ *North Terrace; tel: (08) 8207-7000; www.artgallery.sa.gov.au. Open daily 1000–1700.*

Tandanya arts complex $$ *253 Grenfell St; tel: (08) 8223-2467. Open daily 1000–1700.*

Migration Museum $$ *Kintore Avenue; tel: (08) 8207-7570. Open Mon–Fri 1000–1700, weekends and public holidays 1300–1700.*

Historical Aviation Museum $ *Ocean Steamers Rd, Port Adelaide; tel: (08) 8240-1230. Open daily 1000–1700.*

Port Dock Station *Lipson St, Port Adelaide; tel: (08) 8341-1690. Open daily 1000–1700.*

The South Australian Maritime Museum $$ *126 Lipson St, Port Adelaide; tel: (08) 8207-6255.*

Adelaide Botanic Gardens $$ *North Terrace; tel: (08) 8228-2311. Open Mon–Fri 0800–sunset, Sat–Sun 0900–sunset.*

Zoological Gardens $$ *Frome Rd; tel: (08) 8267-3255. Open daily 0930–1700.*

arts, European and Asian decorative arts and painting and sculpture. The collection of Australian art is particularly strong and has the world's most comprehensive collection of Aboriginal artefacts. Aboriginal art is a continuing tradition, with a growing number of enthusiasts. One place to see it is **Tandanya✦✦**, which is an Aboriginal multi-arts complex including galleries, a workshop and performing areas. If you make an appointment, Aboriginal guides will give introductory talks on various aspects of their heritage and culture. There are several exhibitions as well as work for sale, and a daily didgeridoo performance.

Adelaide's former Destitute Asylum has been transformed into the **Migration Museum✦✦**. A chronological walk through the history of immigration and settlement in South Australia since 1836 offers many moving stories from the nation's migrants. Aviation played a major part in the history of Australia which is reflected in the **Historical Aviation Museum✦**, which has everything from early prop planes to over 50 rockets and missiles. For train-spotters **Port Dock Station✦✦** is a mini-heaven, for there are 26 locomotives on various track gauges – Australia once had different gauges for each state for years – and there are two steam trains that you can ride, if only for a short distance.

The South Australian Maritime Museum✦✦ is not a traditional museum, spread over several sites, including an 1850s bond store, the 1869 lighthouse and a wharf with vessels moored alongside. A life-size model of a ship which brought convicts to Australia provides an insight into the horror that that journey must have been.

Adelaide is a green city with plenty of air and space. It has the **Adelaide Botanic Gardens✦✦**, which were begun in 1855, almost with the founding of the city. It boasts the oldest greenhouse in a botanic garden in Australia and the Bicentennial Conservatory next door is built in a giant arc and holds a tropical rainforest. Nearly as impressive are the **Zoological Gardens✦✦**, which are among the oldest in Australia. Animals are housed in moated enclosures, walk-through aviaries and an excellent reptile house. A pleasant 35-minute boat ride on the *Popeye* launch will take you there from the city centre.

Right
Adelaide's market

Angaston❖❖

Angas Park Dried Fruits Centre $
Murray St, Tanunda. Open Mon–Sat 0900–1700, Sun and public holidays 1100–1700.

Collingrove Homestead $$ *Eden Valley Rd; tel: (08) 8564-2061. Open weekdays 1300–1630, weekends 1100–1630.*

Homely and small, Angaston is an ideal base for exploring the Barossa. The main street is a feast of small shops and fine public buildings, which are mapped in a self-guided walk. Numerous art and craft shops, galleries, tearooms and a blacksmith make it a pleasurable stroll. Visit the **Angas Park Dried Fruits Centre❖❖** and view the production area. Dried fruits, nuts and confectionery are available from the factory. The Zion Lutheran Church has a bold façade of pink marble, quarried from nearby rocky hills. **Collingrove Homestead❖❖** – which was built in 1856 by the Angas family, and remained in their possession until it was given to the National Trust in 1976 – is now a languid guesthouse where visitors can wander through English-style gardens and imagine the lifestyle of wealthy English settlers.

Barossa Valley❖❖❖

Barossa Wine and Visitor Centre 66
Murray St, Tanunda; tel: (08) 8563-0600; www.barossa.mtx.net. Open weekdays 0900–1700, weekends 1000–1600. This centre services the entire Barossa Valley.

Balloon Adventures $$$ *tel: (08) 8389-3195; fax: (08) 8389-3220. Discover the beauty of the Barossa from the air, drifting above the vineyards at a sedate pace.*

The Barossa Valley, Australia's best-known winemaking region, is only an hour's drive north of Adelaide. The valley is bordered by rolling hills, and magnificent old churches, wineries, European-style villages and farm cottages are scattered amongst vineyards, in a manicured landscape. Hot-air balloons are common, particularly in May when the annual balloon regatta is held. But mostly, the Barossa Valley is about wine and food. Begin your gourmet journey at the **Barossa Wine and Visitor Centre❖❖** to talk about winemaking with an expert and learn the history of the wine industry. Last century, wealthy British settlers employed Silesian religious refugees to run their vineyards. The two cultures have blended to create unique regional cuisine, wines and lifestyle, all available throughout the Barossa in abundance. There are about 50 wineries producing world-class wines which welcome visitors, including Yalumba and the internationally famous Jacob's Creek. Some offer tours, picnic facilities, restaurants, as well as cellar door tastings.

Burra❖❖❖

Burra Tourist Office *Market Square; tel: (08) 8892-1254. Purchase your Burra passport here ($$$); a refundable deposit for the passport key is required.*

Burra is a popular tourist destination because of its fascinating history, mainly centred on the discovery of copper here in 1845. The entire town is on the National Estate Register, and many buildings are owned by the National Trust. A caring community has ensured the character of historic Burra remains intact. The Burra Passport enables visitors to drive or walk an 11-km trail past 43 heritage sites, seven of which can be entered with the passport key. The **Bon Accord Mine Complex❖❖❖**, representative of Burra's eclectic history, is best viewed by climbing to the platform of the well-lit vertical mine shaft. The

Bon Accord Mine Complex $$ *corner of West and Linkson St; tel: (08) 8892-2056. Open weekdays 1230-1430, weekends 1230–1530.*

Paxton Square Cottages $$ *Paxton Square; tel: (08) 8892-2154. Open Sat 1300–1500, Sun 1030–1230.*

tiny **Paxton Square**✦✦ cottages must have seemed palatial to the families who had lived in **Miners' Dugouts**✦✦ along the river bed. As part of the Burra Heritage Trail, one cottage is a museum with a mine captain's furniture, and it is also possible to visit some of the dugouts which housed up to 2000 miners and their families. The **Police Lockup and Stables**✦✦, and the **Redruth Gaol**✦✦ (location for the Australian film, *Breaker Morant*) show the grim reality of 19th-century prison conditions.

Right
Seppeltsfield Winery, Barossa Valley

CLARE VALLEY✦✦✦

Clare Valley Tourist Information Centre *Town Hall, 229 Main North Rd, Clare; tel: (08) 8842-2131; www.clarevalley.com.au. Open Mon–Sat 0900–1700, Sun 1000–1600.*

Sevenhill Jesuit Monastery $ *College Rd, Sevenhill; tel: (08) 8843-4222. Open weekdays 0830–1630, Sat and public holidays 0900–1600.*

The picturesque Clare Valley is a 90-minute drive north of Adelaide. Famous for its verdant vineyards and excellent crisp white wines, the Clare Valley is also renowned for its old stone buildings, many on heritage registers. The valley's commercial centre, **Clare**✦, is set in a wooded valley among orchards and 30 vineyards, many boutique winemakers. Further south, in the tiny township of Sevenhill, discover the oldest Clare Valley winery, the **Sevenhill Jesuit Monastery**✦. The region's wine producing history can be further explored at the **Old Clarevale Museum**✦ ($$ *Lennon St, Clare; open daily*), a restored co-operative winery which also houses a gallery and restaurant. It is worth investigating the **Old Police Station Museum**✦ ($$ *West Terrace, Clare; open weekends*), with exhibits illustrating the district's colourful history. **Wolta Wolta**✦ ($$ *West Terrace, Clare; open Sun 1000–1200*) and **Bungaree**✦ ($$ *off Main Rd, 12km north of Clare; tel: (08) 8842-2677; open by appointment*) are working sheep stations which provide an insight into the glory days of farming.

HAHNDORF✦✦✦

ℹ️ **Hahndorf Visitors' Centre** 64 Main St; tel: (08) 8388-2285.

🏛️ **The Cedars** Heysen Rd, Hahndorf; tel: (08) 8388-7277. Closed Sat. Gallery free, open 1000–1600, guided tours ($$) 1100, 1300 and 1500.

Only 28km from Adelaide, in the Adelaide Hills, Hahndorf has become South Australia's most popular tourist town. It was settled by 187 German Lutheran settlers escaping religious persecution in their homeland in 1837. In their new isolated valley home they created a unique north German-style village. Hahndorf is now a listed Heritage area, and Australia's oldest German settlement. A simple walk along shady Main St, lined by century-old trees, provides hours of entertainment wandering through art and crafts shops, gift shops, galleries and museums. Original buildings feature *fachwerk*, timber framing with wattle and daub infill. Taste a variety of local and imported beers at the **German Arms Hotel** ($$ *69 Main Street; tel: (08) 8388-7013*), six-times winner of South Australia's best hotel award, or sample traditional German cuisine in the many bakeries or cafés.

Built in 1858 on the outskirts of Hahndorf, **The Cedars✦✦** was home for Australian landscape artist Sir Hans Heysen from 1912 until his death in 1968. In the chalet-style studio on a wooded slope he painted the works which brought him fame.

NURIOOTPA✦✦✦

🏛️ **Luhrs Pioneer German Cottage** $$ Light Pass. Open weekdays 1000–1600, weekends 1300–1600.

🥩 **Linke's Central Meat Store** $ 47 Murray St, Nuriootpa.

🍴 **Linke's Bakery and Tearooms** $–$$ 40 Murray St, Nuriootpa.

🍷 **Penfolds Winery** Barossa Valley Way, Nuriootpa; tel: (08) 8560-9408; www.penfolds.com.au. Open Mon–Sat 1000–1700, Sun 1300–1700.

The Nuriootpa Plains are covered by extensive areas of vineyards that can be viewed from the Barossa Valley Way. Nuriootpa is the commercial centre for the Barossa Valley, and just the place to stock up on local fare at the cornucopia of butchers, bakers and wineries. Even before European settlement, it was a place of barter for Aboriginal tribes, with Nuriootpa meaning 'meeting place'. Nearby, the **Luhrs Pioneer German Cottage✦✦** is a heritage-listed mud and straw building which is filled with German artefacts. **Linke's Central Meat Store✦** has a fabulous selection of traditional German meats and sausages, and its *jaegerbraten* (stuffed pork belly) is legendary. **Linke's Bakery and Tearooms✦** sells mouth-watering pies, bread and *bienenstich* cake. Buy some *bratwurst*, smoked chicken or pork sausages, to take to nearby Coulthard Reserve for a lovely picnic. **Penfolds Winery✦✦** at Nuriootpa is the valley's largest winery complex, and home of the world-famous Grange Hermitage wines, which can be best appreciated by taking the Great Grange Tour ($$$; available by appointment only, and requires at least five people).

RIESLING TRAIL✦✦✦

The Riesling Trail, which passes through the Clare Valley, is of course named after the prized, dry crisp local wine. The trail is suitable for recreational walkers and cyclists; it meanders through about 27km of

ℹ Clare Valley Tourist Centre
Town Hall, 229 Main North Rd, Clare; tel: (08) 8842-2131. Open daily.

picturesque winegrowing and grazing country, and past the wineries between Clare and Auburn. Worth seeing along the trail are the Sevenhill Jesuit Monastery and Winery built in 1851, and **Martindale Hall**✢✢, the classic 19th-century mansion used in the film *Picnic at Hanging Rock* (tel: (08) 8843-9088; open 1100–1600).

TANUNDA✢✢✢

ℹ Barossa Wine and Visitor Centre *66 Murray St; tel: (08) 8563-0600; www.barossa-region.org. Open weekdays 0900–1700, weekends 1000–1600.*

Tanunda is the heart of the Valley, and the most German of the Barossa towns, even though its name is derived from an Aboriginal word meaning 'watering hole'. A leisurely stroll through its back streets is an instant reminder of the importance of northern German culture to this region; visit the National Trust-listed Langmeil's Goat Square, Rose Bridge, Kegel Alley and the four Lutheran churches.

WALKING TRAILS✢✢✢

ℹ State Government Information Centre *77 Grenfell St, Adelaide, 0930–1700; tel: (08) 8204-1900; www.barossa-region.org. Weekdays only.* Copies of maps ($) are available for the **Heysen Trail**.

◉ Walking Website *www.recsport.sa.gov.au* For good information about other walks in SA.

◔ Maggie Beer's Farm Shop *Pheasant Farm Rd, off Seppeltsfield Rd, Nuriootpa; tel: (08) 8562-4477.* Maggie Beer, famed as a chef, sells her popular Pheasant Farm paté, verjuice, quince paste, mushroom paté and smoked kangaroo through this shop, which is a foodies' heaven.

The patchwork landscape of Barossa Valley vineyards contains beautiful conservation parks. The **Kaiser Stuhl Conservation Park**✢✢ is a rugged mountain park, south of Tanunda on the Tanunda Creek Rd. Walking trails cross bush, rocky outcrops, creeks and open grassland. Look for wedge-tailed eagles, finches, blue wrens and parrots. The **Stringybark Loop Trail** is most enjoyable at dusk, when there is an abundance of kangaroos; there are directions at the park entrance. The **Heysen Trail**✢✢✢, named after the famed landscape painter, is the world's longest walking track. It begins at Cape Jervis and concludes 1500km north in the Flinders Ranges – not that you have to walk the entire length. The trail passes through the most scenic parts of the state including national parks and tourist regions. The many access points in the Adelaide Hills and the Barossa Valley are clearly marked by a red logo or markers. Information signs, stiles, bridges and other trail furniture assist the walker. The trail caters for serious backpackers and day walkers, and is divided into 15 sections, each having a detailed map. There are numerous huts, hostels, home and farm stays along the way. The trail is closed from November to March due to the risk of bushfires.

Accommodation and food

1918 Bistro & Grill $$$ *94 Murray St, Tanunda; tel: (08) 8563-0405.* A casual and friendly atmosphere, local wines and fantastic food.

Barossa Motor Lodge $$ *182 Murray St, Tanunda; tel: (08) 8563-2988.* Surrounded by vineyards and within walking distance to local wineries. Family-friendly, with in-house restaurant.

Bungaree Station $$ *off Main Rd, 12km north of Clare; tel: (08) 8842-2677.* A historic Merino sheep station near Clare, with heritage accommodation for up to 80 guests staying in shearers' quarters or self-contained cottages.

Collingrove Homestead $$$ *Eden Valley Rd, Angaston; tel: (08) 8564-2061, fax: (08) 8564-3600.* Grand guest rooms are decorated with period furniture and the gardens are wonderful; a special experience.

The Lodge Country House *Seppeltsfield Rd, Seppeltsfield; tel: (08) 8562-8277; fax: (08) 8562-8344; email: thelodge@dove.net.au.* Opposite Seppeltsfield winery, stay in luxury in a bluestone country manor.

Skillogalee Winery and Restaurant $$ *Hughes Park Rd, Sevenhill; tel: (08) 8843-4311.* One of Clare Valley's favourite restaurants, located in a 150-year-old Cornish miner's stone cottage.

Cockatoo Valley

Picturesque Cockatoo Valley, between the Barossa Valley and Gawler, abounds with birdlife and enchanting scenery. Gold mining history is explained on several intriguing walking loops at Parra Wirra Park, in the south of the Cockatoo Valley, which provide fascinating information boards along the way. North of the gold fields, the **Whispering Wall** is the retaining wall for the Barossa Reservoir, visited for its amazing acoustic ability. Its shape enables a whispered message at one end to be heard 140m away at the other end.

Suggested tour

Total distance: 199km, 408km with detours.

Time: Three hours driving without stops, but it is worth spending 2 or 3 days to leave room for plenty of wine tasting. The detour to Burra and Clare would fill another 2 days.

Links: Returning to Adelaide after this tour, travellers can link into the Coorong to Coonawarra route leading down SA's southeast coastline (*see page 252*), or head north towards the Flinders Ranges (*see page 242*).

Route: From Adelaide take the winding Eastern Freeway through the Adelaide Hills, turning left at the well-marked exit to **HAHNDORF ❶**, 25km from the city. After spending time in Hahndorf, head back towards Adelaide for 3km, and turn right to reach **Mt Pleasant ❷**, driving over bare grassed hills, before entering the **Eden Valley** with its park-like paddocks of pasture and red gums. If you have time, stop at the **Herbig Family Tree and Heritage Centre** to see a 500-year-old hollow red gum, the first home for German settler Friedrich Herbig.

Yalumba *Eden Valley Rd, Angaston; tel: (08) 8561-3299. Open weekdays 0830–1700, weekends 0900–1700. Guided tour $$ daily 1015, 1045, 1315, 1415, 1515.*

Kev Rohrlach Technology and Heritage Centre $$ *Barossa Valley Way, Tanunda North; tel: (08) 8563-3407; fax: (08) 8564-2941; www.marble.mtx.net/ museum. Open daily 1100–1600, Sun 1000–1700.* This superb private collection includes rockets, missiles and satellites, solar-powered technology, vintage cars, tractors, military machines, as well as artefacts once used by Barossa Valley pioneers.

National Motor Museum $$ *Main St, Birdwood; tel: (08) 8568-5006. Open daily 0900–1700.* Australia's largest collection of motor vehicles from 1899 to the present day.

At Eden Valley turn left to **ANGASTON ❸**, and enjoy the landscape change yet again, as vineyards begin to dominate. **COLLINGROVE HOMESTEAD** is on the way into Angaston, and the magnificent **Yalumba Winery** is the first Barossa Winery on the road. From Angaston, travel west on the Angaston Rd to **NURIOOTPA**. **Luhrs Pioneer German Cottage** and two charming Lutheran churches are at **Light's Pass**, on the right.

Continue along Murray St to **TANUNDA**, with the opportunity to call into about 12 wineries between the two towns. Base yourself in one of these three Barossa Valley towns, allowing yourself the time to discover this fascinating region.

To return to Adelaide, take the Barossa Valley Way, past **COCKATOO VALLEY**, and **Lyndoch** and out of the Valley. Continue over bare plains and on to the historic town of **Gawler ❹** – reputed to be the first country town in South Australia – where there are many self-guided walks. The Barrier Highway returns to Elizabeth, and then the Main North Rd leads back into Adelaide.

Detour: At Nuriootpa, take the Stuart Highway east for 10km, and turn left to **Kapunda ❺**, a historic town with grand architecture, reflecting a prosperous copper mining past. Australia's cattle king, Sir Sydney Kidman lived at Kapunda. If you enjoy country back roads, drive through **Marrabel** and **Saddleworth**. The roads are narrow, but in reasonable condition. Otherwise continue to Tarlee, and the Barrier Highway to **BURRA ❻** through rolling hills dotted with the merino sheep for which the region is world famous.

From Burra head south on the Barrier Hwy, turning right at **Hanson** to reach **CLARE ❼**, 44km away. Once again the landscape changes dramatically approaching the Clare Valley, with vineyards taking over from pasture. The bypass road heads south to the town of **Auburn**, at the edge of the valley, which has some of South Australia's finest stonework buildings. The bypass road rejoins the Main North Rd, heading south to Adelaide.

Also worth exploring

Morgan✦✦ is 100km north of Nuriootpa, and worth exploring to appreciate the mighty Murray River, and the gateway to the orchards and irrigation country of the Riverland. It was settled in the 1870s, and in its heyday was the second busiest port in south Australia. Today, Morgan keeps its heritage alive with a dockyards for river ferry construction and heritage displays. The Morgan Heritage Trail, notable for its fine views, is a walk through history past the railway and wharf areas and along the waterfront.

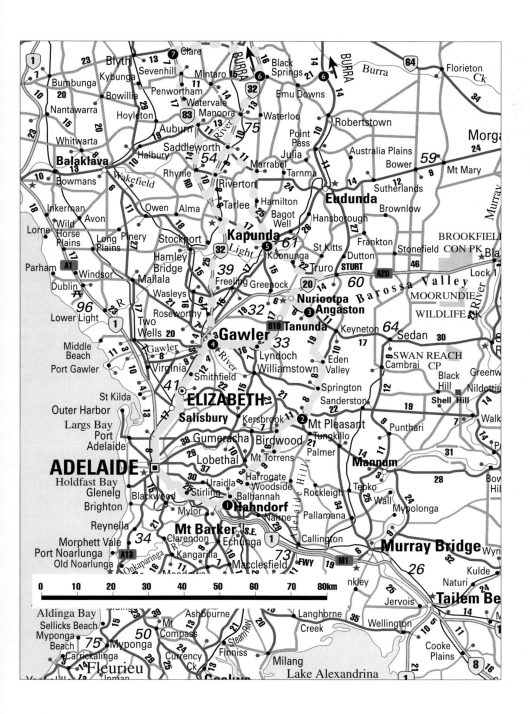

The Flinders Ranges

Ratings

Geology	●●●●●
National parks	●●●●●
Outdoor grandeur	●●●●●
Scenery	●●●●●
Walking	●●●●○
Wildflowers	●●●●○
Food and wine	●●●○○
History	●●●○○

This is a drive for anyone willing to travel 400km north of Adelaide to get a rugged taste of the South Australian outback. The Flinders Ranges have a majesty and beauty all of their own – there are ancient hillsides billowing wildflowers, jugged, rugged red ridges jutting against a hard blue sky, cool deep gorges lined with white-trunked river gums, and wide expansive valleys with purple ranges soaring on both sides above the good gravel roads. This is a land of ancient Aboriginal culture and of the broken dreams of pioneer settlers. Explore the magnificence of Wilpena Pound and the quiet serenity of Brachina Gorge. While spring has a reputation for carpets of wildflowers, the Flinders Ranges has sunny, warm appeal all year round, except perhaps in late January and February when the sun is simply too hot for outdoor activities and the land too parched to enjoy.

ARKAROOLA❖❖❖

 Arkaroola Wilderness Sanctuary $–$$
Arkaroola, Northern Flinders Ranges; tel: 1800-676-042 or (08) 8648-4848. Accommodation, tours, flights and walking.

Known as the jewel of the northern Flinders Ranges, Arkaroola is a large privately owned and run **Wilderness Sanctuary and Resort❖❖**, adjacent to the Gammon Ranges National Park. For a friendly, really remote outback experience, stay at Arkaroola for a day or two. The highlights of this 610-sq km resort are fascinating rock formations, gorges, vast salt lakes, prolific wildlife and some lovely swimming waterholes. It also has its own astronomy observatory for watching the stars which seem to be all the more magical in this remote region. The famous Ridgetop Tour takes visitors in Arkaroola's fleet of 4WDs along rugged and steep ridges to the spectacular Silliers Lookout. Echo camp and Bararranna gorge are great to explore, as are the Bolla Bollana waterholes and the Paralana Hot Springs; or you can take a scenic flight. As well as camping and lodge accommodation there is a restaurant, and an information centre.

**ℹ Flinders Ranges
and Outback
South Australian
Tourism Centre** *41
Flinders Terrace, Port
Augusta; tel: 1800-633-060
or 142 Gawler Place,
Adelaide; tel: (08) 8223-
3991.*

**South Australian
Travel Centre** *1 King
William St, Adelaide; tel:
1300-366-770.*

**Flinders Ranges Road
Conditions** *hotline tel:
1300-361-033.*

**Flinders Ranges
Tourism** *www.
flindersrangestourism.com.au*

**South Australian
Tourism Commission**
www.southaustralia.com

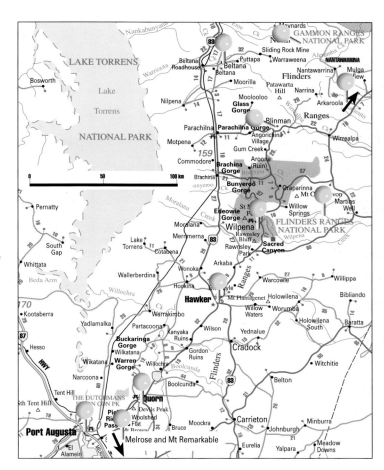

BELTANA ❖

Most of the stone buildings in this historic little ghost town were built between 1855 and 1877, when more than 400 people lived here working rich copper diggings, before disastrous floods in 1877. When John Flynn started his Royal Flying Doctor Service for the outback in 1911, he used the old Beltana mission church as his base. The main ruin now is of the 1874 Rock Hotel. The hills behind Beltana have twice been the setting for the marvellous Opera in the Outback concerts, with NZ soprano Dame Kiri Te Kanawa singing on an outdoor stage.

BLINMAN AND BRACHINA GORGE❖

North Blinman Hotel tel: (08) 8648-4867.

Oratunga Station tel: (08) 8648-4863. Homestead and shearers' quarters accommodation.

Founded in 1859 when Robert Blinman discovered copper here, quiet Blinman still has several 1860s miners' cottages in its main street, as well as the North Blinman Hotel, the Police Station and the Post Office. The Blinman mine was the largest in the Flinders Ranges until it closed in 1906; now a historic reserve, it has an interesting walking trail with interpretative signs both above and below ground. To the west of the town explore Glasses Gorge, the spring-fed Blinman Pools and the old ruins of Artimore, while head northeast on a good gravel road to reach Chambers Gorge and the Gammon Ranges National Park. On the road heading south back towards Wilpena Pound (*see page 248*) are the huge natural rocky battlements poking out of a spine of rolling grassy hills known, not surprisingly, as the Great Wall of China.

You can drive from Wilpena Pound, past the gnarled old Cazneux Tree, through Bunyeroo Valley to spectacular and ancient Brachina Gorge. The scenery is sensational as the tall walls of the Flinders Ranges close in, or the purple rocky spines of the distant Bunker and Heysen mountain ranges give an overwhelming feeling of space and majesty. The road – quite rough in parts – that runs along Brachina Gorge is a complete contrast, with its cliffs, rockpools and quiet river.

FLINDERS RANGES NATIONAL PARK❖❖❖

This 93,000-hectare national park is a wild and ruggedly beautiful part of Australia, offering ancient landscapes, soaring cliffs and ranges, the geological wonder that is the walled Wilpena Pound, and prolific

ⓘ **Flinders Ranges National Park** *SA National Parks and Wildlife Service (NPWS) office, Wilpena Pound; tel: (08) 8648-0048.*

◑ **Rawnsley Park Station** *Rawnsley Bluff, just south of Wilpena Pound; tel: (08) 8648-0008. Accommodation, camping, horse riding, tours.*

Left
Brachina Gorge

wildflowers and wildlife. Formed between 650 and 700 million years ago when the earth's crust rose above the sea, split and was pushed up to form the mountain ridges of the Elder, Chase, Heysen and Bunker ranges, the National Park is a geologist's paradise containing fossils, gold, opal, copper, quartzites, dolomites, shale and granite. Wind, water and rain have cut out deep valleys and smooth gorges over the years, giving the landscape stunning variety and some naturally formed walking trails through the rugged hills. Aboriginal people have lived here for more than 40,000 years and evidence of their occupation and art remains in many caves and rock art galleries.

There are hundreds of walking tracks within the park, including the final section of the 1500-km long Heysen Trail (details are available from the Wadlata Information Centre in Port Augusta or at the main Flinders Ranges National Park Centre at Wilpena Pound). The highlight for most visitors to the park is a walk up into the serene beauty of the Pound itself (*see page 248*), but it is worthwhile exploring Brachina Gorge and other more remote areas of the park on its northern fringe around Blinman (*see page 244*).

GAMMON RANGES NATIONAL PARK✧✧

ⓘ **Gammon Ranges National Park** *SA National Parks and Wildlife Service (NPWS) office, Balcanoona; tel: (08) 8648-4829.*

The ancient granite peaks of the Gammon Ranges are estimated to be more than 1.6 billion years old, rearing up jagged between the great salt lakes of Lake Frome and Lake Torrens on either side. This 128,000-hectare National Park is believed to be one of the oldest places on earth, with deep gorges, high ranges, dry, arid country and plenty of untamed wilderness. Much wilder and less developed than Flinders Ranges National Park to its south, Gammon Ranges is best explored on foot, with great bushwalks to places like Weetootla Gorge with its abundant wildlife. Other popular and lovely walks are Italowie Gorge (16km one-way, so park a vehicle at either end) and Grindells Hut. National Park rangers and the visitor information office are based at Balcanoona, where you will be given excellent maps and advice on where to go; however, most people planning to explore Gammon Ranges head for the town of Arkaroola (*see page 242*).

HAWKER✧✧

ⓘ **Hawker Tourist Information Centre** *cnr Elder Terrace and Wilpena Rd. No telephone. Irregular opening hours.*

Hawker is the small sleepy town at the southern end of the Flinders Ranges National Park where the main road junction forks, the left road leading up to Leigh Creek and the right-hand fork to Wilpena Pound. Nearby is the lovely Moralana scenic drive with superb views from Black Gap lookout; to the south are Aboriginal paintings at the Youramballa Caves. Hawker is also a base for some excellent tours. One of the best is Grant Campbell's **4WD SkyTrek Tour**✧ which

Skytrek-Willow Springs 4WD tours $$ *Hawker Caravan Park; tel: (08) 8648-4006.*

FRAY Aboriginal cultural tours *Hawker; tel: (08) 8648-4122, call for ticket details.*

Arkaba Station and Woolshed *Hawker; tel: (08) 8648-4217.*

explores the wilds of nearby 40,000-hectare Willow Springs including the high ridges of Mt Carnarvon.

Aboriginal tours* are also available to learn about the 40,000 year-old Adnamatna culture of the Flinders Ranges traditional people. Just north of Hawker is the historic **Arkaba Station***, with its 1856 woolshed built by grazier Thomas Elder, founder of the Elder's Empire, now a gallery and café. Arkaba Station also has accommodation and 4WD tours over the top of the jagged Elder Range.

Right
Mountaintop tour

MELROSE**

Melrose Tourist Information Centre *Melrose Caravan Park, Joes Rd; tel: (08) 8666-2060.*

Noel Battersby's Leisuretime 4WD tours *tel: (08) 8666-2017.*

Melrose is the start of the glorious but often ignored Southern Flinders Ranges region. This is a more benign area than the drier, craggier rocks of the central gorges around Wilpena Pound, two hours to the north. Melrose is more about grassy green, flower-covered hillsides, mellow sandstone cottages besides streams and the thick bush-covered hills of Mt Remarkable National Park (*see page 247*). The oldest town in the Flinders Ranges, Melrose is a small, low-key tourist village with plenty of accommodation, eating and tour options. Attractions include the Melrose Museum, once the local police station and courthouse, and the working 1860s blacksmith at Bluey Blundstone's.

Melrose is also a great base for bushwalkers wanting to explore Mt Remarkable National Park, while the 1500-km Hans Heysen walking trail passes through the town. Local resident **Noel Battersby** offers tours in his 4WD up over the hills to visit some of the best lookouts, creeks and old abandoned cottages amid beautiful scenery, not normally accessible to visitors.

Mt Remarkable National Park❖❖

ℹ Mt Remarkable National Park
NPWS offices, Mambray Creek; tel: (08) 8634-7068.

Named by explorer Edward John Eyre for its extraordinary beauty, Mt Remarkable National Park can be reached from either Melrose or Wilmington to its east, or from the Port Wakefield road via Mambray Creek on its western edge. Divided into several different sections, it has lovely trails of varying degrees of difficulty for hikers and family walkers.

From Melrose, it is a steep but rewarding climb of about four hours there and back through grassy fields and wildflowers along the Hans Heysen trail to the top of Mt Remarkable (956m).

Famous Alligator Gorge can be reached by car along a scenic drive from Wilmington. From the gorge, it is a short walk downstream to The Narrows – where the walls of the gorge close in – or upstream for 2km to the Terraces. More adventurous or overnight hikers can tackle the 15-km Hidden Gorge and Battery Ridge Trail in the western Mambray Creek section of the park.

Port Augusta❖

ℹ Tourist Information Centre *Wadlata Outback Centre, 41 Flinders Terrace; tel: (08) 8641-0793.*

🏛 Wadlata Outback Centre $ *41 Flinders Terrace; tel: 1800-633-060 or (08) 8641-0793. Open Mon–Fri 0900–1730, Sat and Sun 1000–1600.*

Royal Flying Doctor Service $ *St Vincent St; tel: (08) 8642-2044. Open 1000–1500.*

School of the Air $ *59 Power Cres; tel: (08) 8642-2077. Daily tour at 1000.*

Australian Arid Lands Botanic Gardens *Stuart Hwy; tel: (08) 8641-1049. Open Mon–Fri 0900–1700, Sat and Sun 1000–1600.*

The largest city in outback South Australia, Port Augusta, is situated at the head of the Spencer Gulf and is often described as being the town at the crossroads of Australia because it stands at the junction of the continent's main north–south and east–west routes. From Port Augusta, the Stuart Highway heads north to Alice Springs and Darwin; the Eyre Highway to the west crosses the Nullarbor Desert to reach Perth; the Port Wakefield road to the south leads to Adelaide, while the Barrier Highway heads east towards Broken Hill and Sydney. Founded in 1852, the town has always been a major port, a road and rail junction, a regional centre and important for its power generation.

The first thing to do in Port Augusta is to visit the outstanding, award-winning **Wadlata Outback Centre❖**, with its fascinating 'Tunnel of Time' which provides an entertaining way of learning about Aboriginal culture and its history, the geology of the ancient landscape of the Flinders Ranges, the environment and much more. The centre also houses the main office of the Flinders Ranges and Outback Tourism Office and the Port Augusta Tourist Information Centre.

A two-hour heritage walk of Port Augusta's grand 19th-century buildings is available, and you can visit the **Royal Flying Doctor Service❖** and the **School of the Air❖** to see how these vital services to outback families operate. Just north of Port Augusta is the magnificent 200-hectare **Australian Arid Lands Botanic Gardens❖❖**, with its excellent visitor and interpretative centre. See the bright Sturts Desert peas flowering all year round, and explore the walking tracks through a profusion of other flowering desert plants.

Quorn❖❖

ℹ **Quorn Tourist Information Centre** *Seventh St; tel: (08) 8648-6419.*

🚂 **Pichi Richi railway** *$$ Quorn Station; tel: (08) 8395-2566 for excellent 24-hour recorded information, or tel: (08) 8648-6598 on train days. Trains run between Easter and Oct, most weekends and during school holidays.*

For steam train enthusiasts, anyone with children, or just the young at heart, the town of Quorn – on the road to the Flinders Ranges – is well worth a stop. This is the home base of the wonderful little Pichi Richi steam train which chuffs from Quorn, along the old 1879 Great Northern railway route, across trestle bridges and through the spectacular Pichi Richi Pass to Woolshed Flat and back again – a distance of 33km, which takes about 2½ hours. A guided tour of the steam train workshops is also possible (*tel: 08-8352-5230*).

Near Quorn, the Devils Peak and Waukerie Falls loop track is a popular, easy grade walk (18km) reached from the Richman Valley Rd; watch out for fossils in the 700-million-year-old quartzite deposits.

Right
Pichi Richi steam train

Wilpena Pound❖❖❖

ℹ **Flinders Ranges National Park** *SA National Parks and Wildlife Service (NPWS) office; tel: (08) 8648-0048.*

According to Aboriginal lore, the elevated, mountain-ringed Wilpena Pound (known as Ikara) was formed when a giant dreaming serpent spirit, Akurra, encircled the dancing of a big corroboree being held by the local Yura people. Akurra went to sleep, forming the mountain ranges around the rim, and creating a spring which is the font of all life, within the sacred pound. More prosaically, geologists believe the rim to be the stumps of massive mountains, eroded down from a height that once approximated the Himalayas, all that remains of a huge dome of rock that was pushed up from the ocean bed 650 million years ago.

Now the Pound is a collection of cracked, split and weathered peaks whose colours change chameleon-like with the sun; the highest is St Mary's Peak, which Aboriginal people believe should not be climbed. The wooded, grassy interior of the quiet, serene Pound is 11km long and 8km across. It is only accessible through the narrow neck of Sliding Rock Gorge along a gentle 2-km walking track from the resort and camping ground below. A good view of this geological wonder rising out of the surrounding flat plains, can be gained from Wangara Lookout, on the rim of the Pound itself, although the best way to appreciate it is from the air, on a half-hour scenic flight.

Inside the Pound, visit the restored cottage of the Hill family, who farmed sheep here in the late 19th century, with 12-year-old Jessie keeping house all alone for her five older brothers.

Kangaroos and euros (small wallaby-like marsupials) bound among rampantly yellow wattle trees, pampas grass and wildflowers in spring, giving something of a quiet, 'lost-world' feel. In season, there are the brilliant reds and pinks of Sturt's Desert pea, Flinders Ranges bottlebrush, hopbrush and Sturt's Desert rose. This birdwatchers' paradise also has 97 species of birds.

Accommodation and food

Arkaba Station $–$$ *via Hawker; tel: (08) 8648-4195.* Cottage accommodation at historic working sheep station.

Arkaroola Wilderness Sanctuary $–$$ *Arkaroola, Northern Flinders Ranges; tel: 1800-676-042 or (08) 8648-4848.* Accommodation, camping, walking, tours and flights.

Bluey Blundstone's Blacksmith's B&B $$ *Melrose; tel: (08) 8666-2173.* Romantic cottage overlooking bush garden.

The Old Ghan Restaurant $$ *Leigh Creek Rd, Hawker; tel: (08) 8648-4176. Wed–Sun lunch and dinner.*

The Prairie Hotel $$ *cnr High St and West Terrace, Parachilna; tel: (08) 8648-4844.* Since the Fargher family transformed this 1876 golden sandstone pub into a restaurant serving kangaroo, emu and other bush food, the award-winning Prairie Hotel has become a centre for gourmands and the occasional country-and-western outdoor concert tour.

Rawnsley Park Station $ *Rawnsley's Bluff, just before Wilpena Pound; tel: (08) 8648-0008.* Cabins, caravan sites and camping in a magnificent outback setting. Also horse rides, 4WD tours and flights.

Wilpena Pound Resort $–$$ *Wilpena Pound; tel: (08) 8648-0004 or 1800-805-802; www.wilpenapound.on.net.* Comfortable resort with family suites, motel units, restaurant, caravan park and camping.

Suggested tour

Distance: Wilpena Pound at the centre of the Flinders Ranges is 450km north of Adelaide, while Arkaroola in the Gammon Ranges is another 200km to the northeast. This tour, depending on which route options are taken, is more than 1000km from Adelaide as a return loop.

Most roads are sealed or good gravel roads, accessible for conventional 2WD cars. However a 4WD drive is needed to explore some parts of both the Flinders Ranges and Gammon Ranges national parks. Taking a 4WD day-tour with a local is an even better option.

Time: Given the distances involved, this route should only be attempted with a four-day time frame.

Links: Just one hour's drive south of Melrose is the Clare Valley wine-growing area, where this route joins up with the drive through the Barossa Valley and Adelaide Hills (*see page 232*). Alice Springs and the Red Centre driving tour (*see page 182*) is 1224km directly up the sealed Stuart Highway from Port Augusta.

Route: From Adelaide, it is 140km via the main highway through **Gawler** to the Clare Valley, and another 120 picturesque kilometres to the historic town of **MELROSE** and the start of the southern Flinders Ranges region. Stop here to explore **MT REMARKABLE NATIONAL PARK**, before driving another 80km on the main sealed road through Wilmington to **QUORN** ❶ with its little steam Pichi Richi railway.

Detour: Drive west through Horrock's Pass to the plains and regional centre of **PORT AUGUSTA**, some 60km away. Return to the main route.

After visiting Quorn, it is time to start the really spectacular drive towards the central Flinders Ranges region. At the little town of **HAWKER** ❷, 100km further on, the road forks to the right, running beneath the foothills of the **FLINDERS RANGES NATIONAL PARK**. Continue for another 52km along the sealed road and down a short turn-off to the left to **WILPENA POUND** ❸ with its resort, camping ground and national park office. Explore the Pound on foot and from the air before driving down the good gravel road through the **Bunyeroo Valley** to the see and feel the peaceful beauty of **BRACHINA GORGE**. Later, head back towards the Great Wall of China on the Wilpena Pound Rd and visit the little old mining town of **BLINMAN** ❹.

Detour: For those with a little more time on their hands, a good sense of adventure and preferably a 4WD vehicle, consider detouring from Blinman north for 125km – seeing Chambers Gorge on the way – to reach **GAMMON RANGES NATIONAL PARK** and its headquarters at

Balcanoona. It is then another 50km on dirt road to wonderful **ARKAROOLA**. Drive home on the sealed road via **LEIGH CREEK** and the ghost town of **BELTANA** before joining up with the main driving tour route at Parachilna.

Follow the road west for another 70km towards the Prairie Hotel in **Parachilna** ❺ – a true gourmet oasis – checking out **Glasses Gorge** and **Parachilna Gorge** along the way. Back on the main Leigh Creek sealed road, it is a 200-km drive south, past the old ruins of the Wonoka and Kanyaka homesteads, to reach Quorn.

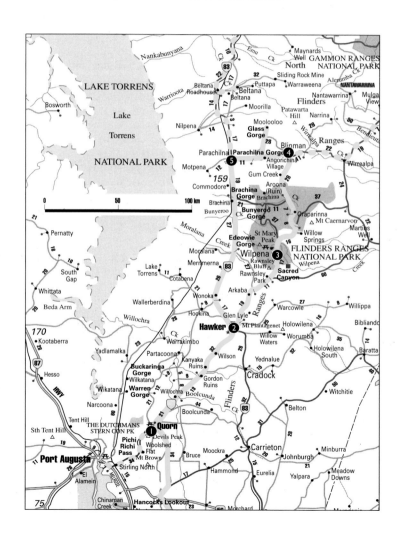

Ratings

Coorong to Coonawarra

Beaches	●●●●●
Scenery	●●●●●
Vineyards	●●●●●
Wildlife	●●●●●
Coastal villages and towns	●●●●○
Art and crafts	●●●○○
Food and drink	●●●○○
History	●●●○○

The drive from Adelaide to the famous vineyards of Coonawarra provides spectacular scenery and vibrant contrast. At the start of the journey, rolling hills, orchards and vineyards are soon replaced by the pounding surf beaches and secluded bays, unspoiled lakes and dunes of the coast. Watch southern right whales at Victor Harbour, or take a ferry cruise to see the magnificent wildlife on Kangaroo Island. Don't miss Coorong National Park and the mighty Murray River. Travel on to the resorts of Kingston, Robe and Beachport. At Port MacDonnell eat fresh crayfish and abalone, then head north to the volcanic sink holes and bright blue lakes of Mount Gambier, and to Penola, home of Australia's only saint. Finally, meander through the cherished vineyards of the Coonawarra, with its prized *terra rossa* soil that is the envy of hearty red wine makers the world over.

CAMP COORONG ABORIGINAL CULTURAL CENTRE✦✦✦

◑ **Camp Coorong Aboriginal Cultural Centre** *tel: (08) 8575-1557. Cottage and dormitory accommodation.*

A visit to Camp Coorong provides a glimpse into the Aboriginal heritage of the Ngarrindjeri people, the original occupiers this 145-km long narrow waterway where the Murray River attempts to reach the ocean, separated only by blindingly white sand dunes and beaches. The cultural museum is fascinating and free.

COONAWARRA WINERIES✦✦✦

ℹ **Penola-Coonawarra Visitors' Centre** *27 Arthur St, Penola; tel: (08) 8737-2855; www.coonawarra.org. Open weekdays 0900–1700.*

There are about 30 wineries in the Coonawarra region, famous worldwide for its award-winning mighty red wines, especially its cabernet sauvignons. The wineries are easily found as they follow a straight road north from Penola, a pleasant drive through vineyards edged with roses or poplars. Maps are available from the **Penola-Coonawarra Visitors' Centre**.

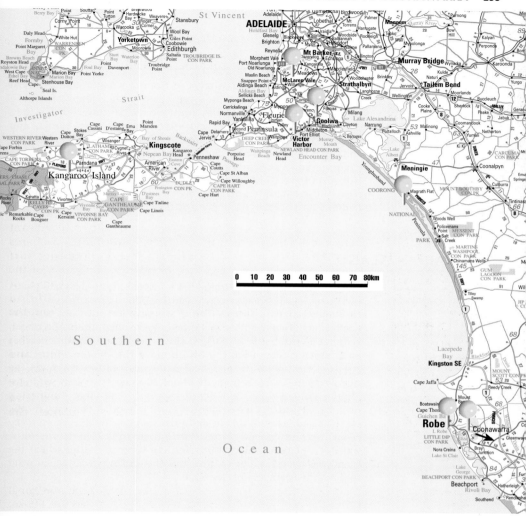

THE COORONG❖❖❖

Coorong National Park *Meningie; tel: (08) 8575-1200.*

Coorong Nature Tours $$$ *tel/fax: (08) 8574-0037; mobile: 015-714-793.* Tours with experienced guides.

The **Coorong National Park** is a mystical place, its name spoken with reverence by those who have taken the time to visit and discover it. The Coorong is a land-locked sliver of water, bounded on the seaward side by large sandhills. At most just under 3km wide, the Coorong's pristine white beaches stretch 145km from the mouth of the River Murray. The Park's 47,000 hectares are a wetland of international significance and, with more than 230 bird species, a mecca for bird lovers from around the world. This is Australia's largest, permanent breeding colony of pelicans.

GOOLWA✧✧

Signal Point River Murray Interpretative Centre
$$ *Goolwa Wharf; tel: (08) 8555-3488. Open daily 0900–1700.*

Cockle Train $$$
operates Sun, public and school holidays from the Goolwa Wharf.

The charming sandstone cottages of Goolwa wrap around the final stretch of Australia's longest river, the Murray. Goolwa is now a junction for the **Cockle Train**✧, a historic holidaymakers' steam train that travels between Goolwa and Victor Harbour every Sunday and during school holidays. From Goolwa, the paddle steamer Mundoo and other vessels leave for day trips or longer to cruise the lakes, the Coorong and the Murray River. The **Signal Point River Murray Interpretative Centre**✧ brings to life the history of the original Ngarrindjeri people and the river trade settlers. High-tech and traditional techniques relate Aboriginal legends and cultures.

KANGAROO ISLAND✧✧✧

Kangaroo Island Gateway Visitor Information Centre
Howard Drive, Penneshaw; tel: (08) 8553-1185. Open weekdays 0900–1500, weekends 1000–1600.

Kangaroo Island National Parks and Wildlife *Dauncey St, Kingscote; tel: (08) 8554-8381.*

Kangaroo Island Sealink Ferries
tel: (08) 8553-1122.

The isolation of Kangaroo Island has protected the animals and plants of this wilderness area magnificently, making it a haven for an enormous variety of species. The 18 conservation and national parks on this large island off Victor Harbour cover one-third of the island, giving it a wild, bush feel. Rugged cliffs, roaring surf, pristine beaches and dramatic caves form the backdrop for the wildlife which have attracted visitors for decades. **Seal Bay Conservation Park**✧, on the island's south coast, is home to about 500 rare Australian sea lions; regular guided tours take visitors close to the large, lumbering mammals. **Flinders Chase National Park**✧ is another sanctuary for the sea lions and sea birds that lie and soar around its weather-worn rocky coastline and coastal dunes. Further inland, koalas, possums, wallabies, platypus, many birds and the kangaroos after which the island was named can be spotted from the walking tracks which wind through the heath and mallee scrub.

MCLAREN VALE✧✧

McLaren Vale and Fleurieu Visitor Centre *Main Road, McLaren Vale; tel: (08) 8323-9944. Open daily.*

This is a haven for lovers of good food and wine, with almost 50 wineries offering tastings and cellar door sales on the outskirts of town, and a wide choice of coffee shops and restaurants in McLaren Vale itself. To get the feel of the countryside, the **Almond Train Walk**✧✧ is an easy amble along the old railway line, flanked by vineyards, almond groves, wild olive trees and twisted old gum trees. Two annual events, the **Almond Blossom Festival** in July/August and the **McLaren Vale Wine Bushing Festival** in October/November, celebrate McLaren Vale's gourmet bounty.

ROBE❖❖❖

Robe Tourist Information Centre Mundy Terrace; tel: (08) 8768-2465.

This pretty seaside village has been a holiday destination for 150 years. Even the colonial governors spent their summer holidays at Robe. It is also a lively fishing port. During the warmer months, an early morning stroll to the port is rewarded with a chat to the fisherman as they unload their lobster pots. At the port, it is also possible to purchase 'spiders' – lobster legs filled with the sweetest meat – for a reasonable cost.

Right
Stock up on seafood

VICTOR HARBOR❖❖

Victor Harbor Tourist Information Centre Flinders Pde, Victor Harbor; tel: (08) 8552-5738.

The favourite summer holiday playground for Adelaide families, Victor Harbor sits on the wide sandy arc of Encounter Bay, close to pounding surf beaches. There's an enjoyable 15-minute walk across the causeway, or for a small cost take the historic horse-drawn tram to Granite Island, home for the delightful **Fairy Penguins**❖❖. Every dusk, a small group is taken on a foreshore tour, to watch the penguins emerge from the ocean and return to their nests. Now a commercial

**Fairy Penguin
Dusk Tour $$$**
*Granite Island; tel: (08)
8552-7555. Daily.*

fishing port, Victor Harbor was once a whaling and sealing depot. Whales still play an important role however, as tourists enjoy viewing the southern right whales which visit each year and the **Whale Centre** is worth visiting.

Accommodation and food

The Barn $$ *Main Road, McLaren Vale; tel: (08) 8323-8618.* Open daily for lunch and dinner, this is one of South Australia's best-known restaurants and galleries. A popular day outing for Adelaide dwellers.

Grey Masts Restaurant and Guesthouse $$$ *1 Smyllie St, Robe; tel/fax: (08) 8768-2203.* Built in 1847 and listed on the national heritage register, this boutique guesthouse really pampers, and packages are available. The food is excellent, and the coffee invigorating. It is certainly worth stopping here for a meal, but if time is short, coffee and cake will suffice.

Penguini's Bistro $$ *Granite Island, Victor Harbor; tel: (08) 8552-8311.* Food with a pleasant view of Victor Harbour.

Punters Vineyard Retreat $$ *V & A Lane, Coonawarra; tel: (08) 8737-2007.* A magical self-contained escape, surrounded by gum trees and vineyards in the heart of the Coonawarra. Highly recommended.

Whalers' Inn Resort $$$ *The Bluff, Encounter Bay, Victor Harbor; tel: (08) 8552-4400; fax: (08) 8552-4400.* Base yourself in Victor Harbor to explore the Fleurieu Peninsula. There are two-storey apartments at this resort, or .choose the gorgeous one-bedroom settler's cottage. All rooms overlook Encounter Bay, as does the restaurant.

Suggested tour

Total distance: 490km, 540km with detours.

Time: It will take about 6 hours to travel the main route from McLaren Vale to the Coonawarra, not including stops. The trip to Hindmarsh Island including the punt is only 5 minutes each way. The detour to Beachport will add 30 minutes travelling time, and Bool Lagoon is 15 minutes from Penola.

Links: From Adelaide, head south on the Main South Road for 30km, turning left to McLaren Vale. This drive links up with both the Barossa Valley drive (*see page 232*) and the Flinders Ranges tour (*see page 242*), through Adelaide. From Penola, the route to Melbourne (*see page 115*)

Right
Victor Harbor horse-drawn tram

Bompa's on the Beach $ 3 Railway Tce, Beachport; tel: (09) 8735-8333; fax: (08) 8735-8101.

Penola-Coonawarra Visitors' Centre, the John Riddoch Interpretive Centre, and the Penola Hydrocarbon Centre 27 Arthur St; tel: (08) 8737-2855. Open weekdays 0900–1700, weekends 1000–1600, closed Christmas and Good Friday.

through Hamilton provides superior scenery to the better known Western Highway, with magnificent red gum grazing country, and the unsurpassed southern view of the Grampians mountain range.

Route: From **McLAREN VALE** ❶ take the McLaren Flat Rd through vineyards, rolling hills and grazing country, and turn right to the seaside holiday town of **VICTOR HARBOR** ❷ 53km to the south. From Victor Harbor, hug the coast along Port Elliot Rd, through pretty seaside villages to the delightful **GOOLWA** ❸. Drive past old stone buildings, paddle steamers and the yacht club, before the road heads inland 34km to **Strathalbyn**, a heritage registered town with strong Scottish associations.

Detour: From Goolwa, a free 24-hour vehicle ferry will take you to **Hindmarsh Island**, a large island impeding the flow of the Murray River before it reaches the ocean. From the island, the views of the river mouth are superb. A large marina has been constructed on the island and aquatic bird habitats ensure the island is popular with bird watchers.

Back on the main route, it is 49km from Strathalbyn to the punt at Wellington, a leisurely way to cross the River Murray as it enters Lake Alexandrina. Then continue on to the Princes Highway (Highway 1). If you are planning to explore the **COORONG**, stop at **MENINGIE PARK RANGER HEADQUARTERS** ❹ for details about access, camping and walks. After another 188km past sand dunes and fishermen's huts, the road reaches Kingston, marked by the giant lobster on the town's outskirts. Take the Southern Ports Coastal Highway to the fishing village of **ROBE** ❺, where you can climb the **Beacon Hill** lookout tower for a lovely view over the small bay.

Detour: From Robe take the Coastal Ports Highway towards **Beachport** ❻. A further short detour leads to the extraordinary **Woakwine Cutting**, a testimony to human endurance. This man-made Grand Canyon is Australia's biggest one-man engineering feat, where M B McCourt spent three years on a bulldozer, and drained a large swamp area, opening it up to farming.

Beachport, a whaling station in the 1830s, has an extremely long jetty which is lined with anglers. Aboriginal shell middens are easily found in the sand dunes, and a number of nature walks lead you through coastline and bushland. The **Artefacts Museum** features an Aboriginal collection and, if there's time, the conservatory at **Bompa's on the Beach** is a nice spot for coffee. Drive east from Beachport, cross the Princes Highway, and turn right to Penola at the next intersection. All roads are clearly marked.

Detour: The 102-km drive from Robe to **Penola** ❼ takes you through sheep and cattle farming plains. Turn left into the town and visit the **Penola-Coonawarra Visitor Centre** for further information about accommodation and attractions. Penola is a good base if you are intending to visit the Coonawarra wineries, which start on the edge of the town, and it has much good historic sandstone architecture. From **PENOLA**, travel north along the Riddoch Highway. The drive through the **COONAWARRA** wine region is lovely when the roses fronting the vineyards are in bloom. After 20km turn left to **Bool Lagoon**, designated by UNESCO as a wetlands of international significance. It is a breeding ground for thousands of birds, fish and other wildlife. There are guided tours along a boardwalk.

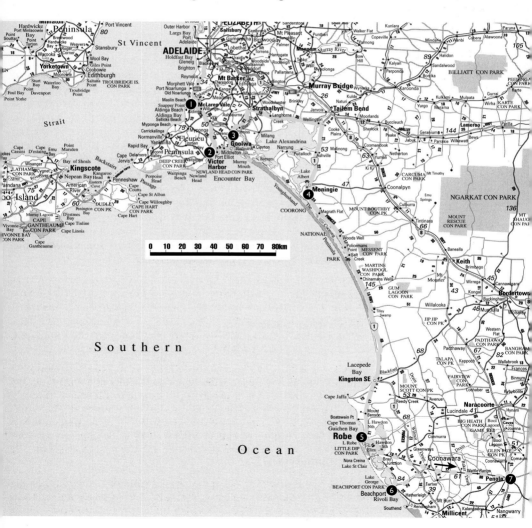

Hobart

The magic of Hobart lies in the union of its very English beginnings and its setting at the edges of isolation and wilderness. The allure of Australia's second oldest city is as much in the natural beauty of the Derwent River estuary and surrounding landscape as in its intriguing past. Situated beneath towering Mount Wellington, the purity of southern light air lends the quality of fantasy to the historic streets, docks and estuary shores of Tasmania's capital city. Hobart's location as Australia's most southerly major city also means that cold winds blow in from the Southern Ocean during the icy winter! On such days, the hardships of an isolated colony may seem more tangible, but it is these same cold winds and encroaching wilderness that gives Hobart its slightly Irish character, warm pubs and cosy, café culture. Good food, good coffee and stories of wilds beyond.

Sights

ℹ **Tasmanian Travel and Information Centre**
20 Davey St, one block east, then one north from the Customs House Hotel and Salamanca Place; tel: (03) 6230-8233; fax: (03) 6224-0289; email: tassouth@tasvisinfo. com.au

Tourism Tasmania
www.tourism.tas.gov.au

Battery Point Village***
Besides being modern-day Tasmania's premier real-estate, Battery Point has numerous streets lined with carefully preserved or renovated cottages dating from the 1820s onwards; when the neighbourhood was mainly inhabited by sailors, traders and their families. Among the most interesting streets are Hampden Rd, Portsea Terrace, Cromwell St and Arthurs Circus. There are many excellent antique shops within the Battery Point village precinct, and the historic **Shipwright's Hotel**** makes a good place for resting and refreshment.

Constitution Dock**
Adjoining Victoria Dock on the walk towards Salamanca Place, Constitution Dock is the centre of Hobart's waterfront district and the keeper of its proud maritime traditions. This is also the place for fish and chips in Hobart, with a series of floating punts selling fresh and

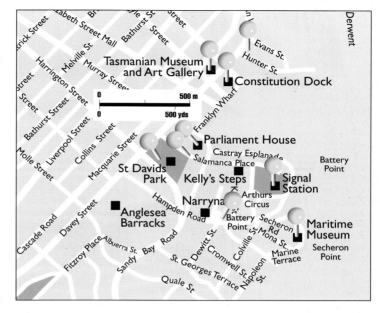

Tasmanian National Parks
www.parks.tas.gov.au

Mures Upper Deck Restaurant $$
Constitution Dock; tel: (03) 6231-1999; fax: (03) 6231-1420. Quality seafood restaurant and a Hobart waterfront institution.

Drunken Admiral Restaurant $$ Hunter St; tel: (03) 6234-1903. Character-laden seafood restaurant run by film producer.

Customs House Hotel $$ 1 Murray St, Hobart. Open daily 1000 till late. Times vary in winter.

Shipwright's Hotel $ Trumpeter St, Battery Point. The 'Shippie' dates to 1846 and is still a mariners' hotel. Mure's ship-building yard is two blocks below the pub, maritime memorabilia weighs heavily on the walls. A Battery Point institution.

cooked seafood along with the famous **Mures Seafood Centre and Upper Deck Restaurant★★**. Each year, it becomes the hub of the city's huge New Year's Eve party, with exuberant yachties who have just finished the gruelling and world-famous Sydney-to-Hobart Yacht Race moored alongside, showering onlookers with champagne and the local Cascade Beer.

Hunter Street★

Hunter Street is best known as home to the Tasmanian Centre for the Arts. This four-storey high row of warehouses, reflected in the waters of Victoria Dock, makes for one of the most evocative snapshots of historic Hobart. The **Drunken Admiral Restaurant★** strikes an entertaining balance between old-world charm and kitsch.

Parliament House★★

The impressive sandstone Parliament House, opposite Salamanca Place and overlooking Constitution Dock, was built in 1836 as the Customs House. Since 1856, it has been home to the Tasmanian State Parliament. Until 1999, Tasmania was widely considered to be over-governed for a state of 450,000 people, but cutbacks have now reduced the Lower House to 25 and the Upper House to 15 members. Across the road to the east is the **Customs House Hotel★★**, a character pub popular with the town's movers, shakers, journos and lawyers.

Down by the waterfront near Parliament House is Macquarie No 2 Warehouse on the dock, where the annual **Taste of Tasmania Festival** is staged between 26 Dec and 3 Jan (*open from 1000 until late every day during the festival*). A huge New Year's Eve party is staged at the Taste venue, but tickets need to be purchased from the Hobart City Council weeks, if not months, in advance. The warehouse is completely filled with the finest Tasmanian foods. The festival is supported by a huge cast of quality busking acts and bands and attracts tens of thousands of people each year.

Salamanca Market $ *Sat 0900–1600, year-round.*

Knopwood's Retreat $ Popular after-work drinks with upstairs live performance venue.

Lebrina $$ *New Town Rd, New Town; tel: (03) 6228-7775.* Consistently rated as one of Tasmania's best restaurants; classical cooking using seasonal produce. A memorable dining experience.

Nicklebys $ *217 Sandy Bay Rd; tel: (03) 6223-6030. Opening times vary according to season.*

St Ives Hotel $ *Sandy Bay Rd; tel: (03) 6223-3655.* Restaurant and nightclub.

Wrest Point Casino $$ *Sandy Bay; tel: (03) 6225-0112.*

Salamanca Place***

For scenery, atmosphere, food, arts and crafts and history, Salamanca Place is where you'll feel Hobart's heartbeat. At the western end of the waterfront's Franklin Wharf, rows of original sandstone warehouses (1835–60) mark what was the centre of commerce in early Hobart, teeming with grain, wool, timber and fruit traders from around the world. The wonderfully preserved buildings, now housing galleries, theatrettes and cafés, stand opposite ample parallel car parking and leafy park space. Every Saturday, the broad cobble-stone street between is filled with colour, craft and the sweet sounds of music, theatre and fresh produce spruikers. Most consider Salamanca to be Australia's best outdoor market and it is particularly interesting for the often highly individualistic art and craft it helps to foster. There is also plenty of home-made produce, flowers, fruit and second-hand fashion. With a bit of hip and radical and a lot of the home-spun cottage crafts, the market day encapsulates the old and new of Tasmanian life. This is also one of the premier eating and night-owl precincts, with the most central drinking establishment being one of the most historically significant in town. **Knopwood's Retreat**** was once owned by a pillar of early Hobart society, the Reverend Robert Knopwood. On a warm summer night, revellers spill over from the pub to jam the pavement. The diverse galleries along the Salamanca stretch showcase the arts on all levels. An on-off alternative cinema and small theatre also find a home here.

Sandy Bay Road*

Beyond Battery Point is the suburb of Sandy Bay, the home of the University of Tasmania and a number of nightspots made popular by its students. There are many good places for a drink, and a few dining options along Sandy Bay. Good nightspots include the **St Ives Hotel**** and **Nicklebys***, both of which are right on Sandy Bay Rd. Continuing further out of the city but still within easy walking distance is the distinctive tower of the **Wrest Point Casino****, a 24-hour affair with gaming rooms and a number of bars and convention areas, a disco and a revolving restaurant on top. It was the only known nightspot of any significance in Tasmania when it was first built in 1967 as Australia's first casino. Today, the casino concept seems a little tired against the increasingly vibrant scene around Salamanca Place, but it remains the only real non-stop party in town.

Tasmanian Maritime Museum $

Secheron Rd and Clarke Avenue entrances, off Hampden Rd; tel: (03) 6223-5082; email: maritimetas@ozemail.com.au. Open daily 1000–1630.

Tasmanian Museum and Art Gallery $$ 40

Macquarie St; tel: (03) 6235-0777. Open daily 1000–1700.

Above left
Salamanca Place

Signal Station*

The oldest existing building in Battery Point, the Signal Station in Princes Park, was built in 1818 as a guardhouse for soldiers. It was one of a series of buildings to be converted into similar stations with tall masts used to relay flagged messages about shipping movements, convict escapees and other fast-breaking news. Messages were relayed as far away as Port Arthur, where the most notorious Australian penal settlement was sited.

St David's Park*

This lovely, sloping parkland between Salamanca Place and Sandy Bay Rd was the original burial ground in old Hobart. It was converted to a public park in 1926 and usually offers plenty of space. A huge band rotunda at the centre suggests a grand early vision but ultimately, this is a leafy peace in the middle of the city. The first recorded burial on the park was that of a young child in 1804. The tombstones of the explorer and whaler James Kelly, and of David Collins, an early Governor of Van Diemens Land (the old name for Tasmania, used until 1856) are among many still preserved in the park.

Tasmania's only Royal (Real) Tennis Court and Australia's oldest is opposite the park in Davey St. Pop inside and ask for a look at the complex, centuries-old indoor game, which has evolved into the multi-million-dollar version we know today. The rules are very strange!

Tasmanian Maritime Museum**

Part of the Battery Point experience and well worth a close inspection, this museum is an important guide to understanding the history of Hobart and its deep seafaring roots. Situated inside Secheron House (1831), a fine example of early Georgian architecture, the museum houses photos, shipping relics, and implements of the whaling and convict history. It explains Hobart's key role as a Southern Ocean port, the base for Antarctic expeditions, men-o'-war and a rich local tradition of wooden boat building. Another bonus is that most of the volunteers who man the front desk are still salty, walking, talking exhibits in themselves. Don't be shy, ask for a story.

Tasmanian Museum and Art Gallery**

While not one of the great museums or galleries of the world, the Tasmanian Museum and Art Gallery is well worth the short detour, two blocks from the waterfront, to the entrance on Davey St. The lovely old timber-floored rooms are a treasure-trove of Tasmanian natural history and old-world style – you can still just about smell the formaldehyde used for preserving botanical specimens. If you are curious about the legendary Tasmanian tiger, you can see a stuffed one here. For real excitement, ask directions to the tiger's prehistoric ancestor – it is three times the size of the modern beast and looks to be stalking you.

Above
Boats in Hobart Bay

Accommodation and food

Hotel Grand Chancellor $$$ *1 Davey St; tel: (03) 6235-4535.* Multi-storeyed international hotel with epic views of the docks and the Derwent Estuary. The complex features a selection of bars and dining options to suit different budgets and has the advantage of its own off-street parking. It's a short walk from here to just about anywhere in the docks precinct or central city.

Jackman & McRoss Bakery $$ *Hampden Rd, Battery Point; tel: (03) 6228-4688.* Absolutely mouth-watering bakery fare from Hobart's most celebrated restaurateur, Chris Jackman, whose Mit Zitrone restaurant ($$) in North Hobart has won many accolades *(tel: (03) 6234-8113).* From the front door of the bakery, just after sunrise, you can watch Mt Wellington glow and cottages on Hampden Rd catch their first glancing rays. Inside, great coffee and exceptional bakery fare at a reasonable price. Having to choose is hard.

Kelley's Seafood Restaurant $$ *5 Knopwood St, Battery Point; tel: (03) 6424-7225; fax: (03) 6224-7226.* Simply the best seafood dining in a place where great seafood is always on offer. Try Atlantic salmon and ocean trout, baby octopus and trevalla. Classy but with chatty, smiling service.

Lenna of Hobart $$ *20 Runnymede St, Battery Point; tel: (03) 6232-3900.* The name is Aboriginal for house. This particularly large house was built in a classic Italianate style for the early merchant and ship-owner, Alexander McGregor. Retains its dignity and usually the services of some of the best chefs in Hobart.

The Sydney–Hobart yacht race

Some of the fastest yachts in the world participate in this challenging race, which can face huge seas as it crosses treacherous Bass Strait between the mainland and Tasmania. The race starts in Sydney at the Cruising Yacht Club on Rushcutters Bay on Boxing Day, with the fastest yachts taking less than three days to complete the race. Even the smallest yachts have usually finished by New Year's Eve, a time of great celebrations on Constitution Dock at Hobart's waterfront. The 1998 race brought disaster and tragedy as massive seas, walls of waves and cyclone-force winds swamped and capsized even the biggest boats, with the loss of more than eight boats and six lives. Only one-third of the fleet of about 80 boats finished that race.

Another, even more challenging yacht race is the Melbourne to Hobart west-coaster, which sails down the rugged west coast of Tasmania before finishing on New Year's Eve at Hobart. The arrival of both fleets in Hobart coincides with the Taste of Tasmania food festival, also on the Salamanca waterfront, making the Tasmanian capital city a great place to be in the New Year.

The Retro $$ *Salamanca Place.* Just roll up to Hobart's hippest café, right at the heart of Salamanca. The decor is arty but easy-going. Service is always good, the menu simple and the coffee close to the best in town. They don't do dinner.

The Wursthaus $$ *1 Montpelier Retreat; tel: (03) 6224-0644.* Best delicatessen in town. Great for prepared gourmet treats to take back to a room and quality wine and cheese for picnics.

Suggested walk

Total distance: About 3km easy walking, with time to stop, look, wonder or eat.

Time: Four hours, comfortably. With 2 hours on the meter, you should be back from the Battery Point leg before the nice man from the Hobart City Council arrives! Put another 2 hours on the meter and continue.

Route: Ideally begin from **SALAMANCA PLACE ❶**, where you should be able to get 2 hours' free parking. Explore the shops as you head south to where Runnymede St curls up and to the right, then pass through charming **Arthur's Circus**, a story-book of cottages, flowers and swings, on the way to Hampden Rd.

Turn right into Hampden Rd and enjoy the atmosphere of **BATTERY POINT's ❷** busiest and often most dramatic street. **Mount Wellington** is usually framed neatly between the closely rowed cottages, and in winter will often have some covering of snow. All along the street are a selection of old-style corner shops, antique stores and restaurants, including the Jackman & McCross bakery.

Detour: Turn right off Hampden Rd into **South St**, for a taste of what locals refer to as 'the village', a narrow laneway of tightly packed terraced cottages many of which date from 1840 to 1850. Turn left and immediately left again into **Kelly St** for more of the same feel, bringing you back to Hampden Rd.

Continue along Hampden and turn left into Dewitt St and left again into Cromwell St. Along Cromwell you will pass **St George's Anglican Church** (1846). Two famous architects of early Van Diemens Land, John Lee Archer (the church's nave) and James Blackburn (tower and porch), were involved in the design. Turn left into Colville St and right into Trumpeter St, where the **Shipwrights Arms** stands on the corner. Pop in and browse around the extensive collection of maritime pictures, including some of world-beating Tasmanian catamaran ferries built by the Incat company.

Above
Constitution Dock

Detour: Wander along Napoleon St and down to a small beach and park on the Derwent's harbour (about 15 minutes return) or continue along the waterfront to **Wrest Point Casino** on **SANDY BAY ROAD** (40 minutes return if you don't gamble).

Turn left into Marine Terrace, a particularly leafy street, and continue for 10 minutes into Clarke Avenue and the **TASMANIAN MARITIME MUSEUM ❸**. From the museum, return to Hampden Rd via Secheron Rd and turn right. Five minutes along, it becomes Castray Esplanade by the entrance to **Princes Park**. Walk through the park, following signs to the **SIGNAL STATION ❹**. Rejoin the Esplanade and continue back to Salamanca Place and the tick, tick, ticking meter.

Detour: Walk to **ST DAVID'S PARK ❺**, on the left at the uphill end of

**Cadbury's
Chocolate Factory**
$ *Cadbury Rd, Claremont;
tel: (03) 6249-0111. Open
Mon–Fri, hourly tours. First
tour starts 0900, last tour
starts 1300.*

SALAMANCA PLACE. In 10 minutes you can check out some of Hobart's most historic tombstones and a rather peaceful park.

Continue north from Salamanca Place toward the distant **HUNTER ST** ⑥ . Many information display boards along Franklyn Wharf further explain the history of the waterfront. Ferry services leave from near Brooke St Pier, with day and lunch cruises on the Derwent and to **Cadbury's Chocolate Factory** (plenty of free chocolate tastings) the most popular.

Detour: Turn left from Franklyn Wharf into **Elizabeth St** and then right into **Macquarie St** to visit the **TASMANIAN MUSEUM AND ART GALLERY.** Return to the main route.

Head south once more to the docks and investigate the picturesque **Victoria** and **CONSTITUTION DOCK** and the **HUNTER ST** row of warehouses. More information boards abound and for lunch, eat fish right where the entire Hobart fishing fleet takes shelter.

Also worth exploring

Drive to the summit of **Mount Wellington** for an unforgettable view. Allow half-an-hour for the drive up, and don't be alarmed by the steep road, hairpin bends and sheer drops – the view at the end is more than worth it.

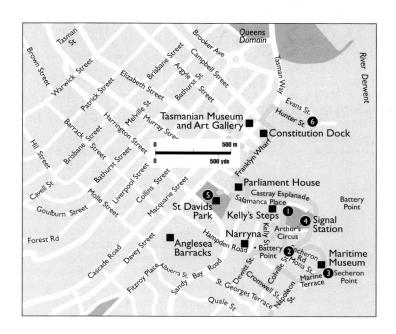

Southeast Tasmania

Ratings

Scenery	●●●●●
Walking	●●●●●
Beaches	●●●●○
Coastal villages	●●●●○
History	●●●●○
Outdoor activities	●●●●○
Children	●●●○○
Food and wine	●●●○○

Travellers lured by an island dot on the map are invariably amazed by the diversity they find in Tasmania. This relaxed drive along sealed but not too busy roads offers some of Tasmania's best scenery. The sunny Freycinet Peninsula and its glorious national park, near the small fishing and holiday town of Coles Bay, is surrounded by white sand, the aqua-blue Tasman Sea and a granite coastline splashed with colourful lichens. Beautiful, sand-rimmed Wineglass Bay is a Tasmanian highlight. The early and brutal history of the penal colony, a deterrent hell at the end of the earth, can still be seen in its own vivid and colourful details, especially at the atmospheric Port Arthur penal settlement and the beautiful little rural village of Richmond. Today, Port Arthur is a peaceful place to visit, and one of Tasmania's must-see tourist attractions.

BREAM CREEK AND WIELANGTA FOREST✢✢

> **ⓘ Tasmanian Kaleidoscope Factory** tel: (03) 6253-5304. Best by appointment.

The Bream Creek area east of Copping, is one of the numerous unsung corners of Tasmania. A simple rural district, it is popular with artisans and Hobart professionals who commute from this rural haven. The views here are across farmland to Marion Bay and the rugged coastal cliffs to the north. Be sure to drop in to Strato Anagnostis's **Tasmanian Kaleidoscope Factory**✶ to view wildly innovative toys-as-art, made with local native Tasmanian timbers. The narrow country road heading north links with the Wielangta Forest Rd, a most rewarding alternative route to Orford. Although the road is gravel, it is typically in good condition and takes you through some beautiful tall eucalyptus forest. Three Thumbs Lookout offers big views of a secluded coast, but requires a 2-hour return walk from the road. Towards Orford, at the road's end, pass by some 19th-century farmlets and quiet beaches with views to Maria Island.

COAL MINES HISTORIC SITE⁺

Tasmanian Devil Park and World Tiger Snake Centre $$
Arthur Highway; tel: (03) 6250-3230. Open daily 0900–1700. The Coal Mines site is free.

The coal mine, worked with convict labour back in the 1830s, is well worth a look, though it is not a patch on the much larger Port Arthur settlement as a spectacle. On the way, drop into the **Tasmanian Devil Park**⁺⁺ at Taranna, to see an array of local wildlife including devils and literally hundreds of tiger snakes, farmed and milked of their venom for use in the development of anti-inflammatory drugs.

COLES BAY⁺⁺⁺

Tasmanian Parks and Wildlife Service *tel: (03) 6257-0107 for information.*

Freycinet Lodge $$ *Freycinet National Park; tel: (03) 6257-0101.*

Freycinet Marine Farm $$ *Pelican Flats, Coles Bay; tel: (03) 6257-0140. By appointment.*

Nestled into the low, forested hills of Coles Bay, the town's greatest asset is the looming view of the Hazards Mountains, a major feature of the Freycinet Peninsula National Park. Fishing, swimming, walking in the national park and lying relaxed on beaches are the main activities here. There are great campsites right on the beach here, tucked amongst its little coves lined with granite boulders, as well as the impressively situated and award-winning **Freycinet Lodge**⁺⁺⁺, at the edge of the far side of the bay, within the national park itself. There are a couple of restaurants in the township and for great value, the **Coles Bay Café Bakery** does gourmet pizza and coffee. It is located next to the **Iluka Tavern**, the local waterhole. For a real treat, ring Andrea Cole of **Freycinet Marine Farm**⁺⁺ and book a guided tour. Watch plump oysters being pulled from the water and taste them within 10 minutes.

EAGLEHAWK NECK⁺⁺

Eaglehawk Café $$ *A9; tel: (03) 6250-3331. Groovy café-restaurant right next to the isthmus.*

This huge sweeping beach, thickly-forested to its edge, holds as much raw beauty as historic significance. At one point, the beach narrows to form an isthmus, less than 50m wide which marks the junction between the Tasman Peninsula and the rest of Tasmania. In the 19th century, the only way for Port Arthur convicts to escape the Tasman Peninsula was via this point, which was guarded with vicious dogs and mantraps (the steel-jawed rabbit-snapping variety, only much bigger).

A small fishing fleet now shelters in Pirates Cove, at the southeast end of the surf beach, and just around the corner are some impressive coastal cliff formations, such as Tasman Arch, the Blowhole and the Devils Kitchen. There are excellent walks right along this coast, with an easy one being the 3-km return **Waterfall Bay** track, beginning at the Devil's Kitchen. If you stop off at the Lufra Hotel, look out for the unusual criss-crossed rock formation, dubbed the Tessellated Pavement, on the foreshore below.

FREYCINET NATIONAL PARK❖❖❖

ⓘ Freycinet National Park *National Parks and Wildlife Service office; tel: (03) 6257-0107. For camping, walking and other information.*

◑ Freycinet Experience and Friendly Beaches Lodge $$$ *Friendly Beaches; tel: (03) 6223-7565. This unique ecofriendly lodge set in the bush is an excellent base for expertly guided walking tours.*

If you love coastal environments and particularly if you like to walk, Freycinet National Park is not to be missed. Tasmania has a huge expanse of coastline, rich with such untouched beauty, but for most people this is the jewel. From the Coles Bay gateway to the peninsula, the first most obvious beauty is the Hazards Mountains (Mt Amos and Mt Parsons), closely bunched granite peaks that rise almost straight from the Tasman Sea. The **Wineglass Bay** walk across the Hazards is the favourite here, involving a short, but steep climb to a saddle in the Hazards; from here, the striking beach with its curved white sand rim and blue water glows pristine, and from this height, it is also in a shape very much true to its name. These days, the beach is an icon, just about as familiar as the famous Cradle Mountain. It can even get a little busy in summer. Serious walkers can plan to walk to Mt Graham or Mt Freycinet (must take water!), but for armchair-wilderness, the **Cape Tourville Lighthouse** and **Sleepy Bay** are short trips from Coles Bay, offering bracing views – especially Cape Tourville – and an often sheltered solitude in the cooler months.

ORFORD AND TRIABUNNA❖❖

ⓘ Triabunna Visitor Centre *Charles St; tel: (03) 6257-4090.*

Maria Island National Park *tel: (03) 6257-1420.*

Orford is a low-key coastal town on the Prosser River, surrounded by peaceful beaches. The narrow roads to the south and east of the town centre are well worth exploring with quiet coastal nooks and beaches (south and north) offering much peace. The **Old Convict Road**, a 40-minute return walk along the Prosser River bank, is pleasant if mainly for its sense of history. Only 8km to the north of Orford is the small fishing village and port of **Triabunna** where fresh fish is landed daily, as are the crayfish for which the area is famous.

Maria Island National Park❖❖❖ is a short, half-hour ferry trip from Louisville, just south of Triabunna. The island shows few marks of modern times, with no electricity, no shopping, just fantastic coastal scenery, plentiful wildlife and the fascinating ruins of a convict settlement built in 1825. Particularly spectacular are its multi-coloured wave rocks and the walk to the towering cliffs and column formations at the easterly end of the island.

PORT ARTHUR HISTORIC SITE❖❖❖

Australia's most infamous penal settlement was Australia's best-known historic site well before the tragic massacre of 35 tourists and locals there by a deranged gunman in 1996. Port Arthur is a place that was central to the difficult birth of Tasmania, and consequently is steeped

 **Port Arthur historic site $$**
Arthur Highway (A9); tel: 1800-659-101. Open daily 0830–dusk. Restored buildings and tours open 0900–1700.

 Boat tours operate at 1400 most days between Nov and Mar and at weekends for the rest of the year, although crossings can be rough. To reach the ferry, turn right off the A3 to Louisville Resort.

Right
Convict re-enactment at Port Arthur

in history and symbolism. More than 30 historic ruins, dating back to 1830, are spread over 40 hectares of lush green parkland. From 1833 onwards, convicts from Great Britain were transported en masse to this site. Australia itself was initially settled for the purpose of establishing a penal colony. It was an era when rapid social change was causing crime on the English streets to get out of control – even prison hulks anchored in the Thames, became overcrowded. The method of dealing with the problem seems radical today, as do some of the methods used in the earliest days of this infamous prison. Situated on the Tasman Peninsula, the site itself fronts sheltered Mason Cove in Carnarvon Bay. Ferries leave daily for the **Isle of the Dead**, across the bay, where the graves of both convicts and authorities are well preserved. In its earliest years Port Arthur was notorious for brutal floggings of the convicts transported from England – one of the reasons why Tasmanians went so far as to change the settlement's name to Carnarvon after it closed in 1849. Guided walking tours leave the visitor centre each day, taking in most of the site.

RICHMOND✦✦✦

Of the many historic villages in Tasmania, Richmond lays claim to being the most significant and intact. The elegant convict-built **Richmond Bridge** (1823) with its three sandstone arches is the oldest

Richmond Tourist Information Centre *Olde Hobart Town Model Village; tel: (03) 6260-2502.*

still standing in Australia. The town itself is lined with elegant sandstone Georgian homes dating from a similar period. The well-preserved convict jail features many relics and even diaries of former inmates and overseers.

SWANSEA✧✧

Swansea Bark Mill *$$ tel: (03) 6257-8382. Open daily 0900–1700. Tourist information available.*

Kate's Berry Farm *$$ tel: (03) 6257-8428. On the way to or from Spiky Bridge. Signed on the highway, just south of Swansea, for freshly picked berries at the 'farm gate', plus great preserves. Seasonal.*

Like so many small Tasmanian towns, what makes Swansea so delightful is simply its location. Sheltered by the hook of Great Oyster Bay, the views from everywhere in Swansea, even the fuel stops, are dominated by the mountains of the Freycinet Peninsula, across the bay to the east. The town itself retains some wonderful historic buildings including the still operating **Morris' General Store** (1834) and the **Swan Inn** (1841). The town is the centre of Australia's oldest rural municipality, Glamorgan. The Tasman Highway hugs the coastline for nearly 20km on the south side of the town, making for a most spectacular scenic drive past oyster farms, sheltered coves and beaches. Much evidence of the rural heritage dots the coastline, with ruins of little farms and shearing sheds standing stark against the sparkling blue ocean. The **Swansea Bark Mill**✧✧ dates from 1885 and recreates faithfully the process used to process black wattle bark for tanning leather. An excellent town to stay in overnight, and dine on fresh Tasmanian oysters and seafood.

Accommodation and food

Kabuki by the Sea $$ *Framoine, Tasman Highway; tel: (03) 6257-8588.* Japanese restaurant on coastal cliff-top by Tasman Highway. Magic views. Also offers traditional Japanese accommodation.

Mrs Currie's House $$ *Richmond; tel: (03) 6260-2766.* Intimate bed and breakfast style. Log fires and your own peaceful garden add to the feeling of home.

Port Arthur Holiday World $$ *Stewarts Bay; tel: (03) 6250-2262.* Though the name might be off-putting, this simple but very comfortable cluster of units has the advantage of one of the best positions on the Tasman Peninsula. Set among fragrant eucalyptus, the cabins enjoy views over Stewarts Bay and its sheltered white beach. The 18 well-spaced apartments can cater for up to 80 guests and the restaurant is good enough to keep you from what is a near-fruitless search for alternatives.

Schouten House $$ *1 Waterloo Rd, Swansea; tel: (03) 6257-8564.* A striking historic house which stands stark against the ocean. The thick, stone walls make for four cosy en-suite rooms and the restaurant, specialising in Italian and seafood, is very good.

Suggested tour

Total distance: 350km driving north via Sorell or 310km driving north via Wielangta Forest. The detour to Saltwater River is an extra 30km. Detouring to the Friendly Beaches will add 17km.

Time: The main route will take 4 hours to drive. A tour of several days is highly recommended, including overnight stops at the Tasman Peninsula, Richmond, Swansea and Coles Bay.

Links: This route connects with the walk along the Hobart waterfront (*see page 260*).

Route: From **Hobart**, head east over the Tasman Bridge, following the signs toward Sorell on the A3. After 10km, turn left on to the B31 and follow it for 13km to RICHMOND ❶. Continue through Richmond towards Sorell, crossing the **Richmond Bridge** and turn right at the A3 after 14km. Drive through Sorell and follow the follow the A9 – the Arthur Highway – all the way to EAGLEHAWK NECK ❷, about 50km. Now on the Tasman Peninsula, continue following the A9, 21km to PORT ARTHUR ❸.

Detour: a right turn on to the B37 shortly after the **Tasmanian Devil Park** will take you through nondescript Koonya and Premaydena. Turn right at the latter and drive 8km on sealed road to **Saltwater River** followed by 4km of gravel to the COAL MINES HISTORIC SITE ❹. Continue to **Port Arthur** via the B37 through Nubeena (approx the same distance as returning to A9).

From the **PORT ARTHUR HISTORIC SITE**, backtrack to the north on the A9 as far as Copping. Here you must consider two alternatives for reaching the East Coast. One option is to keep back-tracking to Sorell and follow the A3 to ORFORD ❺, a route of average interest. Alternatively, you can drive through the stunning **Bream Creek** area, looking over **Marion Bay**, linking with the gravel-surfaced Wielangta Forest Rd. The main highway is sealed, is usually in good condition and passes through miles of tall eucalyptus forest eventually to reach the pretty and secluded beaches south of **Orford**, the fishing village of **Triabunna** and the ferry to **Maria Island National Park**.

Continue north on the A3 to SWANSEA ❻, stopping by the roadside for such features as **Kabuki by the Sea** and **Spiky Bridge**. Visit the **Swansea Bark Mill** or simply enjoy the ambience of this old town with ocean lapping at all sides. It is a further 33km to the COLES BAY turn-off.

Detour: Turn left, 10km into Coles Bay Rd and take the 9km of gravel nice and slow (mainly because the track is narrow) to **Friendly Beaches**. Park at Isaacs Point for easiest beach access or camping. Return via same route.

Spiky Bridge

Spiky Bridge is one of the stranger convict-built constructions in Tasmania. Situated right next to the highway, just south of Swansea, it was built by a convict work gang as part of a coach route from Swansea to Little Swanport, 30km south. Just why strange upstanding points of rock cap each side of the rough-stone bridge remains a mystery to this day. Almost directly opposite is a short road to Spiky Beach, a good place for a stroll, or even a swim in summer.

Friendly Beaches

The Friendly Beaches National Park is a fantastic spot for day-trips, walks and camping. The major feature is simply the beaches themselves, which sweep grandly from Freycinet in the south to Cape Lodi in the north. The whitest sand and crisp blue water can add a touch of Eden to a walk on the beach here. Camping is excellent at Isaac's Point. National Park entrance fees apply.

Drive to **COLES BAY** ❼, a further 21km. From the township, follow the sealed road to the right, tracking eastwards around the bay to enter the **FREYCINET NATIONAL PARK** ❽. Continue on to the gravel to reach **Freycinet Lodge**. Turn up the hill and follow signs to **Cape Tourville Lighthouse** and **Sleepy Bay**. Looking south from the lighthouse you will get a partial view of **Wineglass Bay**.

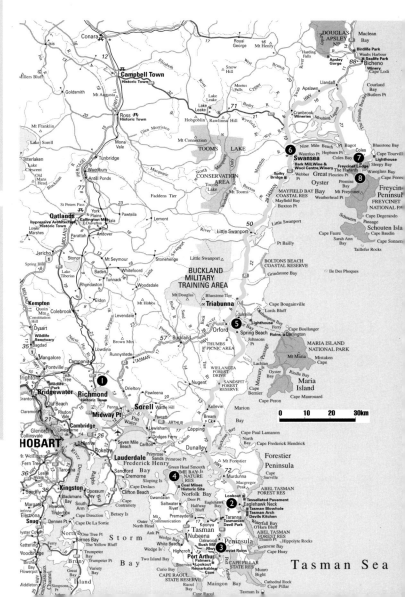

Northern Tasmania and Cradle Mountain

Ratings

National parks	●●●●●
Scenery	●●●●●
Walking	●●●●●
Antique shopping	●●●●○
Fly-fishing	●●●●○
Mountains	●●●●○
Architecture	●●●○○
Food and drink	●●●○○

If the green, wilderness island of Tasmania had a symbol, it would be the beautiful curve of Cradle Mountain, reflected in the cool, clear waters of Dove Lake. The surrounding wilderness national park has extensive walking tracks to explore. The mountains are almost totemic to locals and form a natural barrier between elegant Launceston, Tasmania's second largest city, and the wild interior. Along the northern coast, west of Devonport, there are safe beaches, tame river estuaries and salt air. The peaceful fishing village of Stanley, where 19th-century cottages cling to the base of a mammoth rock called The Nut, is perfectly Lilliputian and is claimed to have inspired Jonathan Swift's *Gulliver's Travels*. Travellers with more time on their hands, should venture down the western side of Tasmania, to explore its beautiful forests and mountains, stunning Macquarie Harbour and the picturesque fishing village of Strahan.

CRADLE MOUNTAIN❖❖❖

ℹ Cradle Mountain National Park information tel: (03) 6492-1133.

Lake St Clair Visitor Information Centre tel: (03) 6289-1137. For off-peak schedules or bookings.

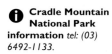 **Idaclair Ferry $$** 0900, 1230, 1500 *during summer months.*

The epic view of Cradle Mountain's distinct crag, from the shores of Dove Lake is the best-known image of Tasmania and its wilderness. It is undoubtedly a spectacular sight at any time, but particularly in the mid-autumn, when the turning leaves of deciduous beech saturate its flanks with reddy gold colours. An early snow can cap off the ultimate vision of Tasmania's ultimate icon. Many who visit Cradle Mountain are serious bushwalkers or those who want to be, just once. Preparation is required for the Overland Track, a wild trek of 80km, from Lake Dove to Lake St Clair. Day-trippers and overnighters will find plenty of enjoyment in the shorter walks close to Cradle Mountain. Among the best is the straight-forward circuit around Lake Dove. **Marions Lookout** can be included or made a separate trek in itself. **Twisted Lakes** was a favourite haunt of the famous wilderness

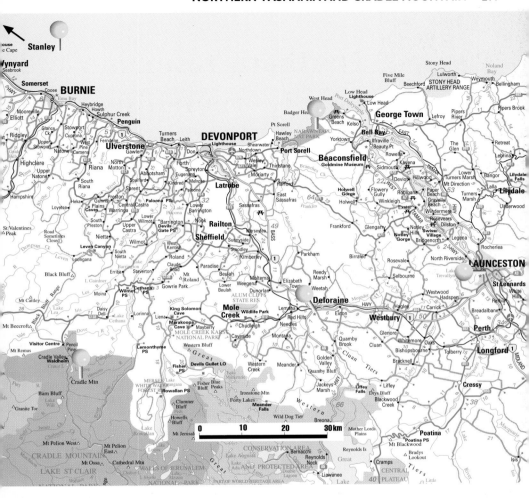

Cradle Mountain Lodge $$$;
tel: (03) 6492-1303;
Lemonthyme Lodge $$
tel: (03) 6492-1112;
Cradle Mountain Tourist Park and Campground $$
tel: (03) 6492-1395.

photographer, Peter Dombrovskis. **Crater Lake** offers dramatic views but quite steep climbs, while the **Ballroom Forest**, closer to Cradle Mountain Lodge, is both easy and fairy-tale pretty. None of the walks requires more than 3 hours, without detours. The mix of alpine rainforest, layered mountain views and abundant wildlife make for the quintessential Tasmanian wilderness experience. Anyone with an interest in the history of the park must also see **Waldheim Chalet**∗ (*always open*). This is the charming, restored cabin of Gustav Weindorfer, the man who pioneered living in the Cradle wilderness and fought for its protected status, early this century.

DELORAINE***

Trowunna Wildlife Park $$ tel: (03) 6363-6162. Open daily 0900–1700.

King Solomons and Marakoopa Caves $$ tel: (03) 6363-5182.

Café Country Style $$ 5km from Deloraine on the Bass Highway; tel: (03) 6362-2186.

In the heart of the northern rural belt, Deloraine is one of the prettiest little towns in Tasmania. Centred around the banks of the Meander River, the town features lovely church spires and stone-built mills against the backdrop of the Western Tiers mountain range. The town itself has a number of antique stores, most of which are within easy walking distance of each other near the centrally located bridge over the Meander. A short drive to Mole Creek will get you to excellent attractions like the **Trowunna Wildlife Park***￼ and **King Solomons and Marakoopa Caves***, where guided and self-guided tours are available.

LAUNCESTON**

Tasmanian Travel and Information Centre cnr St John and Paterson St; tel: (03) 6336-3122; fax: (03) 6336-3118. Open Mon–Fri 0900–1700, Sat 0900–1500, Sun and holidays 0900–1200.

Gorge Restaurant $$ Cataract Gorge; tel: (03) 6331-3330. Open Tue–Sun for lunch and dinner.

Tasmania's northern 'capital' is a rural supply city of 80,000 people. Its historic Boags Brewery produces a world-acclaimed Premium beer, while the city's most obvious charm is the abundance of architectural heritage, particularly the many intact Victorian streetscapes in the inner city. The **Cataract Gorge***, with its suspension bridge and plunging chasm, is a beautiful natural asset, just a short walk from the city centre. The South Esk River sometimes floods violently through the dolerite gorge, which stretches back several kilometres south from its juncture with the broad Tamar. Just upstream, the gorge opens into beautiful, peaceful parkland and gardens fronting the **First Basin** swimming hole. The longest single-span chairlift in the Southern Hemisphere offers dramatic views over the basin and gorge, while a historic suspension bridge offers an equally gratifying experience. A lunch kiosk and the **Gorge Restaurant***￼ are situated in the midst of the parkland. The central city also features two excellent historic parks, **City Park** and **Princes Square**. A great day trip is north along the east bank of the Tamar, where numerous vineyards are flourishing and excellent wines can be tasted free. Ask at information centres about the 'Wine Route'.

NARAWNTAPU NATIONAL PARK***

Narawntapu National Park office tel: (03) 6428-6277.

Narawntapu National Park (formerly known as the Asbestos Range National Park), is well worth a visit for some of the island's best wildlife and beach experiences. At dusk, the number of wombats, wallabies, brush-tail possums and large Forrester kangaroos has to be seen to be believed. A huge inland lagoon is also central to the small park and a fantastic boardwalk and bird-hide allow a close peek at numerous wading species, transient parrots and cockatoos and impressive sea eagles. **Bakers Beach*** is the other key feature of the park, stretching for several kilometres and usually offering sheltered swimming in summer. Just west, the perfect beaches continue along the Western bank of the **Rubicon Estuary** at beautiful **Holey Beach***. Here, even more protection from wind and swell make for wonderful family beach days, amidst the ambience of a quaint shack village, gardens and protective she-oak trees.

STANLEY***

Stanley Tourist Information and Nut Chairlift $$ *tel: (03) 6458-1286. Open daily (weather permitting).*

Highfield House $$ *tel: (03) 6458-1100. Open daily Oct–Apr 1000–1700, May–July 1000–1600.*

Joe Lyons' Cottage $ *tel: (03) 6458-1145. Open daily 1000–1600.*

Stepping out of the car here is like stepping into a storybook. Stanley is set around the base of a massive volcanic plug called **The Nut**, separated from the mainland by a long, sandy isthmus called **The Neck**. With wild Bass Strait lapping – or lashing – on either side, rows of fishermen's cottages cling to its base like barnacles. The wharf, in the southern shadow of The Nut, is popular with local fishermen. Historic **Highfield House (1835)***, from which the Van Diemens Land Company launched many pioneering explorations of the North and West, sits high on another green hill, 2 minutes' drive west. It is open for inspection, with the views back to the township, across a windswept beach, reward enough for many. The **Nut Chairlift**** offers an easy ride to the top of The Nut. The steep walkway option is a hard but relatively short work, for the same amazing views. Among the numerous cottages and appealing craft shops, the **Tasmanian Shell Shop**, in the middle of the main street, stands out for quirky found objects and quality craft. **Joe Lyons' Cottage***, near the wharf, was the birthplace of the only Tasmanian-born prime minister of Australia.

WYNYARD**

Wynyard Tourist Information Centre *Goldie St; tel: (03) 6442-4143.*

Table Cape Tulip Farm $ *tel: (03) 6442-2012. Tours and inspections in spring.*

This small town marks the start of the wilder, greener end of the North West coastal strip. The Inglis River snakes out to a pretty wharf and sea-entrance where a few local fishing boats are moored. Just west, rising straight out of the ocean, is Table Cape, a high rocky headland which – as a backdrop for a fishing and farming village – could make those from the British Isles misty-eyed for home. For often dazzling rural views against the sparkle of Bass Strait, take the scenic route over Table Cape as you head west. The remarkably fertile, volcanic red soil helps make the huge and multi-coloured **Table Cape Tulip Farm**** a must-see in September and October. The **Wynyard Tulip Festival*** is staged in the township in early October each year. Just 5 minutes further west, be sure to stop in at **Boat Harbour Beach*** and **Sisters Beach***, the former like a mini-Mediterranean beach town and the latter a thickly forested beachfront stretching out to the headlands of **Rocky Cape National Park***. Both beaches are great for swimming, as are most North Coast beaches, for Bass Strait quickly becomes placid between storms. The national park, accessed further west on the highway, is of particular interest for its caves and Aboriginal history.

Suggested tour

The Old Cable Station $$ West Beach Rd, Green Hills, near Stanley; tel: (03) 6458-1312. Four rooms with en suites, one with double spa and all with sea views.

The Maldon $$ 32 Brisbane St, Launceston; tel: (03) 6331-3211. Victorian bed and breakfast with self-catering suites.

Larooma Cottages $$ Larooma Rd, Hawley Beach; tel: (03) 6428-6754. Gorgeous cottages in an even better setting overlooking the blue waters of the Rubicon Estuary and the adjacent Narawntapu Ranges.

Dangerous Liaisons $$ 28 Forbes St, Devonport; tel: (03) 6424-6431. Quirky bar-restaurant run by eccentric but talented Scottish chef, John Grant. Chatting in the small bar before eating is half the experience as the chef holds court – and a glass of wine. The food is always innovative and utilises best available local seafood and farm produce.

Calabrisella $$ 56 Wellington St, Launceston; tel: (03) 6331-1958. As the name suggests, an Italian restaurant based on the cuisine of its owners who came from the Calabrian region. Unpretentious, good-value Italian with warm rooms and an atmosphere completely infused with garlic.

Total distance: The main route is 255km, with a near-essential detour to Cradle Mountain adding 110km, or to Great Lake, 132km.

Time: About 3 hours, without stops, from Launceston to Stanley via Sheffield. Detouring to Cradle Mountain or Great Lake will add 2 hours extra driving time. It's a good idea to stay one night up high or at Stanley. Detouring to Asbestos Ranges National Park and Hawley Beach will add 2 hours.

Links: This tour connects to the Hobart walking tour (*see page 260*) and the southeast Tasmania tour (*see page 268*) along the Midlands Highway from Launceston to Hobart.

Route: From **LAUNCESTON** ❶ head south on Highway 1, taking the left ramp at the top of the Launceston outlet, signed to Devonport and Burnie. Continue through small, rural towns and English hedgerows to pretty **DELORAINE** ❷ . The **Western Tiers** mountain range is the predominant feature to the south from here on to Devonport.

Detour: From the **Meander River Bridge** in Deloraine, head south on the A5 towards **Great Lake** ❸ , via pretty Golden Valley and through a steep winding climb with pockets of rainforest, to the high plateau. It is about an hour to Liawenee, with the last 30km on gravel. Some snow is usual in winter but rarely blocks the road.

Continue on Highway 1 to **Latrobe** ❹ , with great antique shopping. Turn left at the west end of town on to the B13, then follow a 20-minute stretch to **Sheffield**, where you might want to stop to see the historic murals painted on shop and barn walls, or visit Mount Roland, a massive monolith of a mountain to the south.

Detour: On the east side of Sheffield, turn south toward **Mt Roland** and follow signs toward **CRADLE MOUNTAIN** ❺ . The road runs right by the base of Roland before climbing and weaving through rainforest to **Moina**. Turn left on to **Cradle Link Rd**, which can be snow-affected in winter. The turn-off to the national park is a further 21km.

From **Sheffield**, take the B14 east and then north to **Devonport** ❻ , a small river port with pretty beaches and the terminal for the Bass Strait vehicular ferry, *Spirit of Tasmania*. The **Don River Railway**⁺ is worth a visit (*tel: (03) 6424-6335; open daily 1000–1600*) and the **Tiagarra Aboriginal Centre**⁺ (*tel: (03) 6424–8250; open daily 0900–1700*).

Detour: From Devonport, backtrack 2km on Highway 1 to the airport turn-off. Drive 15km to Hawley Beach. Alternatively, turn right at the roundabout, 400m from the highway, and drive 18km to the **NARAWNTAPU NP** ❼ turn-off. It's a further 9km to the park entrance, with the last few kilometres on good gravel surface.

Also worth exploring

Spirit of Tasmania
$$ *Bass Strait vehicular
ferry, tel: 13-2010. Leaves
Tasmania on Tue, Thur and
Sat. Overnight trip.*

Tasmania's west coast, and particularly the beautiful harbour village at
Strahan, demands a separate trip rather than a detour. This is the
home of Tasmania's wildest rainforest, beaches and rivers. The easiest
route is south from Burnie on the A10 (2¹/₂ hours to Strahan) but you
can also get there by continuing on the Cradle Mountain link road to
rejoin the A10 near Tullah. Don't miss the moonscape surroundings at
the old mining town of Queenstown, a harbour and river cruise on
Macquarie Harbour, and a fishing trip from Strahan.

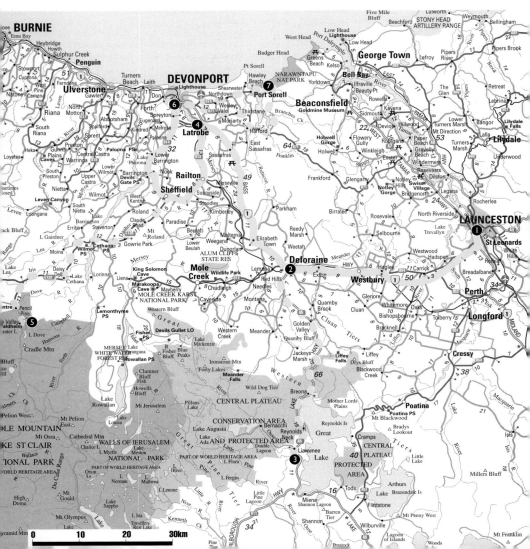

Language

Australians speak English. That is the first fact most travellers will be told when they start planning a trip Down Under.

In essence, it is true. English is the official language of Australia, the first language and the mother tongue. It means anyone who speaks English will manage fine, if not without some misunderstandings, as soon as they land on antipodean shores.

But while English is undoubtedly the main language spoken in Australia, in the two centuries of white settlement of this massive, isolated island continent Australian-English has developed a life and zest of its own – not to mention the unique Aussie accent.

Call it strine, or call it bastardised English, but the Australian language spoken by locals is so colourful and so full of local idioms, abbreviations, expressions, slang, new words or old ones adapted from some of the 250 Aboriginal languages that were spoken when Europeans landed in Australia, that it can sometimes seem like a foreign tongue.

In addition, while English is the first language, 23 per cent of Australia's population was born overseas, and for 10 per cent of Australians, English is a second language. This diversity means it is easy to find speakers of more than 200 foreign languages in Australia, with strong Italian, Greek, Vietnamese, Chinese, Middle Eastern and central European communities active across society. Most non-urban Aborigines in northern Queensland, the Northern Territory and the Kimberley also speak their own mother tongue – and sometimes two or three other Aboriginal languages as well – that belongs to one of the 50 main language groups still spoken in Australia today.

Never assume that a word, saying or expression in English from your own country still means exactly the same in Australia, after 200 years of bastardisation and mangling. But there are a few simple rules. Most words are cut short (afternoon becomes *arvo* as in 'arvo tea'), words are made more diminutive (presents become *pressies*, motorbike riders are *bikies* and environmentalists are *greenies*), Christian names are always abbreviated (David become Davo, Barry is Bazza), and obscure and long-forgotten Cockney rhyming slang is still current ('got an Oxford scholar?' means 'have you got a dollar?'). And never, ever, call everyone 'mate' just because they do in *Crocodile Dundee* – you must know them for at least five seconds before assuming such closeness akin to friendship.

Some helpful translations

Avagoodweekend?: a traditional Monday morning greeting
Back o' Bourke: out in the middle of nowhere

Bush: the bush is an Australian term for a forest, but when it is used in the sense of 'I'm going Bush' it means to get away from the city, or to go off by oneself for a while
Bush-bash: to try and find a path through thick scrub or forest
Bushie: a person who comes from the country
Dag: literally a shearing term, meaning a bit of wool caked in sheep dung. Now used to describe, usually affectionately, a person or friend who is a bit behind the times or socially inept
Dead horse: tomato sauce, from Cockney rhyming slang tradition
Dob: to tell on your mate, as in 'to dob in' to the police
Drongo: a dumb, stupid or weird person
Dunny: an outdoor toilet, usually in a little shed made of corrugated iron
Fair dinkum: to be absolutely true and committed to something
Furphy: a red herring or false rumour
Grog: encompasses all forms of alcoholic drink
Gunna: to be always intending to do something; now used to describe a type of person
Larrikin: a likeable rogue
Never-never: even more outback and remote than the outback
No-hoper: a loser, someone who will never amount to anything
Ocker: a loud, boorish, beer-swilling Australian
Paddock: the Australian equivalent of a field, but it can be thousands of hectares in size
Pom: an English person. Possibly derived from convict days when clothes were stamped with P.O.M (Prisoner of His Majesty)
Sheila: a term for an Australian woman or girl used by ockers or bushies
Shonky: a bit underhand, fake, illegal or a product that is not working properly
Smoko: morning and afternoon tea break
Strewth: exclamation of wonder, developed from 'God's truth'
Tall poppies: high fliers and achievers who then get cut down to size (a national pastime)
Thongs: flip-flop footwear that is always worn by slobs or ockers
To cark'it: to die, or kick the bucket
Two-up: the betting game invented by Australian soldiers in World War I, involving betting on the toss of two coins
Whinge: to complain or moan incessantly; usually attached as an adjective as in 'whinging Pom'
Yakka: hard work, derived from an Aboriginal word
Yobbo: a really uncouth ocker, often violent
Yonks: ages, a long time, as in 'I haven't seen you for yonks'

Index

Acknowledgements

Project management: Cambridge Publishing Management Ltd
Project editor: Karen Beaulah
Series design: Fox Design
Cover design: Liz Lyons Design
Map work: Pumpkin House/Cambridge Publishing Management Ltd
Repro and image setting: PDQ Reprographics/Cambridge Publishing Management Ltd
Printed and bound in India by: Replika Press Pvt Ltd

We would like to thank Ethel Davies for the photographs used in this book, to whom the copyright belongs, with the exception of the following:

Front cover: Kangaroo warning sign on the Uluru ring road, Ayres Rock, Uluru Kata Tjuta National Park, Northern Territory, Nic Cleave Photography/Alamy

Back cover: Aborigine Space Throwing Boomerang Tjapukai Dance Group, Uluru, Ayers Rock, Northern Territory, SCPhotos/Alamy

Australian Tourist Commission (pages 5 and 17)

Tourism New South Wales (pages 78 and 147)

South Australian Tourism Commission (pages 132, 242, 244, 246, 248, 252 and 255)

Parks Victoria (page 138)

Tourism Queensland (page 177)

Pictures Colour Library (pages 22, 102, 104, 106, 108, 110, 134, 136, 142, 144, 150, 166, 225, 260, 264, 266 and 268)

Alan Jones (pages 162, 163 and 168)

www.bigfoto.com (page 165)

Trevor Phillips (pages 227 and 228)

Geoff Murray (page 262)

Feedback form

If you enjoyed using this book, or even if you didn't, please help us improve future editions by taking part in our reader survey. Every returned form will be acknowledged, and to show our appreciation we will give you £1 off your next purchase of a Thomas Cook guidebook. Just take a few minutes to complete and return this form to us.

When did you buy this book? ....
....

Where did you buy it? (Please give town/city and, if possible, name of retailer)
....
....

When did you/do you intend to travel in Australia? ....
....

For how long (approx)? ....

How many people in your party? ....

Which cities, national parks and other locations did you/do you intend mainly to visit?
....
....
....
....

Did you/will you:
❏ Make all your travel arrangements independently?
❏ Travel on a fly-drive package?
Please give brief details: ....
....

Did you/do you intend to use this book:
❏ For planning your trip?   ❏ Both?
❏ During the trip itself?

Did you/do you intend also to purchase any of the following travel publications for your trip?
A road map/atlas (please specify) ....
Other guidebooks (please specify) ....

Have you used any other Thomas Cook guidebooks in the past? If so, which?
....
....

Please rate the following features of *Drive Around Australia* for their value to you (Circle VU for 'very useful', U for 'useful', NU for 'little or no use'):

The *Travel facts* section on pages 14–23	VU	U	NU
The *Driver's guide* section on pages 24–29	VU	U	NU
The *Highlights* on pages 40–41	VU	U	NU
The recommended driving routes throughout the book	VU	U	NU
Information on towns and cities, National Parks, etc	VU	U	NU
The maps of towns and cities, parks, etc	VU	U	NU

Please use this space to tell us about any features that in your opinion could be changed, improved, or added in future editions of the book, or any other comments you would like to make concerning the book:

....
....
....
....
....
....
....
....
....
....

Your age category: ❑ 21-30   ❑ 31-40   ❑ 41-50   ❑ over 50

Your name: Mr/Mrs/Miss/Ms ....
(First name or initials) ....
(Last name) ....

Your full address: (Please include postal or zip code)

....
....
....
....
....

Your daytime telephone number: ....

Please detach this page and send it to: The Series Editor, Drive Around Guides, Thomas Cook Publishing, PO Box 227, The Thomas Cook Business Park, 15–16 Coningsby Road, Peterborough PE3 8SB.

Alternatively, you can email us at: books@thomascook.com

We will be pleased to send you details of how to claim your discount upon receipt of this questionnaire.